RELIGION, TOLERATION, AND BRITISH WRITING,
1790–1830

In *Religion, Toleration, and British Writing, 1790–1830* Mark Canuel examines the way that Romantic poets, novelists, and political writers criticized the traditional grounding of British political unity in religious conformity. Canuel shows how a wide range of writers including Jeremy Bentham, Ann Radcliffe, Maria Edgeworth, and Lord Byron not only undermined the validity of religion in the British state, but also imagined a new, tolerant, and more organized mode of social inclusion. To argue against the authority of religion, Canuel claims, was to argue for a thoroughly revised form of tolerant yet highly organized government, a mode of political authority that provided unprecedented levels of inclusion and protection. Canuel argues that these writers saw their works as political and literary commentaries on the extent and limits of religious toleration. His study throws new light on political history as well as the literature of the Romantic period.

MARK CANUEL is Assistant Professor in the Department of English at the University of Illinois at Chicago. He has published numerous articles and reviews on Romantic writing in journals, including *ELH*, *Nineteenth-Century Literature*, and *Studies in Romanticism*.

This series aims to foster the best new work in one of the most challenging fields within English literary studies. From the early 1780s to the early 1830s a formidable array of talented men and women took to literary composition, not just in poetry, which some of them famously transformed, but in many modes of writing. The expansion of publishing created new opportunities for writers, and the political stakes of what they wrote were raised again by what Wordsworth called those "great national events" that were "almost daily taking place": the French Revolution, the Napoleonic and American wars, urbanization, industrialization, religious revival, an expanded empire abroad, and the reform movement at home. This was an enormous ambition, even when it pretended otherwise. The relations between science, philosophy, religion, and literature were reworked in texts such as *Frankenstein* and *Biographia Literaria*; gender relations in *A Vindication of the Rights of Woman* and *Don Juan*; journalism by Cobbett and Hazlitt; poetic form, content, and style by the Lake School and the Cockney School. Outside Shakespeare studies, probably no body of writing has produced such a wealth of response or done so much to shape the responses of modern criticism. This indeed is the period that saw the emergence of those notions of "literature" and of literary history, especially national literary history, on which modern scholarship in English has been founded.

The categories produced by Romanticism have also been challenged by recent historicist arguments. The task of the series is to engage both with a challenging corpus of Romantic writings and with the changing field of criticism they have helped to shape. As with other literary series published by Cambridge, this one will represent the work of both younger and more established scholars, on either side of the Atlantic and elsewhere.

For a complete list of titles published see end of book.

RELIGION, TOLERATION, AND BRITISH WRITING, 1790–1830

MARK CANUEL

The University of Illinois at Chicago

CAMBRIDGE UNIVERSITY PRESS

PUBLISHED BY THE PRESS SYNDICATE OF THE UNIVERSITY OF CAMBRIDGE
The Pitt Building, Trumpington Street, Cambridge, United Kingdom

CAMBRIDGE UNIVERSITY PRESS
The Edinburgh Building, Cambridge CB2 2RU, UK
40 West 20th Street, New York, NY 10011-4211, USA
477 Williamstown Road, Port Melbourne, VIC 3207, Australia
Ruiz de Alarcón 13, 28014 Madrid, Spain
Dock House, The Waterfront, Cape Town 8001, South Africa

http://www.cambridge.org

First published 2002

Printed in the United Kingdom at the University Press, Cambridge

Typeface Baskerville Monotype 11/12.5 pt   *System* LaTeX 2$_\varepsilon$ [TB]

A catalogue record for this book is available from the British Library

Library of Congress Cataloguing in Publication data
Canuel, Mark.
Religion, toleration, and British writing, 1790–1830 / Mark Canuel.
p.   cm. – (Cambridge studies in Romanticism ; 53)
Includes bibliographical references and index.
ISBN 0 521 81577 0
1. English literature – 19th century – History and criticism.   2. Religion and
literature – Great Britain – History – 19th century.   3. Religious tolerance in literature.
4. Religion and literature – Great Britain – History – 18th century.   5. Religious
tolerance – Great Britain – History – 19th century.   6. Religious tolerance – Great
Britain – History – 18th century.   7. English literature – 18th century – History and criticism.
8. Romanticism – Great Britain.   I. Title.   II. Series.
PR468.R44 C36   2002
820.9'382 – dc21   2002023444

ISBN 0 521 81577 0 hardback

Contents

Acknowledgements

Like any first book, this one is the result of many visions and revisions during the years I wrote it. My primary debt is to Frances Ferguson, who provided encouragement, read multiple drafts, and often made it possible for me to realize what, after all, I was trying to say. Jerome Christensen was a most meticulous and engaged reader. Stephen Engelmann, Andy Franta, Jonathan Gross, Allen Grossman, Michael Macovski, Sandra Macpherson, Don Marshall, Mary Poovey, Larry Poston, Mary Beth Rose, Jim Sack, and Karen Weisman made invaluable suggestions on, and challenges to, various parts of this book at different stages. Robin Grey read a late draft of the entire project and made more helpful ideas for revision than I can adequately thank her for. The readers at Cambridge University Press, Kevin Gilmartin and Paul Hamilton, offered still more useful advice. Linda Bree has proved to be an attentive and thoughtful editor, and I am grateful for Audrey Cotterell's detailed copy-editing. Although they have become my colleagues in Chicago at too late a date to have influenced this project, I would be remiss if I did not express my gratitude for the friendship of Jennifer Brody, Sharon Holland, E. Patrick Johnson, and Dwight McBride. I wish to thank University College London for allowing me to use their collection of Bentham's manuscripts; I also made extensive use of the Newberry Library, The Regenstein Library at the University of Chicago, and the Richard J. Daley Library at the University of Illinois at Chicago. A year-long fellowship at the Institute for the Humanities at the University of Illinois at Chicago helped me to finish the typescript. Finally, I wish to thank my parents, George and Mary, who continue to offer love and their own form of tolerance. The book is dedicated to them.

I wish to thank the trustees of Boston University for permission to reprint material from an earlier version of chapter 2, which appeared as " 'Holy Hypocrisy' and the Government of Belief: Religion and Nationalism in the Gothic," *Studies in Romanticism* 34 (Winter 1995); a shorter version of chapter 3 was published in *ELH* 68 (Winter 2001).

Introduction

Toleration, political theorists tell us, is a philosophy of government that asks people to get along with others who differ substantially in their backgrounds and preferences. In our day, such a goal, even if it seems attractive (and it may not be for everyone), is elusive. We are continually reminded, first of all, that the impulse to share the benefits of social life so widely – among persons racially, ethnically, sexually, and religiously diverse – is not always widely shared. Many political regimes have taken it upon themselves to suppress the activities of groups or sects whose beliefs they regard to be subversive of social stability; territorial wars inspired by racial, ethnic, or religious differences continue to define the climate of contemporary political life in many regions of the world. But even more perplexing may be the fact that even ostensibly tolerant societies exert a considerable level of suppression of and control over beliefs, dispositions, and expressions – a practice from which the theory of toleration apparently tries to extricate itself.[1] This is why much of our common experience of secular institutions shows that such institutions – even while they accept persons with different backgrounds and beliefs – also remain hostile to those who wish to express, or act upon, their affiliations openly. School districts in the United States, for example, regularly limit the expression of the very religious beliefs that they apparently tolerate. In India, the practice of ritual self-immolation or *sati* has been banned since 1829 in the interests of democratic freedom. In Turkey, ethnic Kurds have been sentenced to prison terms for publicly exposing sectarian differences or for criticizing secularism.

This book does not try to comment on any of today's practical puzzles of toleration – puzzles that require us to make vexing distinctions between other tolerant and intolerant governments or to make difficult decisions in our own communities about what can and cannot be tolerated in order to achieve the goal of toleration. Neither does it rigorously study, or adjudicate between, current theoretical views of the subject or

1

present cases that such views attempt, correctly or incorrectly, to address. Instead, *Religion, Toleration, and British Writing* provides something of a genealogy for such puzzles and theories. It takes the specific issue of *religious* toleration, an issue attracting increasingly heated debate throughout the late eighteenth and early nineteenth centuries, as one of the Romantic period's most compelling occasions for exploring the extent of, and limits upon, the liberality of liberal government.[2] The central argument of this book is that much of the writing that emerged in this period is important not merely because it advocated specific kinds of beliefs or interests, but because it advocated a new way in which different beliefs could be *governed* under the auspices of tolerant institutions. Or, to put it another way, this book, rather than a study of political or religious beliefs, is a study of emergent beliefs about the *position* of beliefs in modern society more generally.

The four decades I study in this book witnessed some of the most intense and creative challenges to the authority of the confessional state – the monopoly of the Anglican church, enforced through oaths, tests, and penal laws, over all regions of British civil and political life. From the political writings of Jeremy Bentham to Lord Byron's *Cain: A Mystery*, the works I study in this book portrayed the conventional structure of establishment as a "tissue of imposture" (as Bentham put it). But these works also revealed established religion to be a spectacular political failure: an attempt to produce order that resulted in chaos, an attempt to establish legal control over regions of consciousness which continually eluded all legislation. In a joint enterprise of literary and political speculation, the discourse of toleration reimagined the lineaments of British government as a social entity that was both more permissive *and* more orderly – a nation-state that included and coordinated multiple, diverging beliefs and alliances within a set of accommodating institutional environments, from schools and workplaces to parliament and the church itself. Toleration emerged, in other words, neither as a naive commitment to individualism nor as an oppressive ideology. Rather, incommensurable and contentious beliefs provided writers of the day with the impetus to propose revised and expanded institutional organs of the state, which could assume the responsibility of coordinating a range of incompatible moral and religious doctrines and perspectives. Jeremy Bentham thus envisioned his schools, prisons, and "pauper management" schemes not merely as tools of "normalization" (as Michel Foucault has described them) but as the vital means through which individuals holding divergent beliefs might simultaneously gain social admission and achieve public recognition within the "connexions and dependencies of the several parts of the admirable whole."[3] Maria Edgeworth adopted a similar strategy in her fiction by showing how Irish Catholic culture could preserve and embellish its distinction precisely by being included in Britain's economy and British secular institutions. Even the late Wordsworth, well known for defending the established church in his later poetry, frequently regarded the ecclesiastical institution as a source of social value only because it served as a foundation for tolerant government. In *The Excursion*, a poem so frequently dismissed by critics as a piece of dry and sterile propaganda for orthodox Anglicanism, the church does not merely identify and exclude enemies from an ideal communion; it instead absorbs and protects even the most mutinous and recalcitrant subjects within the church-guided "powers of civil polity."[4]

As frequently as the topic of this book may bring it into contact with terms such as "liberal," "liberalism," and "liberality," I insist upon the particularity of the discourse of toleration, inherited from the writing of Milton and Locke and given further shape by writers from Joseph Priestley and George Dyer to William Godwin and Bentham. This is because of the distinctive challenges that religious belief posed (and still continues to pose) to philosophies of liberal government.[5] Religious toleration, so often confronting writers as the paradox of tolerating the intolerant, presented specific problems that required specific institutional remedies. Because I do not frame toleration as an issue that could be separated from an institutional construction of it, however, I offer an account of toleration that is somewhat different from that which is found amongst the works of political theorists who either support or criticize philosophies of liberalism. I have already said that I do not propose to offer a theory of toleration in this book, but I can still say more precisely how the historical work of this study supplements more abstract accounts of the subject. From differing and occasionally contending positions, writers such as Stanley Fish, Kirstie McClure, Robert Post, Michael Sandel, and Charles Taylor argue that toleration is only a version of – or is at least difficult to separate from – assimilation.[6] To tolerate others, they claim, we need to agree on the terms of toleration in advance; we therefore only tolerate others who share our own beliefs or perspectives.

What these arguments have in common is their commitment to framing toleration as a political value so pure that it is conveniently unreachable; they describe it as an ideal that seeks to be "neutral with regard to truth" (McClure) and that can therefore be criticized from a more skeptical or pragmatic position – one that shows how social arrangements are actually the product of "indoctrination" (Fish) or specific group interests.[7] I might add here that studies of "liberalism" in eighteenth- and nineteenth-century writing – by critics including Julie Ellison, William Jewett, and Celeste Langan – follow this line of reasoning by making liberalism look like a commitment to purely autonomous individualism and thus rather obviously like a political impossibility.[8] Generally speaking, a historical perspective on the issue shows that defenders of toleration seldom subscribed to unsophisticated commitments to abstract values of freedom or neutrality. More specifically, though, the focus of this book shows how the discourse of toleration elaborated towards the end of the eighteenth century promoted liberal inclusion not as mere permissiveness but as the foundation of institutional strength and security. Such strength and security, moreover, was viewed as the very means to achieve toleration – rather than as an embarrassing excrescence on an otherwise perfect utopia. The Romantic discourse of toleration pursued a seemingly inextricable dual commitment to individual freedom and the social organization and facilitation of that freedom.

The chapters that follow regularly engage with criticism of Romantic writing that has explicitly or implicitly addressed the issues at the center of this project; the main lines of the polemic are worth emphasizing here, though. I address a critical tradition – visible in the work of writers such as M. H. Abrams, Harold Bloom, and Geoffrey Hartman – that insists upon the context of Romantic poetry within the Christian tradition, and, more specifically, within the history of Protestant Dissent.[9] M. H. Abrams describes Romantic poetry as a "secularized form of devotional experience," an internalization and privatization of religion that allows the poet's "mind" to take over "the prerogatives of deity," a view carried forward into the late nineteenth century in J. Hillis Miller's Heideggerian account of the "disappearance of God."[10] My own view reorients this perspective on secularization and thus on the connection between "Romanticism" and the "secular." While very much about the "secular" innovations in British literary and cultural productions, this book regards the secular as a specific *institutional achievement* rather than an individual or psychological phenomenon or act of individual "devotion." Although I refer throughout the following chapters to "secular" institutions and "secular" government, then, I am arguing that secularization did not emerge as a change in individuals' beliefs, or a change in collective beliefs, but as a shift in the means through which distinct beliefs could be coordinated or organized under the auspices of more capacious and elaborate structures of government.

Now it is precisely this dimension of my argument – a redefinition of Romantic writing by contextualizing it within accounts of the extent and limits of toleration – that aims to address more recent historical views of the Romantic period. These have tended to focus on the alliances that writers form with currents of religious or political radicalism or with hegemonic ideologies of one kind or another – whether those ideologies are defined as bourgeois, paternalistic, nationalistic, or imperialistic. I respond, first of all, to important work by critics such as Robert Ryan and Martin Priestman, who have examined the correlation between poetry and religious or anti-religious commitments during the Romantic period.[11] Other critics, such as Kevin Gilmartin, Steven Goldsmith, Ian McCalman, and Nicholas Roe, more consistently link religious beliefs with political and economic struggle; they reveal that the work of writers such as William Blake, Percy Shelley, and John Keats participate in trends of radical thinking promulgated through ventures (in writing and publishing) of figures such as Richard Carlile, Daniel Isaac Eaton, and William Hone.[12] Whether considering religious beliefs in the abstract or as connected to political movements, these critics provide nuanced readings of the relationships between literary works and specific group interests: how writers (as Kevin Binfield succinctly puts it) strive to form a "community of value" with a shared "core of belief and behavior."[13]

Second, though, I mean to respond to the line of critical discussion of the "nation" or "empire" in the work of Saree Makdisi, Michael Ragussis, Cannon Schmitt, and Katie Trumpener, to name a few.[14] As useful as this work may be in helping to move our attention from the issue of personal belief to large-scale social formations, it tends to read the organization of these larger entities as if such entities necessarily flattened out or erased identities within the nation's or empire's separate parts. These critics show, in other words, how the formation of a national or imperial public requires the erasure or suppression of separate publics. Romanticism, on these terms, can either be a support for or resistance to the "production of homogeneous abstract space and the attempt to paper over or incorporate heterogeneous and differential spaces and times."[15]

While this book speaks of the British "nation" and "empire," it shifts attention away from discussions of nationalism or imperialism: the collective search for an "essence and inner virtue of the community" or "collective self-consciousness" as nationalism is described by Gerald Newman.[16] Whereas views of Romantic religion, politics, nationalism, or imperialism emphasize either a private counterpublic or suppressive hegemonic public, I study the development of the nation-state in different terms – not defined according to the relatively homogeneous beliefs and alliances that it traditionally demanded, but according to altering technologies of social order that both permitted and encouraged heterogeneity and dis- agreement. This is not a book on "Romanticism and religion," then, and not a book on "the politics (or ideology) of Romanticism." Rather than attempting to identify the particular beliefs and alliances of individual writers, I show how these writers took an interest in the organization of those beliefs within the larger entity of Britain's secular institutions.

To some extent, this means that the writers on whom I concentrate differ from those that are featured in many other studies of the period. The work of Bentham, for example, is far more central in my argu- ment than the work of Thomas Paine. Paine's writing (in the tradition of the French *philosophes* and British skeptics) was primarily concerned with religion's epistemological invalidity, and not necessarily as a force to be organized by the state. There is also no extended discussion of the work of William Blake, who (as many critics have successfully argued) more consistently maintained the energies of seventeenth-century agrar- ian radicals than the authors treated in this book.[17] Ultimately, however, these differences derive from a new perspective from which to view the interconnected commitments of a range of genres from nature lyrics to national tales, Gothic novels to historical dramas. In chapter 1, I demon- strate how the political and aesthetic imperatives of Britain's confessional state were defended, and how Romantic reformers from Priestley to Ben- tham opposed those imperatives by redescribing the aims and functions of civil government. Edmund Burke, I argue, provided a remarkably nuanced but problematic apology for the alliance of church and state. Established religion was such a traditional part of British national def- inition that it seemed natural, thus helping to preserve "the method of nature in the conduct of state."[18] At the same time, the church required a variety of artificial mechanisms – oaths, tests, and penal laws – in order to maintain its unassailable position. I show how reformers of the late eighteenth century pointed out, first of all, that the supposedly natural authority of the church suppressed the actual diversity of beliefs that ex- isted within Britain's shores. But such arguments, most fully developed in the work of Jeremy Bentham, also surprisingly proposed that the artifice and tyranny of established religion could be counteracted by the still more powerful and vitalizing artifice of secular government. Although Bentham is frequently considered an enemy of Romanticism's emphasis on individual volition and imagination, I contend that his work is as crucial to understanding the writers of this period as the enthusiasm of his most overt admirers, including Leigh Hunt and Percy Shelley, would suggest. For in Bentham's plans for poor houses, hospitals, and schools – from the *Panopticon* papers (1791) to *Chrestomathia* (1815–16) – he modeled communities that could abridge the need for religious agreement: indeed, the goal of institutions was frequently described as "social cooperation" itself. At the same time, the intricately orchestrated exercises and employment in such institutions offered a system of "dependencies" so vital that the beliefs and dispositions of their members required communal inclusion in order to become visible and meaningful to others – or even to themselves. Bentham's most significant contribution to Romantic writing can be discerned in his simultaneous advocacy of an increased freedom of expression and a rigorous program of institutional reform as a creative way to manage and accentuate divergent beliefs and interests.

In chapter 2, I show how debates about religious toleration that I mention in the previous chapter – debates usually receiving scant attention by literary critics – frequently indulge in the sensational rhetoric of the Gothic novel. What makes this practice appropriate is that Gothic novels are not merely sensational but promote an intriguing social logic of their own. Although many recent accounts of the Gothic have viewed it as a champion or enemy of social conformity, I argue that the genre is better described as an attempt to identify and manage the adherents of diverse, incompatible beliefs. The Gothic presents monastic institutions as fascinating sources of danger, but not because the genre seeks to suppress Catholicism as a set of alien beliefs. Instead, even early examples of the genre by Horace Walpole and Clara Reeve frequently identify monasticism as a private and self-enclosed structure of confessional authority, visible in Britain itself, that the Gothic novel participates in dismantling and modifying. I focus on Ann Radcliffe's novels – beginning with *A Sicilian Romance* (1790) and in particular on *The Italian* (1797) – in order to demonstrate how the Gothic secularizes ecclesiastical authority rather than opposing or eliminating it, making the church counteract its own traditional confessional networks of power in order to provide a stable and inclusive source of social order. *The Italian*'s romantic heroes, Ellena and Vivaldi, are not only lovers but also lovers of justice, and they eventually become the beneficiaries of the tolerant administration of justice procured by the Inquisition itself. Although agents of the church persecute these characters throughout the novel for their blasphemy and recusancy, *The Italian* achieves a resolution by revising the Inquisition as a secular form of legal intervention that punishes persons for harmful actions rather than offensive beliefs, and that convicts murderous clerics rather than heretical heroes.

As much as writers such as Samuel Taylor Coleridge and William Wordsworth may have denigrated the popular genre of the Gothic, I demonstrate how they nevertheless return to its tolerant logic. In chapter 3, I show how Coleridge's early journal *The Watchman* (1796) argues against the authority of the state to command belief; his later work, although frequently deemed conservative by many critics, actually bears a closer resemblance to his early radicalism than to defenses of established religion by Burke and other eighteenth-century Anglican apologists. Coleridge does indeed declare in the 1790s that he has put aside his "baby trumpet of sedition,"[19] but his works from *The Friend* (1808–10) and the closely related *Lay Sermons* (1816, 1817) to *On the Constitution of Church and State* (1829) are far from traditional: indeed, they suggest that he understood his own defense of the church as a way of undermining the legacy of forced and falsified religious conformity. These commentaries on ecclesiastical government – further pursued in poems like "Religious Musings" and "Fears in Solitude" – defend the church only insofar as it upholds and cultivates dissent from any established code of belief. Coleridge repeatedly idealizes the religious climate of the reformation because of the "warmth and frequency of . . . religious controversies" and the "rank and value assigned to *polemic divinity*."[20] And he projects this into a revised mission for the national church, whose "clerisy" provides nonconformity with a new vitality while serving as a public "guide, guardian, and instructor."[21]

My discussion of Coleridge's writing suggests that his early arguments *against* established religion and his later arguments *for* it actually offer compatible perspectives on the relationship between secular government and religious belief. This aspect of Coleridge's work helps us to see an analogous convergence between the radically secular project of the "national tale" and the apparently more conservative support for the established church in Wordsworth's later work. Chapter 4 shows how the Irish national tale, as it was practiced by writers such as Lady Morgan and Maria Edgeworth, participates in the discourse of toleration by making fiction both intensify and organize differences in Catholic and Protestant beliefs and alliances. Although Irish Catholics were viewed as a potentially destabilizing *imperium in imperio* that might threaten the 1800 union of Britain and Ireland, the national tale – a genre frequently depicting the reconciliation of an Anglo-Irish landlord with his Irish tenants – makes Ireland into a distinctive member of an expanding

Britain precisely by virtue of its inclusion in Britain's mutually supporting economic relations and secular institutions. Critics frequently read national tales as either advocates of national sentiment or collaborators in the imperialistic suppression of that sentiment; I contend, however, that novels such as Edgeworth's *Ennui* (1809) and *The Absentee* (1812) subtly make local Irish "habits" and the "multiplicity of minute . . . details"[22] visible to the landlord – and to us as readers of fiction – only because of the landlord's attention to "business" and economic "affairs." The heroes of such novels are as notable for their strong attachments to Ireland as they are for their accommodation within the marketplace. I end this chapter by re-evaluating the relationship between national tales and Scott's historical novels. My account of the national tale's interest in the contours of tolerant government, rather than its interest in any straightforward celebration of nationalism, allows us to achieve a clearer view of the national tale's relation to the historical novel. As in *Old Mortality*, Scott's characters do not only express or value their personal beliefs. They must also negotiate a place for those beliefs within new structures of government that preserve and regulate them. Modern British institutions, submitting all religious communities to their rule, are thus said to commit "a rape upon the chastity of the church," since their goal is not to preserve a uniform religious chastity but to "tolerate all forms of religion which [are] consistent with the safety of the state."[23]

The aggressively secular perspective of the national tale – which led to complaints by many reviewers who faulted Edgeworth for her irreligion – complements rather than contradicts Wordsworth's view of the established church itself. Chapter 5 argues that the often-noted religious orthodoxy of Wordsworth's later writing does not hail the triumph of any particular doctrine as much as it discovers divergent beliefs to be assimilable within a pattern of actions that forms the recognizable basis of Britain's national community. *The Excursion* (1814), I argue, shows dissent to be an essential feature of this community. The recalcitrant character of the Solitary (a religious dissenter) does not merely act as a citizen in need of conversion. In fact, his separation from community makes him "pious beyond the intention of [his] thought": a suitable – perhaps even an ideal – subject of Britain's church-guided "powers of civil polity" (*The Excursion*, 4.1147–48). I show how this logic animates works that preceded *The Excursion*, such as *The Prelude* (1805), and those that followed it: *The Ecclesiastical Sonnets* (first published in 1822) and other poems displaying a similar preoccupation with the church. In these later works, religious establishment is not naturalized, as it is in Burke; nature is made to seem religious. The church in the landscape, a predominating image providing "rich bounties of constraint" ("The Pass of Kirkstone"), suggests that the church can be seen as a "frame of social being"[24] that minimizes – just like a landscape – its demands upon an individual consciousness.

In the last two chapters of this book, I discuss the continuing appeal of the Gothic novel's treatment of religion for writers of poetry and drama. In chapter 6, I argue that Byron and Keats capitalize on Gothic scenarios of religious violence and subterfuge; but this interest in contending beliefs – beliefs that seem socially and poetically destructive – actually expresses a profound confidence in poetry itself. The literary aims of both poets accompany a sympathy with religious tolerance, Byron arguing in parliament on behalf of Catholic Emancipation, and Keats declaring his contempt for parsons, who must be "a hypocrite to the Believer and a coward to the unbeliever."[25] And I contend that these opinions only begin to assert the more profound ways in which both authors view their poetry as literary instances of the logic of toleration. In *Childe Harold's Pilgrimage*, Byron connects his ambition for poetry with the demise of the self-determining authority of religious beliefs. Decaying monuments attract the poet's notice precisely because of their ruin: they are not the representatives of any living and animating beliefs, but examples of "mouldering shrines" that are the homes of "shrinking Gods."[26] Keats makes *The Eve of St. Agnes* and *Lamia* (1820) assert poetic power as a contrast to the dramas of belief and skepticism that they depict: contending prejudices seem conspicuously dead or hollow in relation to the poems that represent but also outlast those prejudices. Keats associates *Lamia*'s status as a literary work, for instance – a fictional "tale" inherited from Philostratus and Burton – with the palace and palace furniture that persists after Lamia "withers" and vanishes. He thus contrasts the durable fabric of his own imaginative work with the skeptical beliefs that might seek to undo its power.

I conclude this book in chapter 7 by returning full circle to the Gothic's methods of surveying, enclosing, and regulating the terrors of confessional uniformity. I examine a common practice on the Romantic stage that linked it to the Gothic novel: the practice of representing Inquisitorial politics for the consumption of a British audience. Lord John Russell's *Don Carlos* (1822), Shelley's *The Cenci* (1819), and Byron's *Cain* (1821) – a more disguised Inquisitorial drama – invite an audience to encounter the technology of confessional government, and conscript the audience as participants in the enclosure and regulation of that government. Russell's *Don Carlos*, although ignored by critics, provides a particularly compelling starting point for illustrating this technique. One of the most outspoken and eloquent parliamentary defenders of religious toleration, Russell has his eponymous hero argue against the Inquisitorial *auto-da-fé* not simply because it is unjust but because it is inefficient: toleration, he argues, is "more politic than force."[27] Shelley's *The Cenci* and Byron's *Cain*, I contend, depict an analogous enclosure of a confessional power structure by a more "politic" tolerant government, but with more tragic and disturbing dimensions. *The Cenci* makes the Inquisition itself into the guardian of tolerant policy; it sentences Beatrice to death for parricide according to a typically liberal demotion of Beatrice's claims to religious and moral purity. In *Cain*, the blasphemous hero – in many ways identified with Byron himself – finds the ultimate expression of his rage through a murder which, he insists, is unintentional. God's punishment of Cain represents the furthest reach of the Inquisitorial drama's logic of toleration: Cain is accused of his crime regardless of his intentions, but he is also treated with God's leniency in a way that resembles the tolerant state's limitless and utterly inescapable inclusiveness. Inquisitorial drama, I conclude, conveys a British commitment to tolerant government at the same time that it frequently registers the uneasiness with which writers regarded the ability of tolerant regimes to alter and transform the significance of personal beliefs.

CHAPTER I

Romanticism and the writing of toleration

A CHIMERICAL PROJECT

By 1800, members of Britain's House of Commons could confidently refer, with approval or dismay, to a "spirit of toleration." What was this "spirit," and why was it invoked either as the key to the nation's dazzling future – or as the source of its ultimate corruption and defeat? The spirit of toleration, as this chapter will discuss it, could be viewed as a series of legislative enactments extending from the Act of Toleration in 1689 to (and beyond) the repeal of the Test and Corporation Acts and Catholic Emancipation in 1828 and 1829. These were, briefly put, legal measures that made it possible for adherents of different religious beliefs to worship freely, to participate in political, military, and educational institutions, and to assume a wide range of offices in civil government. Many of those legal provisions will be described somewhat later in this chapter. But the spirit of toleration needs to be understood in another way, too: as a new and controversial way of imagining the lineaments of British government.

Indeed, nothing less than the very survival of Britain's social body seemed to be at stake. Those who so vigorously opposed toleration could very effectively argue that the British nation – indeed, any nation – was a community by virtue of its religious communion. This was a unity dependent upon a uniformity of belief, and supported by sanctions designed to enforce that uniformity: what J.C.D. Clark and other historians refer to as Britain's "confessional state."[1] Unsettling that uniformity by admitting adherents of nonconforming faiths would endanger not only the "security of church and state" but Britain's "national humanity." Defenders of Britain's Protestant communion, however, were not the only ones to use this kind of high-sounding language. *Not* to tolerate Catholics could be diagnosed by some liberal reformers, for instance, as a sickness in Britain's "moral body": it would "narrow the field of intellectual exercise and free discussion" and would only punish a group of persons who were "as harmless and as loyal as any one class of his majesty's Protestant subjects."[2] Arguments about toleration were not arguments about preserving or abolishing the authority of the state, but arguments about how that authority was to be conceived.

In order to prepare the way for the discussion in the following chapters, this chapter aims to show exactly why it may have been plausible for Bishop Butler to proclaim in 1747 that "a constitution of civil government without any religious establishment is a chimerical project of which there is no example."[3] It shows, in other words, why defenders of the established church might have had understandable reasons to believe that the nation, as they had come to conceptualize it and value it, could be threatened or at least compromised by tolerating adherents of religious beliefs outside the Anglican communion. I then want to trace the fitful emergence – in its intricately entwined political and literary shapes – of the counter-confessional discourse of toleration. Romantic writers who gave voice to this discourse would reimagine government, it could be said, in a "chimerical" form. For just like that fabled monster of Greek mythology – a beast composed of many beasts – tolerant government was imagined to be composed of the adherents of many different beliefs, without being determined or controlled by any one of the beliefs that it so generously accommodated. The Romantic government of religion was not a rule by belief, in other words, but a secular rule *over* belief.

This chapter begins by explaining the political importance of the church as it continued to be perceived throughout the three decades that I study in this book.[4] The Church of England, an element of British custom so traditional as to seem like something natural, supposedly provided a prepolitical basis for Britain's national institutions. As a naturalized tradition, one might argue, it was less important for assuring the salvation of British souls than for procuring and extending the present social order. Edmund Burke will provide my central example of one of the church's most eloquent and successful defenders during the period studied in this book. I then move my discussion towards an account of how the discourse of toleration, as it came to be elaborated by political reformers and adherents of different religious groups, came to attack what they perceived to be the injustices wrought by established religion. The burden of my argument will be to illustrate, first of all, that proponents of toleration could routinely show how unnatural the traditional structure of the church actually was: they could contend that the beliefs supposedly held by the nation's public were not actually held by that public. Reformers could thus regularly point accusingly at the church's artifice and its tyrannical authority – an artifice supported by mechanisms of power, and mechanisms of power that enforced their legitimacy through artifice. But then there is a second, more important, set of observations that this chapter makes: observations that constitute the core of this book's argument. As much as the discourse of toleration opposed the power of confessional regimes, it eventually contended that British government was brutal and excessive precisely because of its weakness. Arguments against the power of the confessional state, such as those of Jeremy Bentham (who provides the most compelling examples of the logic I am describing), ultimately exalted and aggrandized the very sources of state power that they might have seemed to oppose. Still more, the tolerant opposition to the falsity of ecclesiastical authority was conducted by enhancing, rather than diminishing, the artifice of government. The adherents of tolerant reform resisted the conceit of confessional uniformity with a vigor matched only by their intriguing and paradoxical faith in the providential sustenance of secular institutions.

The authority of religion in the conduct of British government must certainly be viewed in terms of its most ancient defenses: its ability to provide an Aristotelian hierarchy of goods – a *summum bonum* for individuals that Thomas Aquinas adapted in his account of the church's role in defining a higher good that could in turn orient human actions towards a higher end.[5] But the defenses of, and arguments against, the Anglican church revolved specifically around its political instrumentality: its function in having provided social order in the past that needed to be continued into the future. The more abstract defense of the church on religious grounds, in other words, was inseparable, in the arguments I discuss, from the historical emergence of state religion – a religion that ostensibly took on those ancient forms of care for the soul but that had been directed towards the more pragmatic end of maintaining social stability and national distinction.

Even so, it was in fact necessary for defenders of the Protestant establishment to claim that the church was *not* simply a matter of political convenience but was in fact "essential" to the state, as Henry Phillpotts (ultimately Bishop of Exeter) put it.[6] Thinking of the Protestant church may have been impossible without thinking of politics: from Henry VIII's separation from Rome and Elizabeth's elevation of the church's national importance with the 1559 Act of Supremacy, to the Glorious Revolution and beyond. But the advocates of establishment could typically brush aside the politicization of the church and put greater emphasis on the natural continuity of the church's inextricable connection with the state. Its defenders, imbibing a political tradition handed down from Hooker and Filmer, continually invoked a lexicon of natural imagery, likening the church and state to a plant or human body. The emancipation of Catholics could thus be said to lay an "axe" to the "root" of the British constitutional "tree";[7] liberal attitudes towards religion could be said to be "preying on the vitals of the country."[8] The church, according to Linda Colley's account of British nationalism, could be valued because of its efficacy as a "vital part" of Britons' present life and "the frame through which they looked at the past."[9]

But perhaps the range of Colley's unstable expressions – first "vital part" and then "frame" – attests to the way that the rhetoric of nature defended the church's explicitly political work: its role in securing the "peace, order, and happiness of the community."[10] Indeed, the notion of the church as a vital part of the British nation helped to make the adventures of history seem like a political prescription, a recipe for future harmony. After all, Anglicans could look to the church as a time-honored source of national unity and distinction, an example of "Divine favour and protection," as the Prince Regent put it in 1819, that secured "the principles of religion, and . . . a just subordination to lawful authority."[11] Established religion continued to strengthen, and be strengthened by, the union of England with Wales, Scotland, and Ireland in 1536, 1707, and 1800, respectively: the church, its supporters argued, was a "fundamental part of the Union" that also remained a consistent influence in the governance of the colonies.[12] Although the union of England and Scotland preserved the Scottish Church intact, religious oaths, tests, and other mechanisms of exclusion maintained the political dominance of the Anglican establishment. I will thus continually make reference to the hegemony of the Anglican church in *Britain* rather than merely in *England*; it is only as a *British* church, moreover, that writers such as Coleridge and Wordsworth could reimagine its social purposes. Within these growing boundaries of Britain, David Hempton suggests, the influence of the church could be measured by the way it "was intimately involved in the life of the community through its uncontested monopoly over the rites of passage, its provision of welfare and education, its widespread distribution of popular forms of religious literature and its thorough identification with the political, legal, and social institutions of the state both at the centre and in the localities."[13]

An established religion could thus seem as natural to the population of Britain as the landscape that surrounded them – and we will see, in chapter 5, how a writer such as Wordsworth drew on this traditional view of the church even while departing from it in order to reach surprising poetic results; churches in his poetry look natural so that the church seems as inclusive as nature itself. But the point that bears some emphasis at the moment is that the church, defended as natural, could never seem entirely natural enough. That is, if established religion were to persist as a natural community of believers, it needed to confront the limits of its own logic. Beliefs having acquired the status of nature did not merely describe the beliefs of Britain's population; they needed to be turned into a political imperative or prescription. And the result was that persons needed to function not as independent agents of belief but as representatives of beliefs held in the past: persons in the present were required to engage in a political *mimesis* of past beliefs.

At the most general level, this could be rationalized because religion itself (whatever the doctrinal content might be) appeared to be a welcome stabilizing instrument: all nations, in order to be nations, needed to be defined in terms of common religious beliefs – hence Bishop Butler's comment on the "chimerical" project of imagining a government without an established religion. It seemed to go without saying, moreover, that the "establishment" required for Britain was a Christian church, and this was because the social structure of Britain was inseparable from the Christian beliefs that had informed it. The Christian religion was so central to the order of the state that Lord Chief Justice Hale held that "Christianity is part of the laws of England and therefore to reproach the Christian religion is to speak in subversion of the law."[14] In his *Commentaries on the Laws of England* (1765–69), William Blackstone later concurred that "the preservation of Christianity, as a national religion, is . . . of the utmost consequence to the civil state."[15]

Blackstone's view of religion's "utmost consequence" was not merely a handsome turn of phrase. It summarized a profound political logic according to which belief could be imagined as if it generated its own consequence in the form of the state – a political logic that resonated throughout defenses of the confessional state and informed Romantic responses to them. If Blackstone's argument was that specific beliefs carried specific consequences, then it could also be argued that Britain's government was not merely Christian but specifically Anglican. Britain's laws were the consequence of specific (Protestant) codes and doctrines, held by others in the past, that needed to be reproduced in the present. British law – the foundation for the national community – *was* belief, or at least had its own foundation in it. And if Britons could look at the established church and see it as a natural part of national society, they were continually reminded that it could only *seem* natural if it received the support of their present beliefs. What was natural and thus beyond the reach of human agency contradictorily required the effort of human agency in order to maintain its natural status.

ESTABLISHING PREJUDICE: EDMUND BURKE AND THE LOGIC OF PROTESTANT LEGACY

Religious prejudice, then – the body of beliefs held in advance of social action – was a national resource as treasured as the ownership of private property. Maria Edgeworth's writing will show us, in chapter 4, how fruitfully the conflation of property ownership and religious prejudice could be examined and challenged in her fictions. It was Edmund Burke, however, who launched perhaps one of the most successful and enduring defenses of the political instrumentality of prejudice in the eighteenth century. It is this defense, developed from the tradition of Anglican ideology that I have briefly traced out so far, that will be relevant to every chapter of this book. Crucial to Burke's typically delicate and complex defense of the political role of the church – "the first of our prejudices" – was its resistance to dogmatism and its apparent achievement of a limited form of toleration.[16] First of all, he was able to articulate a defense of religion *in general as* the outcome of the customs and traditions of specific nations. Burke appointed himself as a defender of "the whole of the national Church of my own time and my own country, and the whole of the national Churches of all countries" (*Works*, VIII:40), and spoke in the broadest of terms of how religion was "one of the bonds of society" that secured "peace, order, liberty, and . . . security" (X:44). Statements of this kind showed how Burke effectively adopted a genial relativism with respect to religious belief, enabling him to argue in his speeches on the trial of Warren Hastings that colonial administration had unjustly deprived the people of India of their native beliefs and cultural practices.[17] He was just as notable for defending the claims of Catholics in Ireland; Catholicism in Ireland – like Protestantism in England – was handed down "from time immemorial" (IX:433).

Burke could relativize beliefs *among* nations, but it was quite another matter to do the same *within* them. The world and its collection of separate entities was not like a person – and thus could not have distinct beliefs assigned to it – but nations and their institutions were. This is why Burke could personify the Church of England as a parent to the

nation's children and a repository of proper values and human affect.
In a particularly resonant characterization, he saw the church as the
nation's author as well as its guardian or protector: a "wise architect"
of the state, the church labored "like a provident proprietor, to preserve
the structure from prophanation and ruin" (v:176). It could thus provide
Britain with protection from infidelity – "the harlot lap of infidelity and
indifference" – in the comforting "maternal bosom of Christian Charity"
(x:38). Burke's suggestive yet scattered figures indicated how important
it was for him in many cases to make the nation into something that
seemed natural because traditional – a "structure" that existed before its
inhabitants and thus prohibited human questioning. In one of his celebrated formulations, society was a "fixed compact sanctioned by the
inviolable oath which holds all physical and all moral natures each in
their appointed place." Only an inheritance to which one was bound by
an "inviolable oath" could furnish the "method of nature in the conduct
of the state"(v:184,79). At the same time, however, Burke's cluster of personifications of the church as architect, as proprietor, or as mother served
to show how truly vulnerable the structure was – how susceptible it might
be to "prophanation and ruin." The church was thus a crucial part of the
nation because it was the "proprietor" of the structure, making the structure look more like a person endowed with specific mental states that
continually needed to be defensively reproduced in, or countersigned by,
the members of the national population. The inviolable oath for which
Burke argued was strangely deficient in that it continually needed to
shore itself up by procuring oaths against its violation.

Now Burke's support for religious establishment was, as I suggested
earlier, a support for religious toleration. We will have ample opportunity
to see how his account of this establishment was not simply rejected
but modified by the writing of Coleridge and Wordsworth, who also
declared the church to be the very guarantee of tolerance. Following an
extensive lineage of Protestant apologists (such as Milton, who argued
for a limited freedom of the press based precisely upon principles of
Christian virtue), Burke argued in his "Speech on a Bill for the Relief
of the Protestant Dissenters" (1773), "I would have toleration a part of
Establishment, as a principle favourable to Christianity, and as a part
of Christianity" (*Works*, x:25); intolerance, conversely, was "inconsistent
with the interests of Christianity" (x:35, punctuation altered).[18] The point
towards which Burke continually drew, though, was not that the purpose
of government was toleration, but that Britain's national church was
the Anglican church, and that the Anglican church happened to be a

tolerant one. Tolerance, in other words, was merely the outcome of a fortunate historical accident. What is particularly important about this line of reasoning is that Burke was not in any sense defending toleration as a vantage point on belief (since toleration itself could not be defended as a value); rather, he maximized the importance of Protestantism as a specific *kind* of belief (a tolerant one) that could – just like the intolerant beliefs in other nations – provide Britain with its "moral basis." Its moral basis derived exclusively from its historical basis.

It should be clear enough at this point that explaining Burke's position has necessarily required a confusion between "the Church of England" and "Protestantism," a confusion between a Protestant institution and Protestant beliefs: indeed, Joseph Priestley later would criticize him for making "no difference between christianity and the civil establishment of it."[19] This confusion was a particularly instrumental one. For the institution of the church, even while its status as historical enabled it to seem larger than any person, also seemed – thanks to Burke's strategy of personification – to be very much like a person: a person, moreover, endowed with specific beliefs. Interpreters of Burke routinely point out that these religious beliefs are unsystematic in his argument and that they do not amount to any coherent doctrine.[20] Perhaps this could account for his opposition in the *Letters on a Regicide Peace* to the "doctrine," "abstraction," and "wretched system" behind French Revolutionary politics and the sympathizers with those politics in Britain (*Works*, x:8,10,23). But this really only explains a fraction of Burke's view. Those beliefs, while seemingly unsystematic and attached to conveniently imprecise terms such as the "public," or the "common sense of mankind," could nonetheless provide justification for the exclusion of impious or nonconforming members of the national community (x:71,81). And this strategic lack of doctrinal systematicity could regularly be invoked as a way of making the operations of prejudice seem attractive and benign rather than exclusive or injurious.[21]

The point I need to make about the place of religion in Burke's account is that the very demonization and denial of doctrine in fact shows us how important he actually deemed specific sets of beliefs or dispositions to be. Burke's defense of a shallow form of consensus, that is, required a much more comprehensive sense of agreement: British institutions routinely emerged in his arguments as forms that threatened to become so emptied of moral and religious content that they required refilling by the dispositions of the persons over which they ostensibly governed. "Our own dispositions" – dispositions constituting proper

notions of "humanity, morals and religion," he argued – "[are] stronger
than Laws" (x:111). Or, in another instance, he claimed that it was in the
"Christian Religion" that "all our laws and institutions stand as upon
their base" (IX:126). This was what made the Protestant establishment in
particular "a great national benefit, a great publick blessing," whose "existence or . . . non-existence . . . is a thing by no means indifferent to the
publick welfare" (x:59). And this is what made Burke continually frame
his politics in rigorously religious terms: "We are protestants, not from indifference," he wrote in the *Reflections*, "but from zeal" (v:174). "Zeal," furthermore, was to arise not only from personal conviction but from public
enforcement: if the Protestant establishment was a "national benefit,"
it remained that way because it was "publicly practised and publicly
taught," and this in turn required that public institutions "have a power
to say what the Religion will be" (10:17).

IMPERIUM IN IMPERIO; OR, THE LOGIC OF ANGLICAN PANIC

Burke's arguments are worth lingering over, I think, because of the frequency with which they tend to be invoked as cornerstones of Romantic political and aesthetic theory.[22] Certainly critics have not mistaken
Burke's influence on his contemporaries, judging from the extent to
which writers felt compelled to respond to the *Reflections on the Revolution in France* following its publication. On the other hand, though,
many students of Romanticism have too quickly taken "Burke" to be the
metaphorical representative of "Romanticism" – thus accepting Burke's
politics and aesthetics as the repository of historical truth – without considering him as a participant in the context of political debate. What
frequently gets lost in this tendency is any attention to the extent to
which Romantic writers renewed a discussion of the relation between
religious belief and the institutional organs of the state that – in Burke's
argument – had been treated as a complex but highly problematic relationship of identity. Far from merely extending the Burkean account,
as I will be arguing throughout this book, Romantic writers are most
notable for exerting an intriguing and transformative pressure on it: for
negotiating the relationship between belief and the tolerant institutional
organs of government.

I will be turning to this point in a moment, but – before moving further – I wish to emphasize how important it was for Burke's argument
to be supported by, and give support to, a whole range of official and
unofficial mechanisms that collectively excluded unnatural and perverse

elements from Britain's naturalized Protestant communion. Burke could on the one hand argue for tolerating some kinds of dissenters (Methodists, for example), but not others (Burke was particularly unwelcome to toleration for Dissenters after the outbreak of the French Revolution). Those who refused subscription to the 39 Articles were "infidels," he argued, and thus "outlaws of the Constitution; not of this Country, but of the human race. They are never, never to be supported, never to be tolerated" (*Works*, x:38). The rationale for exclusion and discrimination received considerable support from the likes of Thomas Hobbes in his *Leviathan* (1651), who opposed all those with "erroneous doctrines" who would "obtain dominion over men in this present world."[23] William Warburton – whose name will appear in discussions of Coleridge and Byron and who influenced Burke's thinking considerably – claimed in his *Alliance of Church and State* (1736) that there could be no society without "a RELIGION BY LAW ESTABLISHED," and that established religion required a "TEST-LAW for her security."[24] In Burke's day and long afterwards, parliamentary speakers and writers of all kinds, could continually invoke dissensions among beliefs as threats to national integrity. "Every kind of separation from the Established Church," one pamphleteer remarked in 1801, "by narrowing the ground on which that Church stands, tends to weaken the foundation on which the government of this country is built."[25] In 1879, one contributor to *The Nineteenth Century* could summarize – and still defend – this logic by stating that a religious establishment was necessary to the nation, and that intolerance was necessary to uphold such an establishment: "No matter what the creed be of the nation we are considering... let the nation be but convinced of the truth and the importance of it, and they will persecute for heresy, as surely as they will prosecute for theft."[26]

The British church had traditionally distinguished itself with increasing vehemence by demonizing Rome in particular as the "Antichrist," a supple term deployed to sensational effect in the most popular of religious tracts, such as Martin Bucer's *De Regno Christi* (1557) and John Foxe's *Acts and Monuments* (1563); these and other writings like them continued to hold the attention of Romantic readers and writers.[27] A history of prejudice against Catholics in Britain remains outside the scope of this project, but it is in fact closer to my purpose to note that well into the nineteenth century, Protestant Britons commonly recalled a colorful history of Catholic subversion: the Gunpowder Plot of 1605, the Irish rebellion of 1642, the Popish Plot of 1678. That history – added to Britain's multiple and protracted military engagements with Catholic powers on the continent – made skirmishes in the past seem like a prediction of future subversion and consequently as the fodder for anti-Catholic paranoia.[28] Catholics were collectively associated with deception and manipulation: "casuistry," "extreme flexibility," and "deluding slipperiness."[29] They were charged with tendencies to idolatry, mental slavery, disloyalty, and intolerance; and their spiritual affiliation was assumed to entail a political subversion that affected every aspect of their lives even outside the church. For the likes of Michael Sadler, an evangelical "Ultra" Tory, Catholicism's historic association with "cruelty, tyranny, and arbitrary power" was enough to undermine "that allegiance which is due to the sovereign power of this Protestant empire."[30] Lord Eldon likewise maintained that "the Roman Catholics had systematically pursued the accomplishment of their own objects and the destruction of our national Church, through every obstacle and without difficulty." He therefore refused to accept the vows of those who disclaimed the influence of papal authority, insisting, "There was no proof that any change had occurred in their religious principles."[31] The worst, some said, was yet to come: "The more they gain," Robert Southey wrote, "the more strongly will it be considered a point of honour for them to pursue their advantage"; Catholic ambitions would not be satisfied until they had "gained the ear of queens and kings" and taken "control of the kingdom."[32]

Before, during, and after Britain's 1800 Union with Ireland, Ireland's large population of Catholics, tenuously coexisting alongside their Anglo-Irish Protestant landlords, offered a steady source of inspiration for anti-Catholic hostility; and it is to these predispositions that national tales like Edgeworth's and Morgan's responded. Irish Catholics could not be put on an equal footing with Protestants, for they were considered to be fundamentally unsuited for civil society; throughout Ireland, Francis Jeffrey confirmed, "a Protestant alone is qualified with the appellation of an honest man, and, in common speech, the Catholics are still designated by terms of contempt and abhorrence."[33]

Still more, Ireland seemed to offer a peculiarly vivid and compelling example of an *imperium in imperio,* a state-within-a-state. This presented, in miniature, the challenge repeatedly confronting adherents of religious toleration: how could the state rule over conflicting religious rules that lurked within its boundaries? For Lord Redesdale, Catholics were "a great and compact body, a species of corporation, with all the forms and gradations of a distinct and firm government," and he believed that the native Irish, if given sufficient power, would rise in rebellion against the Union in order to reclaim church lands and endowments.[34] William

Phelan charged in his *History of the Policy of the Church of Rome, in Ireland* (1827) that Catholic "government" was a "HIEROCRACY; swaying a compact mass of five millions of people, with a plentitude of dominion which might be envied at Constantinople, and breaking down all distinctions among their vassals into the same abject prostration before their insolent supremacy."[35] The political sympathies of Irish Catholics only aggravated the popular perception of this threat. Fears of a French invasion of Ireland in the 1790s, along with a rebellion of Irish Catholics in 1798, bolstered arguments on behalf of the "Protestant Ascendancy" against emancipation; like Luddism and other workers' movements during the early years of the nineteenth century, Catholics were regularly suspected of Jacobinism. The political insubordination of forty-shilling freeholders against their Protestant landlords in 1818 and 1823 – encouraged by support of the Catholic bishops – increased the popularity of pro-Catholic candidates for parliamentary seats in Ireland and encouraged further worries about Catholic political alliances.

Although anti-Catholicism may have been the more conspicuous source of exclusionary national definition (especially appropriate given its Catholic neighbors on the continent), it was just as important for Britain to distinguish itself through its hostility to various forms of Protestant Dissent. The association between Protestant Dissent and lower-class unrest could easily be recalled by writers of the day for dramatic effect; subversive movements by "Levellers" and "Diggers," though seemingly buried in the nation's past, showed how dissenting sects were all "equally fierce and intolerant."[36] Like Catholics, they could be accused of "the grossest superstitions" and fantastic manipulative powers.[37] The "popular eloquence" of Methodist preachers, one *Quarterly* reviewer reported, "strikes, inflames, and leaves no time for the mind to cool, or for the excited passions to subside." "We are strongly opposed to the nonsense of Methodistic experience, which makes the effect of obstructed bile, and the state of the animal spirits, the test of religion."[38]

A variety of different forms of Protestant nonconformity, moreover, could also be regarded as infectious growths within the state, competing with the established church for power. Southey charged in his *Life of Wesley* (1820) that Methodists, just like Catholics, were a troubling "*imperium in imperio*," and – in agreement with Burke – he insinuated connections between British Dissenters and the French Revolution.[39] Lord Redesdale asserted that political freedom for Dissenters would necessarily result in an attempt to obtain power; religious liberty meant "the possession of political power; for political power, and nothing else, was manifestly the aim of those who petitioned in favor of [toleration]."[40] For the Bishop of Bristol, the danger of religious freedom could already be observed in the education of children outside the supervision of the church. Dissenters, he declared, were "a powerful body. . . . [t]hey had great control in many places": a control enabled, in part, by the way they had "established schools in various parts of the country, and they frequently kept the children at those schools on the Sunday when the service of the Church was going on, by which they were deprived of religious instruction."[41]

I have here addressed only two of the prominent targets of Anglican panic for Romantic poets and political theorists, and surprisingly similar exclusionary arguments could be applied to a whole range of adherents of nonconforming religions. Jews, for example, could be regarded as "a distinct and separate nation" within Britain with "their own purposes and speculations" which included a project to "unchristianize themselves and the country."[42] Such rationalizations for exclusion, however, were not merely personal opinions. They gave support to, and were supported by, an impressive array of coercive legal devices that kept the "inviolable oath" of society intact. The inseparability of church and state was secured by the revolutionary settlement and the institution of the Coronation Oath of 1689, which stipulated that the sovereign would "maintain the laws of God, the true profession of the Gospel, and the Protestant reformed religion established by law." The function of that settlement, Sadler claimed, was to "exclud[e] from power . . . the devoted adherents of a cruel, tyrannous, and superstitious church."[43] Long before the revolutionary settlement, the predominance of the Anglican church had been secured by a whole range of legal measures including the 1662 Act of Uniformity, the Corporation Act of 1663, the Conventicles Act of 1664, the Five Mile Act of 1665, and the Test Act of 1673, all of which rearticulated the persecuting spirit directed against both Catholics and Protestant Dissenters dating back to the reign of Henry VIII. These acts imposed limitations on travel, public worship, the transfer of property, and participation in public offices. Acts in 1678 and 1689 prohibited Catholics from entering parliament. The Blasphemy Act of 1698 barred from office all those, educated as Christians, who denied (in conversation, speech, or print) the doctrine of the Trinity, the truth of Christianity, or the divine authority of the Bible; this routinely shaped the law of libel, which protected the reputations of individuals, but of Christianity as well – as the blasphemous libel trials of those including John Taylor (1676), Edmund Curll (1727), and Thomas Woolston (1729) amply showed.

This is not to say that the efforts of English reformers before the nineteenth century were not successful. The Toleration Act of 1689 was itself an attempt to unite Dissenters within the Church of England; but this was a "Bill of Indulgence" rather than a repeal of oppressive acts, and it excluded Catholics from the scope of its reliefs. Limited concessions were provided by the Relief Acts of 1774, 1778, and 1791: acts that repealed certain components of the penal code, and thus provided for freedoms of religious teaching, the saying of Mass, and the transfer of Catholic property. The Franchise Act of 1793 afforded parliamentary suffrage for Catholic forty-shilling county freeholders in both Britain and Ireland. Although the effects of the penal code had been eased, Catholics and Dissenters were still denied seats in parliament by the acts of 1678 and 1689; and they were also excluded by means of the Test and Corporation Acts – which required oaths and declarations that they could not conscientiously provide – from holding civil posts such as Chancellor, Commissioner of the Seal, Lord High Treasurer, along with numerous judicial and military posts.[44] The legislative measures prior to the nineteenth century, important as they were, had provided private freedoms while maintaining public discrimination.[45]

LOCKE AND THE CONSTRUCTION OF RELIGIOUS FREEDOM

What stands out above all, from the sketch that I have provided of these policies of exclusion, is that the legal apparatus providing the means for exclusion was understood merely to reflect popular prejudices – as Francis Jeffrey claimed, the prejudices of British society were not the result of "directly imposed" laws but instead "originate[d] ... in the habits and feelings which the law originally suggested, and still encourages and foments."[46] At the same time, though, this apparatus needed to enforce the very prejudices that were assumed to stand at its base. Laws governing exclusion did not only represent beliefs that were the "basis" (to use Burke's terminology) for British society; they tended to require and construct an exclusive basis, through political means, that could in turn be claimed to act as their prepolitical foundation.

This point needs to be emphasized in order to prepare our return to the question with which I began this chapter: what was the "spirit of toleration" that seemed to threaten the comforting basis of British society in its time-honored prejudices? In one very popular view of intellectual history, the late eighteenth and early nineteenth centuries were characterized by a diminished belief in religious modes of authority.[47] Obviously this perspective finds support from the frequently noted decline in public commitment to the Church of England in the late eighteenth century.[48] Thomas Mozley, for example, sadly reported in his *Reminiscences* that the number of communicants attending Easter Sunday services at St. Paul's had dropped to 6 by 1800. He blamed the poor showing, in fact, on the church's lack of faith in itself: non-resident benefices had become the norm rather than the exception, and pastoral duties were therefore performed only "intermittingly and cursorily."[49] Nineteenth-century observers continually took note of how this decline in commitment to the church merely reflected a collective lack of faith that had come to invade British society. By the mid-nineteenth century, Engels speculated that the nation had been infected with the spirit of "continental skepticism in matters religious," attributing the changes that could be observed in British institutions to a universal change of mind – an increasing skepticism, disenchantment, or "loss of belief."[50]

Observations such as these certainly lend support to still broader statements that historians have made about the "secularization" of European culture during this period. Scholars such as Keith Thomas and Brian Singer, for instance, associate the rise of secular institutions with a growing enlightened scientific perspective on nature and social organizations: the decline in religious authority, in this view, can be attributed to a growing realization of the powers of the individual rational mind.[51] Or – from the Marxist perspective adopted by historians such as Isaac Kramnick – the same phenomenon can be attributed to the development of a bourgeois liberalism that emphasized individual self-advancement over more abstract and distant theological foundations of social unity.[52] Both explanations press rather hard on the uniformly altering set of beliefs that accompanies historical change; but it should not escape our notice that the lack of commitment to established religion recorded by nineteenth-century observers such as Engels did not in any way imply a lack of commitment to religious belief more generally. Just the opposite, really: Joseph Priestley could describe the church establishment that Burke defended as an "old and decayed . . . building" attended by "few persons of rank"; but "Dissenters of one denomination or other, are very much increased of later years."[53] By 1851 (according to some reports), half of the nation's population was nonconforming.[54] The eighteenth-century decline in Anglican church attendance was joined by a rapid increase in sectarian activity, a revival of evangelical spirit within the church itself (not to mention the rise of the more conservative "Oxford" movement in the nineteenth century) – developments that should add a significant amount of historical complexity to the picture of religious life in Britain. But if toleration could be understood merely as diversity – the sheer multiplication of religious groups that could be observed in British social life – it was also something more: it consisted of new conditions under which religious beliefs could be practiced, and altered protocols through which beliefs could be assigned social value. As one writer in *Blackwood's* put it, toleration was "a new method of managing the interests of England."[55]

It would obviously be a mistake to suggest that toleration was simply *completed* during the period that I am studying. Indeed, it would be easy to point to any number of ways in which intolerant acts of legislation, judicial decisions, and practices of government continued throughout the nineteenth century. The continued availability of blasphemy as a criminal offense – as the trials of figures such as Daniel Isaac Eaton, William Hone, and Richard Carlile demonstrated – suggests that I am not describing a straightforward progress. The infamous Six Acts, with their restrictions on seditious meetings and on blasphemous and seditious expression, were passed into law in 1819, and the Alien Bill was renewed in 1820; both would add further complication to such a claim. At the same time, however, I do in fact want to account for toleration in terms of a set of specific legal and political achievements to be observed from the 1790s to Catholic Emancipation in 1829 – achievements that established a precedent for related measures throughout the nineteenth century. I also want to account for toleration as an available discourse – defending, explicating, and facilitating those achievements – that can be analyzed in terms of a specific kind of logic: a logic that permits us to see why toleration was considered chimerical or novel (and why historians have continually viewed the events of the early decades of the nineteenth century as a turning point in the re-evaluation of the confessional state's traditional methods for securing social order).

We should thus acknowledge the importance of an entire complex of legislative enactments that very gradually awarded religious freedoms and that also institutionally supported and managed those freedoms. The Trinity Act of 1813, for example, relieved adherents of different religions – including Unitarians but also Jews, Muslims, Deists, and so forth – of certain criminal penalties; the 1828 repeal of the Test and Corporation Acts (of 1661 and 1673), and the 1829 removal of Catholic disabilities (including the Test Act of 1678 and oaths of abjuration), produced significantly expanded freedom to participate in government offices. Later in the nineteenth century, a bill for the further relief of restrictions against Jews was passed in 1858; and laws against blasphemous libel were substantially relaxed. At the same time, a coordinating series of acts provided for expanded activities of government, from the development of housing for the poor and improving prison conditions to planning a system of national education and expanding resources for public security. It is not entirely surprising – from the vantage point that I will be taking in this book – that the year of Catholic Emancipation was also the year of the establishment of a full-time London police force. Lord Russell, one of the leading proponents of the repeal of the Test and Corporation Acts (and author of *Don Carlos* [1822], to be discussed in chapter 7), soon followed up the establishment of this force by appointing a commission to address the development of similar forces throughout England and Wales.[56]

These developments that I have only briefly described were significant, I would argue, not because they consisted of new beliefs (whether scientific or self-interested), but because they combined to promote a new *relation* between beliefs and institutions of secular government. Toleration was thus envisioned less frequently as an altered set of personal dispositions, than as an altered disposition of government towards belief that provides a genealogy for John Rawls's account of the liberal state's ability to "allow for a diversity of doctrines and the plurality of conflicting, and indeed incommensurable, conceptions of the good."[57] In order to expand upon this argument that I have so far only described in the most abstract terms, I do not aim to provide a history of liberal toleration in Europe or in Britain. Instead, I want to draw attention to the intensifying discussions of the subject in the late eighteenth century by first addressing some crucial features of John Locke's *A Letter Concerning Toleration* (1689). Locke's text articulated a disposition towards religious belief – a belief about the institutional significance and positioning of belief – that would continue to resonate throughout the later works of Romantic political speculation that I explore in this book.

However frequently Locke has been extolled or vilified as an early apostle of possessive individualism, his importance in the Romantic account of toleration can be understood in quite different terms.[58] We can certainly see how welcome the *Two Treatises of Government* (1690) have been to historians who view Locke as an early and influential defender of the middle class – especially when he states (in chapter 5 of the *Second Treatise*, "Of Property") that every man "has a *Property* in his own *Person*. The *Labour* of his Body, and the *Work* of his Hands . . . are properly his."[59] The *Second Treatise* extended the *First Treatise's* opposition to Filmer by insisting that God's law is not a law of the divine right of kingship, but a law of individual ownership: "God, by commanding to subdue, gave Authority so far to Appropriate" (*Treatises*, 292). If it was clear enough that the right to subdue might continually engage one person's claim to property into a conflict with another's, Locke turned to contract, to "compact and agreement" between social agents, as a resolution to the ever-present problem of scarcity. The obvious problem of contract – that even in securing personal liberty it would in no way guarantee the equal distribution of resources – was very neatly resolved in the *Second Treatise* by differentiating between tacit and explicit contract. No self-interested social agent would ever simply agree to fewer resources than another agent, but all agents tacitly agreed – a "tacit and voluntary consent" – to the economic system that placed them in unequal positions. That "tacit and voluntary" amounted to an oxymoron – because tacit agreement was not in fact an agreement but consisted of the "bounds of Societie . . . without compact" – was precisely Locke's point. Tacit agreement was an agreement beyond agreement, or a "conveniency" that preceded individual claims of "right" (302).

The especially important feature of tacit consent was that it made the "bounds of Societie" and modes of "conveniency" not merely into tradition or immemorial custom (as in Burke) but into the governmental regulation of contract itself, which is why the earlier chapters of Locke's treatise continually argued for the capacity of "government" to act as the overarching organization of individual claims to property. The "state of nature" did, in a sense, consist of a state of disconnectedness and disorganization that preceded the foundation of a "Politick Society." But what was even more crucial was that this very same state of nature, in Locke's conception of it, required notions of "Peace and Safety" tailored to the "preserv[ation] of mankind in general" in order to be defended. Nature needed to enlist the presence of society as the organ to which individuals might look for "assistance" and "reparation" for their "injury." While "Civil Government" seemed to arise out of the consent of individuals, it was also – in a paradoxical way – a necessarily anterior structure that preceded and regulated consent (273–77).[60]

It is precisely on this point that we find the connection between the two *Treatises* and Locke's work on toleration. For the *Treatises* (which, according to some scholars, were drafted before *A Letter Concerning Toleration*) developed an argument not only about individual possession but also about the appropriate *regulation* of possession that occupied his thinking in the *Letter*. Locke, that is, arrived at a correlation between religious belief and property ownership, but not a correlation that depended merely on the identification of both belief and property as private. It was a correlation that depended instead upon his ability to mark out a domain of patterned relations between social agents that in fact restructured the significance of belief in such a way as to render its meaning in terms of its social effectiveness. Locke did, of course, defend religious belief as the internal property of individuals, for "true religion consists in the inward and full persuasion of the mind; and faith is not faith without believing."[61] The magistrate was therefore forbidden from intervening in the religion of political subjects, "which, whether it be true or false, does no prejudice to the worldly concerns of their fellow-subjects, which are things that only belong unto the care of the commonwealth" (*Letter*, 60).

Nevertheless, Locke continually demarcated a sphere of government intervention for the "care of the commonwealth" that *never* treated belief as a matter of only private ownership.[62] When Locke used the word "prejudice" in the passage from which I just quoted, he might have very easily substituted the word "injury," or "harm." And the substitution serves to show us how "prejudice" had shifted in his argument from a word that described the individual mental dispositions of political subjects – inclinations that might be either "true or false" – to a word that described an inhibition of movement in worldly affairs.[63] The further discussion of religion in the *Letter* goes on to show in even more striking terms how prejudice was transformed from an issue of religious relevance at the level of psychological disposition into an issue of *social* relevance insofar as it might inhibit or "prejudice" the movements effected by other people's prejudices.

Locke thus anticipated an argument about the sanctity of private worship in this way:

You will say . . . if some congregations should have a mind to sacrifice infants, or, as the primitive Christians were falsely accused, lustfully pollute themselves in promiscuous uncleanness, or practice any other such heinous enormities, is the magistrate obliged to tolerate them, because they are committed in a religious assembly? I answer. No. These things are not lawful in the ordinary course of life, nor in any private house; and, therefore, neither are they so in the worship of God, or in any religious meeting. (47).

Toleration emerged in Locke's argument, then, not as a right to privacy but as a legal *enclosure* of the private that both enhanced private religious choices but produced an extra-religious legal registration and restriction of those choices according to their contribution to the "public good" (43). Making all aspects of "the ordinary course of life" into the province of legal differentiation – regardless of its religious value or its place in the privacy of the home – he could actively promote the restriction of harms to infants, as in the example above. And he could, in contrast, identify rituals such as "the washing of an infant with water" as an "outward worship" that should be unhindered by the magistrate's intervention; but there was still an important exception. For "if the magistrate understand such washing to be profitable to the curing or preventing of any disease that children are subject unto, and esteem the matter weighty enough to be taken care of by a law, in that case he may order it to be done" (42–44). Locke continued this line of reasoning to insist upon the "extreme difference" between this example and a law that would require "that all children shall be baptized by priests, in the sacred font, in order to the purification of their souls" (44). And we can consequently see how the privacy of religion became important in his argument not as a place of self-definition by religion's own "nature" but as the site for a whole apparatus of distinctions that treated personal belief as an ever-receding vanishing point or blind-spot for public redefinition. Toleration did not arise from the magistrate's indifference but from a legal and institutional construction that *produced* a region of indifference precisely by virtue of its ability to account for "extreme difference." The subject of tolerant government was conceived as freely worshiping, while also continually looking to the apparatus of government as the resource for a social construction of the meaning of worship.[64]

I have spent these pages interpreting Locke's account in order to emphasize what would turn out to be an influential interest in the inclusive forms and constructive purposes of tolerant government. It was this, and not a defense of possessive individualism, that made him "that great man Locke" to writers such as Philip Furneaux towards the end of the eighteenth century.[65] By this time, as I suggested in the opening pages of this chapter, it was common to understand toleration as a far more pervasive "spirit": a spirit that could not be understood as a collective consciousness but as a commitment to a structure of social relations dedicated to accommodating and managing disparate consciousnesses. The writers forming the intellectual milieu for early Romantic poets and novelists continually opposed themselves to the traditional logic of the confessional state by pointing, first of all, to its obvious falsity.[66] Daniel Isaac Eaton called the church "a patent for hypocrisy; the refuge of sloth, ignorance and superstition, the cornerstone of tyranny," an argument that was repeatedly articulated in the work of Paine, Hone, and other radicals – and that clearly inspired the antinomian energies of William Blake.[67] At this level of argument, such writers could keenly respond in

kind to the claims that the church establishment was a thing of nature –
asserting that, while religion was natural, establishment was not. William
Cobbett's *History of the Protestant Reformation in England and Ireland* (1824–27)
showed how the Protestant establishment had only been secured through
the imposition of military force.[68] The "unnatural mixture" of church
and state, Priestley claimed, consisted of "a *fungus* of establishment upon
the noble plant of christianity, draining its best juices."[69]

Still further, though, it was possible to suggest that the confessional
state was not merely a misrepresentation of people's actual beliefs; it in
fact *encouraged* the misrepresentations that it ostensibly set out to remove.
This was an argument that differed substantially from Locke's. Locke's
Letter repeatedly pointed to intolerance as an evil because it violated
Christianity itself (*Letter*, 25); even the likes of Richard Price thought of
"religious liberty" primarily in terms of "different persuasions of Christians," thus necessarily excluding Catholics with their "shocking rubbish"
of Popery.[70] But it was also possible to show how the logic of confession –
the very attempt to impose uniformity through accumulating oaths, tests,
and penal laws – entailed a far more disturbing and disabling dilemma.
For if it seemed from one point of view as if a fundamental obscurity of
belief demanded that the law multiply the means of ensuring religious
uniformity, it seemed from another quite different point of view that
the traditional means of ensuring religious uniformity elevated and enhanced belief as something obscure and problematic. In his *Enquiry Concerning Political Justice* (1793), William Godwin summed up an increasingly
widespread view of oath-taking: the Thirty-Nine Articles as a statement
of personal belief, he claimed, actually created a division between public
statement and private belief. Oaths and sacramental tests only "make
men hypocrites," he wrote; they functioned merely as inducements to
secrecy since they already produced "a perpetual discord between our
professions and our sentiments" – a disparity between form and content,
statement and belief. On this account, the relation between individual and community was rather plainly structured as institutionalized
hypocrisy – the necessity of lying.[71]

The outlines of this logic continually appeared in the writings and
speeches of critics and reformers. Lord Russell, for example, pointed out
that doctrinal requirements for office created a "temptation to abuse
the sacrament," for they made oaths into a mechanism of "patronage
and profit." Even a "regular communicant" could be hostile to the beliefs of the Church of England, he claimed; even conformity might hide
deeper levels of nonconformity.[72] But there is an even more intriguing

dimension to many of the popular critiques of religious establishment that needs to be emphasized here. The argument against the false and tyrannical mechanisms of Britain's confessional state was also an argument against its weakness. This should not, of course, detract from the very important methods through which reformers continually identified the establishment of religion as not merely un-Christian but also destructive of personal liberty.[73] The very condition of liberty necessarily depended upon the disestablishment of the church – or, at least, a drastic reduction or elimination of its traditional powers. Joel Barlow wrote in his *Advice to the Privileged Orders* (1792–93), for example, that "*The existence of any kind of liberty is incompatible with the existence of any kind of church.*" "By *church*," he continued, "I mean any mode of worship declared to be national, or declared to have any preference in the eye of the law."[74]

This way of arguing against government as a false imposition, though, reveals only part of the story. For the point that these writers frequently wished to make was that national institutions needed to be expanded and strengthened rather than contracted. Priestley's *Essay on the First Principles of Government* (2nd edn., 1771) contended that a "full toleration" for Catholics – something that Locke was not able to contemplate – would in fact enlarge the power of government over the nation's population: "We should, at least, by this means, be better judges of their number, and increase." If Locke was concerned about the extent to which Catholics did not merely practice a religion but wished to overthrow the government, Priestley suggested that toleration would enable the government to "keep a watchful eye over the papists." Furthermore, toleration would necessarily produce allegiance rather than demand it: "they would not only cheerfully acquiesce in, but would become zealously attached to our excellent form of *free government*."[75]

Other pleas for tolerance tended to follow suit: pleas that continually linked the advocacy for freedom with an advocacy for government to act as a "guardian" that could secure "distributive justice" and supply a protection from "physical evils."[76] William Frend defended his opposition to oath-taking at Cambridge precisely by arguing for the coherence of the University's "discipline," with its differentiation of subjects and degrees, which could render all concerns with the "*Unity of Truth* in the Church" irrelevant.[77] Dyer's *Complaints of the Poor People of England* (1793) campaigned against the power of religious establishments but also advocated a new and still more extensive system of national education, national charity, and police forces that would include and superintend adherents of all beliefs.[78] The direct response to Burke, then – and to a

whole tradition of defenses of religious establishment – was to disaggre-
gate religion from government; not just to procure increased liberty but
to redescribe government's "proper end."[79] The state would no longer
establish and perpetuate religious consensus, but would provide "whole-
some laws to prevent men from injuring one another," and "execute
those laws, so as to preserve the *peace of society.*"[80]

These altered views of the aims of secular government with respect to
religious belief cannot be described as an attempt to impose a superior
kind of moderate temper or rationality on a national population – and it
is here that I must emphasize the distinction between these aims and numerous intertwined strains of thought that intellectual historians group
together under the term "enlightenment." The names of Gibbon, Hume,
Rousseau, and Voltaire (among others) find their way into discussions
in the following chapters, but they continually appear as figures whose
ideas require either opposition or adjustment. There are important reasons for this. Hume's equation of social refinement with "mildness and
moderation," for instance, required an art of government hostile to all
forces of excess: indolence and innovation, fanaticism and superstition.[81]
Rousseau's consistent emphasis on the formation of society as a kind
of rationalized religion required "transforming" particular wills into the
collective will; he thus went so far as to say that a diversity of "motives"
and "opinions," leading to "long debates, dissensions, and tumult" contributed to the "decline of the state."[82] To be sure, the writers I have
been discussing could routinely point to the alliance of church and state
as a mere superstition – or plead with their readers to honor "truth"
and "nature" above a blind adherence to conventional beliefs.[83] Such
arguments, it might be said, clearly anticipated John Stuart Mill's more
systematic defense of liberty for the sake of achieving "truth" or "a rational assurance of being right"; for him, freedom yielded an increasing
number of "doctrines which are no longer disputed or doubted."[84] But
what I have been arguing is that the admittedly powerful urge towards
the advancement of knowledge was necessarily tied to a support of tolerant government that was in fact designed to relieve its participants from
adhering to a specific kind of truthful or untruthful knowledge. Toleration was envisioned as a way of organizing the adherents of different
beliefs regardless of the individual claims that those beliefs might have
to truth or falsity, rationality or irrationality.

At no point in the argument in this chapter or in those that follow do
I want to suggest that this technique of toleration was able to free itself
of hostility towards different kinds of religious beliefs. The marginalized

position of Catholicism in the Gothic novel, continued in the work of
Wordsworth and Coleridge – or the offensive representations of Jews in
the novels of Edgeworth – will show us how inaccurate such an idea
would be. Although I will be more explicit about the meaning of these
regions of hostility in those discussions, I wish to emphasize here that the
discourse of toleration engaged in a *redirection* of hostility. For the opposition to Catholicism and other supposed forms of religious aberrations or
nonconformities continually emerged throughout the period as an opposition to a specific relation between belief and government, not only
an opposition to belief itself. Robert Robinson wrote in his *Ecclesiastical
Researches* (1792) that

that kind of religion, which the Catholics always propagated, ought to be considered, as it really is, not merely a religion, but as a species of government,
including in it a set of tyrannical maxims injurious to the lives, liberties, and
properties of citizens in a free state, and tending to render the state dependent
on a faction called the church, governed from age to age by a succession of
priests.[85]

As I will discuss more fully in the next chapter, the hostility towards
Catholicism was most important in this period as a suspicion of the
monastic retreat from society: not because monasticism subverted normative beliefs, but because it sought to form a society governed by its
own beliefs that it privileged over all other values. Monastic environments
could thus attract criticism for self-enclosing practices such as celibacy,
precisely because celibacy signaled one amongst many withdrawals from
social contact overseen by the state. Marriage in the Gothic novel, we
will see, is less important as a celebration of privacy and domesticity than
as a solicitation for, and confirmation of, public regulation.

By the same token, Isaac Taylor's *Fanaticism* (1833), while viewing fanaticism as "unreasonableness" and "perversion," more frequently saw
it as a fundamental resistance to social stability that was a great deal
more general: a "valour of the clan" mixed with "unsocial emotions,"
a "rancorous contempt or detestation of mankind."[86] With a rich and
transformative networking of religious offenses into criminal offenses,
Taylor came to see fanaticism and "clerical arrogance" as a tendency to
"confound all distinctions, violate all modesty, and in the interested idolatry of human excellence commit frightful outrages upon the just rules
of piety." These "just rules of piety" were less significant as religious piety
than as an extra-religious code of law. For fanaticism involved a desire
to act "as proxy for the minister of Justice in his own case" – a "hope of

abating the demands of justice in the region of chastisement." For the fanatic, "there is no murder in murder . . . but the perpetrator is inflate with the persuasion of himself being a demigod in goodness."[87]

In the logic of toleration, I am arguing, Catholicism, fanaticism, and other non-normative beliefs were not used to characterize a hostile "other" that required exclusion for the sake of national consolidation. Instead, these beliefs – including the tenets of Anglican orthodoxy themselves – could be mobilized as a receding but nonetheless volatile vanishing point serving as a focus for the more capacious organizational functions of British government. The hostility towards specific kinds of beliefs was a hostility towards a government-by-belief that continually found an antidote in social intercourse itself. Such beliefs provided an occasion to intervene within the closed structure of confessional organizations: an intervention that simultaneously separated individuals from the privacy of confessional arrangements (hence the common distinction between tolerating "Catholics" rather than "Catholicism," a belief but not a government) and yet also exalted the secular pressures of government as a vital resource for distinguishing and articulating the very personal beliefs that were "freely" practiced.

An insistence upon religion as the province of personal belief, coupled with an insistence upon society and its institutions as the indispensable resource for the meaning of those beliefs: this was the logic underwriting the discourse of Romantic toleration that will serve as a guide for the discussions in the following chapters of this book. In one sense, this line of thinking could find expression as a series of paradoxes. For Priestley, the avoidance of Catholicism required the toleration of Catholics; and this was because "liberty" was inevitably combined with "union," or "felicity" with "security."[88] The problem with the alliance of church and state, for Barlow, could be located not in only in its religious prejudices but in its prejudice against religious prejudices: its attempts to "extirpat[e] the idolatries of ancient establishments."[89] What is interesting about these expressions, I think, is the way that their constructions repeatedly draw attention to the way that government itself could be understood as a kind of fiction – or, at least, as a realm of organizational functions decidedly removed from the personal and empirically centered vantage point of belief. Even as reformers regularly criticized the church establishment for its artificiality, that is, tolerant government could be defended by opposing the artifice of confessional regimes only to reassert it in a new and more absorbing way. The problem with the confessional structure of government – that individuals were continually forced to adhere to a

specific doctrine in order to participate in government and in civil institutions – could be solved by the capacity of a tolerant regime to abridge
the need to correlate religious doctrines with the vital and facilitating
artifices of government. The individual subject of tolerant government
was to be recognized as "a kind of artificial being, propelling and pro-
pelled by new dependencies, in which nature can no longer serve . . . as
a guide." And the proper sphere of government was to supplement the
"*physical and moral powers*" of persons with "artificial aid" and "artificial
industry": providing each subject with a sustaining "art or trade," while
also securing "personal protection and public happiness."[90]

BENTHAM AND THE RULE OF BELIEF

This notion of society's artificial aid – amounting to a reorganization
and redirection of belief in a sphere of "new dependencies" – brings the
Romantic discourse of toleration into connection with a trajectory of
thought that could extend from Adam Smith's *Theory of Moral Sentiments*
(1759) to Emile Durkheim's *Division of Labor in Society* (1893) and beyond.
Smith, that is, celebrated the economy as an "art or contrivance" that
allowed persons to act in concert without "pure sympathy" with others;
Durkheim would later look back on the nineteenth century as the rise
of "organic solidarity," a mode of social organization, centered in public
institutions, that linked together "dissimilar natures" and insisted upon
only "a minimum number of similarities from each one of us."[91] These
"new dependencies," furthermore, would be described and appreciated
still later in different terms in Louis Althusser's account of "ideological
state apparatuses" and Marcuse's account of "Repressive Tolerance" –
both perspectives viewing an eighteenth-century solution to religious
intolerance as a renewed form of oppression.[92]

The direction of this book's argument can be clarified best, however, first by distinguishing the claims I make about Romantic writing
in the following chapters from claims that have frequently been made
about the politics of literature during this period. It is often the case
that both critics and historians describe the French Revolution, and
Britain's entry into war with France in 1793, as an occasion for radical
writers either to maintain their pro-revolutionary advocacy or establish a counter-revolutionary position of reaction. The chapters in this
book intervene in this common mode of thinking in order to suggest
that such accounts of the opposition between what Marilyn Butler calls
the "stubborn individualism" of Dissenters and the "twin hierarchies

of aristocracy and church" exclude a prominent – I would argue, per-vasive – way that Romantic writers depicted the relationship between nonconformity and the institutional organs of the state.[93] This does not mean that I am merely focusing on moderate rather than radical wri-ters. In fact, what I have been arguing is that even writers such as Dyer and Priestley – frequently understood as political radicals – were perhaps more interested in describing a revised relation between individuals and the state rather than merely campaigning for the rights of individuals or specific groups of individuals. Such writers sought to revise govern-ment – not oppose it – in order to embrace nonconformity within newly broadened and invigorated structures of social cooperation.

I can clarify this argument still further, however, by turning to the figure who can provide an even more precise insight into the specific features associated with the discourse of toleration that I wish to exa-mine in the following chapters: Jeremy Bentham. Michel Foucault has emphasized the importance of Bentham's *Panopticon* as an institutional model that effected an "individual transformation" to "habits of order and obedience"; but I am viewing the importance of Bentham's contri-butions in a different way.[94] They were less remarkable, I would suggest, for promoting specific individual "habits" than for schematizing social environments as complexes of cooperative activities that in fact dimi-nished the need for inculcating norms or habits. It is still crucial to return to Foucault's emphasis on Bentham's accounts of communal structures – schools, workhouses, hospitals, and prisons, and so forth. But this branch of Bentham's thinking must be considered in light of the specific roles that such institutions took on as solutions to what he saw as the shortcomings of the church establishment and its influence on affairs of state.[95] In *Church of Englandism and its Catechism Examined* (1818) – a frequently quoted text in Leigh and John Hunt's *Examiner*, which published extended extracts from the book in 1825 – Bentham continued and extended Godwin's arguments against the use of oaths, tests, and penal laws designed to en-force religious uniformity.[96] Bentham's work, although specifically tar-geted at the practices of the National Society for the Education of the Poor in the Principles of the Established Church, argued even more ge-nerally that public tests of faith were reminiscent of the Inquisition, "the mode of inquiry employed in foreign parts" for the purposes of "clearing the country of persons guilty of thinking differently from what was pro-fessed to be thought by the Church of Rome."[97] Britain's rehabilitated Inquisitorial tribunals were not only oppressive, to Bentham's mind, but incoherent. For the attempt to guarantee the integrity of the nation through religious uniformity either eliminated persons from any political or civil identity whatsoever, or produced the "mendacity and insincerity" that religious uniformity was designed to avoid; it was an "exclusionary system" that was only a "tissue of *imposture*, and if not of direct *forgery*, then something extremely like it."[98]

This writing on religion continually showed that Bentham's line of attack was not aimed against the irrationality of belief (although he admired Paine's *The Age of Reason* [1793] and its deistic attacks on the absurdities of Christian doctrine), but against the more fundamental technologies through which belief was constructed as socially meaningful and influential. He thus drew particular attention to the church's historic limitation on public inquiry that made dissenting belief into a "calamity" in advance of its effects, or its traditional oppositions to beneficial medical and scientific discoveries that it considered libelous.[99] In a similar spirit, he urged specific reforms such as the decriminalization of actions such as usury – a practice that had been associated with Jews and with moral prodigality – on the basis of what he understood to be its useful social effects. Or, in another instance, he argued against laws restricting blasphemous speech, "portions of discourse, by which, with or without production of uneasiness, offence has been supposed to be given to God, or to the Saints, or to both."[100] He was also an energetic supporter of Carlile (for publishing *The Age of Reason*) during his various trials for blasphemous and seditious libel.[101]

Such arguments for reform, with all of their apparently vigorous advocacy for freedom of speech and freedom of the press, constitute a significant part of Bentham's *oeuvre* not because they merely sought to remove unfair restrictions on the members of Britain's national community, but because they accompanied a more pervasive set of commitments to tolerant institutions and legal procedures.[102] These institutions and procedures were designed, first of all, to enhance the inclusiveness of government with respect to belief. Government, Bentham commented, should not be "designed to distinguish what doctrinal opinions are true." In accordance with Locke's argument, governments should relinquish any attempt to control specific beliefs, not only because matters of belief were to be left up to the relation between humans and God, but also because prejudice was an ineradicable aspect of human psychology: private "duty" and "self-regarding interest" would inevitably lead an individual – in a way that was "natural, and even, morally speaking, excusable" – to embrace personal prejudices and hostilities.[103]

Perhaps it might be said that the tolerant institution on Bentham's terms resembles Michael Walzer's recent claim that "toleration in nation-states" is established by liberating individuals from "old corporate communities" and inserting them in a new "circle of rights" with new "citizenly duties."[104] Certainly this line of argument was not foreign to proponents of toleration such as Anna Laetitia Barbauld, who urged readers "to bury every name of distinction in the common appellation of citizen."[105] Bentham's plans for institutional and legal reform both established a point of contact with this way of thinking about the "citizen" – so obviously inspired by French revolutionary values – and also departed from the ideology of sincerity, authenticity, and transparency that the discourse of citizenship frequently recommended.[106] Bentham thus opposed the mechanisms of confessional government as mere bugbears and superstitions that this son of the Enlightenment could brush away as absurd misrepresentations of real interests. But the advantage of the citizenly duties proposed in his schemes of social cooperation consisted in their capacity to provide new positions for individuals that did not merely represent their pre-institutional or authentic beliefs. Bentham's arguments opposed the mechanisms of confessional government, in other words, precisely by investing the structure of institutions with the capacity to abridge – through the convenient and functional artifice of a whole range of cooperative activities – vastly different orientations in sentiment, interest, or disposition.

Another way of framing the issue would be to say that Bentham countered the artifice and tyranny of the confessional state by reimagining government as an even more exalted and productive force of artifice – an extension and more complete elaboration of the emphasis on public union, felicity, and security found in the works of earlier writers.[107] If it is true in one sense that toleration disaggregated religion from government, it is true in an even more powerful sense that it reaggregated religion and government. Government, that is, became a source of social belonging more vital than any religion; at the same time, the authority of religion itself could be affirmed insofar as it could achieve the status of a secular, tolerant institution (thus Bentham did not merely dismiss the existence of the church but sought to reorient its function).[108] One of the key advantages that Bentham ascribed to his institutional plans – again, this is where the distinction from Foucault's account is most apparent – was that they facilitated relations between persons by diminishing the prejudicial force of their personal differences. The model of the Panopticon, for instance, was a prison plan that Bentham proudly claimed to be applicable to other institutional contexts – to poor houses, hospitals, and schools. But this owed less to its demand for conformity than to its function as a community with only imperfect communication – an order permitting a significant degree of disorder. The Panopticon, that is, offered a scheme of movements that, in its minimization of "troublesome exertion" and face-to-face "communication," was able to provide a means of organizing the actions of persons who stood in "predicaments" that were vastly "dissimilar" (*Works*, IV:41,44). William Hazlitt's *Spirit of the Age* (the essay on Bentham appearing first in the volume, published in 1825) remarked on how Bentham "had struck the whole mass of fancy, prejudice, passion, sense, whim, with his petrific, leaden mace," and reduced "the theory and practice of human life to a *caput mortuum* of reason, and dull, plodding, technical calculation."[109] Dickens followed suit by providing perhaps one of the most memorable and unforgiving portraits of utilitarianism with his fact-mongering Gradgrind in *Hard Times* (1854); even J.S. Mill, one of Bentham's more fervent disciples, admired him primarily for his "skeptical philosophy" and eminently "practical mind" that had dealt a deathblow to ancient superstitions.[110] But it turns out that Bentham viewed the institution as something more than just a way of forcing individuals to become cookie-cutter products of a rational, unemotional set of routines. The notions of economy and efficiency put forward in these programs were actually aimed to unburden individuals from having to conform to any preordained standard.

There is still a second aspect of *Panopticon* and its related projects that needs to be explored, however. For at the same time that institutions on this model were to be admirably inclusive, the very validity of their inclusiveness depended upon their constructive capacities: their capacities to increase, rather than obscure or normalize, the visibility and distinctiveness of belief. We find this, among other places, in the principle of "Separation and Aggregation" – the separation of individuals into protected and differentiated spaces and the aggregation of those individuals within a series of orchestrated group actions (*Works*, VIII:372). The institution, as Bentham put it in his *Tracts on Poor Laws and Pauper Management* (not collected until 1843), was first and foremost a way of combining "interests" and "duties" in such a way as to make the privacy of the individual dependent upon the protections afforded by institutional integration, at the same time that communal "aggregation" consisted of heightening the significance of individual differences. Turning private disposition into institutional "employment," the Benthamite institution did not simply represent individual predicament; it provided a "particular *means* for the *direction* of it," a means through which "ability" might be "directed into particular *channels*" of constructed activity or employment (VIII:382). In "a system of such a magnitude," he enthused, "not the

motion of a finger – not a step – not a wink – not a whisper – but might
be turned to account" (VIII:382).

Now we are brought closer to the significance that I want to locate
in Bentham's thinking: its methods of social inclusion, facilitation,
and differentiation. The institutional "economy" described in his writing might provide a means of accounting for "every *fragment* of ability, however minute," so that the deaf, the blind – even "classes of the
insane" – would not be excluded from participation but would find a
place within its sublime orchestrations (VIII:382). Perhaps there was no
institutional scheme that so vividly illustrated this kind of facilitation as
Bentham's *Chrestomathia* (1816), his plan for a school derived from the
work of Joseph Lancaster and Andrew Bell, whose work showed him a
model of education as enticing for its "cheapness" as for its ability to
accommodate large numbers of students.[111] Bentham's school was to be
built in his own garden, Hazlitt observed, where John Milton's house
once stood and where the "*Prince of Poets*," as a marker in the garden described him, once "breathed the air of Truth and Heaven for near half a
century." There, in "the cradle of Paradise Lost," Hazlitt went on to say,
was to be built "a thoroughfare, like a three-stalled stable, for the idle
rabble of Westminster to pass backwards and forwards to it with their
cloven hoofs." For Hazlitt, Bentham's Chrestomathic scheme perfectly
displayed his cold-hearted rationalism, his neglect of "the refinements
of taste or fancy."[112] But these observations, uncharitable as they may
seem, cannily pointed to Bentham's secularization of the Prince of Poets,
Chrestomathia operating in the most baldly literal terms as an opening of
the heaven-directed *hortus conclusus* to the devilishly heterodox "cloven
hoofs" of the lower classes.

Although Bell and Lancaster would eventually be polarized in a debate
over the role of the Anglican church in a system of national education,
Bentham's openly acknowledged debts to both writers – the Anglican
Bell and Quaker Lancaster – showed that it was precisely the fine-tuned
mechanisms of tolerant inclusion in both writers' schemes that inspired
him and that inspired others such as Edgeworth and Wordsworth. (It is
especially peculiar that *Church of Englandism* may have been designed as
an appendix to *Chrestomathia*, since it suggests that Bentham saw Bell as
a more problematic or at least ambivalent advocate of the church than
his supporters such as Sarah Trimmer did.) Indeed, the special feature of
Bentham's plan that is worth some emphasis was its ambition to produce
a system of tolerant "social co-operation" that was utterly inseparable
from the project of education (*Chrestomathia*, 31). In *Chrestomathia* could

be observed the most intriguing complex of features I have described so far: a hostility towards religious belief that finally manifested itself as an enclosure and management of belief within the secular auspices of the institution. This was an institution, furthermore, that both emphasized its distance from any determination by religious belief at the same time that it attempted to direct those beliefs into an increasingly dynamic interchange within the context of the school. Bentham continually promoted the plan as an enlightened project which could afford "security . . . against groundless terrors, mischievous impostures, and self-delusions" (29). Such delusions were associated with irrational fears and hopes – for example, of "unembodied beings, of various sorts, actuated by the desire, and endued with the power, of doing mischief to mankind" (29–30). Setting himself at odds with specific kinds of beliefs that he regarded to be inimical to his educational project, Bentham occasionally seemed to be repeating the traditional doctrines that he ostensibly opposed: in his denunciation of "irreligion . . . heterodoxy . . . schism" and other "abominations," he made himself sound oddly like his Anglican enemies. But the point of all this was that such religious (or anti-religious) teachings needed to be resisted, not because they were irrational or dangerous beliefs, but because they were "dissocial passions" leading to "jealousy" and "wretched envy" (51). Such "dissocial passions," he imagined, posed a danger only because they might undo the mechanism of the educational scheme itself.

What might seem like a hostility towards various kinds of beliefs, then, ultimately contributed to the inclusive logic of the institution. The Chrestomathic scheme was thus a response to apparent errors of belief that in fact differed substantially from philosophical rationalism – even though Bentham warmly welcomed the scientific investigations of Humphry Davy and Edward Jenner (47, 56). The solution to the problem of delusion (or "perverted religion" [30]) turned out to be nothing other than toleration itself, as if the fear of delusion were a primary cause of delusion. The "supposed error" of others was not understood as a deluded state of mind to be removed through education, but to be considered "free . . . from all moral blame," an occasion for "forbearance . . . which men are so ready to preach and so reluctant to practice" (30).

Toleration was so important in Bentham's argument because it could continually appear as a measure of institutional effectiveness and could be intriguingly construed as the very object of education itself: the object of instruction was a "social co-operation from which labour receives so much relief, and pleasure so much increase" (31). The ends and means of education thus converged at toleration, which was both an efficient method of instruction as well as its ultimate goal. Whenever he drew attention to the school's "largeness of scale," or the "magnitude of scale," it was also to convey the school's ability to accommodate differences – allowing students to pass the time "in company with so many hundred fellow-labourers and coadjutors" (31,32). Although Bentham sought to exclude "controverted points of *Divinity*" (89) from the Chrestomathic curriculum, then, the particularly striking feature of the school was that it guided students into patterns of action – according to the principles of "separation and aggregation" – that in turn coaxed disposition into visible effects. The school had the useful advantage of bypassing the need to have comprehensive doctrinal agreements in place in advance of instruction, while also offering a system of institutional dependencies so vital that the very beliefs or dispositions of individual members seemed to rely upon communal inclusion in order for those beliefs to become visible or meaningful to others – and to the adherents of such beliefs themselves. Just as Bentham had described institutions generally as ways of bringing the deaf and blind into a socially facilitating set of discursive relationships, he envisioned the school as a means of absorbing and registering the effects of individual actions in the context of others' actions – through the "forthcomingness of Evidence" of those actions in an "easily accessible shape."[113] This brought "*bodies* . . . into some new form," or shaped "bodily organs" into "exercises" that would reveal "the connexions and dependencies of the several parts of the admirable whole" (98,121).

COMMUNITY BEYOND COMMUNION

My aim in focusing on Bentham in this way is to suggest that he was not merely an isolated figure during the period; his notions of tolerant government in fact distilled a more pervasive disposition towards belief – one that was visible not only at the level of specific acts of legislation, but also at the level of political argumentation. To advocate toleration was to advocate for a seemingly unavoidable set of interlocking commitments to religious freedom and to an institutional facilitation and management of that freedom. On the one hand, then, reformers such as Charles James Fox insisted that "whatever a man's opinions might be . . . no harm could possibly arise from them to the state, unless they should be brought into action."[114] Lord Holland later argued in a similarly liberal spirit against sacramental tests designed to exclude Catholics and Protestants as well as Jews and those of other religious orientations; oaths "on the true faith of a Christian," he claimed, unfairly implied that "a particular religious faith was necessary to the due discharge of civil duty."[115] The validity of such statements, though, depended upon a sphere of governable "action" and "civil duty"; toleration could not emerge without a specific institutional context – educational, military, parliamentary, and religious – in which adherents of beliefs could be tolerated. Lord Plunkett argued for Catholic emancipation in 1829, for example, in order to secure "public safety" and "public prosperity" within Britain's expanding and diversifying boundaries; Francis Burdett sponsored the Catholic cause precisely in order to encourage Catholics to participate more fully in "the constitution of the country" with a proper measure of "quiet enjoyment."[116] The freedom ultimately granted to Dissenters to be married in their own chapels, moreover, was only possible because of a sophisticated strategy for "universal registration": computing numbers of persons and licensing ministers within Dissenting congregations.[117] Toleration for Jews, both in the eighteenth century and the nineteenth, was defended because it would be an advantage to "commerce" and would help to solidify Britain's "navigation and . . . maritime power."[118]

Although this chapter may have brought us closer to understanding the political discourse of toleration that emerged during the late eighteenth century, another question still remains: how is the discourse of toleration that I am describing explicitly a literary discourse – especially since I have located the most compelling defense of toleration in the work of a writer who apparently regarded poetry as no better than push-pin?[119] The answers that this book puts forward in each chapter do not imply that discussions of toleration influenced literary production – as if the poems, novels, and dramas that I discuss mirrored political logics. Rather, the writers I study sustained a consciousness of the "literary" as neither identical to nor utterly distinct from politics; writers of genres commonly known as "literary" knowingly exploited the literary status of their works in order to comment on the conventional relationships assumed to exist between the beliefs that individuals held and the institutions in which they participated. Novels, poetry, and drama were instrumental in giving shape to the discourse of toleration, at the same time that toleration provided these writers with repeated opportunities to assert the position of their own works in a marketplace inhabited by adherents of different beliefs.

The point I make here differs substantially, then, from the practice of historicism summed up in Edward Said's claims about the "worldly" quality of literary texts – their status as "enmeshed in circumstance, time, place, and society" – and followed out in the work of critics of Romantic writing.[120] Clifford Siskin, for example, has shown how the domain of literature participates in the formation of specialized "disciplines" and "norms" in the marketplace of print culture; James Chandler's refinement of this view interprets Romantic literary work as a self-conscious exploration of the historically contingent conditions of representation.[121] In contrast to these views, I am suggesting a position for the "literary" that is in fact more historical; this is because, rather than relativizing the notion of literature with respect to culture or history, my vantage point discloses Romantic literature's interest in an institutionalized relativism. I show that a range of Romantic writers viewed their works as distinctive contributions to debates about toleration because of distinctive potentialities that they attributed to literary form. Reminding their readers of the separateness and incompatibility of their beliefs while also bringing such beliefs into a new set of relations and articulations within their works, a whole range of writers constructed texts that were both reflections upon – and instances of – toleration.

Two well-known texts, Jane Austen's *Mansfield Park* (1814) and Percy Bysshe Shelley's *Prometheus Unbound: A Lyrical Drama* (1820), will begin to illustrate this point. These works provide a particularly appropriate coda because their mutual immersion in the techniques of the Gothic novel will forecast discussions in the following chapter – and in the last two chapters, where the Gothic's religious politics return with startling force in the poetry of Byron and Keats and in the mode of dramatic writing that I call the "Inquisitorial stage." Still more, however, I want to exploit a contrast in the interests of commentary: a contrast between Austen's moderate respect for the established church (the novel, she writes in a letter, was to be about "ordination") and Shelley's outspoken opposition to it.[122] My aim is not to provide detailed readings of these works, but to show that their treatments of religion are in fact complementary rather than opposed, and that they offer illuminating explanations of each other's insights. The scene to which I want to draw attention in Austen's novel is, of course, the visit to Sotherton – the Rushworth estate – when Mrs. Rushworth (in chapter 9 of volume 1) takes the guests from Mansfield on a tour of the house that includes a visit to the family chapel. Here is a novel in which the main character's judgments on moral virtues are routinely and profoundly conflated with judgments on spaciousness, lighting, and interior design – and this scene is certainly no exception.

What immediately strikes Fanny about the chapel is its lack of grandeur; and (in ways that foreshadow future turns of events in the novel) her observations on the neglected room are both supplemented by Edmund's defense of her perspective and played off Mary Crawford's contrasting contempt for organized religion. "There is nothing awful here, nothing melancholy, nothing grand," Fanny complains. "Here are no aisles, no arches, no inscriptions, no banners."[123] Edmund glosses her comment by suggesting to her that the lack of grandeur reflects its function "for the private use of the family" (*Mansfield Park*, 72); but Mrs. Rushworth's helpful comments as tour guide reveal that the chapel itself, even for its limited purposes as a religious community within the home, has been abandoned by the late Mr. Rushworth (73).

This development – one of the "improvements" of the last generation, as Mary lightly puts it (73) – accompanies a more general social trend that the characters observe and continue to comment on: a trend that seems to lead towards an autonomous sphere of private worship on the one hand and an autonomous sphere of public preaching and oration on the other. Mary thus gleefully remarks on the way that religion has left people "to their own devices," and on the way that "every body likes to go their own way – to chuse their own time and manner of devotion" (73). At the same time that she describes a public freed from an oppressive religious orthodoxy, moreover, she describes the unwelcome persistence of a religious orthodoxy that is so formal as to be utterly without influence: with the "influence and importance" of the British clergy in a state of decline, "One scarcely sees a clergyman out of his pulpit" (78).

Now Edmund is quick to contradict Mary Crawford's analysis of the clergy, and Fanny is just as quick to register her assent to his opposition. Mary (according to him) has mistaken the clergy's lack of influence in the city for its lack of influence in the country and in Britain more generally; Edmund proceeds to extol the clergy's role in terms that explain precisely how appropriate it is that he enters the church – and precisely why there could be no better husband for Fanny than a clergyman. This contrast in views – the contrast in descriptions of the clergy having subtly shifted into a struggle over prescriptions for it – often strikes critics of the novel as a contrast between the conservativism of the country and the radicalism of the city, between Tory and Jacobin, or between the values of the gentry and the rising middle class.[124] But the case turns out to be significantly more complex. Edmund begins to describe the clergyman in terms that are inseparable from the "neighbourhood" in which he works: in such a "neighbourhood," a population will be able to know the clergyman's "private character" and "observe his general conduct," while at the same time the clergyman will be able to inculcate "good principles" amongst his parishioners (78). The conflicting accounts of the clergy – and the conflicting approval attached to those accounts – actually show that Edmund and Fanny defend the church not because it imposes a particular set of doctrines, but because it provides the opportunity for public interaction – within a "neighbourhood" – in a far more general way.[125] Fanny, that is, assumes the chapel to function for "a whole family assembling regularly for the purpose of prayer" (73).

This can hardly satisfy Mary, who continues to argue in radical fashion against "the obligation of attendance, the formality, the restraint, the length of time" that the church requires; "altogether it is a formidable thing and what nobody likes" (73). But what becomes particularly clear from the argument I have been pursuing is that the practice of social interaction in this scene – indeed, throughout the novel – tends to provide a subtle counterpoint to Mary's claims. It is precisely the organized, assembled activities of touring a house and engaging in conversation that allow Austen to set up contrasting viewpoints, and to give an airing to Mary's argument *against* such social activity. *Mansfield Park* as a novel, we might say, trumps Mary's perspective. Still more specifically, though: the position that Fanny and Edmund take, a position on the value of "assembling" in general, places a value on social obligation that Mary – seeing it as mere hypocrisy – ignores at the cost of society itself.[126]

Austen, that is, deftly ties Mary's criticism of the church to her tendency to engage in a regular pattern of injuries to her family and friends, injuries that she both fails to recognize and yet also attempts to conceal. When Henry Crawford elopes with Edmund's married sister towards the end of the novel, Mary reacts in a characteristic fashion. Even after her brother has perpetrated a palpable "wound" or "crime," she continues to suggest that Fanny should quietly accept her brother's suit. To Edmund, this only advocates "a compliance, a compromise, an acquiescence, in the continuance of the sin." With alarming consistency, Mary Crawford's approval of private worship accompanies, and indeed excuses, an approval of Gothicized violence behind a false conformity or "compliance" (376–78). Although Lionel Trilling's account of the novel insists that Austen's drive towards conformity exhibits "the Terror which rules our moral situation," he misidentifies terror's source.[127] Mary's apparently liberal attitude towards freedom from public worship comes to look less liberal and more like a recommendation for the most extreme form of protected patriarchal brutality; the opposition to the church looks like a support of domestic violence. Her "perversion of mind" thus turns out to have less to do with any deviance in her thoughts than with her violence against society (376); the respect that Fanny and Edmund show for the church has less to do with a respect for conventional communal traditions or beliefs than with a respect for community itself.[128]

Shelley's *Prometheus Unbound* converges with the kind of support Austen provides for established religion even while apparently undermining it. Some of the most ambitious recent scholarship on Shelley – by Paul M.S. Dawson and Timothy Clark, for example – has tended to view his work within a tradition of radical skepticism gleaned from the works of Drummond and Volney: an intellectual heritage that can be discerned in the author's political and aesthetic leanings, and in his own writing on religion.[129] There are certainly compelling reasons for reading *Prometheus Unbound* in this manner. The preface to the work reveals just how earnestly he wanted it to be a catalyst in a gradual loosening of the power of "the most oppressive form of the Christian religion," a "fervid awakening of the public mind," in which Milton – "a republican, and a bold inquirer into morals and religion" – also participates. Presumably Shelley wishes to further his own drama's radical potential by choosing Prometheus as the protagonist rather than Satan; Prometheus "is, as it were, the type of the highest perfection of moral and intellectual nature, impelled by the purest and the truest motives to the best and noblest ends." And the drama purportedly improves upon Aeschylus to maintain this level of moral commentary by making Prometheus refuse to compromise with Jupiter: "The moral interest of the fable which is powerfully sustained by the sufferings and endurance of Prometheus, would be annihilated if we could conceive of him as unsaying his high language, and quailing before his successful and perfidious adversary."[130]

Furthermore, there are ways in which we might see the drama extending the preface's stated aims, depicting an ideal state of moral purity that in turn achieves political gravity because of its uncompromising opposition to tyranny. The drama trains this opposition on the ultimate goal of "disenchantment": a liberation from the "hypocrisy and custom" that make people's "minds / The fanes of many a worship, now outworn" (*Prometheus Unbound*, 1.1.621–22). This freedom is to be accomplished by Prometheus's refusal of "submission" (1.1.395) to Jove's "faithless faith" (3.3.130) – a refusal which is apparently in sympathy with the "one voice" of nations that call for "Truth, liberty, and love" (1.1.651).

And the new community of "linked brothers" (1.1.571) imagined in Shelley's work keeps being described in terms of a freedom from external control over thought: the "change" wrought in the world is not merely in "outward things" (3.4.100,130) but in the mind's freedom from outward coercive authority.

This logic would seem to find its ultimate expression in the world as observed by the Spirit of the Hour in Act 3:

> I looked,
> And behold! thrones were kingless, and men walked
> One with the other even as spirits do,
> · None fawned, none trampled; hate, disdain or fear,
> Self-love or self-contempt on human brows
> No more inscribed, as o'er the gate of hell,
> "All hope abandon ye who enter here."   (3.4.130–36)

I will return in a moment to this reference to Dante which both registers an affiliation with and distance from Dante's cosmogony. But it should suffice to say that this speech appears to work through a series of negations that seemingly typify Shelleyan freedom: a freedom from traditional symbols of power that the Spirit continues to catalog in the following lines: "Thrones, altars, judgement-seats and prisons," "Sceptres, tiaras, swords and chains, and tomes / Of reasoned wrong glozed on by ignorance" (3.4.164–67). "Altars" are now "soiled and garlandless" (3.4.186); "shrines" are "abandoned" (3.4.189); and, in a particularly Burkean image, the "painted veil" "Which mimicked /All men believed or hoped, is torn aside" (3.4.190–92). The "Loathsome mask has fallen," so that "man," while not "Passionless," "remains / Sceptreless, free, uncircumscribed – but man: / Equal, unclassed, tribeless, and nationless, / Exempt from awe, worship, degree, – the King / Over himself" (3.4.193–98). In an echo of Mary Wollstonecraft, perhaps, the Spirit reports that women, likewise, are "From custom's evil taint exempt and pure; / Speaking the wisdom once they could not think, / Looking emotions once they feared to feel, /And changed to all which once they dared not be, / Yet being now, made earth like heaven" (3.4.156–60).

The nature of this exemption from obedience to external powers also frees the world from the falsity of all conventional inscriptions on the human body itself. The Spirit proclaims each individual's brow to be cleared of the woeful Dantean inscription, and goes on to proclaim how the "subject" free of tyrannous authority is a subject free of false language – presumably the false language of oaths and religious tests: "None wrought his lips in truth-entangling lines / Which smiled the lie his tongue disdained to speak" (3.4.142–43). Still further:

> None talked that common, false, cold, hollow talk
> Which makes the heart deny the *yes* it breathes,
> Yet question that unmeant hypocrisy
> With such a self-mistrust as has no name.
>
> (3.4.149–52)

What becomes particularly clear in these lines is that Shelley must recover bodily organs and movements from their own propensity to falseness: the falsifying "heart" needs to be divided from its truthful "*yes*" of its own breathing; the "lips" need to be separated from the more honest "tongue." This logic insists so valiantly upon the subject's freedom from the falseness of its own confessions, in fact, that it becomes more and more difficult to locate any self at all: the very ability to think of the self freed from false sources of authority entails thinking of a self drained of all resources for its selfhood. The unsettling outcome of Shelleyan brotherhood is that it may require an absence of other persons hostile to one's self – and even the absence of a self and its perpetual falsifications.

Shelley's iconoclasm – which seems to lead at this point to an unsettling, self-destructive minimalism – perhaps carries us very far from the way that Austen has her characters celebrate the shrines and altars that *Prometheus* destroys. But if the drama would seem to wish for the freedom of persons by freeing them from the false beliefs supporting conventional oppressive governments, there is yet another direction of argument in the work – and within the very speech of the Spirit of the Hour itself – that makes the very existence of Shelleyan brotherhood even more fully dependent upon the artifice that seemed to be its enemy. We cannot help but notice, first of all, that Dante's language is not merely dismissed but preserved in this passage. The "gate of hell" with its Dantean inscription actually stands utterly intact, preserved and regarded by those who have refused its inscription on their brows – as if the very notion of religious opposition depended upon retaining the integrity of the structure that it apparently opposes. Certainly this reasoning comports with Prometheus's recantation of his curse, his refusal to participate in a reciprocal pattern of abuse and revenge. And the passage above continues by not merely dispensing with the modes of worship that it attacks but strangely sustaining them. The images of power are not in fact erased: they "are now/But an astonishment," they "Stand, not o'erthrown, but unregarded now" (3.4.176–79). The word "astonishment" to describe objects is particularly interesting here, since "astonishment" connotes not only a new and unparticularized affect but (thanks to its root in *astony* in Chaucer's English) a religion turned to stone or art. The images are "unregarded" in that they are not part of a religious observance, an "awe," or a compulsion to obey. They are the subject of a different kind of observation – a beholding and looking: "I looked, / And behold . . ."

Would it be appropriate at this point to say that Shelley's very opposition to established belief requires a logic of isolation and alienation that can be healed only through a repetition of religion itself? Perhaps, in the terms offered by Harold Bloom, this is the logic of Shelley's "mythmaking."[131] Or, as a deconstructive turn on such an argument might suggest, the very opposition to religious icons or "tools" that we observed in the passage eventuates in the drama's advocacy of a new, equally illusory, and perhaps parodic form of consecration.[132] The reign of "love" that succeeds Jove's fall is yet another form of "worship," for example (3.3.59), with its own "temple" graced by "Phidian forms" (3.4.112). But this religion is most consistently described as a mode of attention – a beholding or viewing that is not necessarily connected with any particular belief or myth. It is hardly surprising that Shelley's letters contemporaneous with the writing of *Prometheus Unbound* show his sustained appreciation of "public buildings," places of assembly that reveal "the excellence of the ancients."[133] For the drama itself finds its most resonant portrayal of a harmony between individuals through their mutual acts of following, looking, listening, and wondering. What holds characters together is nothing more than their "assembling," as Austen's characters describe it. *The Mask of Anarchy* – written in 1819, not published until 1832 – explicitly refers to a "vast Assembly," and a "great Assembly . . . / Of the fearless and the free" not in order to *reject* the "old Laws of England" (and thus not on the model of the National Assembly in France) but to reconsider and reapply them (*Poetry and Prose*, 262,295). Repeatedly catching up its *dramatis personae* in collective acts of beholding and attending, *Prometheus Unbound* offers a consistent and profound set of related injunctions to "behold," "look," "see," "listen," "wonder," and so on. "Apollo/Is held in heaven by wonder," for example (2.5.10–11); Demogorgon directs Asia to "behold" (2.4.130); Ione asks Panthea, "Behold'st thou not two shapes from the east and west . . . " (1.1.752). The exchange of speech in this work, in fact, most frequently amounts to a direction to direct attention.

All of these states of attention, it could be said, engage the speakers in what the drama understands as "enchantment" ("Two visions of strange radiance float upon / The ocean-like enchantment of strong sound," Panthea reports [4.4.202–03]; "My soul is an enchanted boat," says Asia [2.5.72]). Like Shelleyan "astonishment" with its etymological underpinnings in "stone," "enchantment" denotes something more formal than psychological: an engagement with *chant* or song.[134] There are at least two points that need to be made in order to characterize this kind of enchantment, or re-enchantment, further. First, the "change" to which the poem looks forward is so resistant to the idea of specifying a content for that change that change must be understood as a conversation about change rather than a change itself. Prometheus thus looks forward to a time "where we will sit and talk of time and change / As the world ebbs and flows, ourselves unchanged" (3.3.23–24). And in the next scene the Spirit of the Earth describes how "ugly human shapes and visages" are only "somewhat changed"; even "toads, snakes, and efts" have become "beautiful" from "little change in shape or hue" (3.4.65–76).

Second, Shelleyan brotherhood looks like a secular religion that provides an alternative to, rather than a mere repetition of, religious communion, for it aggregates a community of different and seemingly incompatible elements: it is precisely in this way that Shelley imagined the drama "harmonizing the contending creeds by which mankind have been ruled," as he wrote to Thomas Love Peacock in 1819.[135] *Prometheus Unbound* assembles a reconstituted family in which the Earth becomes the "fair dam" with "sustaining arms" to "all plants, / And creeping forms, and insects rainbow-winged / And birds and beasts and fish and human shapes" who will be treated as "sister antelopes" (3.3.90–98). (The antelope is particularly striking here due to its status as a creature found in nature *and* in heraldic or legendary imagery, thus condensing the poet's impulse to accommodate real beings in an ideal society.) If conventional religion in this poem keeps getting associated with a false uniformity, Prometheus describes "Strange combinations out of common things," and "harmonies" that are created "From difference sweet where discord cannot be" (3.3.32, 39–40); the Earth speaks of "Man" as a "harmonious soul of many a soul" (1.4.400). The "mighty Power" that is "Love" is not a universalized affect, but the very possibility of registering affect: "a sense of words" and a "universal sound like words" (4.510, 517–18); not thought itself but "a chain of linked thought" (1.4.394). "Language," in one of the drama's most emblematic passages, "is a perpetual Orphic song" that provides new ways for registering previously suppressed thoughts; it "rules with Daedal harmony a throng / Of thoughts and forms, which else senseless and shapeless were" (4.416–17). The fall of Jupiter comes to achieve the most significance in this drama because of the rise of a previously submerged possibility of discourse itself: it is poetry's version of removing blasphemy law, an equivalent to the "legislative enactment" that Shelley wished for, a law "framed to erase this scandal [of blasphemy law] from our age."[136]

What I have been saying is that Shelley's drama meets the logic of Austen's novel by affirming the social value of a specifically Romantic disposition towards belief – rather than advocating a specific belief or set of beliefs. Critics have understood *Mansfield Park* as a novel that confirms a conventional ideology of church and state against the exercise of personal freedom – and they have understood *Prometheus Unbound* as a poem that confirms very much the reverse. Donald Reiman, for example, provides a particularly resonant contrast between Austen's "pastoral" mode, depicting a world where "men are guarded from danger by pastors," and Shelley's more subversive "Gothic" mode, portraying a "dangerous and hostile" world requiring "heroic struggle."[137] But both works, it turns out, transform these apparent oppositions by both soliciting dangerous "Gothic" forces and enclosing them within a secularized pastoral authority – a logic that I will associate in the next chapter with the Gothic novel itself.

At no point in this book do I mean merely to suppress or erase important distinctions between political or religious vantage points in order to say that works such as Austen's and Shelley's are simply "the same." I do, however, wish to emphasize a previously unexplored convergence between seemingly discrepant allegiances. These works exert a pressure on the logic of confessional government that is not simply disruptive of the social order; instead, this pressure frees individuals from conformity to conventional beliefs while asserting an even more powerful and compelling social unity. They arrive at this position, to be sure, from opposite directions, Austen arguing on behalf of religious establishment and Shelley arguing against it. But the striking feature of both works is that arguing "for" or "against" establishment amounts to compatible alternatives. If Austen imagines a church that has evolved into a kind of secular government – an embrace of persons that would guarantee the visibility of the person in conversation – Shelley's secular opposition to establishment conjures a Providential level of authority so extensive that it is exempt from requiring religious uniformity in order to secure its invulnerable position. In Austen's "assembling" or in Shelleyan "enchantment," confirmation and opposition meet in an approval of a community beyond religious communion.

CHAPTER 2

"Holy hypocrisy" and the rule of belief: Radcliffe's Gothics

THE GOTHIC CONSENSUS

What is there left to say about the Gothic novel's shopworn images of clerical abuse – the forced confessions and tortures of the Inquisition, the confinements and seductions in convents and monasteries? Some time ago, Montague Summers made an effort to stifle idle speculations about their meaning by arguing that they are mere "absurdities," and that "it is folly to trace any 'anti-Roman feeling' in the Gothic novel."[1] That advice, however, has hardly dissuaded other critics from rounding up any number of political referents for those supposed absurdities: in many such accounts the Gothic wields its images of monastic terror to figure its fear of revolutionary upheaval or its mirror-image, oppressive authoritarianism; the remedy to that fear is a typically British "moderation," perhaps, or "repression," or "ideology."[2] These alternatives do not, of course, add up to a summary of the criticism of the Gothic. Yet they do indicate the ways in which advances in historicist criticism, by viewing the genre primarily as a way of distinguishing one society from another – Britain from the continent (France, say, or Spain), the free from the oppressed – essentially see it as a means of establishing social consensus. On a model familiar to us from the likes of Freud, René Girard, or Clifford Geertz, the Gothic functions within the realm of ritual, wherein the novel represents and reinforces a set of common beliefs, and conveniently (albeit suspiciously) sounds an alarm against a host of social outcasts.[3]

Those accounts, I think, too quickly assume that British society – and the Gothic novel's representation of it – required an attempt to unify beliefs among a public and remove the presence of dissent as a consequence. And in doing so, such accounts tend to ignore the important position the Gothic assumed in the debates on religious toleration that I surveyed in chapter 1.[4] The rise in popularity of Gothic novels during the latter half of the eighteenth century, it turns out, coincided rather conspicuously with the increasingly heated discussion of the importance of established religion to Britain's self-constitution. And while the Gothic has often been understood as the archetypal paranoid genre in its attempt to establish uniformity (of manners, of custom, of ideology), I believe that the Gothic novel generally – and I will turn to Ann Radcliffe's 1797 novel *The Italian* as a specific example – leads us towards an altogether different account of the genre and the social organization that it envisions. Monasticism, the images of which are pervasive enough in Gothic novels to look like one of the most conspicuous features of the genre, arose as a subject of concern not because monasticism could be separated from British customs (in order to separate Britain from Catholic countries, or fan the flames of anti-Catholic sentiment at home): not, in short, because monasticism was the representative of a certain (Catholic) set of *beliefs*. Rather, it was a subject of concern because it represented a mode of *governing* the beliefs of political subjects, visible in Britain itself, which the Gothic novel participated in dismantling and modifying. In their fictional renderings of monasticism, writers from Walpole to Radcliffe and beyond depicted the political mechanisms of confessional regimes of power that continually demanded, and attempted to enforce, a uniformity of belief amongst members of the national community. The innovative response taken by the Gothic novel was to expose what it deemed to be a terrifying logic of confessional government and then to assume – precisely as a remedy to the anxieties about Catholicism it generated – a more tolerant relation to religious belief. With their plots as well as their elaborate prefaces, Gothics used the imagery of monastic terror in order to distinguish a confessional rule by belief from their own alliance with a more expansive secular rule *over* belief: a practice of government that exposed religion itself to new techniques of observation, analysis, and manipulation.

In the previous chapter, I wanted to describe the general shape of Romantic debates about religious toleration, and show why those debates might have seemed important to writers of poetry and novels. In this chapter, I extend my discussions further to account for the more specific relations between those debates and the Gothic novel. The Gothic can illuminate certain logical and rhetorical features of the toleration debates, just as it can reveal (or at least begin to reveal) how the toleration debates offered an occasion for writers of this period to re-examine the disposition of institutions – and literary texts – towards incommensurable beliefs. In the chapters following this one, moreover, we will see how the Gothic reemerges as a source of fascination for Romantic writers:

not just because of its psychological charge (procured thorough its violence, sexuality, and supernatural effects) but because the Gothic makes psychological states – the beliefs or dispositions of the person – into sites of social, rather than merely personal, attention and regulation. The Gothic's enduring attraction for the writers studied in this book can be measured by its ability to serve as the occasion for defining the extent of, and limits upon, secular technologies of public order.

Some of the relevance of the debates over Britain's oaths, tests, and regulations on speech to the Gothic can be discerned in the rhetoric of the debates themselves, which became immersed in, and fascinated by, the devices the genre afforded. Advocates on both sides of the issue of Catholic Emancipation – perhaps the most relevant of the debates to the Gothic – saw the genre as an appropriate way of heightening the villainy of their opponents. Proponents of establishment conjured up a host of ghastly images of religious dissent; the parliamentary petitions of Catholics, Robert Inglis declared, "are . . . shrouded in clouds and darkness; and it is hardly possible to say to what extent they aspire." Concessions to Catholics had only released a body that took on the attributes of a monster, which, with its "violent sentiments," "went forth without fetters among the people" to endanger the empire.[5] Contemporary journalism, playing off the religious valences of both domestic and international conflict, related tales of seduction and torture in Catholic houses of religion; popular prints by artists from Hogarth to Cruikshank inflamed hostility by representing monks armed with instruments of torture, or personifying Catholicism as a grisly Satan.[6]

The Gothic was just as easily accommodated to the aims of the reformers. In chapter 1, I showed how Bentham's *Church of Englandism* accused the establishment of replicating the very structure of the Inquisition it opposed; William Empson in *The Edinburgh Review* even more explicitly wove his criticism of establishment into the structure of the Gothic plot. After the Catholic claims had been provisionally resolved with Emancipation in 1829, he cheered the demise of established religion, "that nodding and impending danger, which, like the mysterious helmet in the Castle of Otranto, was enlarging every hour before our eyes . . ."[7] Despite this facility with which reformers handled the conventions of the genre, the Gothic was singled out in their arguments for a reason that – as both Empson's and Bentham's claims showed – differed from that of their opponents. For if the defenders of establishment incited a fear of Catholic monstrosity, reformers made that fear itself into something monstrous. More precisely, it was commonly the case that a discourse of liberal tolerance defined itself by calling attention to the way that the Anglican establishment deployed fear and panic as a political instrument. For them, the Gothic quality of the religious establishment did not derive from a belief that was to be feared, but from the equally – if not more – terrifying specter of the political demand for uniform belief. Parliamentary reformers thus pointed (sometimes with ridicule) to conservatives' manipulation of Gothic images and, in a more important sense, their tendency to *believe* in them: Thomas Spring Rice contemptuously dismissed widely distributed propaganda relating the plight of "victims of papal vengeance" and the Satanic practices of Catholics, whose religion entailed "all the tortures that the fiends of hell could invent."[8] Others observed how writers acquired the "habit . . . of exciting horror by the narration of cruelties perpetrated upon the Protestants, especially in the reign of the Queen Mary."[9] And in Lord King's opinion, the "tales" of Catholic subversion were "handed down by tradition from one old woman to another; and, in truth, they were fit only to frighten old women."[10]

King's description is surely interesting for its misogyny, its stereotyping of the female gossip; but it is even more interesting for the way that it identifies the defenders of the establishment with a particular way of reading the Gothic novel. That identification is not produced by associating them with monstrous Gothic characters, but, more profoundly, by associating them with a compulsion to believe – not merely a tendency to believe but to make others adhere to their beliefs. The transmission of the Gothic plot is a transmission of private belief "handed down by tradition." And thus the criticism of the anti-Catholic, intolerant vision of society is linked to the functionality of text as an instrument of belief – discourse that is moved by belief in order to replicate belief. More than just a symptom of misogynistic paranoia, the "old woman" emerges as a Burke-like figure of social relations built upon domestic privacy and the confessional structure through which those relations demanded conformity from their members.[11]

SOUTHEY AND THE MONASTIC ENCLOSURE

Perhaps no writer figured so prominently in the debates over Britain's established church as Robert Southey; and perhaps no writer moves us closer to an understanding of the impact of the discourses that shaped these debates on the Gothic novel. For some time cleansed of his radical sympathies, Southey tendered his support for the established church with a series of articles so virulent in their accounts of monastic madness, masochism, and torture that they apparently disturbed even the editors of the Tory *Quarterly Review*.[12] And Southey's defense of establishment was still more incisively expressed in his widely read and controversial *Book of the Church* (1824). As much as Southey defended himself against detractors who faulted the author's anti-Catholic hysteria, the *Book* flaunts a spectacular Gothic compendium of Catholic impositions and deceptions. Cardinal Crima and Saint Dunstan, for example, emerge as doubles of "Monk" Lewis's Ambrosio. Crima "delivered a discourse upon the wickedness of marriage in the clergy" and in the evening "he was discovered . . . in bed with an harlot."[13] Southey later recounts – once more in the sensational idiom of *The Monk* – the story of Dunstan's imaginary encounters with the Devil, who tempts him in a variety of seductive and sexually ambiguous forms outside his cell at the Cathedral. His "easy frauds" on the king and his subjects, coupled with his hypocritical oratory, make him "a . . . complete exemplar of the monkish character, in its worst form" (*Book of the Church*, 1:98–113).

But Southey's aim is not merely to demonize a *particular* form of belief, in order to privilege Protestant over Catholic doctrine; it is, rather, to criticize the relationship between civil institutions and belief in general. The Protestant establishment wins his favor not because of its origin in tradition but because it provides the groundwork for an essentially secular account of national institutions (it was for this reason that Wordsworth, as I shall discuss in chapter 5, likened his own *Ecclesiastical Sonnets* to Southey's work but also sought to take Southey's point still further). Southey's historical argument is instructive here, because he consistently understands a Protestant establishment in terms of a spirit of resistance to established belief, while Catholicism can be connected to Druidical worship because of its means of *government*: an analogous Druidical and Roman "hierocracy" which secures a "portentous tyranny . . . not over the minds of men alone, but in all temporal concerns." The persistence of heterodoxy against this "hierocracy" comes to define the British church establishment itself (1:189–90). When St. Augustine converts King Ethelbert of Kent to Christianity, that is, the king refuses to compel the conversion of others, "having learnt from his teachers that the service of Christ must be voluntary" (1:31). While Ethelbert's conversion appears to be accomplished through the mediation of Rome, Southey essentially contends that Ethelbert was not converted to "Roman" Christianity – or, that Ethelbert was already practicing a more tolerant form of Christianity once he was converted. Southey's history thus traces back

in the succession of English kings a resistance to papal authority long
before the Reformation. The result is that Protestantism comes to look
British not because it describes a coherent system of beliefs, but because
it represents a community in the absence of religious conformity, a community that looks "voluntary" precisely because of a lack of any actual
agreement.

Southey's hostility to the notion of religious establishment as a consensus informs his more rigorous hostility to monasticism, since monasticism
is less worrisome for any Catholic doctrines that it might recommend
than for its private environments in which and through which it enforces
a conformity of belief. But this hostility actually has a constructive purpose. Catholicism enters into his account as an occasion for rigorous
observation rather than exclusion, a hierocracy which the combined efforts of British law and the Protestant establishment continually attempt
to penetrate and regulate. Visitors to England's monasteries, he relates,
"found parties opposed to each other, and cruel abuse of power, which
dreaded no responsibility. Coining was detected in some houses; the
blackest and foulest crimes in others" (II:55). Coining appears more central than incidental in this list of crimes, for monasticism appears most
disruptive because of its attempt to replace a national economy with a
privately generated system of values, an attempt by a single privileged
group to re-create an economic system in its own image. And in a way
that becomes resonant in Gothic novels themselves, Southey continually
paints a picture of monasticism as a creation of uniformity at the expense
of a blindness to, or protection of, the "abuse of power" and the "foulest"
of criminal actions.

Considering Southey's reputation as a conservative apologist for the
establishment, it will no doubt seem strange that I have implied in this
account that his way of thinking was closer to an argument against traditional established religion than it was to an argument for it. Yet Southey's
work is of interest here because of the way it indicates the church itself
as a crucial point of differentiation between secularized and confessional
institutional structures (and the claim that I attribute to Southey lends
support to the work of historians such as David Zaret who have suggested that the "bourgeois" public sphere defined by Habermas may in
fact have emerged from within religious discourse itself).[14] As much as
The Book of the Church defends the church, it does so by imagining the
church as a structure of all religious structures: an intervention within
and protection against the pressures of private religious organizations.
This helps us to see exactly why it is that the debate over the Monastic

Institutions Bill in 1800 (a bill "to prevent any addition to the number of Persons belonging to certain foreign Religious Orders of Communities lately settled in this Kingdom, and to regulate the Education of Youth by such Persons") ignited a parliamentary discussion concerning the degree to which the establishment of Catholic institutions in Britain would conflict not merely with an ideal uniformity in Protestant belief but with the secular auspices of British government. For in that debate, it was particularly important for the Bishop of Rochester to point out how the "zeal" of Roman Catholics "is not in itself criminal," and that "to be reconciled to the pope or see of Rome" "is no longer an offense to be prosecuted under . . . any . . . statutes." His impassioned argument against the bill's policy of "persecution," however, was also nevertheless an argument in favor of an increased level of attention to the requirements of "public safety" that "must not be trusted to the discretion of individuals." Monastic institutions, even while they had to be tolerated, needed to be subjected to the active intervention of government regulation. The object of the bishop's concern was not a dangerous doctrine but a private legal code. The system of penance, he argued, was a code "administered . . . by the order and direction of the superior" and that "often consists in imprisonment for any length of time, and in other corporal severities." Granting monasteries a government "licence" – in accordance with one part of the bill – might only be a license to "imprison and otherwise maltreat the persons of his majesty's subjects."

The Bishop of Rochester's reasoning did not imply that monastic institutions should be either suppressed *or* freed from control; it implied that private religious activity should be – indeed, already was – underwritten by an analysis and observance of religion within the realm of social effects. What was at stake, in other words, was not a privilege of the hegemonic Protestant religion over the dissenting Catholic religion, but a more comprehensive view of the alliance of church and state that allowed Catholicism to be included, observed, organized, and regulated. This point becomes particularly clear in the Bishop of Rochester's suggestion to extend greater tolerance to "Roman Catholic schoolmasters and schoolmistresses," a suggestion aimed to protect the right to private religious education but at the same time aimed to enhance the structure of dependency between individual religious communities and the state. "I think it would be very proper that government should be informed from time to time of the actual state of all Roman Catholic schools," he urged, and this should be only "a part of a general bill for the regulation of all schools."[15]

Like Southey's account, this opinion on the Monastic Institutions Bill revealed monasticism to be both a form of resistance to the exertions of secular government and a place of intervention and organization: both a private religious community and the ultimate site of an extra-religious rule of law. This way of summarizing the bent of these discussions, I think, helps to explain their relevance to the subject of this chapter, the Gothic novel, which continually casts the church in an analogously complex and fluctuating role – wavering between an acquiescence to, and a control of, the conformity exacted by private affective associations within familial and religious groups. While Richard Hurd's *Letters on Chivalry and Romance* (1762) sees Gothic writing as a vigorous promotion of Britain's traditional social order, and while literary critics continually regard the Gothic novel as a more or less conservative endorsement of this view, the Gothic novel just as often identifies the private sphere of traditional feudal alliances as the very source of its terror.[16] The place of church authority in the Gothic emerges most distinctly in its alternating roles in relation to these alliances: the ecclesiastical institution is, on the one hand, the model for an oppressive conformity demanded by the family unit with which the church then competed for allegiance. On the other hand, the Gothic accompanies this gesture by imagining ecclesiastical government as if it could oppose – indeed, as if it could serve as an *antidote* for – the terror inspired by mutually reinforcing and competing religious and familial authorities. Serving both as an enforcement of confessional regimes of power and ultimately as capable of fortuitous reversals and enclosures of those regimes, the ecclesiastical institution in the Gothic plays off the affective bonds of family and faith in order to represent – and indeed exalt – the more secularized functions of ecclesiastical government. To put it yet another way: religion is most important in these fictions not as a belief but as a point of fracture between belief and government, between a self-enclosed confessional authority and a more comprehensive, inclusive rule over that authority.[17]

If the Parliamentary debates of the late eighteenth and early nineteenth centuries mobilized the plots and images of the Gothic novel, the Gothic novel itself in still more obvious ways betrayed an unusual fascination with scenarios of religious – and particularly Catholic – subversion and oppression. With monastic settings populated by savage monks and nuns bringing violence upon over-credulous victims, the novels of Radcliffe and Lewis attracted an enthusiastic readership long after 1800; shortened "blue-book" versions of these novels attempted to reproduce the shocking effects for an even wider audience. Writers with an enduring reputation such as William Godwin and Charles Maturin invoked the conventions of monastic settings, and countless anonymous productions with titles such as *The Midnight Assassin, Almago and Claude; or Monastic Murder*, and *The Abbott of Montserrat, or the Pool of Blood* appeared in the early 1800s as variations on familiar Gothic themes.[18] As I have already suggested at the beginning of this chapter, the immense popularity of the Gothic genre – just like the Gothicism of parliamentary debates and popular journalism – could be interpreted as a highly politicized means of exposing and excluding certain modes of unenlightened or irrational beliefs. But, from another point of view, it would be possible to see that even early instances of the Gothic novel deploy monastic settings and devices as a more complex way of exploring the relationship between beliefs and social groups more generally.

Horace Walpole's *Castle of Otranto* (1764) and Clara Reeve's *The Old English Baron* (1778; previously published as "The Champion of Virtue" in 1777) present their figures of ecclesiastical authority – Father Jerome in Walpole and Father Oswald in Reeve – as oddly poised between a condition of powerlessness and power, hostile competitors with the authority of the family yet ultimately the guarantors of secular order. In *Otranto*, the "subterranean passage" between the castle and the church conveys some of this ambiguity surrounding the place of ecclesiastical government, for the entire novel shows the church to be either a mutable, infinitely corruptible mirror-image of patriarchal power or a foundation for legitimate authority. The "sacred" offices of Jerome, that is, are at first threatened by the "profane" power of the state embodied in the tyrannical figure of Manfred. As Manfred's power exercised in pursuit of an heir manifests itself in the most extreme forms of brutality, the church's role eventually becomes defined as a protection against feudal brutality.[19] The novel procures a resolution to the problem of ecclesiastical power in a way that is typically Gothic: for the church eventually proves its long-established relation to legitimate succession as Jerome reveals his protection of and devotion to Theodore, the rightful heir of Alfonso. By supporting parental authority, however, the church also sets a limit upon it, protecting legitimate succession by supervising it and limiting its excesses. Similarly, *The Old English Baron's* Father Oswald acts not only as a confessor, but also as an agent of detection who brings the violence of private relations under public scrutiny; the church does not merely support claims to heredity but superintends them and serves as a "witness" to the rightful heir Edmund Twyford's claims to legitimacy. The lofty references to the "conduct" of "Providence" or the all-seeing "eye of heaven" is thus consonant with the rational, meticulous guidance of the church.[20] The novels, in short, eventually implicate the ecclesiastical institution within a disintegration of the family – a disintegration that continually clears the way for the reintegration or reconstruction of new domestic arrangements under the auspices of secular government.

The prefaces to these novels do just as much – perhaps even more – to accentuate the Gothic's interest in identifying the terror of religious uniformity by describing the literary text itself as a possible instrument for enforcing that uniformity. Walpole, masquerading as the manuscript's editor, prefaces the first edition of *Otranto* with the claim that the work had been produced by "an artful priest" in order to "confirm the populace in their ancient errors and superstitions." The preface, that is, inserts the text within a confessional scenario: a scenario in which the text represents a consciousness that it seeks (in the hands of an "artful priest" in an "ancient catholic family") to reproduce in the "vulgar minds" of readers. Yet for Walpole, the interest of the novel can be located elsewhere – in the way it produces a kind of "entertainment" that is not merely the communication of doctrine. The ability of the novel to be appreciated as entertainment, moreover, derives from its connection to the "flourishing state" of "letters" in a public sphere (a circulation further enhanced by the mass-produced print of Walpole's "edition" of the text), as if the status of the novel as a novel rather than doctrine depended upon a sufficient level of publicity.[21] A similar logic informs the prefatory matter to Reeve's *Baron*. It proclaims itself to be a more "credible" version of Walpole's novel; because of its likeness to the actual world, it appears to be able to "excit[e]" the reader's "attention" and direct it towards "useful" ends, and thus it brings the element of "romance" in the "Gothic story" into a closer connection with the realist techniques of the "modern novel." The preface may seem to insist upon the credible, and on the way that the narrative has been adjusted to suit the beliefs of rational readers; it may seem to emphasize the text's credibility as a *credo*, a body of rational and virtuous beliefs to be recognized and imitated by the reader. But just as notable is the emphasis the preface puts on the ability of both Reeve's work and Walpole's to capture the reader's "attention" to, or "enchantment" with, the work itself – an attention that is reducible neither to religious delusion nor a rational response to such delusion. Instead, Reeve wishes continually to emphasize nothing other than the fact of reading: she depicts herself as an attentive reader of other Gothics (Walpole's in particular), just as she regards her own novel as a work that has been read. At the end of the preface, she claims to have written *The Old English Baron* only after submitting the unfinished manuscript to a "circle of friends" that urged her to continue – as if the work owed itself to its effect upon a reading audience. And when Reeve finds occasion to criticize Walpole, she does not simply imply that his work has failed to conform to our supposedly rational beliefs about the world. In fact, her complaints refer to the way that *Otranto* relies upon a lack of correspondence between its own images and human normative measurements in order to produce shocking effects upon the reader ("A sword so large as to require a hundred men to lift it"). The problem with the novel, as she sees it, is not that it is incredible but that its emphasis on normative proportion and disproportion makes belief – credibility and incredibility – into such a relevant issue that it detracts from the work's "enchantment"; such an emphasis must "destroy the work of imagination," and dissipate the reader's "attention."[22]

While the most pressing issue in both Walpole's and Reeve's prefaces might appear to be the distinction between romance and realism (an issue discussed in the prefaces of Defoe's and Fielding's novels, and which Walpole discusses further in the second of his prefaces, where he reveals his own authorship of the work), the more fundamental distinction seems to be between the novel as literature and the novel as catechism. The Gothic novel seeks to image itself within a discourse that emphasizes comprehensiveness not by achieving a consensus among beliefs, but by valuing the literary – and the regime in which literature makes its appearance – precisely in its separation from doctrinal compulsion.[23]

RADCLIFFE'S *JOURNEY* AND THE REGIONS OF BELIEF

Ann Radcliffe's Gothic novels develop a particularly sophisticated account of an institutional disposition towards religious beliefs, just as much as they draw attention to their own self-conscious disposition, as novels, towards those beliefs. Before proceeding to examine those novels, though, we should take note of how Radcliffe's strategies in fiction emerged alongside a similar strategy in her travel writing as she practiced it in her *Journey Made in the Summer of 1791* (1795). The association between fiction and travel writing is certainly already implicit within the structure of the Gothic novel itself, which – especially in Radcliffe's handling – was often set in foreign locations among foreign cultures: locations and cultures to be displayed before the eyes of British readers. Indeed, it is the travel narratives' observations and analysis of social life – above the observation of landscape or architecture – that is particularly relevant to the Gothic novel; places are occupied by consciousnesses that require translation or negotiation by the author (and reader). In one sense, the logic of travel narratives appears to be appropriate for the aims of the Gothic because of the way that foreign cultures are made to seem more foreign: the descriptive techniques of many travel narratives exoticized and distanced the foreign even in the process of describing it. Thus, as Mary Poovey argues, Johnson's *Journey to the Western Island of Scotland* (1775) continually sets Highland custom under the lens of traditional classical learning, gauging its progress – and lack of progress – according to a British standard of improvement.[24] To be sure, some other travel writings such as Lady Mary Wortley Montagu's *Letters* (1763–67) may seem rather different from Johnson's enterprise because of their tendencies to locate *both* the rationalities and irrationalities of foreign customs and to find fault with Britain's own unenlightened state of affairs. But what unites these strategies is their way of making travel narrative into an occasion for comparisons of national character: comparisons that, in turn, depend upon comparisons of local customs and beliefs.

Radcliffe's travel writing likewise devotes a considerable amount of energy to distinguishing the author's beliefs (as a rational British Protestant observer) from different – often inferior – forms of religious and moral belief or conduct. Although the lineaments of British character are not always plain in the *Journey*, they are nevertheless implied by an insistent observation of other, non-British, patterns of affiliation. A series of comparisons thus yields notions, for instance, that British laborers are more industrious than Germans, or that the British have more sensibility than the economically efficient yet self-interested Dutch.[25] Yet the *Journey* is significant not only in its rehearsal of distinctive beliefs that constitute different national characters. It continually takes an interest in distinguishing forms of government that are not simply identical to beliefs: an interest, that is, not merely in how beliefs are different in different places, but in how different beliefs are governed differently in different places. A British perspective is defined not simply by expressing a difference in beliefs, but by expressing differences in the way that beliefs are *managed*. The unusual extent of religious "toleration" in Holland, on the one hand, is criticized for the way it empties the nation of its spirit, of all that is "magnificent" or "grand" (*Journey*, 59,60,76). Her visit to a Capuchin church in Bonn, on the other, is plagued by a kind of religious excess. She recounts her visit as an extravagant Gothic encounter: as if reading a novel, she is drawn to the church in order to gratify her "curiosity" and "love of surprise." A monk's praise of relics, however, provokes her to condemn such an attempt to make relics "preten[d] to a connection with some parts of Christian history, which it is shocking to see introduced to consideration by any means so trivial and so liable to ridicule." If the encounter with the monk begins by looking like a novel, it ends by directly contrasting her own sense of enchantment with the monk's forced and coercive attempt to inspire religious awe (124–26).

The *Journey* turns the interest in comparing governments away from an interest in comparing beliefs. And in doing so, it presents contrasting but complementary institutional formations: on the one hand a Dutch version of "toleration" that has emptied the nation of all beliefs – or at least made those beliefs seem irrelevant – and on the other hand a monastic regime that, by making belief seem like the *only* relevant aspect of political organization, attempts to enforce religious uniformity through coercion. If the *Journey* offers these two (presumably unacceptable) alternatives, Radcliffe's more celebrated works – her novels – adopt a disposition towards religious belief that modifies both: a disposition that advocates neither a mere suppression of religion nor a conventional state religion. *A Sicilian Romance* (1790), the second of her novels and yet the first to assure her preeminence in Walter Scott's estimation as a master of the Gothic, firmly identified the peculiar construction of the genre with a peculiar discourse on religious toleration.[26] The novel's brief preface establishes a fictional provenance similar to *Otranto*'s, and further emphasizes the importance of that provenance as a way of advertising the secular credentials of the work. Here, the first-person narrator in the opening pages obtains the "history" from a "superior" at the convent near the ruins of the Mazzini castle.[27] As in Walpole's narrative, the circumstances of transmission center around the problem of privacy, and the extent to which privacy involves an account of the text as an attempt to compel belief. The movement of the narrative – a "manuscript" in the convent "library" – from the hands of the "superior" to the fictive editor associates the very text of the novel with an opening of the private to public view, a shift of the narrative's function from the confessional uniformity of the convent to the diverse readership in the literary marketplace (*A Sicilian Romance*, 1–2).

If the novel's appearance in public circulation removes it from its prior institutional position as the extension of an agent's desire to compel belief, the significance of Radcliffe's appropriation of the Gothic preface unfolds in the novel's plot – a plot which continually makes the conformity demanded by religious and familial groups into occasions for concern and intervention. The *abate* at the abbey of St. Augustin, for example, becomes a model of tyrannical authority that places him in competition with the nobility. He offers temporary protection for Julia (recently escaped from the power of her father, who wishes to force her consent in marriage to the Duke de Luovo) because of his "pride" in his "religious authority" (129–30); yet it was an identical "pride" that led the Marquis to demand obedience from his daughter in the first place. As a figure of ecclesiastical authority, in other words, the *abate* differs from feudal authority only to repeat it and compete with it. This logic in which monastic protection merely doubles the violence of feudal power relations governs nearly every aspect of the *Romance*. The Castle of Mazzini, a "scene of dissension and misery," finds its complement in the monastery where Luovo seeks shelter, with its "wild uproar" and "profusion and confusion" (90). The abbey of St. Augustin itself, moreover, is a "proud monument of monkish superstition and princely magnificence": with its fortress-like exterior, the abbey turns out to be too much like a castle, the *abate* too much like a prince (116).

The competition between mirroring social organizations – between the castle and the church – plays out over the course of the novel as a competition over the allegiance of individuals. And the attempt to create uniformity continually produces an opposition between the beliefs, desires, or alliances of individuals and the demands of the group: an opposition that the confessional technology of government creates even in its attempt to overcome that opposition. The crimes of the Marquis's family, for example, are kept in secrecy by "vows," an "oath," and a "secret pledge of honour": pledges of allegiance that seem quite directly to oppose the beliefs and interests of society (52). Even the castle's architecture itself – which could be analogized to the text as a vehicle of belief as it was described in the preface – appears to be an instrument designed to enforce political and religious conformity. Like the abbey, whose "solitude and stillness conspired with the solemn aspect of the pile to impress the mind with religious awe" (116), the architecture is repeatedly characterized as a structure that bears and enforces specific dispositions. When Julia's mother is secretly imprisoned in the castle of Mazzini, her captivity is accompanied by a host of Gothic effects observed by the other inhabitants – unexplained lights, figures, and midnight noises of which she herself is the cause. The coupling of imprisonment with popular superstition clarifies the point that superstition is not merely a psychological but a *social* phenomenon. Secret imprisonment is the sign of a social exclusion that finds its complement in popular superstition, for superstition is less significant as a kind of belief than as a complement to coercion:

belief compelled by the demand for political and religious conformity. Superstitious explanations turn out to be extensions of a social organization regulated throughout the novel by "customary amusements" and "dull uniformity" which keep its members "veiled in obscurity" (7, 23). And thus the very existence of persons in this version of community repeatedly coincides with their obscurity or invisibility.

To frame the issue more precisely, Radcliffe's novel is perhaps less concerned with the epistemological distinction between true and false belief than with the degree to which social conditions permit beliefs – whether true or false – to be exposed and exchanged. Julia's discovery of her mother in the castle, then, at once makes her presence public and simultaneously erases the mystery behind the previously unexplained – or supernaturally explained – events (174–83). But this intervention does not merely give a more real or more scientific explanation of those events; it does not, in other words, merely provide an account of supposedly supernatural effects to show how they originated from natural causes. (Indeed, Radcliffe cleverly makes the Marquis into the novel's most vocal advocate of "reason" and the "senses" over a "timid imagination" that might tempt others to expose his crimes [48–49].) And this is because the epistemological concerns here and elsewhere in Radcliffe's writing – her widely acknowledged skeptical position in relation to supernatural devices that supposedly distinguished this novel so strongly from Lewis's *The Monk* – can never be extricated from the more explicitly social concerns about confessional uniformity, a concern with the ways in which individuals might need to be converted into the representative consciousness of the group. Julia's discovery of her mother's secret imprisonment is not only a way of revealing superstition as a false consciousness: it is a way of making her mother's consciousness *count* as an individual consciousness, regardless of what her beliefs might be. We cannot help noticing that, throughout this novel, Julia and Hippolytus are described as having an ample share of "religion" and "devotion," but their piety manifests itself as an opposition to piety as a foundation for community (114). Their devotion, perhaps, is to something more general: the care for and protection of a population.

THE ITALIAN AND CRIMES OF BELIEF

It is still not altogether clear, at this point, what Radcliffe's Gothic offered as an alternative to the confessional model of social organization that it identified and repudiated; nor is it clear how such an alternative

might differ from the equally unacceptable tolerance of the Dutch in
the *Journey*. It is crucial, however, that the framing device of the *Romance*
formulates a concern with the publicity of text; and it is essential that
this concern is taken further in the novel itself as a concern with the way
that the publicity of institutional arrangements plays an important role in
reorganizing the confessional relationship between individual consciousness and communal formations. In this respect, the *Romance* anticipates
the direction of the similar yet more elaborate novel *The Italian*, which
appeared with its full title of *The Italian, or the Confessional of the Black
Penitents* in 1797. The preface to the novel rehearses the text's relationship
to monastic privacy that, at this point, should now be familiar to us. In
The Italian's preface, however, is an even greater investment in defining
British institutions on a secular rather than a confessional model, for it
implies that the very survival of a national population hinges precisely
on the difference between these models.

The preface consists of a conversation between an English tourist, one
of a group of "English travellers," and an Italian friar in the church of
Santa Maria del Pianto; and their conversation ultimately leads to an explanation of the source of the novel that follows. In a sense, the scenario
leads to a delineation of character on the level of stereotype. In keeping
with the novel's title, which sets up a category applicable to any of its
characters (although presumably the "Italian" is Schedoni, the novel's
arch-villain), the preface refuses to particularize the two interlocutors
beyond their identity as "Englishman" and "Italian." Aside from describing discrete national characters, the preface seems pointless; there
is no attempt (as in Walpole's novel) to establish the text as a translation,
to explain its transmission from one culture to another. And the emphasis
on national difference ultimately revolves around the issue of different
ways of schematizing institutional authority. Monasticism's emphasis on
uniform belief looks like a blindness to criminal action, a privilege of
private association over public harms. When the friar explains to the
English tourist that the stranger attracting his attention is an "assassin"
who seeks "sanctuary," the Englishman suggests that this role for the
church undermines, rather than supports, civil government: "of what
avail your laws," he asks, "if the most atrocious criminal may thus find
shelter from them?" The friar claims that the church violates the law to
protect life: "if we were to shew no mercy to such unfortunate persons,
assassinations are so frequent, that our cities would be half depopulated."
Yet the Italian's logic reveals to the Englishman that if the law destroys
populations, the church's remedy to the law is even more destructive in

the way that its private alliances and sympathies "shelter" the criminal from any accountability for the consequences of criminal action.[28]

The preface to *The Italian*, as it sets up distinctions between confessional and secular institutions, anticipates distinctions that pervade the novel itself. The plot will seem familiar, if not predictable, enough: against the wishes of his parents, a young nobleman, Vivaldi, pursues Ellena Rosalba, bereft (she thinks) of her parents and living with a distant relation. The Marchesa, Vivaldi's mother, is aided by the evil monk Schedoni in arranging Ellena's imprisonment in a monastery, since the family disapproves of her; she is eventually rescued by Vivaldi yet recaptured under the auspices of the Inquisition. After Vivaldi submits to the Inquisitorial tribunal and after Ellena only narrowly escapes death at the hands of Schedoni, the obstacles to marriage are quickly overcome: Ellena is reunited with her mother, her noble lineage is revealed, Vivaldi and Ellena are wed.

I will discuss some of these familiar features of the Gothic plot – the separation of children from families, the romance that initially appears as class transgression and then is revised as class misrecognition – in a moment. Yet another device of the Gothic novel more obviously touches on our concerns: the Inquisitorial regime and the specific technologies of the Inquisitorial tribunal, which figure so prominently in other examples of the genre yet perhaps nowhere so brilliantly as in *The Italian*.[29] The emphasis on uniformity is continually represented as a strategy of ecclesiastical government that extends into the structure of the family. It is true that *The Italian* – like other Gothic productions – occasionally shows the family to be a place of aristocratic stability and comfort; some critics have concluded from this that Radcliffe awards it the greatest privilege as a basis for social order.[30] In Radcliffe's first novel, *The Castles of Athlin and Dunbayne* (1789), such a view seems to be justified by the way in which the "bosom" of the "family" affords Matilda protection from the tyranny of her husband's murderer in "the ancient seat of feudal government."[31] In Radcliffe's 1794 *Mysteries of Udolpho*, the protracted plot of Emily St. Aubert's imprisonment is finally resolved by her return to her family estate.[32] The catalogue of crimes in *The Italian*, moreover, consists of outrages against the family: Schedoni arranges the murder of his brother; the Marchesa plots (unsuccessfully) the murder of her son's lover. Thus the family, as an ostensibly natural collection of persons, falls victim to interests and ambitions that appear foreign to it.

Yet if the family appears at one moment to provide a source of domestic comfort, it reveals itself to be a social group that continually violates the

desires and interests of its members. The Marchese's "confidence" in
Vivaldi is an implicit command for him to abide by his father's choices:
"you belong to your family," he asserts, "not your family to you" (*The
Italian*, 29). The Marchesa follows the same logic as her husband, however
"more subtle in her whole conduct" she may be (33). Her solicitous regard
for the protection of her family only reveals, as Ellena finds out, that
"mercy" is only a "colouring" for actual "injustice," and that "generosity"
only adds "softening tints" to "acts most absolutely tyrannical" (83).
What the Marchesa calls "justice" is in fact only "sternness" and "callous
insensibility" (111).

The church – as in *A Sicilian Romance* – acts as a shelter from feudal
power only by doubling it. In the monastery of San Stefano, for example,
Ellena witnesses a form of feudal hierarchy in the "nuns of high rank"
and the "favourites" who attend the Abbess (124). The Abbess "believed
that of all possible crimes, next to sacrilege, offences against persons
of rank were least pardonable" (67). The "*Father-director* and his flock,"
whom Vivaldi and his servant encounter in their search for the kidnapped
Ellena, admit them into their company only because Vivaldi appears to
be of noble birth, and thus confirm the sense that the church does not
"protect" against the family with all its prejudices and exclusions, but
colludes with it in all of its crimes (114).

Monasticism's centrality in the novel is owing not only to its tendency
to double the tyranny of the family, but to its even more conspicuous
technology for securing the uniformity exacted within familial privacy:
it most clearly embodies a social model that – as I have been arguing –
seeks to elicit a uniform consciousness from the members of a group. For
Ellena, the deep level of psychological conformity within the monastic
institution in fact serves as both an initial source of comfort and eventual
source of terror. The "sanctuary" she finds in the convent is "especially
adapted to the present state of her spirits" (57); when she is kidnapped
and brought to the monastery, the songs she hears are in "perfect unison
with her feelings" (65). The notion of the institution as a correspondence
between minds, however, is ultimately less comforting when considered
from the vantage point of a nun she observes, "characterised by a gloomy
malignity, which seemed ready to inflict upon others some portion of the
unhappiness she herself suffered" (66).

It is Schedoni, moreover, the Marchesa's confessor and the most
prominent figure of priestly authority, who repeatedly asserts the claims
of uniformity on individuals within a community in the most terrifying ways. The already established network of the family allows him to

command a whole series of obligations from its members, as he "steals into the bosom of a family only to poison its repose" (51). When Schedoni restrains himself from murdering Ellena according to the Marchesa's plan, it may initially appear as though familial affection has conquered sinister ambition. When he recognizes a portrait miniature of himself hanging around Ellena's neck, that is, he mistakenly assumes that she is his daughter, and thus lavishes on her his "paternal affection" and "father's tenderness" (237). Yet, from another point of view, it is precisely Schedoni's fatherly role – a position acquired from monastic privilege – that makes it possible for him to exercise that power. The familial interest that saves Ellena complements rather than contradicts the ambition that initially motivated Schedoni to put her to death. His aid to Ellena is indeed "paternal affection," but the very terms of that affection are consistent with his "selfish apprehension" (288); his newly-formed plan to unite Ellena with Vivaldi resembles fatherly concern but is also a "grand design" and an "erroneous ambition," motivated by the expectation of "immediate preferment" (290). Ellena's portrait miniature, then, is a mark of descent: yet it is not so much a sign of security in one's lineage as it is a sign of past and future obligations. Even though the portrait initially saves Ellena's life, it is nonetheless a reminder that the lineage that produces one's security can also lead to one's death – one's inability to escape the obligations incurred by that lineage.

If the function of the portrait was to suggest how Schedoni's act of sympathy only more clearly shows the relevance of an individual's prior affiliations for inclusion within a community, the point it makes about the mechanisms of confessional government is taken still further in the episodes of Inquisitorial confession and forced conversion. The scene of confession demands not so much a truth of the individual as a truth held by the tribunal *itself* in order to confirm that authority (it is in possession of a person's "most secret offences" to which they are expected to confess even if innocent [205]). The crime of which Vivaldi is accused – and this is crucial – is a crime against religion and thus a crime against society; it is his "horrible impiety" rather than any offense against a person that is a violation of the "public good" (111). However the Inquisition may attempt to uphold this good by upholding a uniformity of belief, it only abounds in the deceptions and dissimulations that Bentham and other reformers would later claim to be central to Britain's own confessional government. It abounds, that is, in a proliferation of "figurative signs," a "dark and circuitous" line of questioning that seems to proceed in a language as private as a single consciousness (346). Even the innocent are urged to "become criminal, and assert a falsehood, that they might be released from anguish, which they could no longer sustain" (200). The Inquisitorial procedure is thus not merely engaged in the removal or prevention of dissimulation; it actively produces and perpetuates it.

Ellena's confinement in San Stefano sharpens the novel's representation of this mode of government. For one of the struggles that arises over the course of her confinement in the convent is not simply over the physical limits of her imprisonment, but over her coerced noviciation – a struggle that must end in her being "sacrificed" if she refuses (126). The regime of the Inquisition in general and the monastic structure of San Stefano in particular place Ellena as a figure outside the community in need of conversion, and in this sense her resistance to noviciation points towards the imperfection of those institutions. For the potential advantages of monasticism are at first visible in the way that it provides a new identity for its participants (by removing them from the pressures of families and other prior alliances); at the same time, it eventually *reinforces* the importance of those alliances by attempting to guarantee uniformity – which mirrors and in fact supports the feudal hierarchy in the world outside.

THE GOTHIC PURSUIT OF JUSTICE

The Italian's interest in the various incarnations of monasticism that I have been describing appears to be an interest in a particular relation between individual and community, in which the relevance of agreement to the formation of community entails either an exclusion from community or an inclusion that inevitably produces hypocritical subjects. The thrilling *mise-en-abîme* effected through this institutionalized hypocrisy has been identified by readers of the Gothic such as Eve Sedgwick and Anne Williams as a predominant feature of the genre.[33] The Gothic emphasis on impenetrable surfaces, in those accounts, demonstrates a kind of truth about the human subject's position within a matrix of linguistic signs: it points, that is, towards the ontological problem of character's essential unknowability. Those accounts (and post-structural accounts more generally) emphasize the apparent hold that mental states have over "personal identity," precisely in order to show how the language of fiction – in the Gothic, a numinous language that is "only barely writing" – unsettles that hold.[34]

Rather than revealing a truth of language, *The Italian*'s focus on dissimulation has more to do with a specific historical logic of government:

what links the practices of the Inquisition to the traditional confessional practices of the British state. But if monasticism is a focus of interest in *The Italian* because it represents a confessional model of government, it is also a focus of interest because the novel likewise identifies it as a solution to the problems with that model. Radcliffe, that is, mobilizes monasticism both as a confessional structure and as its antidote in a more tolerant form of government. To begin with, the novel is not without an actualized institution as an alternative to monastic organization: the convent of Santa della Piéta, where Ellena finds refuge after narrowly escaping death at the hands of Schedoni, embodies an order and stability that contradicts monasticism's rigidly patriarchal authority. Piety – as in the *Sicilian Romance* – is equated with a form of supervised freedom from doctrinal prohibition. The convent's superior acts as an agent of reformation, with a religion "neither gloomy nor bigoted"; her latitudinarian principles inform her "lectures," which "seldom touched upon points of faith, but explained and enforced the moral duties, particularly such as were most practicable in the society to which she belonged" (*The Italian*, 300). The way that the convent provides an appropriate refuge for Ellena suggests that her resistance to noviciation during her imprisonment in San Stefano – her "repeated rejection of the veil" (95), her "protest against vows which my heart disclaims" (119) – is neither merely a plea for truthfulness, nor the assertion of an honest individual against a corrupt society. It is the assertion of a different relationship between individual and society, one that does not involve the practice of "dissimulation" for entry within a system of social organization, but allows the "heart" to remain "unchanged" or to change at will because those beliefs and predispositions are no longer the basis for communal membership (95,120).

If we take note of Ellena's individual refusal of conformity, and of the actual incarnation of the secular institution at the Santa della Piéta, we must even more carefully attend to the ways in which the novel takes care to distance the relations between certain characters, its representations of "justice," and its own narrative strategies, from the logic of confession. We should note, for instance, how individual characters outside the mechanisms of the Inquisition become intelligible to us and intelligible to each other in a way that consistently distinguishes a definition of character from a definition of mental states. The irreducible particularity of individual psychological states is continually indexed to exchangeable forms, as if to make the language of characters seem like a geometrical pattern rather than the obscure, unreadable language that the novel associates with Inquisitorial authority. When Vivaldi visits Ellena, for instance, "he trembled as he took up the lute she had been accustomed to touch, and, when he awakened the chords, her own voice seemed to speak" (23). The particularity of Ellena's voice comes to be available through a replicable form or "chords" (chords that are interestingly ambiguated by Vivaldi's name – are they the character's invention or are they the publicly circulated work of a famous composer?); and in this sense Vivaldi's encounter with her "voice" implicitly invokes an earlier moment when he had serenaded her under her balcony (17). There, Ellena's absence during Vivaldi's performance prevents Vivaldi from "judging" its "effect" on Ellena. Both instances work to release intelligibility from a reliance on a full exchange or communion of minds; they imply an account of identity that is more formal than psychological.

Even the surroundings in Ellena's house, described a moment later during Vivaldi's first visit, seem to participate in this strategy. We should look back to the episode concerning the portrait miniature to emphasize the way Radcliffe's novel – and other Gothic novels such as *Otranto* – employ the portrait in order to mark a particular vision of society as an adherence to established norms: society, that is, as a replication of identical selves that are affiliated with the portrait. The ancestral portrait resembles to some degree the very structure of the confessional state itself, in the way that the Burkean "oath" attempts to image future generations as the projection of a single body of beliefs. In Ellena's house, however, Vivaldi discovers an altogether different relationship between artistic production and reception that in turn corresponds to a different model of social relations. There, every object is a "copy": the "dancing nymph" on a stand is a drawing that is a "copy from Herculaneum." Upon closer examination, Vivaldi "perceived this to be one of a set that ornamented the apartment, and observed with surprise, that they were the particular subjects, which adorned his father's cabinet, and which he had understood to be the only copies permitted from the originals in the royal museum" (24). The Marchese's "copy" is, in a sense, a copy that attempts to deny its meaning as a copy; he attempts to view the copy as if he could claim a unique property right in the representation. (Ironically, we are earlier told that "the copies . . . which ornamented a cabinet of the Vivaldi palace, were drawn by her [Ellena's] hand" [9]). The copy, by the Marchese's reasoning, would be assimilated to the system of inheritance suggested by the ancestral portrait. Yet for Ellena the "copy" becomes a way of decreasing the importance of exclusive ownership, and a way of accommodating individual versions to the general type, for the "copy of Herculaneum, though a copy, was touched with the spirit of original genius." Ellena's copies, in other words, demonstrate the convergence between individual volition and categorical expression; her craft is an expression of the "industry" which makes her supremely individualized and utterly typical (24–25). (Radcliffe's own use of quotations throughout the text – from works of Shakespeare, Milton, Walpole, and others – including herself – develops an analogous position with respect to literary history. For the quotations preceding individual chapters are devoted less to continuing a canon of taste – on the model of a pseudo-religious literary establishment – than to imagining the productions of others in an enabling relationship to her own constructions.)

These instances repeatedly represent Vivaldi and Ellena as participants in an accessible public language – a language that becomes both the emblem and vehicle of the novel's more pervasive representations of justice. Although the novel refers to justice on the level of character – so that the Marchesa's prejudices can be contrasted with Ellena and Vivaldi's "love of justice" (84) or with Vivaldi's refusal to make himself an "instrument" of the Inquisition's injustices (321), justice in fact has very little to do with affection or a sympathy between minds. Instead, it has more to do with removing judgments of innocence or guilt – or judgments of character in general – from the beliefs or associations formed by individuals prior to their actions. While Schedoni earlier in the novel claims protection from accusations of guilt by asserting affiliation with a particular monastic order, the method of achieving "justice" in the novel is in a crucial sense separated from the set of private affiliations and personal beliefs that come into play in that account (50). In the Inquisitorial tribunal, Vivaldi's main angle of protest against its procedures focuses on its protection of "religion" from "heresy" rather than persons from "injuries," on the criminalization of beliefs rather than actions (314). And the lengthy Inquisition scene continues to distinguish between the tribunal's attempt to privilege the testimony of particular individuals, while Vivaldi insists upon the necessary partiality or interestedness of testimony.

Vivaldi, however, only carries out a vision of justice that is more generally located on the level of narration that is itself a practice of justice. Vivaldi demonstrates his devotion to justice through his devotion to the "circumstantial," to careful and detailed description; Ellena likewise attends to the degree to which her own romantic love will be "vexatious in its consequences" (122,333). And they do so, interestingly, in imitation of the novel's own practices: its corroborating emphasis on the circumstances and consequences of the actions of its pious schemers.[35] The third-person narration self-consciously intrudes within the protected "spheres" of familial and monastic authority with all of their private demands for "obedience" (121), and thus the novel can provide accounts of sanctified dispositions that are nevertheless "vicious in [their] consequence[s]" or persons who cloak themselves with ecclesiastical authority but who are "injurious" in their "conduct" (122).

This perspective – a secularizing perspective adopted by Vivaldi, Ellena, and the narration itself – ultimately defines the very operations of the Inquisition. Vivaldi, Ellena, the Inquisition, and the narrative slowly converge and collude with each other in the third volume of the novel in order to expose a narrative of "circumstances." Monastic secrecy, previously unexamined or unchallenged, is now laid open to view by the procedures of the Inquisitorial tribunal that fold into the procedures of Radcliffe's narration. The court records of the Inquisition are supposed to be virtually interchangeable – they are "nearly in the following words" – with the novel's own fictional point of view (337). And in this maneuver, I would argue, *The Italian* does nothing less than perform a fictional equivalent to removing the benefit of clergy in the law: the traditional means of obtaining pardon by appealing to the influence of the church, but to which charges of capital offense became immune in the eighteenth century.[36] The Inquisition essentially turns into a public trial; and while the emphasis on the administration of oaths in monasticism nurtures "prejudice" and "indulgence" (180), the novel consistently distributes justice by moving towards a narrative of actions that defeats the contradictions of hypocritical testimony. The collusion of fictional narration and public trial finally is able to "unmask" Schedoni, to "strip [him] of [his] holy hypocrisy" (103–04).

There is an important and revealing similarity between the plots of *The Italian* and *The Romance of the Forest*, Radcliffe's novel of 1791. The novel's hero, Adeline, is saved by the La Motte family – who are at first kind to her but then conspire with the Marquis de Montalt to arrange a "fictitious marriage" with her.[37] After escaping from the Marquis, she discovers shelter finally in the tranquil company of the La Luc family, which is primarily characterized by its tolerance, its "philanthropy" which is "diffused through the whole village," and by its active engagement in commercial enterprises (277,296). As in Radcliffe's other Gothics, the security of domestic arrangements continually relies upon a vocabulary of "sincerity," of friendship and trust, at the same time that such arrangements – and the oaths and declarations supporting them – are shown to be conspicuously and dangerously fragile (121,125,224). The ruin of the abbey in which La Motte holds Adeline captive only emphasizes the disintegration of the faith-based relationships that are part of the abbey's history. As if to revive that history, the La Mottes continually strive to rejuvenate the crumbling rooms with rugs, furniture, and tapestries; Adeline (like Ellena in *The Italian*), however, is marked by her refusal of vows in the convent in which her father – following her mother's death – had placed her. The family of La Luc offers the most suitable environment for the novel's young hero, since it bears the strongest resemblance to *The Italian*'s convent of Santa della Piéta in its regulation by "principle" and "systems" that are "rational and sublime" (245).

And perhaps the most striking resemblance of all appears in the manner in which the novel's Gothic terror finds a resolution in a public trial. In a "public court of justice," the Marquis, who killed Adeline's father, has his crimes "exposed to the public eye" (342); La Motte is justly convicted of assault and robbery (317–19); and Theodore, Adeline's lover, is convicted of misconduct against the Marquis – his colonel in the military whom he injured in a tavern brawl (325). In this respect, *The Romance of the Forest*, like *A Sicilian Romance* and *The Italian*, moves the center of attention to a prosecution of crimes against persons and property rather than crimes of heresy, blasphemy, or other crimes against a nebulously defined public good. It is at this very moment, though, that we come to the important point of distinction between *The Romance of the Forest* and *The Italian*, and see how the later novel enhances or accentuates the operations of law as a secular ordering of private familial and religious spheres of authority. For the resolution to the earlier novel is achieved *outside* the law: while it is affirmed that "justice will overtake the guilty" (*The Romance of the Forest*, 343), the novel nevertheless represents the judicial system as a tool to be manipulated by the interests of private individuals with private interests. After the Marquis dies, his malevolent influence in court is removed, and the novel proceeds towards a wholly new outcome. Adeline procures a pardon for Theodore and La Motte obtains a relaxed sentence of banishment (353).

The task of *The Italian*, however, is to make the Inquisition work, paradoxically, against the traditional confessional mechanisms of the Inquisition itself; the Inquisition becomes synonymous with a law that encloses, includes, and regulates all religious and domestic attachments within its scope. The operations of justice that work against the operations of the Inquisitorial demand for conformity (and in fact turn the very methods of the tribunal against itself) are tellingly portrayed on the surface of Schedoni's body. The monk's monastic authority had earlier appeared to make him "super-human," and to endow him with the capacity to "triumph" over the "tempers and passions of persons," even while his internal sense of guilt for murdering his brother causes a "hideous gnawing" at his "conscience" (*The Italian*, 34–35). Yet the novel's unraveling of Schedoni's crime – his true guilt for having murdered his brother – eventually makes his body shrink back into itself: he appears "almost to writhe" under the strenuous pursuit of "justice," as if the workings of justice have literally constrained his own voraciously expanding body.

The closing chapters of the novel in fact continue this logic through which social arrangements move sacred communities into altered positions; Schedoni's writhing body becomes a miniaturized version of effects of the secular mechanisms of justice. A brief synopsis of the plot of these chapters helps us to perceive this point. *The Italian* ends rather precipitously with the sudden exposure of Ellena's noble birth. She is, after all, neither the daughter of poor parents nor the daughter of Schedoni; she is the offspring of Olivia (the nun Ellena meets at the convent of San Stefano) and the Count di Bruno. Following these revelations, the Marchese di Vivaldi sanctions the couple's marriage. Now this relation of the facts might seem to confirm that Radcliffe's Gothic is as conventional as critics have previously claimed.[38] But the meaning of this apparent deference to familial alliances becomes all the more pointed for the line of argument I have been pursuing once we recognize the way that families are reconstructed through their prior estrangement – the way that alliances are restored precisely by reconfiguring them within new modes of social organization. After all, Olivia and Ellena, mother and daughter, become united not within the privacy of the family, but within the "sanctuary of the della Piéta" (372), the novel's single instantiation of a legitimate liberal institution. And, as if in contrast, the Marchesa dies – another withering body like Schedoni's – apparently as a consequence of the family's exclusions that monastic privacy so rigorously enforces. Her doctors, that is, "found out that she had been dying, or as good, for many years, though nobody else had suspected it." The dissimulating conformity that the Marchesa herself has demanded recurs in the way that the physician shows his "regard for [his] lady" by claiming "there was no danger" in her illness (375).

To put these observations somewhat differently, the plot's resolution in marriage eventually erodes the sense of marriage as a private agreement. As if the Marchesa's death did not sufficiently convey the novel's hostility towards the dependence of society upon those agreements, the closing chapters also foreground the presence and peculiar character of its favored forms of social organization. The scene turns, that is, to the church of the Santa della Piéta, the tolerant monastic institution, and to the gardens of the Marchese, the "style" of which is "that of England" (411,412). The restoration of order indeed provides an English answer to the confessional structure of feudal and monastic power; yet it is uniquely English not because of its doctrinal difference from other nations, but because of its uniquely secular character which reduces the requirements placed on individuals in order to participate within the national community.

GODWIN, *MANDEVILLE*, AND THE TRIUMPH OF TOLERATION

What is English about the ending of *The Italian*, I should add, is not merely a *description* of English institutions but a new account of their aims: a new account that would enable a more comprehensive role in expanding *British* dominions. The value of such an account is that – informed as it is by deeply embedded traditions in English philosophical and institutional history – the scope of its organizational powers is not merely limited to the territory of England or to English people. Indeed, the argument I have been making is that the institutions imagined within the Gothic novel, rather than simply props for nationalism or nationalist ideology, dispose themselves towards ideologies in a new way in order to facilitate relations among their diverse adherents.

Up to this point, I have been referring to the Gothics of Ann Radcliffe as paradigms for the way the genre in a more general sense established its stance towards religious belief and its position in relation to modern secular institutions. But now I need to contribute an important nuance to that account before closing this chapter. The point that I have been making is that the church disaggregates itself from the confessional functions of religion and assumes a position of secular government in Radcliffe's fictions. Reconceptualizing both government and the church, Radcliffe's work makes the church become an all-encompassing secular government that extends its protection far beyond the followers of one specific religious doctrine. This secular mission of the church, moreover, reinforces government's own aspirations to be as authoritative and all-commanding as any religion. Stating the aims of Radcliffe's vision of social order in this way helps us to see how her treatment of religious establishment – an establishment beyond establishment – might be very clearly related to the *opposition* to religious establishment in other, apprently more radical, novels.

Very briefly, then, I want to explain precisely how it is that a novel such as Godwin's *Mandeville* (1817) – often known as a "Jacobin" novel, a "philosophical" novel, or even an "historical" novel, but sharing many characteristics with the Gothic – quite clearly shares the concerns of Radcliffe's writing as I have been describing them so far. Yet it departs from Radcliffe's Gothic in a way that will help me to forecast issues that arise in chapter 7 of this book, where I show how toleration assumes a more tragic cast in works such as Shelley's *The Cenci* and Byron's *Cain*. In many ways, *Mandeville* continues themes that the author had explored earlier in *St. Leon* (1799), a novel set during the Protestant Reformation, that repeatedly depicts its hero's persecution at the hands of the Inquisition. In St. Leon's description of it, the object of the Inquisition, defined in a way that might be a paradigm for the Gothic, is "to defend our holy mother, the church, from whatever might defile her sanctity and whiteness. Every thing that calls into question the truth of her doctrines, that pollutes and turns from their original purpose any of her ordinances, or that implies commerce and league with the invisible enemy of saints, it is its peculiar province to investigate."[39] The Inquisition is central in this novel because of the terror it inflicts upon St. Leon in order to discover the secret behind his extraordinary powers (he has received the philosopher's stone and the *elixir vitae* from a mysterious stranger). Ostracized everywhere as blasphemous and irreligious, St. Leon is taught to realize that his supposedly unlimited resources are in fact limited, and this is because those resources are never available simply for the purposes of utility. The suspicion that the hero is in league with "the invisible enemy of saints," that is, counteracts the purposes to which he attempts to direct his infinite resources; even when he acts for the benefit of others, St. Leon is repeatedly viewed as a criminal because of his apparent irreligion.

Godwin's later novel *Mandeville* seems even more appropriate for the direction of my discussion because of the way that it both dramatizes and devalues the logic of confessional politics; perhaps even more important, it finally imagines a secular resolution to religious violence and struggle that relocates, but does not eliminate, the terror of social relations. The novel follows the adventures of Mandeville, the orphaned son of an Irish Protestant, raised in the home of his Protestant uncle, and tutored by the fanatical Protestant Hilkiah Bradford. Like Edgeworth's Harrington (the hero in the novel by that name which I will discuss in chapter 4), Mandeville's education is an education in the decisive importance of religion to social life. "Religion is the most important of all things... All other vices, crimes, profligacies, call them by what name you please, are trifles to this," Godwin has Mandeville declare late in the novel.[40] As important as it may be for social stability, however, religion is more often shown to be the cause of dissension and division. Virtually every aspect of young Mandeville's education turns out to be an education in prejudice and anti-Catholic paranoia. In the first two volumes of the novel, furthermore, he continually finds himself placed in situations (during the wars between Catholics and Protestants in Ireland, under the tyrannical authority of Mr. Bradford, and in school at Winchester and Oxford) where demands for adherence to specific religious and political principles repeatedly require either conformity or exclusion – or even death.

The religious warfare that continues throughout this novel seems, in one way, to be nothing other than the consequence of any attempt to build social units. The experience of living in a social world, it appears to Mandeville, involves finding acquaintances – such as his sister Henrietta – that enable him to "mee[t] with persons of like dispositions to himself" (*Mandeville*, 214). But the disappointing lesson he initially learns is that it is so difficult to find others with similar dispositions (even Henrietta eventually reveals herself to be less sympathetic than he had imagined her to be [312]) that it would be wiser – or certainly easier – to give up the eternal warfare of social relations entirely. It might be wiser, that is, to resign himself to living in utter "solitude" (214).

In another way, however, *Mandeville* presents a very different view of social interaction: a view that emphasizes the overriding power of secular government to organize the adherents of different religious beliefs and alliances regardless of the presence or absence of sympathy among them. Towards the very end of the novel, the hero will in fact declare that there has been little point in his "faith": "Oh, that I had believed nothing, that I had expected nothing, that I had relied on nothing!" (309), he says despairingly. Mandeville's lack of faith in faith is not as significant for making a point about personal faith as it is for making – or at least acquiescing to – a point about the *social value* of faith. Indeed, although Mandeville holds fast to his fanatical religious hatreds, he keeps finding at the same time that inescapable social ties, together constituting a newly visible tolerant regime of government, continually accumulate between himself and others despite his hatreds or his sympathies. The importance of Holloway, the attorney who insinuates himself within and ultimately gains control over the legal and financial affairs of Uncle Audley Mandeville, is to be discerned precisely in the way that he makes Mandeville come to terms with a network of affiliations that are *not* the product of similar beliefs. As he takes control of Uncle Audley's will, Holloway hollows out the hallowed way of religion and religious alliances; he engages the family in an obscure set of property disputes and obtrudes into every detail of domestic movement, causing Mandeville increasingly to remark upon how he is engaged in an "intimate alliance with persons . . . little agreeable to [his] disposition" (231). When Mandeville's arch-enemy Clifford abandons Protestantism and converts to Catholicism, the professional and political success of the "apostate" further demonstrates that the entire structure of modern government itself is defined by a lack of uniformity in belief: a "latitudinarianism and licentiousness" that the hero comes to identify with the policy of toleration itself (252). And when Clifford and Henrietta are engaged to be married, Mandeville appears more or less resigned to accept the call of "justice" over the call of sympathy. Recognizing – at least for a moment – that the couple's ability to "be happy, and to make happy" would be defeated by his desire to keep Henrietta for himself, he declares that his "prejudices" and "groundless fancies" are "on no account to be permitted to become a law, to the sane and effective members of the community of mankind" (298). His prejudices, though deeply felt, have little bearing on the more inclusive operations of the "law" that constructs and binds persons together into new and unexpected relationships.

While he continues to feel "shut out of the pale of humanised society" (253), Mandeville's feeling of exclusion from sympathy only momentarily deflects our attention from the more profound inclusion effected by the social environment that surrounds him, his intimate alliance with persons disagreeable to his disposition. It is this non-intimate intimacy that forms the "sane and effective" logic of Godwinian community. The final, thoroughly stunning, gesture in this novel is to give Mandeville what amounts to the mark of Cain: a mark incurred in an attempt to murder Clifford, and that I think we must see as Godwin's way of remarking upon a religious system of values while also marking *over* those values with the mark of legal sanction. When Mandeville attacks Clifford, Clifford in an act of self-defense inflicts a "deep and perilous gash" that leaves his opponent scarred with "a perpetual grimace" (325). As if to comment on Mr. Bradford's religious harangues in the first book of the novel – discourses that are meant to enforce a proper religious devotion – Mandeville's mark at the end of the novel is a mark of his crime that continues to remind us of his religious predispositions inculcated in childhood. The mark is cleverly described as *une balafré*, a wound given its name "in the French wars of religion in the latter half of the sixteenth century";

and the origin of the term in religious wars serves as the faint echo of the theocratic structure of power that inspired such wars (325). But it is also a mark of the occlusion of that structure of power, the *balafré* acting as the mark of a far more comprehensive legal code. What we realize is that this mark is not merely associated with wars of religion inside or outside of England – wars of religion that seem to inflect all of Mr. Bradford's lessons communicated to his young student at an earlier point in the novel. This is, instead, a scar that is legally sanctioned as punishment for Mandeville's act of violence. It is not the mark of religious demonization and exclusion, but the mark of a legal inclusion that superintends all religious inclusions and exclusions.

The logic of secularization in Godwin's fiction, then, is not at all separable from the tolerant logic of Radcliffe's. The difference between the novels lies in their different vantage points on that logic, in their contrasting tallies of the costs and benefits of feeling intimately allied with persons "little agreeable" to their dispositions. For Radcliffe, lifting the burden of belief is always made to seem like a social as well as a personal gain; the sunny endings of novels such as *The Italian* derive directly from the ability of such fictions to imagine persons becoming more social precisely because they have been relieved of a whole range of demands for social conformity. In *Mandeville*, the zealous hero's dilemma is to feel the pain of exclusion that is actually a painful feeling of the impossibility of ever excluding himself from "the community of mankind": a dilemma that literally drives him to madness. For Shelley, in his review of the novel published in *The Examiner*, Mandeville's situation was the same as the Romantic reader's: "we can scarcely believe that the grin which must accompany Mandeville to his grave is not stamped upon our own visage."[41]

CHAPTER 3

Coleridge's polemic divinity

THE WATCHMAN'S ORGANIZED DISSENT

The modern age's "love of knowledge," as Samuel Taylor Coleridge describes it in the first issue of *The Watchman* (his ill-fated newspaper issued for less than three months in the spring of 1796), did a great deal to weaken the traditional social authority of established religion. But it also did a great deal to sustain the life of *religions*. The philosophy of the modern age did not simply disenchant the world: it did not, that is, replace ancient mythologies with empirical truths, religion with science. In fact, the "love of knowledge" was significant – and it earns a privileged place in Coleridge's initial conceptualization of *The Watchman* – for enhancing rather than suppressing the visibility of religious beliefs and the dissension among them.[1]

The claim I am ascribing to Coleridge first arises in this issue of the newspaper in connection with a story – also told by the likes of Godwin and Hume – about the defeat of Constantinople by the Turks. As a consequence, we are told, learned Greeks were driven west into Europe, an event that happily coincided with the invention of printing.[2] That story does, in fact, look very much like a uniform movement from darkness to light: "The first scanty twilight of knowledge was sufficient to shew what horrors had resulted from ignorance." But it is also true – and certainly more interesting – that what Coleridge really sees in this series of events is less a uniform growth of "knowledge" than a *decline* of any such uniformity: a decline brought about by the interdependent growth of the media and facilities for learning and the growth of religious disputation. The "diffusion of truth," he contends, "was aided by the Lutheran schism"; "literary exertion" was inspired by "the keen goading of religious controversy" (*CW* II:9).

My contention throughout this chapter will be that *The Watchman* pursues an interest sustained throughout Coleridge's long career as a writer of poetry, philosophy, theology, literary criticism, and political commentary: an interest in how modern (specifically British, liberal) society exists not in spite of, but *because* of, doctrinal disagreement. To frame the concerns of Coleridge's writing in this fashion is to emphasize its relation not only to the Two Acts of 1795 against Treasonable Practices and Seditious Meetings, to which the periodical's "Prospectus" explicitly refers, but also primarily to the issue of religious toleration which predates, circumscribes, and conditions treatments of the issue of free speech and freedom of association during the period.[3] As Coleridge continues in this number of *The Watchman* to describe the "diffusion of Knowledge," he characterizes it as the proliferation of religious sects – "the progress of Methodists, and other disciples of Calvinism" – rather than the consolidation of reason. "The most thorough-paced Republicans in the days of Charles the First were religious Enthusiasts," he continues to observe. Religious dissent acquires a positive value in his account because "the very act of dissenting from established opinions must generate habits precursive to the love of freedom" (*CW* II:12–13).

But even more intriguing is a fundamental paradox that emerges in these pages. Coleridge insists that "freedom" is demonstrated by dissent and also by society's internal *organization* of dissent, an organization that furnishes dissent with a distinctive and discernible shape. While the expression of religious belief may provide individuals with personal opportunities for "self-government," it also – in an even more important way – depends upon a facilitating pattern of social movement. For *The Watchman* attends not only to the varieties of personal belief as causes of the "diffusion of Knowledge" but also to the communal structures that regulate – while also producing and enhancing – dissension. The "diffusion of Knowledge" is thus attributed, for example, to a government that protects persons from "the attacks of others," to the "institution of large manufactories" accommodating members of different parties, and to "book societies established in almost every town and city of the kingdom" (*CW* II:13–14). In other words, Coleridge imagines *The Watchman's* affiliations with dissent – conveyed by its exhilarating motto, "That All may know the TRUTH; And that the TRUTH may make us FREE" – in terms of the way that dissent is framed within the social context of the law, the factory system, the institution of learning.

The critical commentary on Coleridge that more or less directly addresses the set of issues I describe often tends either to polarize or collapse discussions of religious belief and discussions of politics or government. On the one hand, critics such as Thomas McFarland and James Boulger

ably chart the gestation of Coleridge's personal religious beliefs or philosophical opinions. With little attention to the political significance of
those beliefs or opinions, they track the movement that Coleridge makes
from unitarianism towards trinitarianism – a movement that accompanies (in complex ways) a shift in philosophical affiliations beginning with
Hartleyan associationism and ending up with Kantian idealism.[4] To discuss Coleridge's politics, on the other hand, has often seemed to require
dismissing the issues of religious belief and philosophical speculation;
or – to be more precise – these concerns have merely seemed like en-
coded forms of radical or conservative politics. The critical attention to
political context, then, tends to view all discussions of religious belief
as mere abstractions and thus distractions from a keener observation of
the political alliances forged throughout the author's career. Critics such
as Nicholas Roe carefully investigate the alliance between Coleridge's
unitarianism and radical politics; Nigel Leask and John Morrow show
how his later conservative politics are the expected extension of later
increasing sympathies with orthodox Christianity.[5]

I would suggest, though, that these arguments, by either dismissing
politics in order to favor belief or making belief look like veiled politics, try too strenuously to resolve one term into the other. They thus
tend to ignore Coleridge's attention to the *negotiated* relationship between
belief and modes of government: the way that beliefs are not simply
self-governing but are governed within the context of different kinds
of political institutions. As a result, such arguments also tend to ignore
Coleridge's more specific efforts – in *The Watchman* and beyond – to defend a tolerant mode of government that accommodates and organizes
adherents of many beliefs and moral standpoints. Coleridge's focus on
laws, factories, and schools in *The Watchman*, in other words, reveals a
preoccupation with the way that secular institutions not only permit but
actively solicit and cultivate dissent. The fact that the mature Coleridge
comes to the defense of the established church – ostensibly a conservative one – should not deter us from noticing how such a defense regards
religious sectarianism as a strength rather than a weakness of British
civil institutions. Nor should it go unnoticed that a whole range of works
from the earliest to the latest stresses the importance of theological disputation in the development of civil society, counting "the number and
respectability of our sects" as one of the predominant advantages of
British social life – and even a protection against Napoleon's invasion.[6]

Coleridge will provide an opportunity for me to discuss in some
detail the manner in which Romantic writers continue to elaborate

upon the Gothic novel's literary and institutional orientation towards religion. To be sure, Coleridge objected to the "meretricious *popularness*" of sensational novels, in *The Friend* (*CW* IV.1:24), just as he anticipated Wordsworth's judgment on such literature in the preface to *Lyrical Ballads* by calling them "powerful stimulants" that "can never be required except by the torpor of an unawakened, or the languor of an exhausted, appetite."[7] Even so, it is important for us also to see that he continues to maintain the Gothic's combined commitment to both facilitating and managing the articulation of contentious religious beliefs, making incompatible religious perspectives *institutionally* compatible. What I claim throughout this chapter is that Coleridge, coming from different vantage points in his different works, engages in a sustained attempt to develop a sophisticated – and quintessentially Romantic – account of the relationship between dissent and secular government. This account, one that develops the Gothic's representations of tolerant legal and ecclesiastical institutions into a comprehensive view of the national church, makes us realize that even the crowning achievement of his defense of the church in *On the Constitution of the Church and State* (1829) has less in common with a theory of cultural hegemony than with a theory of toleration evident in his earliest writing. I locate this claim in relation to Coleridge's two efforts at periodical journalism – *The Watchman* and *The Friend* (1808–10; revised 1818) – along with the *Lay Sermons* of 1816 (*The Statesman's Manual*) and 1817, whose concerns recall those in *The Friend* but anticipate those in the later *Church and State*.[8] While it is not my purpose here to show that all of Coleridge's political opinions remained the same throughout his career, I do want to suggest that arguments depending on rigid or decisive shifts from individual faith to collective faith or heterodoxy to orthodoxy neglect the ways in which seemingly opposed allegiances are actually interdependent. Coleridge therefore realigns conventional oppositions of nonconformity and establishment in unexpected ways. Behind his radical critique of establishment in *The Watchman*, for instance, lies what seems to be a strong urge towards social conformity and religious orthodoxy; but behind the ostensibly more conservative and principled trajectory of *The Friend* and the *Lay Sermons* lies a potentially unsettling commitment to dissent. The purpose of revealing these surprisingly combined impulses is to show that these works do something more than simply oppose government with dissent or oppose dissent with government; they reimagine government itself as a highly productive coordination and facilitation of dissent. This, finally, will lead us towards a picture of Coleridge's political and literary construction of "polemic divinity."

BELIEF AND DISASSOCIATION

Many of Coleridge's works – such as *The Watchman* and the *Conciones ad Populum* (1795), out of which many parts of *The Watchman* grew – partake of a specifically Protestant anti-clerical critique of religious establishments, whether Protestant or Catholic. The Anglican church is criticized and satirized for its corruption: for its excessive worldliness, for its self-enrichment, for its violence and oppression – in effect, for its resemblance to Catholicism. The sheer conventionality of the rhetoric – made familiar through Anglican critiques of Catholicism (in Foxe's *Acts and Monuments*, for example) and through sectarian critiques of the Protestant establishment (in the works of Wycliffe, Tyndale, Whitgift, and others) does not make it any less attractive for Coleridge's purposes.[9] In the "Letter from Liberty" preceding the *Conciones*, the imagery follows the Book of Revelation 17: "RELIGION" appears as "a painted and patched-up old Harlot," and later as a "Religion of Mitres and Mysteries, the Religion of Pluralities and Persecution, the Eighteen-Thousand-Pound-a-Year Religion of Episcopacy" (*CW*1:30,65–66). The extracts from the poem *Religious Musings* in *The Watchman* appropriately echo those characterizations with their references to "PAGEANT POWER" or the image of the church as whore of Babylon, "The abhorred Form, / Whose scarlet robe was stiff with earthly pomp" (*CW*II:64,66). In the "Historical Sketch of the Manners and Religion of the ancient Germans" of March 17, 1796, the anti-clerical position is only slightly less thinly disguised; in the character of Odin, Coleridge finds a figure of a priest showing his skill in "imposture" by presiding over a religion of "error" and "superstition" that worshipped him as a "Supreme Being" (*CW*II:92).

That Odin resembles not only the bishops of the Church of England but the revolutionaries in France – who celebrated their own festival of the Supreme Being so meticulously orchestrated by Robespierre – suggests how broadly Coleridge wishes to oppose oppressive and corrupt institutions. In fact, these attacks would seem to suggest that there is more, or less, at stake here than demonizing structures of authority for their moral shortcomings. Maybe the imagery of the whore of Babylon appears to emphasize lewdness and blasphemy in order to solicit a proper English Protestant disgust and outrage; but Coleridge's more consistent aim in his early writings is not to satirize or demonize the hypocrisy and corruptions of the clergy as errors in either belief or personal conduct. He draws attention to and opposes the still more general confessional logic behind the alliance of church and state. In that logic – as I showed in chapter 1 – the nation could not only be imagined but also *enforced* as a community of like-minded believers with the aid of exclusionary oaths, tests, and penal laws. This made religion corrupt, but not because it was corrupt as a belief. It was corrupt because, in an inextricable alliance with the state, it made political participation depend upon conformity to a specific set of beliefs or doctrines. And this policy in turn either excluded adherents of nonconforming beliefs (from parliament, civil offices, educa- tion, and military institutions) or – at the very best – encouraged people to lie for the purposes of inclusion. The church was guilty, then, not for supporting a sinful or corrupt priesthood; it was guilty of building hypocrisy into its own institutional foundations.

Perhaps Coleridge's most characteristic response to this logic emerges in the second issue of *The Watchman*, where, after the celebrated "Essay on Fasts" (which I will discuss later), he launches a satirical "Defence of the Church Establishment from its similitude to the grand and simple Laws of the Planetary System." The ecclesiastical system is imagined by analogy with the planetary system in which bishops and chaplains revolve around the church as "larger bodies" and "moons" revolve around the sun. With this image – part Newton, part Dante – the satire represents a confessional community as if it were as natural as planetary movement. But the point it finally makes is that the music of the spheres is only a false harmony. Religious uniformity is a cover for a deeper and potentially more disruptive disagreement among the "atheists, papists, jacobites, and jacobines" that are "lured to the Church by hopes of livings and stalls"; the church is set up to fashion Anglicanism into a masquerade for divisive, self-serving interests. Its members accumulate not because of shared beliefs but because of fear and hopes for advancement: "by force of parental authority or apprehensions of starving." Confronted with the available options – dissimulation or exclusion – "many are compelled to subscribe what they cannot but disbelieve" (*CW*II:67–68).

From the point of view of the satirical "Defence," then, corruption turns out to be the necessary attribute of any system that demands uniformity – regardless of the *kind* of uniformity it might demand. This is why *The Watchman*'s recourse against institutional corruption fortifies itself against institutions altogether; or at least this is one way of under- standing why it is that Coleridge continually points to the ways in which the beliefs of an individual might be falsified or betrayed by the require- ments of those institutions.[10] It might be said, in fact, that *The Watchman*'s counter-confessional strategy comes to be defined by assuming a *necessary* disagreement or misalignment between an individual's beliefs and the

beliefs required for group membership. However *The Watchman* may initially align its sympathies in the Prospectus with radical political groups,
the journal's more pervasive strategies install an even more rigorous
logic of disassociation. *Any* association of persons, that is, amounts to a
falsified account of the individuals that contribute to that association,
for Coleridge consistently opposes not merely "metaphysical systematiz-
ers," not merely "party," but even "faction" itself, as though sectarianism
would be defeated once it became a sect of more than one (*CW* II:12,14).
Although he would later characterize *The Watchman* as an effort in journalism that was too highly politicized, the more vexing problem with
the work might be that it pursues its commitment to disassociation so
relentlessly that it threatens to undo any kind of group membership
whatsoever.

Such rigorous sectarianism – a sectarianism too constraining for sect
itself – could be read as an ailment in Coleridge's thinking that *The Friend*
successfully cures. Indeed, he introduces *The Friend* – which he names
partly as a way of paying respect to the Quakers' "admirable discipline"
and less radical position of dissent – as a deliberate correction of the failed
Watchman and all of its "allurements" of divisive, sectarian, "transitory
interests" (*CW* IV.1:244,22). The new journal, the Friend (Coleridge's
persona) announces, will instead be dedicated to the cultivation of
"principles" and the "communication" of truth, "preventing both author and reader from becoming "the unstable Patriots of Passion or Accident" (*CW* IV.1:39,326). But even more interesting than this dramatic announcement of philosophical departure is the crucial aspect in which *The
Friend* nevertheless resembles the earlier enterprise. The first essay of *The
Friend*, with its "Fable of the Madning Rain," insists upon the difference
between "universal" and transitory truth (*CW* IV.1:7–13), and the Friend
continually proclaims the writer's desire to communicate religious – and
specifically *Christian* – truth (in the footsteps of writers such as Luther,
Hooker, Jeremy Taylor, and others). Even so, this is writing that refuses its
own recommendations to universalize – as if (according to *The Watchman*'s logic) encouraging the communication of truth might do nothing
more than encourage lying. The "Fable" depicts a blind, enslaved populace ignoring the words of the prophet; but the words of the prophet, assumed by Coleridge himself, are nothing other than "the Law of my own
mind" (*CW* IV.1:9). And the succeeding numbers of the journal repeatedly
confirm the earlier logic of disassociation: more important than establishing a truth or general principle is the ability – indeed the necessity –
to deviate from any general principle. Throughout this enterprise,

the Friend insists on the value of "freedom of thought" against the "intolerant" (*CW* IV.1:279); the aim of the Friend's inquiries is not to build consensus but to deny it by vociferously insisting on the journal's lack of popularity, its eccentricity, its lack of adherence to any standards of "*plain good common-sense*" (*CW* IV.1:20,24). Indeed, so far is Coleridge from rejecting *The Watchman's* divisive and contentious stance that he just as frequently excuses, extols, and retrieves – rather than merely forswears – an earlier radicalism. While free from the "stains and impurities" of "ordinary fanaticism," he still embraces his "youthful enthusiasm" (*CW* IV.1:224).

It is the extended argument against William Warburton that carries perhaps the greatest burden in *The Friend's* polemic against religious unifomity as it is practiced in the established church. *The Friend*, to be sure, does battle with religious and political extremists by delineating the "PRINCIPLES implanted by GOD in the universal REASON of Man" in essays such as "On the Errors of Party Spirit" (*CW* IV.1:206). But it also deliberately sets itself apart from the way that Warburton's defense of Anglican orthodoxy defends *its* principles and claims to universality. Warburton's *Divine Legation of Moses* (1737–41) would not in fact seem to lack "principle," since something akin to principle guides Warburton's dogged attacks on the "intemperance," "buffoonery," and "strange Propensity to Infidelity" amongst adversaries such as Arthur Ashley Sykes and Nathaniel Lardner; his own polemic offers a salutory "Sobriety, Decency, and good Manners."[11] Few writers were more frequently consulted as oracles of Anglican orthodoxy during the eighteenth and ninteenth centuries than was Warbuton. The Friend however, glosses Warburtonian orthodoxy as "slanderous vulgarity," and "*Warburtonian* arrogance" (*CW* IV.1: 29,30n). I will return to the full import of Warburtonian arrogance at a later moment in this chapter; but what needs to be emphasized for now is that the apparently more universalizing gestures of *The Friend* are accompanied at moments such as these by refusals of universalization. Coleridge argues not merely against Warburton's particular brand of Anglicanism, but against the more general attempt to imagine *any* uniformity in religious belief. As Jerome Christensen remarks on the journal's logic, the freedom from "arrogance" is continually asserted through an opposition to all traditional sources of authority: it affirms its own authority not by forming consensus but by refusing it.[12] So inflexible is this refusal, in fact, that it comes to take on the qualities of a physical principle: a later essay asserts that the position of consensus is as unfathomable as imagining that two bodies could occupy the same space. "That which doth not *withstand*, hath *itself* no standing place. To *fill* a station is to exclude or repel others, – and this is not less the definition of moral, than of material, *solidity*." Far from a position of consensus on religious or moral principle, the Friend can only imagine a state of perpetual and perhaps violent disagreement: "We *live* by continued acts of defense, that involve a sort of offensive warfare" (*CW* IV.1:97).

One way of looking at *The Friend*, as this last quotation would suggest, would be to see how it marks out a path for the two *Lay Sermons* in its peculiar and paradoxical commitment to understanding orthodoxy itself precisely as the most militant form of opposition to any attempt to assimilate beliefs within a single institution. In *The Statesman's Manual*, the apparently conservative underpinnings of the work conveyed on the first page – *The Bible the Best Guide to Political Skill and Foresight* – are immediately forced into a complex and ambiguous relationship with a position of dissent that designs to "repel" rather than attract adherents. As much as the topic of the work seems to be scriptural rather than political knowledge, the first paragraph suggests that the object of the work will not be – indeed *cannot* be – the encouragement of doctrinal conformity. That, indeed, is the object only of the "jealous priesthood" to whom the first paragraph also refers: a priesthood that seeks to use the Bible for specific doctrinal purposes, to "represent the applicability of the Bible to all the wants and occasions of men as a wax-like pliability to all their fancies and presuppositions" (*CW* VI:5). As if to counteract such impulses towards uniformity, Coleridge later takes issue with Hume's *History of England* (1754–61) in a spirit that curiously resembles the way he took issue with Warburton in *The Friend*. "The founders and martyrs of our church and constitution, of our civil and religious liberty, are represented as fanatics and bewildered enthusiasts," he writes of Hume's *History*. Coleridge responds not by diminishing the "enthusiasm" of those founders and martyrs but by insisting upon it – since "nothing great was ever achieved without enthusiasm" (*CW* VI:22–23).[13] Hume thus winds up looking surprisingly Warburtonian in his account of the history of British religious and civil liberty. Humean skepticism looks like a constraining form of religion; Humean doxa or common sense verges on Warburtonian orthodoxy.[14]

This aspect of *The Statesman's Manual* – its defense of church and constitution that glorifies rather than suppresses the dissent that might seem to endanger it – may reflect the tendency that William Hazlitt found in Coleridge's work: a tendency, namely, towards "potential infidelity" (which Hazlitt located specifically in the claim that "Reason and Religion are their own evidence") invading every discussion of the "principles" and "important truths" that the author means to communicate.[15] Indeed, Coleridge's ostensibly conservative later writing was praised even by William Hone, who was tried and acquitted of blasphemous libel in the year of the second *Lay Sermon*'s publication.[16] But what is equally if not more important than heretical or "potential[ly]" heretical doctrine is the way that Coleridge prizes the *position* of infidelity in relation to orthodox systems of authority, a position that registers a lack of faith in system itself. Thus, although it proposes to mine the Bible's "knowledge and information" for the sake of "communities no less than for individuals," Coleridge's advice to a statesman is curiously anti-communitarian: the man of "speculative principles" is not, in fact, to be found among the "cabinets of statesmen" or among the "men of business," but "in the closets of uninterested theorists"; their works are the "visions of recluse genius." Here Coleridge may very well gesture towards one recluse genius – Wordsworth – whom he had once called "at least a semi-atheist." Odder still may be the list of recluse geniuses from Shakespeare that follows: "Lear, Othello, Macbeth, Hamlet," whose "principles of deepest insight and widest interest fly off like sparks from the glowing iron under the loud anvil" (*CW* vi:14–15). But if these choices of characters seem at all striking for their status as murderers, social exiles, and madmen, such choices only confirm the *Lay Sermon*'s more oblique point. Outside the limits of Warburtonian doctrine or Humean common sense, that is, they are the very kinds of social outcasts that speak for the anti-communitarianism of Coleridge's dedication to community.

The first *Lay Sermon*'s peculiar elevation of dissent in the instances I have just mentioned leads to a more consistent, but no less perplexing, characterization of community in the second. For the second *Lay Sermon* returns to and expands upon the subject of the first by idealizing the climate of political and religious life prior to the Glorious Revolution. The purpose, however, is not to pay homage to an age of perfect harmony but to an age of widespread contention among adherents of different beliefs. According to Coleridge's argument, religion was the occasion for dissension rather than communion; churches and homes alike were places where religion was "discussed with a command of intellect that seem[ed] to exhaust all the learning and logic, all the historical and moral relations, of each several subject." Affectionately reflecting on "the very length of the discourses, with which these 'rich souls of wit and knowledge' fixed the eyes, ears, and hearts of their crowded congregations," Coleridge in fact attempts to recover the value of discussion and argumentative discourse which he presumes to be unknown to a nineteenth-century audience. The *Lay Sermon* thus continues by self-consciously associating its position of dissent with a defense of the mechanism of print (something that should remind us of the example from *The Watchman* with which I began this chapter). The period from Edward VI to James II, he argues, was characterized by "the warmth and frequency of . . . religious controversies . . . the deep interest excited by them . . . the importance attached to them . . . the number, and in many instances the transcendent merit, of the controversial publications – in short, the rank and value assigned to *polemic divinity*."[17] Donne and Taylor are singled out as particularly appropriate examples of polemic divinity – not because they provide models of faith, but because they are models of unmodeled faith. Their works presented "excitements to inquiry and intellectual effort" that inspired "enthusiasm" in their audiences. Advancements in print functioned precisely in order to enhance this polemic, as Coleridge suggests by wistfully recalling the "numerous editions of massy, closely printed folios: the impressions so large and the editions so numerous, that all the industry of destruction for the last hundred years has but of late sufficed to make them rare" (*CW* vi:197–99).

LIVING BY FAITH; OR, THE FIRM SOD OF PATRIOTISM

What I have been arguing is that Coleridge produces, even in works that supposedly celebrate religious orthodoxy, a radical disassociation of the individual from civil and political institutional formations. But why, then, do we also find an unsettling and contradictory impulse towards religious conformity – or at least what seems like it – consistently repeated even while it is so strenuously opposed? Perhaps, since critics have often interpreted *The Friend* as a turn towards a more conservative politics, we should not be at all surprised to find it vigorously defending religion as the ground for moral and political conduct, since "religion, true or false, is and ever has been the moral centre of gravity in Christendom" (*CW* iv.1:447). By doing so, this and other subsequent works may in fact adhere to a trend that critics such as Julie Carlson and Jon Klancher identify as the author's increasing distance from the political complications of social action and his movement towards religious principle and moral idealism.[18]

I do not want to dismiss this tendency in Coleridge's thinking – his seemingly paradoxical emphasis on religious conformity – immediately; in fact, we must understand how pervasive it is and how it *could* be interpreted as a contradiction (or at least a severe qualification) of the emphasis on nonconformity that I have been discussing so far. We cannot, for example, ignore the centrality of faith, and the political instrumentality of faith, in *The Friend*. "We live by faith," the Friend declares – a phrase emblematic enough to be repeated in *The Statesman's Manual* (*CW* IV.1:100; 6:20); it is in personal faith, or the lack thereof, that all subjects find the "principle of moral election" or the cause of "human misery" (*CW* IV.1:103). Living by faith routinely enables a distinction between mere "prudence" – actions pursued only for their effects rather than their motives – and morality informed by religion (*CW* IV.1.441). The distinction, permeating arguments throughout this work, corresponds with related discriminations between mere "obedience" and "faith," or between transient "EXPEDIENCY" and those "FEELINGS" that "God has given us" (*CW* IV.1.316). The moral conduct of the individual extends, moreover, to the political conduct of the state. Religion, the "moral centre of gravity in Christendom," shelters the state from the terrifying specter of the French Revolution (*CW* IV.1.447). The state, in turn, must preserve its religion "from foreign and domestic attacks" (*CW* IV.1:252). Napoleon is portrayed as the usurper of traditional national belief, his way having been prepared by others such as Voltaire and Rousseau, the *philosophes* "steered by the compass of unaided reason" (*CW* IV.1.133).

Intolerance of dissent for the sake of religious uniformity thus takes on a distinctive virtue in this argument: how indeed would the brand of patriotism that Coleridge defends have any content without it? In the essay "On the Law of Nations," it becomes clear that the problem with Napoleon and the *philosophes* is not merely that they believe the wrong things, but that they are apostles of "Cosmopolitanism," whose tolerance leads them to permit *any* kind of belief and thus seems unable to provide any sense of true national coherence. "Cosmopolitanism" contrasts with "Nationality," which is necessarily intolerant of dissent. Rather than a community of disputing minds, a nation is imagined at this point as a community of identical passions, interests, or beliefs: a "circle defined by human affections, the first firm sod within which becomes sacred beneath the quickened step of the returning citizen . . . where the powers and interests of men spread without confusion through a common sphere like the vibrations propagated in the air by a single voice, distinct yet coherent, and all uniting to express one thought and the same feeling" (*CW* IV.1:293).

Even though the *Lay Sermons* seem to value Britain's "polemic divinity," a system of relations nurturing religious dissent, they – like *The Friend* – also seem to follow a somewhat contradictory adherence to religion as the "centre of gravity" for moral and political conduct. *The Statesman's Manual* repeats *The Friend*'s commitments to a Christian system of morality and a Christian government, informed by "The great PRINCIPLES of our religion, the sublime IDEAS spoken out everywhere in the Old and New Testament" (*CW*VI:24). These are principles, as the second *Lay Sermon* boasts, that separate the "true friend of the people" from the "factious demagogue" (*CW*VI:131). And Coleridge can imagine such a unity of principle originating from the Bible itself because the reader of the Bible is not an entirely free interpreter of Scripture but a receptacle for its principles. The threat of any disharmony in beliefs and motives instantly dissolves as long as we accept that the individual and her motives are only an "effec[t]" of Scripture: the reader absorbs a "spring and principle of action" from the text (*CW*VI:21). And these motives, "The great principles of our religion," seem like instinct – or, at least, like a form of wisdom that seems only natural: "At the annunciation of *principles*, of *ideas*, the soul of man awakes, and starts up, as an exile in a far distant land at the unexpected sounds of his native language, when after long years of absence, and almost of oblivion, he is suddenly addressed in his own mother-tongue" (*CW*VI:24).

Much more than instinct is involved, though; this much is clear from Coleridge's extravagant and contemptuous attacks on public "irreligion" (*CW*VI:155), suggesting that a Christian community can only consolidate itself either by forcing others to believe in its doctrines or by excluding unbelievers entirely. Making light of popular claims for the "*imprescriptible and inalienable* RIGHT to judge and decide for themselves on all questions of Government and Religion," *The Statesman's Manual* joins *The Friend*'s ridicule of the *philosophes* of "THE ENLIGHTENED EIGHTEENTH CENTURY" (*CW*VI:37), but now with an added twist. The rationalists Voltaire, D'Alembert, Diderot, along with "Frederick [The Great], Joseph [the Holy Roman Emperor], and Catherine [The Great]," are described not only as unbelievers but also as "proselytes and disciples" of a subversive sect that has joined forces with "the banners of Antichrist" in order to further their "schemes of vice and irreligion" (*CW*VI:75). The advocates of "presumptuous and irreligious philosophy," it turns out, appear in this text as odd hybrids of rationalists and idolaters. Coleridge sees in the French a cold rationalism – a "general conceit that states and governments might be and ought to be constructed as machines, every movement of which might be forseen and taken into previous calculation" – but also (quoting here from Isaiah 47:12) a "multitude of . . . sorceries," an "abundance of . . . enchantments" (*CW*VI:34). Unbelief joins forces with extremities of belief; rationalism with superstition and fanaticism. All forms of extremity threaten to undo the "single voice, distinct yet coherent" of the perfectly harmonized national community.

To follow this train of thought is to notice still further how rationalism, in Coleridge's mind, apparently supports not merely a benign secularism but more disruptive forms of belief. Especially earmarked for Coleridge's opposition is Joseph Lancaster – whose "*liberal idea*" of education was so inspiring to Bentham. Offering tentative support for the Anglican Andrew Bell, Coleridge charges Lancaster with "potential infidelity" (the very phrase Hazlitt applied to Coleridge himself); rather than teach religion, Lancaster conveys "those points only of religious faith, in which all denominations agree." But even Bell's system, adopted by the Church of England, is insufficiently grounded in religion. To rely upon any such system as a source of education – even Bell's is a "vast moral steam engine" – would be a "most dangerous delusion," for it might allow too much divergence on points of faith (*CW*VI:40–41). *The Statesman's Manual*'s interest in the place of religion in social reform expands still further in the 1817 *Lay Sermon*, when Coleridge opens fire on the "Masters of Political Economy" portrayed as "noisy and calumnious zealots" and "factious leaders of the populace" (*CW*VI:140,143). Those enemies – unnamed but usually understood to include the likes of Malthus, Cobbett, Burdett, and "Orator" Hunt – are "worthless persons" whom the English public mistakenly views as its "only genuine patriots and philanthropists" (*CW*VI:125n, 144). Like the adherents of cosmopolitanism criticized in *The Friend*, these figures display a public spirit that has no religion attached to it; their public spirit thus takes on the appearance of public disruption and subversion (for the sake of private interest) rather than public improvement. They are "sophists and incendiaries of the revolutionary school," only "Mountebanks and Zanies of Patriotism" spreading their "irreligion" like "drugs" that will "poison" the national community (*CW*VI:125). And like the French *philosophes*, the masters of political economy are guilty not merely of an indifferent secularism but of explicitly *religious* subversion – they are cast as "zealots" and as Satanic figures in order to emphasize their sectarian offense against the socially unifying force of religion (*CW*VI:152).

The threats to national composition that Coleridge identifies, moreover, continually erupt as threats within a reading public located in the destructive influences of dangerous writers and readers. While it is indeed true that Coleridge wistfully invokes the polemical spirit of an earlier age, it is nevertheless also true that the very act of writing in which Coleridge imagines himself to be engaged involves consolidating a group of like-minded believers, or so it would seem when he directs *The Statesman's Manual* towards "a very different audience" from that which he finds in the present British public. Just as a system of education should recognize classes of individuals and educate them according to the "sphere in which the individuals . . . are likely to act and become useful," so should the writer designate a specific audience for his work, an audience comprised of suitable receptacles for the work's principles. Thus the sermon is addressed "exclusively *ad clerum* . . . to men of *clerkly* acquirements, of whatever profession"; but its gesture of widening – to those in "whatever profession" – is also a gesture of narrowing, an attempt to filter out the disturbing elements in a "promiscuous audience" in favor of those men "moving in the higher class of society" (*CW* vi:7,36). The second *Lay Sermon*, even more thoroughly devoted to the state of publication and education in Britain, makes recommendations to "Fellow Countrymen" that are explicitly circumscribed by the assumption that "countrymen" can be defined not only as "the higher and middle classes" but as "English Protestants" and "Fellow Christians" (*CW* vi:119–23,139). Indeed, in his efforts to distinguish true from false religion and exalt the "full faith in the divine WORD," Coleridge seems to add a significant qualification to his nostalgic glance backwards to a period of religious controversy (*CW* vi:175). The sign of national health in the present is in fact to be found in the "numerous large and small volumes composed or compiled for the use of parents" and designed to instill "national honesty and individual safety, private morals and public security" among children (*CW* vi:64–65).

If Coleridge seems to be imagining his works as mechanisms for discovering and confirming religious states of mind in his readers, then his works also direct themselves against the legions of non-adherents who make inappropriate writers and readers, producers and consumers of literary text. He thus adroitly smokes out the "enemies of liberty in general" who are "enemies of the liberty of the PRESS in particular" (*CW* vi:150).[19] The presence of dissent – of "warfare" among beliefs – is revealed to be a circumscribed form of "liberty," so highly regulated that it ceases to look like dissent at all (*CW* iv.1:97). The 1817 *Lay Sermon* sets out to preserve this version of liberty by attacking a "rank and unweeded press" that "freethinking" writers use to influence their "ignorant and half-learned" readers (*CW* vi:152,193). And the pages of the *Lay Sermon* proceed to anatomize radical eloquence by enumerating its multiple evils: the "compound poison," concocted from appeals to the "passions" and "vague and commonplace Satyr" (*CW* VI:152–4). The uncontrolled individual expression of freethinking can only lead to a more dangerously pervasive public freethinking, tantamount to utter disorder; and the sermon nervously foretells how writers will "seek notoriety by an eloquence well calculated to set the multitude agape, and excite *gratis* to overt-acts of sedition or treason" (*CW* VI:145). Coleridge's concerns about the unbridled production and consumption of printed material become so profound that he ultimately seems to argue against the publication and distribution of *any* text. He must therefore oppose the potentially dangerous distribution of Bibles, a practice that encourages the very "polemic" that he had seemed, at other moments, to uphold (*CW* VI:200–1).

Now it may seem plausible, after all, that *The Friend* and the *Lay Sermons*, the very works that tend to be identified with Coleridge's Christian orthodoxy, are in fact orthodox (although the difficulty still remains of reconciling this set of affiliations with the apparent refusal of orthodoxy in the same works). Far more surprising than this, however, is the extent to which even Coleridge's earlier writing can be so deeply immersed in the rhetoric of religious uniformity. If *The Watchman* develops a position outside – or in opposition to – Anglican orthodoxy, this is a position of counter-orthodoxy barely distinguishable from orthodoxy itself. It insists upon a radical division from establishment (indeed, from all forms of religious community) but also imagines that division to occur under the auspices of establishment – or at least with a considerable amount of harmony among religious beliefs.

Perhaps this could be explained in one way by turning to Coleridge's own testimony in his letters. Writing to the Reverend John Edwards in 1796, for example, he said of his 1795 lectures that "the *Sacred* may eventually help off the *profane* – and my *Sermons* spread a sort of sanctity over my Sedition."[20] And the radical tendencies of his writing seemed to be not only disguised but forsworn in his vow to Charles Lloyd's father in 1796 that "I have . . . snapped my squeaking baby-trumpet of sedition, and have hung up its fragments in the chamber of Penitences."[21] Another way of making this point would be to refer back to those instances from *The Watchman* – to the imagery of the Anglican church as whore of Babylon, for example – where Coleridge's opposition to religious establishments actually resembles the Anglican church's own critique of Catholicism. The demonization of high-church Anglicanism as a kind of crypto-Catholicism, it could be contended, does not argue against the Anglican church as much as it merely attempts (like Protestant

Evangelicals) to assert a more purified set of beliefs and practices from within the church itself.

There are still other more pervasive ways, however, in which the range of political positions throughout *The Watchman* quite openly depends upon appeals to religious – Christian, and specifically Protestant – uniformity. *The Watchman*'s ultimate ability to argue against the slave trade, for example, relies upon the authority of Christianity: calling supporters of the slave trade not merely "Atheists" but the "causes of Atheism," Coleridge continues, "I address myself to you who independently of all political distinctions, profess yourself Christians!" (*CW* II:138).[22] Those who are Christians by "profession" are in fact not true Christians and thus do violence to the very notion of Christianity itself:

Gracious Heaven! At your meals you rise up, and pressing your hands to your bosoms, you lift up your eyes to God, and say, "O Lord! bless the food which thou hast given us!" A part of that good among most of you, is sweetened with Brother's Blood. "Lord! bless the food which thou has given us?" O Blasphemy! Did God give food mingled with the blood of the Murdered? Will God bless the food which is polluted with the Blood of his own innocent children? (*CW* II:138–39)

Coleridge's use of "blasphemy," joined to the framework of allegorical reference that casts the English as Cain and the slaves as Abel, shows how slavery might be considered a distinctively *religious* offense because the blessing of food that is "polluted" with the blood of slaves is offensive to God. Coleridge, conflating an offense against persons with an offense against God, might seem to make a social problem into a religious problem: slavery exists because of a lack of proper religious faith. While *The Watchman* appears to be advocating abolition of the slave trade, its liberal sentiments in fact seem to be articulated by an equally strong urge towards religious conformity. Liberty can be advocated for a greater portion of humanity only by suggesting that the response to slavery is to be found in moral purification – "benevolence" and benevolent "self denial" – and that this purification is open only to Christians (*CW* II:140). If the door of humanity is opened to slaves, it is nevertheless closed to non-Christians (and, more particularly, non-Protestants).

The Watchman even more strenuously maintains this position in the essays attacking Godwin and his *Political Justice*: "Modern Patriotism" of 17 March 1796 and "To Caius Gracchus" of 2 April 1796, the latter in response to a letter published in the *Bristol Gazette* that accused Coleridge's first attack of enthusiasm, prejudice, and illiberality. Although the more comprehensive response to Godwin that Coleridge announced in the April issue never materialized, the direction that he was planning is clear enough. "I do consider Mr. Godwin's Principles as vicious; and his book as a Pandar to Sensuality" he writes in "Caius." Godwin inspires Coleridge's opposition because of his radical individualism – his belief that "mind will be omnipotent over matter" – and for his accompanying contempt for all species of conformity (*CW* II:196,197). In "Modern Patriotism," the "Good Citizen ——" to whom the essay is addressed is told that "to think filial affection folly, gratitude a crime, marriage injustice, and the promiscuous intercourse of the sexes right and wise, may class you among the despisers of vulgar prejudices, but cannot increase the probability that you are a PATRIOT" (*CW* II:99). A surrogate for Godwin himself (and for Godwinians such as John Thelwall), the "Good Citizen" is advised that in order to be a patriot, "You must give up your sensuality and your philosophy, the pimp of your sensuality; you must condescend to believe in a God, and in the existence of a Future State!" (*CW* II:100). If *The Watchman*'s rigorous sectarianism seemed to anticipate Coleridge's later account of "polemic divinity," it also anticipates *The Friend*'s attack on cosmopolitanism by viewing religious belief not only as a prerequisite for communal membership but as the very foundation for any humanitarian action.

THE SELF THAT NO ALIEN KNOWS

What can be concluded from these seemingly incompatible directions in Coleridge's thought? What coherence, if any, is to be found in works that advocate both the necessity of dissent and an intolerance of dissent, a simultaneous refusal and embrace of religious conformity? There are at the very least three possible constructions that could be applied to the discussions I have pursued thus far: two are historical, the third formal. One kind of historical argument might suggest that Coleridge's position is quite simply a Protestant one. Seeking echoes of a dissenting tradition in apologies for religious establishment, such an argument would agree with accounts by J. A. Appleyard and John Colmer, which show how Coleridge's writing bears the marks of an Evangelical or Methodist opposition to institutional corruption and affirmation of a more powerful sense of affective religious community.[23] A second line of historical argument might urge us to move from intellectual to economic history: a history that – in the work of Isaac Kramnick, following Max Weber – traces associations between religious dissent and bourgeois individualism.[24] It is this perspective that leads Forest Pyle to read tensions such as those we have observed as proof of ideological contradictions in Coleridge's writing between bourgeois cultural hegemony and dissenting subject, between nations and individuals.[25] Yet another argument – one that is formal rather than historical – would show how the troubled logics in Coleridge's writing are symptoms of its rhetorical slippages. Deconstructive readings by Jerome Christensen, Julie Ellison, and Arden Reed thus point towards the author's precarious attempts to discriminate between the delusions of superstition and the delusions of legitimate religion, between a deluded Catholicism and an equally deluded Protestantism, between enthusiasm and fanaticism.[26]

But there is still another alternative to these explanations which is, I think, more convincing. What we see in Coleridge cannot be summarized merely as an attempt to forge an alliance between belief and government – an alliance reducible to a purified form of the church-state, of Protestantism and capitalism. Nor can it be summarized merely as a contradiction or slippage in terms that would testify to the logical impossibility of forging such an alliance. Instead, it is possible to see how Coleridge participates in the discourse of toleration not only in his early writing but also in his later defenses of the church establishment. This is because Coleridge repeatedly pressures what he sees as a corrupted logic of confessional community while asserting community of a different kind: one that does not merely renew religious affiliation but that enforces an even more powerful sense of obligation and social solidarity in the absence of shared belief.

It is precisely this re-forming of community that gives shape to Coleridge's poetry of the 1790s, poetry that occupies a crucial position in the argument I want to make because of the way that these works – ranging from fervent calls for social and religious regeneration to "confessional" poetry – crucially articulate a sustained tension with confessional politics. The shuttling between personal belief and broader political commitment, first of all, cannot be accomplished without an underlying resistance to the very possibility for personal belief to function as a political norm. Works such as "Religious Musings" (1796), "The Destiny of Nations" (not published alone in its entirety until 1817 but inserted in Southey's *Joan of Arc* [1796] and excerpted, along with "Religious Musings" in *The Watchman*), and "Fears in Solitude" (1798) were frequently defended and quoted by Coleridge throughout his career, as if their critical position in relation to the Anglican establishment could nevertheless be retrieved within the author's support of a radically revised established church.[27] The political and poetic integrity of such works depends upon their highly charged criticism of the traditional technology of oath-taking: "The sweet words/Of Christian promise," described in "Fears in Solitude," that lead to "one scheme of perjury."[28] We must therefore see how Joan of Arc proves to be a fitting epic subject for "The Destiny of Nations" and Coleridge's epic collaboration on *Joan of Arc* with Southey in 1796, since the hero's refusal to comply with the conventional system of religious testing makes her into a particularly compelling image of the dissenting Romantic poet. Elsewhere, we repeatedly find Coleridge framing poetic reactions to the falsity of established religion – as in the opposition to "pageant Power" and "mitred Atheism" (lines 263,334) in "Religious Musings"; the poet's retreat into nature from "Priestcraft's harpy minions /And factious Blasphemy's obscener slaves" in "France: an Ode" (1798); or the seemingly private form of faith purified from this pageantry and subject to the poet's own "abstruser musings" in "Frost at Midnight" (1798).

Second, however, it is just as important for us to see that the *Joan of Arc* collaboration shows how the very independence from established religion makes the hero/poet into an even more compelling advocate for social justice. Although the poem represents her rejection of conventional notions of confessional community – and conventional notions of religious purification or redemption – Joan turns out to be a figure who privileges the security of the "realm" over the domestic comforts of the "home."[29] Elsewhere, Coleridge regularly opposes the confessional technology of oath-taking only to embrace a more accommodating set of associations that bridges across distinct religious and domestic communities.[30] In "Reflections on Having Left a Place of Retirement" (1795), Coleridge departs from the affective alliances of the "pretty Cot," spurning both "cold beneficence" and "sluggard Pity" to seize upon the figure of John Howard, England's great prison reformer, as a model of appropriate social action (lines 49–56). In *The Watchman*, Coleridge would later admiringly invoke Howard's name; there, Howard's "zeal" and "genius" are said to have reappeared in Count Rumford, an advocate of "benevolence" on behalf of the poor and a sponsor of "a new system of order, discipline, and economy" in the Bavarian military (*CW*II:176–77).

"Religious Musings," while instructing its readers in a proper form of Christian worship, also urges a far more inclusive sense of "the moral world's cohesion": a world freed from religious wars and slavery, in which individuals partake of a collective "Self, that no alien knows" (lines 145,154). Coleridge's kinship with Priestley can be found not only in the lines of praise for the "patriot, and saint, and sage" in line 371, but in the combination of religious with secular aims. The work of the poem, finally, is both to clarify the separation between the "redeeming God" and the hierarchies of the established church (line 399), and to effect a reform of earthly government itself.[31] In a similar spirit, "Fears in Solitude" chastises its readers for imagining themselves to be merely pious spectators upon, rather than contributors to, harmful actions; the poem thus accuses Britons of using "holy names" to sanctify and sentimentalize an enterprise that causes "the certain death / Of thousands and ten thousands" (lines 101–04). Coleridge in fact makes poetry seem decidedly opposed to sympathy, whether in the form of prayers or sentimental outpourings of emotion over a child pulling off an insect's leg (lines 105–08). Instead, it accounts for human association on different terms by reading association over or across the lines of religious, moral, and national community; it urges readers to "feel / The desolation and the agony / Of our fierce doings" against France (lines 128–29). While in one sense Coleridge opposes himself to the "abstractions" and "empty sounds" (line 115) of conventional religion, the poem's work proceeds as a politics through an even greater level of abstraction. Transforming inaction into action, virtuous belief into murder, it extends accountability and responsibility for death in order to assert human community in the absence of emotional sharing. Through these means, "Fears in Solitude" asserts its political opposition to France (and its "light yet cruel race" [line 150]) not merely by discriminating between good and evil, but by encouraging Britain to adopt a superior sense of responsibility for past and future crimes. Britain will prove its superiority by "Repenting of the wrongs with which we stung / So fierce a foe to frenzy" (lines 152–53).

It is frequently the case that critics find Coleridge's poetry endorsing a retreat from politics; in their different ways, for example, Kelvin Everest, Tim Fulford, and Paul Magnuson suggest that his poetry cautiously endorses domestic affections as an alternative to broader political engagements. Karl Kroeber takes the more extreme view that Coleridge backs out of social engagement more generally to endorse a thoroughly apolitical individualism. What I am suggesting is that Coleridge's poetry ultimately endorses neither of these views; its achievement is to demote the value of conventional affective relations precisely in order to promote a more profound sense of social obligation.[32] Even in a less politically charged poem such as "Frost at Midnight" (1798), we find a similar logic shaping Coleridge's poetic enterprise: a disengagement from the prejudicial foundations of conventional religious community that only prepares the way for him to enlist the poem itself on behalf of a more inclusive sense of solidarity.³³ The speaker's consciousness, free from the constraints of London's "cloisters dim" and from the "populous village" of Stowey (the motif that would inform the "glad preamble" of Wordsworth's *Prelude*) owes itself, paradoxically, to the reciprocal urgency with which the speaker seeks a sociable foothold in a world that he so earnestly wishes to drain of society. (This is at least one way of understanding the importance of the deliberately fictive "conversation" of the conversation poems more generally: a conversation that both insists upon radical distinction while also requiring communal association.) In "Frost at Midnight," the poem both emphasizes the lack of any consciousness in the present that would compete with the speaker's own freely ranging meditations; yet these meditations also require the assistance of the sleeping babe in order to be formed. The verse oddly confounds the infant Hartley's "gentle breathings" that "Fill up the interspersed vacancies / And momentary pauses of thought" with the poem's own vacancies: its caesuras and abrupt, spontaneous pauses. It presumes, moreover, a future in which the babe will resemble the speaker, not because the child will merely mimick the speaker's consciousness, but because the "universal Teacher" – giving Hartley access to the "lovely shapes and sounds intelligible" in nature – will (Coleridge assures him) "mould / Thy spirit, and by giving make it ask" (lines 54–64). To "ask" is both to participate in a future anticipated by the speaker, and to affirm that such a future contains in itself the possibility of striking out in a new direction.³⁴ In a similar fashion, "This Lime Tree Bower My Prison" (1800) presents a speaker's "joys" that are poetically valuable to the addressee of the poem (Charles Lamb), as they are to the reader, precisely *because* they are joys that "we cannot share"; they are open instead for the reader to "contemplate" in the absence of sharing (lines 66–67). That Charles Lamb was attacked by *The Anti-Jacobin* for his atheism is an illuminating historical detail not because the poem reveals Coleridge's sympathy for Lamb (indeed, Coleridge's letters reveal how urgently he wished to distance himself from the "demagogy and atheism" of Thomas Poole and John Thelwall) but because the poem asserts so powerful a sense of community without evidence of religious sympathy.³⁵ The poem aspires to a discursive equivalent of the image and sound of the rook beating a "straight path along the dusky air / Homewards," for the flying rook provides an opportunity for the speaker to claim reciprocation from Lamb – "to whom / No sound is dissonant which tells of life" – even while the lines simultaneously and conspicuously assert the lack of consonance between consciousnesses (lines 69–76).

These poems suggest that neither radical disassociation nor social homogenization is sufficient to describe Coleridge's disposition towards the social role of religious belief; they undermine the traditional position of religious belief in the British national community while at the same time redefining precisely what members of a community might hold in common. It is neither moral nor religious sympathy but a sense how individuals are parts of a social whole that demands a renewed attention to one's "doings." To be sure, this is a social whole that is both more inclusive and tolerant (since this obligation crosses over the boundaries of confessional communities). Yet it is also less forgiving: the sense of community in these works arises from repeated assertions of a persistent and inescapable web of interdependencies that crosses over and binds together all sympathetic relations between or among believers – regardless of what they may actually share.

The poems that I have only briefly surveyed, I think, should urge us to re-examine the prose works I have been discussing in the previous sections of this chapter in light of their simultaneous refusals of community and reassertions of community on new grounds; the prose works, likewise, will continue to show us how the issues of religious intolerance and tolerance, of confessional and anti-confessional community, informed Coleridge's understanding of poetry itself – or of literature more generally. If we revisit works from *The Watchman* to the *Lay Sermons*, then, we might come to appreciate how Coleridge's tendency to demonize certain beliefs and expressions of belief as blasphemy, idolatry, superstition, or fanaticism does not arise solely from an *opposition* to nonconformity. He is not, in other words, simply opposing violations of a particular category of the sacred, or taking issue with any number of heretical doctrines. At the same time, however, he does not define a radical position against institutionality *in general.* Rather than merely endorsing or suppressing the authority of either dissent or establishment, Coleridge's writings ultimately redefine the kind of work that establishment does. That kind of work requires that Coleridge reconfigure "establishment" on terms that depart from any notion of establishment defined according to specific doctrines that it takes an interest in upholding. For establishment is most vividly conceptualized in these writings as a way of providing contending beliefs with a public context that in turn awards those beliefs with increased distinction, articulation, and protection. Establishment is not defined by collective belief as much as belief is defined by the organs of a radically reformed religious establishment – an establishment not limited to the church but extending its influence to a whole range of secular institutions.

It is particularly crucial for me to emphasize at this point that Coleridge's writing does not conform to the more purely oppositional and self-consciously blasphemous political energies of a writer such as William Hone. It is just as important for me to emphasize, though, that Coleridge was not merely a conventional supporter of religious orthodoxy; in all of its various manifestations from Unitarian to Trinitarian, Coleridge's Christianity insistently opposes Christian *uniformity*. In *The Watchman*'s "Essay on Fasts" of 9 March 1796, for example, Coleridge takes aim at the state-enforced institution of fast-days as a political instrument that is aided by the Two Acts of 1795 in order to create a false sense of uniform support for the war against France. Fasting repeats and sacramentalizes a false harmony that has been achieved through the legal apparatus of censorship: "By two recent Acts of Parliament the mouths of the poor have been *made fast* already." A fast therefore can serve as an expression of national community only because no one in the community can speak against it. Although Coleridge suggests with the support of Scripture that the custom is "superstitious or hypocritical," the object of the essay is not merely to lay siege to conventional religious rituals with beliefs that are truer or more deeply felt. The essay consistently opposes the general logic of confessional community, through which the "sins of our enemies," just like the "incorruptness of our House of Commons," are defined solely through the alignment of prejudicial states of feeling (*CW*ii:54–55). Coleridge, in other words, does not simply oppose political institutions with the strength of personal conviction; the more direct purpose of the essay is to criticize the political *work* of belief.

Despite its apparent affirmation of a community of Christians uniting against slavery, the "Slave Trade" essay follows a similar logic. Coleridge does indeed address his audience as "you who independently of all political distinctions, profess yourselves Christians!" (*CW*ii:138), but his purpose is not to distinguish those who profess truly and those who profess falsely. It is to show the irrelevance of professing *anything*. Only a self-satisfied "bastard sensibility" leads people – such as the merchant, the "citizen at the crouded feast," and the lady sipping tea and weeping over *Werther* – to support the slave trade; they do so as long as it does not present a "hideous spectacle or clamorous outcry" to their "senses," or "disturb their selfish enjoyments." Thus a striking parallel surfaces between "sensibility" and institutionalized religion's own predilection for "ostentatious sensibility." Both are formed through highly theatrical compurgational communities of feeling; both neglect the wider range of effects that such feelings and tastes for luxuries might produce. "Sensibility," the moral feelings communally affirmed in church rituals as well as "selfish enjoyments," is not "Benevolence" (*CW* II:139).

The charge of "blasphemy" in the same essay, from this perspective, does not simply denote a verbal offense against an arbitrary category of the sacred – an attempt to draw a "boundary between the permissible and the prohibited," as blasphemy is described in Joss Marsh's comprehensive study of the subject.[36] The targets of the essay are guilty in at least one more sense, in that they commit an offense against a *public* endowed with sacred significance. And to make this point is to move towards the logic according to which belief appears as both a necessary component of action (indeed, Coleridge insists that we must have beliefs about the morality or immorality of our actions) and yet an insufficient account of action: an account that becomes complete only when the public effects of action are brought into view. A community thus becomes important in Coleridge's view not as the preadjudicated outcome of belief – through communion – but as a means through which belief can acquire a more precise social value. It is for this reason that the very first number of *The Watchman* turns to the way that the proliferation and definition of belief is inseparable from the development of institutions such as factories and book societies, institutions whose significance is not to be found in their suppression of belief but in their ability to produce facilitating relationships through which the *effects* of belief can be more vividly and conspicuously measured.

And it is for this same reason, moreover, that the social connections between agents that *The Watchman* asserts continually emerge as after-effects of belief – after-effects that exceed any doctrinal perspectives while giving a legible shape to them. The "Essay on Fasts," for instance, insists on a logic of accountability that draws the actions of the House of Commons, the "rich and powerful" of the nation, into connection with the "public calamities" for which it is responsible. The government's use of religious belief is only a way of deflecting attention from social inequality and social harm: from crushing poverty and from the devastating effects of war that the fast is meant to glorify.[37] In the essay "On the Slave Trade," moreover, the community of belief is insufficient as an account of community precisely because it neglects a larger community beyond the precincts of professed or confessed Christians. The essay builds out an expanded sense of association by reconfiguring the sugar merchant's "ledger" in order to extend its columns of accounts. If the merchant finds no argument against the slave trade, it is because his ledger – just like the household economy represented by the tea-table – does not spread wide enough to include the cost of human life. Translating single actions into multiple actions, the essay makes the merchant – as well as the feasting citizen and the weeping woman at her tea-table, both of whom purchase and consume the sugar – accountable for the deaths of slaves that only appear to be the remotest consequences of their apparently private activities. If the claim of the essay is finally that benevolence "impels to action," mere benevolent dispositions are insufficient since the essay continually attaches blame to wrongful action rather than wrongful beliefs (*CW* II:139–40).

This line of reasoning also informs Coleridge's argument against Godwinian "Modern Patriotism" that I mentioned earlier. The last lines of the essay – "you must condescend to believe in a God, and in the existence of a Future State" – only imperfectly convey the precise argument against Godwin's position, at least if the lines are understood to recommend belief itself as a solution to social problems. For the "Modern Patriot" is linked surprisingly to the "bastard sensibility" described in the "Slave Trade" essay: "You harangue against the Slave-Trade; you attribute the present scarcity to the war – yet you wear powder, and eat pies and sugar. Your patriotism and philanthropy cost you very little" (*CW* II.99). Part of the cleverness of this criticism derives from Coleridge's ability to turn the circumstantialism of Godwin's own *Political Justice* against itself. If, as Godwin claims, persons are the products of circumstances, circumstantialism seems clearly at odds with Godwinian individualism, exemplified by the claim put forward in *Political Justice* that "we ought to be able to do without one another" and thus seek out society as a mere "luxury" in relation to "purest delight" of "solitude."[38] Individualism on these terms strikes Coleridge as merely sentimental in its efforts to view personal needs and desires apart from social obligation. In the reasoning behind *The Watchman*'s response, the interest of the self cannot be separated from an interest in another with whom the self interacts; interest is inseparable from a coordinating obligation. "Your *heart* must believe, that the good of the whole is the greatest possible good of each individual," Coleridge warns, "that *therefore* it is your *duty* to be just, because it is your *interest*." Godwinian rationalism ends up looking compatible with "sensibility," since it entails a retreat into private taste and feeling, a false separation of domestic consumption from effects on a wider range of persons. The criticism of Godwin for being a "pandar to

Sensuality" (*CW* II.99), then, rather than faulting him for his immorality, instead gestures more persistently towards his lack of attention to the self as a socially involved being.

What this suggests is that Coleridge's interest in belief continually revolves around belief's inseparable social value (the "cost," for example, of Godwinian philanthropy). His object is not to discount the importance of personal beliefs; rather, the significance of those beliefs is reinterpreted within an economy of action that takes a view of their wider interanimating effects. This is why *The Watchman* so consistently understands a range of beliefs to be significant in terms of more expansive costs and benefits, for the meanings of actions cannot be circumscribed by any person's ability to count themselves among a community of Christian believers. "Benevolence" is uncoupled from "sensibility" since it has less to do with what one believes about what one is doing (what amounts to a version of the "private language" argument described by Wittgenstein and some of his interpreters such as Kripke) than with what one has done in the context of other actions that are not necessarily one's own.[39]

Coleridge's apparent willingness to defend religious uniformity in his later work is no exception to this way of thinking. As frequent as his attacks on superstition, atheism, fanaticism, and other kinds of nonconforming beliefs may be, we should not take them as markers of any simple position of religious orthodoxy. We should instead view these attacks in the context of Coleridge's more comprehensive attempt to envision a social *organization* of believers under the tolerant auspices of the state. His characterizations of the "anti-christian priesthood" and "Papal darkness" do not easily resolve themselves into an effort to oppose Catholicism as a belief. Catholicism represents an attempt to enforce conformity through politics; and even the honored "Christian Fathers" themselves come under suspicion (much as this may play into the "seductive arguments of infidelity"), insofar as they employed "artifices" for the control or manipulation of belief (*CW* VI:37–38).

The religious "fanatics" and "empirics" that Coleridge derides in *The Friend*, furthermore, are significant because of their cult-like uniformity, not their dissension: fanaticism presents an example of the very kind of intolerance that it apparently opposes (*CW* IV.1:58–59). The counterpart of the superstitious idolater, the fanatic is one who attempts to transplant her own beliefs into others; she embodies a "satanic pride and rebellious self-idolatry in the relations of the spirit to itself, and remorseless despotism relatively to others." The mind of the fanatic makes all things and persons into a uniform image of itself, adopting a "fearful resolve to find in itself alone the one absolute motive of action, under which all other motives from within and from without must be either subordinated or crushed" (*CW* vi:65).⁴⁰

It is obvious enough that Coleridge's political positions alter substantially among the works that I am discussing, his increasing approval for Britain's war against France being a particularly notable example of this. But if his works seem to adopt a more conventionally conservative political stance on such issues, this should not deflect our attention from the ways in which Coleridge consistently characterizes his adversaries as advocates of religious, or more broadly ideological, uniformity. When he takes issue with religious dissent and philosophical rationalism, it is curiously because he associates these orientations with a logic of religious exclusion. Likewise, Coleridge's apparently increasing sympathies with religious orthodoxy in *The Friend* and the *Lay Sermons* seem far less interested in enforcing a uniformity in belief than in assessing the social value of a whole range of beliefs. The primary aim of the pervasive arguments against idolatry and other forms of unorthodox religious worship derive from their status as social, rather than psychological, phenomena: religious belief is to be judged or measured not merely according to the state of mind that might or might not inform actions, but according to the social benefits or harms that precipitate from those actions.

The relationship between *The Friend* and Quakerism can now come into still greater focus. For it is not just the admirable personal "discipline" of the Quakers that *The Friend* recalls and emulates. It is what Thomas Clarkson perceived as a paradoxical mixture of dissent and compliance built into Quaker society: their aversion to oath- or test-taking coupled with the most fervent dedication to public "happiness" and "security."⁴¹ (A similar reasoning undoutedly lay behind Shelley's account of his own politics as "Quakerish" in a letter of 1812, and behind the figure of Joshua Geddes in Scott's *Redgauntlet* [1824].)⁴² In keeping with such a notion, *The Friend*'s hostility towards "Brahmins" extends beyond any defense of established religion to an attempt to define the limits for tolerating bodily harm. This is not to deny that Coleridge's characterization of the "Brahmin goading on the disconsolate victim to the flames of her husband's funeral pyre" may be the result of his own prejudices – a belief that foreign religions are essentially violent ones. But the focus on violence is interesting in yet another way, since it clearly shifts the argument's attention towards the issue of social protection rather than legitimate belief (*CW* iv.1:99). And as he continues discussing the extent and limits of tolerance, Coleridge once again raises the specters of "witchcraft" and "fetish-worship" precisely in order to counterpoint the private meanings of belief with the public significance of belief; witchcraft and fetish-worship coincide with irrationality only because these forms of worship signify an inattention to "consequences" that are "diffused over a larger space of time," or to the "after harm" of action (*CW* IV.1:105–6). The significance of a belief, in these instances, is to be discerned not only on the basis of their correctness *as* individual private beliefs, but in terms of their contextualization within irrevocably interindividual actions.

The way that Coleridge continually relocates the discussion of non-conformity within a discussion of injury is suggestive of the many ways in which the range of texts we have been examining understands religion itself less in terms of a particular doctrine than in terms of an art of government or civilizing process – what eventually becomes a fully developed account of national religion in *On the Constitution of Church and State*.[43] If this is a civilizing process, however, I do not refer to an improvement or cultivation of manners (as Norbert Elias describes it), to a consolidated middle-class "ideology" or to the triumph of conventionalism. Religion as civilization, rather, consists of an increasingly widened scope for the opportunities, protections, and obligations of civil society – a principle of toleration itself. This is why even the most fervently Christian of Coleridge's political writings – such as *The Statesman's Manual* – rather than supporting politics with belief, envisions spiritualized political organs that would strive to be more capacious than the beliefs they accommodate.

This should not be taken as a way of suggesting that Coleridge's writing is more secularized than critics have previously believed it to be; I am, however, arguing that Coleridgean "religion" might have more to do with tolerance itself than readers have usually recognized. Coleridge's work thus extends the Gothic novel's preoccupations with the formation of social unity in the absence of religious uniformity – the Gothic's decidedly forward-looking interest in the management of populations that are characterized by diversity rather than similarity. By emphasizing this particular aspect of Coleridge's kinship with the Gothic, moreover, I am suggesting an equally powerful affiliation between his writing and the defenses of secular institutions extending from Locke to Bentham. Coleridge himself does little to encourage such comparisons, since he openly expresses contempt for the calculating self-interest that he sees in the work of William Paley, ardent follower of Priestley and Britain's "widely acknowledged representative of the Utilitarian morality" before Bentham.[44] John Stuart Mill confirms the opposition between Coleridge and Bentham, and critics such as Catherine Gallagher, showing how

Coleridge's purified realm of spiritual values contradicts Bentham's nar-row empiricism, only follow Mill's influential interpretive paradigm.[45] I suggested in chapter 1, however, that Bentham's writing is not merely an endorsement of calculating, atomizing self-interest; in this chapter, I have been arguing that Coleridge's writing does not merely champion traditional, normative religious values. The connection between these two apparently opposed figures thus needs to be re-evaluated in terms of the way both authors envision a convergence of, and tactical collusion between, religion and government. Bentham, far from simply hostile to religion, sought to confirm the power of churches insofar as they approxi-mated the aims of secular government; Coleridge, rather than defending conventional established religion, sought to fashion the national church into a tolerant government more permissive than any individual church. For Coleridge, a defense of national religion – religion as a kind of gov-ernment – involves an attempt to see the national church not merely as a belief or as a vehicle for belief, but as a far more capacious organization of beliefs. And if this strategy is visible in the emphasis that his works place on the secular government of religion (as I have been arguing), it is also visible in the way that his works represent the place of *texts* within institutions of government to accomplish what *The Friend* calls "literary toleration." This entails not only a toleration of dissenting points of view, but also a defense of toleration that literature makes for itself – an apol-ogy, that is, for the literary integrity of poetry and philsophical prose that can be articulated only on the condition that such works aspire to a position of toleration (*CW* IV.1:72).

It is precisely such a notion that informs Coleridge's carefully orches-trated negotiation of the status of his own writing in relation to forms of representation that are more explicitly designed for the ritualistic pur-poses of forming communities of belief. What I have been suggesting elsewhere in this chapter – that Coleridge opposes the system of oaths and tests that works to consolidate a false community of "professed" reli-gious believers – only begins to indicate the more pervasive ways in which he aspires to distinguish his writing from versions of oath- and test-taking. The specific criticism of oaths, tests, penal laws, and other mechanisms for the legal enforcement of uniformity, that is, both supports and re-ceives support from a criticism of the textual means of supporting that uniformity. If we return to the subject of "Warburtonian arrogance" that I mentioned earlier, for instance, we see how Coleridge's opposi-tion to the institutionalization of belief has its analogue in a series of observations about writing that seems to have no other purpose besides

consolidating identical religious beliefs. What Coleridge finds objectionable as a true mark of arrogance is Warburton's conspicuous "absence of
logical courtesy" (*CW* IV.1:29). Although "presumption" demonstrates
"a frequent bare *assertion* of opinions not generally received," Coleridge
argues not merely against the content – against different religious opinions – but against the form that those opinions take. The contention
against Warburton, that is, hinges precisely on Warburton's "bare assertion" or "naked assertion" of opinion: bare or naked assertion that
lacks an "argument" since it distances itself from a text on which an
argument might rest, just as it attempts to evade examination by the
argumentative reader. Instead, Warburton's text strives only to foster
prejudices in its audience. Refusing to "prefix or annex the facts and
reasons on which . . . opinions are formed," he only conveys the "bitter-
ness of personal crimination" (*CW* IV.1:29–30). In this way of writing,
Coleridge finds, a difference in "doctrine" is construed as a "weakness
of intellect, or want of taste and sensibility, or hardness of heart, or corruption of moral principle" (*CW* IV.1:29). Concerned only with doctrinal
agreement or disagreement, Warburton strangely lacks adherence to
language itself – to the logical connections between "bare assertions" –
and thus presumes that language functions as an "idolatrous charm"
or "potent Abracadabra." The ideal reader for Warburton's writing is
an idolatrous worshiper who sees language only as "*noise*," as isolated
"empty *sounds*" that are communicative only by virtue of their momentary ability to become charged with supernatural authority, which in
turn commands specific kinds of beliefs from the reader (*CW* IV.1:440).

   It is hardly surprising to find Coleridge in his notebooks associating Warburton and even Evangelicals such as Wilberforce and Hannah
More (as much as he might have agreed with their positions on abolition)
with the "Devil-Worship" of "Savages"; and *The Friend* elsewhere derides
popular journalism not because of its tendencies towards social anarchy but because of its attempts to appeal to an audience's "prejudices"
by articulating "broad avowals of atheism" and reinforcing a fashionable dispositition against Methodism (*CW* IV.1:41–42).[46] These terms
for describing the relationship between textual representation and religious belief are equally important for the *Lay Sermons* and beyond,
for Coleridge's thoughts about what a government's relation to belief
should be is never very far from his thoughts about how writing participates in the formation of that government. *The Statesman's Manual*, for
example, contrasts the Bible itself with objects and actions that purport to
convey powers of a higher authority to the believer: "amulets, bead-rolls,

periapts, fetisches, and the like pedlary, on pilgrimages to Loretto, Mecca, or the temple of Jaggernaut, arm in arm with sensuality on one side and self-torture on the other, followed by a motley group of friars, pardoners, faquirs, gamesters, flagellants, mountebanks, and harlots" (*CW* vi:64–65). The terms that Coleridge uses not only remind us of the opposition to Warburton, but also of *The Friend*'s discourse on witchcraft and sorcery; more than attempts to ridicule foreign or unfamiliar belief, they function as attempts to counteract the compurgational logic that motivates the use of representations for the consolidation of belief more generally. Like Warburton's potent abracadabra, the totems of religious ritual mentioned here function as "*specific* and *individual*" signs that achieve meaning only because they are charged with carrying and compelling specific beliefs (*CW* vi:65); their meaning, in other words, is to be discerned in their power as discrete, autonomous objects.

It is precisely this assumption about the relations between beliefs and representations that can also be found in the writings of fanatics and "political Empirics"(*CW* vi:150). Indeed, we can now more clearly see why the two *Lay Sermons* conflate the rationalist's opposition to religion with an equally powerful and exclusive religion, as I mentioned earlier. The Socinian and the atheistic empiric are characterized in the same terms as Warburton and the idol worshiper (as much as the figures might appear to oppose each other): the Socinian uses the Bible only for its "fragments," in order to "pick and choose" articles of faith from the text; like Warburton, the Socinians "inspir[e] . . . a contempt for the understandings of all who differ from them" (*CW* vi:182,184). If Warburton appears in *The Friend* as one who wields an "idolatrous charm," the political empiric is not simply demonized for opposing religion or for disrupting a perfect religious unity. In fact, the case is quite the opposite: it is the empiric's discourse that seeks to compel or enforce private belief. The empirics are, as the name for them suggests, empirical – relying on "particular Facts" that are "dissevered from their context." But these are also "startling" facts, with the "*sensation*" rather than the "*sense*" of connection; their writing tends only to concentrate on "scenery of local, and particular consequences" rather than a "general and ultimate result" (*CW* vi:153). The "facts" in the empiric's text thus operate as a way of carrying conviction from author to reader – to vehiculate particular kinds of sensations and particular kinds of shock or outrage.

The point of this criticism, finally, is not to delineate and correct beliefs or doctrines, nor is it an attempt to encourage a more moderate, "latitudinarian," or tolerant kind of belief. Instead, these discussions consistently draw attention to the self-contextualizing features of text. The adherents of superstitious and fanatic faiths can only be criticized, that is, insofar as they do not *read* (or, at least, they do not do what Coleridge would call reading) but only see objects, including all writing, as the epiphenomena of belief; hence *The Statesman's Manual*'s criticism of the "Church of Superstition" that "commands" its "vassals" to "*take for granted*" the truths of the church that are distilled from Scripture; hence the second *Lay Sermon*'s criticism of dissenters on the basis of their apparent contempt for "study and research," their lack of attention to reading Scripture which they believe is "easy" to understand (*CW* VI:194). These readers-who-do-not-read stand accused of "superstition" and "idolatry," in other words, not because of a type of belief or disposition that informs their reading of a text, but because they believe that texts *are* beliefs and that they *require* specific beliefs: the argument thus moves towards a general resistance to the functionality of text in a regime of political "servitude" that invests "idols of the sense" and "lifeless images" with the ability to secure religious or political uniformity (*CW* IV.1:518).

Coleridge's fascination with religious fetishes provides a crucial maneuvering point for him to define his poetic and philosophical project. Just as established religion would be a religion over all religions, his writing aims at once to be the "Subversion of vulgar *Fetisches*" and at the same time to be a fetish of fetishes, a fetish object more widely appealing than any particular communal fetish (*Notebooks* II:3156). This finally can be accomplished only by placing the highest value on the reading of text: a text about which beliefs may be formed but that also recontextualizes those beliefs, requiring them to account for their impact in a new set of syntactical relations. And it is for this reason that the Bible, even if it is the best guide to political skill and foresight, can function as such only because Coleridge first specifies that the Bible's significance does not consist in its ability to convey a discrete system of religious beliefs. It would be incorrect, in other words, to say that Coleridge judges the Bible to be a repository of specific lessons for political or religious conduct. Indeed, he criticizes all Biblical scholarship that might judge the authority of parts of the Bible for the sake of "discountenancing" some "doctrine concerning which dissension existed." Even if disbelief in a doctrine may discredit the holders of that doctrine as Christians, the reader must do everything to avoid the "fearful license" of "picking and chusing . . . religion out of the Scriptures" (*CW* VI:57). The licentiousness of license is not to be found in a lack of moral or religious orientation but in the attempt to turn Scripture into a mimetic representation of that orientation. The value of the Biblical text is that it does not conform to the prejudices that individual readers may apply to it.[47]

The Bible more consistently achieves its exalted status in the *Lay Sermons* because of its publicity, its availability to adherents of different faiths: "The Gospel lies open in the market-place," Coleridge declares, "and on every window seat, so that (*virtually*, at least) the deaf may hear the words of the Book!" (*CW* vi:6). Such words urge us to reconsider the meaning of Coleridge's emphasis on the "READING PUBLIC" in *The Statesman's Manual*, along with his efforts to locate a "very different audience" in that public: one that is "*ad clerum*," composed of men with "*clerkly* acquirements, of whatever profession." For the object of reading is not, as I have been arguing, to consolidate an audience of like-minded believers, but to imagine even the Gospel itself – and the institutions in which the Gospel may be read – as a way of attracting and preserving a "polemic divinity." Indeed, the second *Lay Sermon* continues this pattern of thinking against those who use the Scriptures "for the support of doctrines which they had learned beforehand from the higher oracle *of their own natural Common Sense. Sanctas Scripturas frustant ut frustrent*" (*CW* vi:182–83). The importance of the Bible lies not in its doctrinal content (the Latin translating into "they rend the Holy Scriptures to bits in order to render them vain"), but in its formal treatment of individual agency. "In the Bible," he declares, "every agent appears and acts as a self-subsisting individual: each has a life of its own, and yet all are one life" (*CW* vi:31).[48] The "one life" – which we recognize as a principle from Wordsworth's and Coleridge's earliest poetry – reveals itself in this instance as something other than an assertion of a shared consciousness or collective disposition. It is an assertion of connectedness among agents that can be shared in the *absence* of any comprehensive agreements. The Bible asserts omnipresence – an "omnipresent Providence" – not as something that needs to be believed, but as the very condition of belief or disbelief, for it asserts the value of a belief in little more than interconnection itself.[49]

I have said that Coleridge's interest in religion (what is eventually theorized as a national religion) is, from his earliest writing to the *Lay Sermons*, to be understood as an advocacy of "toleration"; I have also said that Coleridge understands *writing* to be engaged in that analogous project of toleration. This direction of Coleridge's thinking shows, first of all, why the poetry I discussed earlier makes claims on behalf of communal solidarity that must simultaneously be juxtaposed with the traditional foundation of national community in religious uniformity. Coleridge's later writing in defense of the established church, moreover, continues to support these claims for toleration, since Coleridge can only understand an established church on terms that radically reconfigure the notion of established religion as established and enforced religious beliefs. The later works that I have been discussing in this chapter also place a crucial emphasis on reading as a cultivation of "polemic divinity"; and this continually reinforces the value of Coleridge's own works – both poetic and philosophical – that aspire to attract the interest of as many readers as the Bible. The celebrated account of poetry as a "willing suspension of disbelief... which constitutes poetic faith" in the *Biographia Literaria* (1817) is informed by Coleridge's aim to refuse appropriation by adherents of either skeptical *or* religious doctrines, whose beliefs might lead them to criticize or neglect writing based upon their predispositions.[50] And it is crucial for Coleridge to continue defending his works by appealing to properly "poetic readers" who would not allow their religious "intolerance" to interfere with their reading of, and appreciation for, his work.[51]

The argument that I have been tracing must also guide us eventually to the *Aids to Reflection* (1825) and *On the Constitution of Church and State*, Coleridge's most comprehensive account of the national church. As sustained and passionate as Coleridge's support for such a church may have been, it was also a support that, as Cardinal Newman described it, "indulged a liberty of speculation, which no Christian can tolerate, and advocated conclusions which were often heathen rather than Christian."[52] Even Mill, so sharply contrasting Coleridge with Bentham, had to admit that Coleridge's views bore little resemblance to those of Anglican apologists such as Eldon or Inglis.[53] *Church and State* can be illuminated by our inquiries into works as early as *The Watchman*, and likewise illuminates those inquiries. Coleridge's final writing on the church and state makes the fundamental distinction between the national church and the church of Christ precisely as a way of indicating that religions are not necessarily tolerant of each other, but that the national church is a mechanism for organizing potentially incompatible religious beliefs. The rhetoric of religious opposition that I outlined in the earlier part of this chapter does not disappear as much as it becomes an animating and distinctive feature of establishment itself. Establishment, meanwhile, does not oppose dissent as much as it encourages and protects it. To the church is assigned the power of holding in suspension tendencies towards permanence and progressiveness; the "clerisy" as a body of persons guiding the "civilization" of the nation comprehends "the learned of all denominations."[54] "Civilization" is brought about by the cultivating agency of the clerisy, which serves as a public "guide, guardian, and instructor" (*CW*x:43). Not to be reduced to a "sect," the clerical guidance of the nation does not enforce doctrine as much as it is "an indispensable condition of national safety, power, and welfare" (*CW*x:61,53).

Coleridge's reservations about Catholic emancipation – the impetus for publishing the work – may in fact suggest that *Church and State*'s apparent liberalism only masks its covert bids for cultural hegemony. Yet what I have been arguing throughout these pages is that such a claim would merely collapse the categories of religious belief and government into each other. *Church and State* advocates not merely a government by belief but *of* belief – a notion that is only imperfectly recognized by Raymond Williams's understanding of this text as an early articulation of national "culture."[55] The claim that I have been making about these works alerts us, first, to the meaning of Coleridge's enduring religious demonizations, which are quintessentially Gothic. Catholicism, like utilitarianism, appears in *Church and State* – as it did in Coleridge's earliest writing – as a possible reduction of community to private sympathetic alliances that do not take account of "enlarged" spheres of action. *Church and State* argues for the exclusion of Catholics, then, not because of its doctrines but because of its "customs, initiative vows, covenants, and bylaws" which – allied to a foreign power – seem to constitute a threat to national security.

Second, however, the meaning of exclusion should be considered in light of the ultimate logic of social allegiance – which once again brings Coleridge back within the realm of the Gothic's tolerant logic. For the "allegiance" required of members of a national community, in fact, is required precisely in order to intervene within the existing "classes or aggregates of individuals" and thus to avoid private and hidden sources of exclusion (*CW*x:79,87). Coleridge's revised version of the national church is universal, but it is universal in a way that differs from the universality of conventional religions. If religious beliefs cross nations and continents (since people share those beliefs in different nations), the national church is both more local – because confined to a territory coextensive with the nation – and more general. It cultivates government as polemic divinity: a government that is, quite simply, beyond belief.

CHAPTER 4

Sect and secular economy in the Irish national tale

THE REGIONS OF PURER INTELLECT

In Lady Morgan's *Manor Sackville* (1833), the Sheriff Job Blackacre comes up with a strange and interesting way of criticizing the opinions of Sackville, a zealous reformer and English lord of a manor in Blackacre's county in Ireland. "Your English notions are very amiable," he says, "and what you call the philosophy of politics sounds very well in an Edinburgh Review, or a national novel; but such views and principles are utterly inapplicable in this country."[1] *Manor Sackville* is not in fact a national novel or a "national tale" (a term also used by Morgan and now favored by critics), but one of the author's *Dramatic Scenes* – a seldom-discussed series of works consisting of dialogue and stage direction. Along with the other works in the collection, it launches a recognizable generic departure for Morgan from the Irish national tale which she developed along with writers such as Maria Edgeworth and Charles Robert Maturin. It also offers some pointed explanation for that departure by making Sackville resemble an author of national tales – often voicing opinions identifiable as Morgan's – and by making Blackacre into a canny critic of the genre. The national tale itself, the Sheriff implies, represents an awkward attempt to apply "English notions," typified by the Whig political philosophy of *The Edinburgh Review*, to an Irish nation where they are "utterly inapplicable."

As if to confirm Blackacre's judgment on the national tale, Morgan uses the preface to *Dramatic Scenes* to insist upon her work's newly asserted distance from the relics (such as national tales) of another "epoch" in literary production: an epoch in which questions about the applicability of fiction to the "country" – to Ireland – were strangely suspended. The "public mind" at this prior point in history (which Morgan never clearly defines) had "leisure to stoop from its high quarry of political change, to sport in regions of purer intellect, and play with interests less mundane and positive" (*Dramatic Scenes*, iv). Her current work, in direct contrast, adheres to a new motto: "Those who would live by the world, must live in it, and with it; and adapt themselves to its form and pressure" (v).

That Lady Morgan imagines herself to be following the latest trend in public taste – living "by the world" – may not surprise anyone familiar with her reputation as one of the most brilliant socialites of her age, celebrated not only for her novels but also for her presence in fashionable circles in Britain and on the continent. But what is undoubtedly more surprising is her perplexing characterization of the national tale, since the preface to *Dramatic Scenes* – and *Manor Sackville* itself – suggest that the Irish national tale is not really about Ireland at all. Instead, it offers "views and principles" that are inapplicable to it; it is less concerned with the region called Ireland than with philosophical abstractions emanating from the "regions of purer intellect." If it is true that the national tale is not about the "real life" of the nation, then what is it about? To put the question even more simply, how and where is the "national" represented in the national tale?

Morgan's most celebrated example of the national tale, *The Wild Irish Girl* (1806), begins to suggest how the genre, in her handling, was by no means a straightforward advocate for, or expression of, the "real life" of the Irish nation. Even though her characters appear to be lifted out of the pages of Irish folklore and speak in "the peculiar idiom of [their] vernacular tongue," Morgan also makes them as cosmopolitan as she was; her heroine Glorvina is a skeptic, a reader of Rousseau, a child of the Enlightenment quoting French literature.[2] The novel most conspicuously renders Ireland as a place of secular learning rather than occult ritual, directing attention to the local and the vernacular precisely through the formal conventions of the epistolary novel and the work's fictive "editor." Horatio, heir to the estate of Lord M – in Ireland and hero of the novel, conveys his account of what is "singular and fantastic about Irish culture" to a "J. D. Esq. M. P.," as if to imply that the observation of local culture is in fact initiated and sustained by an extra-cultural correspondence with a member of the British parliament.[3] The "editor," furthermore, draws attention to Irish vernacular words and phrases by expanding the range of reference far beyond Ireland – to a large and erudite body of scholarship on Ireland, to London fashion, and to European literature and history.

My concern in this chapter is not with Morgan, in fact, but with Maria Edgeworth: a writer who does not resolve the paradoxical mixture of characteristics that I have just pointed out in Morgan's writing but in fact accentuates them. The works to which I devote the most attention in this chapter – *Ennui* (1809) and *The Absentee* (1812) – make the questions I posed about the national tale's unclear commitment to nationalism particularly difficult to answer, since her writing seems to be as devoted to organizing and managing the pressures of contentious local or national identifications as they are to exposing and enhancing them. Even though we will find that Edgeworth's novels appear (even more than Morgan's) to violate conventional definitions of the national tale in interesting ways, my purpose is not to show that they are *not* national tales, nor is it to suggest that they are merely problematic examples of the genre. These works will in fact teach us to understand the genre in a different, somewhat less conventional, way.

To begin my discussion with Morgan's rather strange view of her works may seem counterintuitive, since the national tale has often struck its readers as an obvious outlet for nationalist sympathies. For many nineteenth-century readers, national tales made local color come to life like versions of genre painting. Edgeworth's works in particular were judged to be "pictures of the manners of her country" to Anne Plumptre;[4] they were like "Dutch pictures, delightful in their vivid and minute details of common life" to John Wilson Croker.[5] In *The Edinburgh Review*, Francis Jeffrey fervently pledged his "love" for the "fair writer's country, and her pictures of its natives."[6] And William Butler Yeats later summarized this way of thinking by suggesting that Edgeworth's work brought the country to life with "faithfulness and innocence." It thus joined the legions of Ireland's other "poems and stories" which "came into existence to please nobody but the people of Ireland . . . They are Ireland talking to herself."[7]

As much as Edgeworth's contemporaries may have admired her writing's faithful rendering of Irish life, Edgeworth and her father Richard Lovell Edgeworth (acting in numerous roles as collaborator, editor, advisor) had ways of understanding their collaborative work and Maria Edgeworth's own work that frequently sounded quite different. Rather than merely celebrating the specificity of Ireland and the fruits of its genius, both Edgeworth and her father were eager to imagine their publishing ventures as increasingly universalized forms of address. For example, it was a spirit of internationalism – or, more precisely, a new and more tolerant spirit of British nation-formation – that animated Maria and Richard Lovell Edgeworth's *Essay on Irish Bulls* and *Practical Education*, works that sought out an audience in "England, Wales, and Scotland" and that angled to appeal to readers without regard to "sect or party."[8] In the preface to Edgeworth's *Popular Tales*, moreover, her father described the writing of fictional text as an act conducive to British national unification, thus proving the importance of "popular" in the title of the volume as an antidote to sectarian or socially divisive tendencies. Writing in conventional "polite" circles could "command attention" only by imagining itself as sectarian or un-popular, the communication of a coterie unified by "austere wisdom." The popularity of the *Popular Tales* consisted not in their attempt to promote themselves amongst a broader audience – " not as a presumptuous and premature claim to popularity" – but in their opening of "new channels of entertainment and information" that was furthered by the "art of printing." It opened learning up to those who had previously been "denied admittance."[9]

And a version of that spirit seemed to animate Edgeworth's own explanations of her fiction, as well – even *Castle Rackrent*. The tale's fictive "editor" envisioned an Ireland that would be known only as a distant, but not entirely relevant, memory: "nations as well as individuals gradually lose attachment to their identity," the preface asserted. And however convincingly the editor referred to *Rackrent* as an "unvarnished tale," or touted the "characteristic manner" in which it was told by the narrator Thady Quirk, the preface in fact imagined that his speech and manners were already lost by the readers that might once have adopted them. All that could be asserted was an enlightened distance from national allegiance (the reader will "look back with a smile of good-humored complacency" on the characters in the narrative); the tale's audience had traded in its archaic nationalism for "new habits," finding itself "amused rather than offended by the ridicule that is thrown upon its ancestors."[10]

Edgeworth and her father were not entirely alone in voicing this interpretation of their work. Many of Edgeworth's readers, like Morgan's, tended to fault her for a cosmopolitanism that verged on atheism. While Croker expressed some approval for Edgeworth's work, he could hardly ignore her "systematic exclusion of all religious feeling."[11] William Stephen complained that *Practical Education* "excluded . . . all reference to the subject of religious instruction" and that her tales neglected "a system of manners" that might lead to "difficult or important efforts of virtue."[12] If Edgeworth could be praised as the heartwarming advocate for the native Irish, she could also be viewed as a somewhat chilly formalist: something that Sir Walter Scott – to whom I will return in the final section of this chapter – saw in her as well. Even though Scott joined some critics in commending her for making the English "familiar with the character of their gay and kind hearted neighbours of Ireland," he also hinted that her novels paradoxically contributed to the loss of the very particularity they celebrated. Edgeworth, he claimed, had "done more towards completing the Union [between Britain and Ireland], than perhaps all the legislative enactments by which it has been followed up."[13]

This latter view, I think, echoes in the accounts of some recent critics, even though they tend to describe Edgeworth's writing in less flattering terms. Finding her cosmopolitan rationalism to be overly superficial – or simply condescending – such readers of her work portray her as an apologist for British national and imperial expansion, deaf to the claims of regional and historical specificity. Terry Eagleton thus explains Edgeworth's Anglo-Irish view on Irish culture as an "outside vantage point" that is "also a site of power."[14] Mary Jean Corbett shows how *Castle Rackrent* in particular reveals an author struggling to "secure the superiority of the domestic English reader over the Irish subject."[15] Other critics, however, register an opposing response that renews a line of argument associating Edgeworth's writing with Irish nationalist sympathies. Those critics find Edgeworth to be unusually sensitive, for an author of her day, to the claims of cultural particularity and national difference. In her study of British fiction and the formation of empire, for instance, Suvendrini Perera suggests that Edgeworth unites nationalist, feminist, and emancipationist sympathies, challenging "hierarchical and colonizing systems" with "alliances . . . between the repressed classes (women, menials, blacks, and other non-Europeans) of nineteenth-century England."[16]

Such divided opinions of Edgeworth actually correspond to divided critical assessments of the Irish national tale in general, but these recent contentions over the status of the genre actually show how deeply both sides agree.[17] For whether they view the national tale as an apology for imperialism or a more fervently local challenge to it, these arguments suggest that the genre concerns itself primarily with gathering adherents to a cause: the cause of imperialism or the cause of a nationalist (or regional) resistance to imperialism. I will eventually explain what I believe to be the shortcomings of these perspectives. But for the moment, we should attend to the way that these critics usefully focus on how the genre raises belief to a level of importance that both connects and contrasts with the aims of the Gothic novel discussed in chapter 2. It is certainly illuminating to see how frequently Gothics and national tales rely upon similar imagery, ranging from ancient ruins to picturesque landscapes to guitar-strumming minstrels. This makes it possible for readers of these works occasionally to associate novels such as Radcliffe's *Castles of*

Athlin and Dunbayne (1789), Maturin's *The Wild Irish Boy* (1808), and even Edgeworth's *Castle Rackrent* with either category. The similarities in imagery, moreover, indicate similar interests that both genres take in the *locality* of belief: attitudes, perspectives, or states of mind that are shared, or not shared, by individuals within a specific region. Despite these commonalities, a contrast – maybe the definitive contrast – might be observed between the national tale and the Gothic novel: the national tale frequently manages to overcome the terrifying effects of the Gothic by accenuating and elaborating upon the role of belief in the formation of social groups. Whereas the Gothic presents a picture of society as necessarily conflictual – characterized, at least, by adherents of incompatible beliefs that need to be (somewhat uncomfortably) assimilated to each other – the national tale appears to move in a different direction. It makes beliefs that are religious, or that carry the force of religious beliefs and have a clear alliance with them, into a source of social value and distinction. Such beliefs have a fictional value, too. If the Gothic strives to assert its distance as public literature from a private liturgy, the national tale seems to renew the claims of local beliefs and customs on the language of a literary text: a text that continually expresses such beliefs and customs through dialect, local terminology, and the frequent use of notes by fictive manuscript "editors" who do not merely stand outside the walls of monasteries but in close proximity to a local culture.

This is not to say that the national tale simply becomes an advocate for specific national interests; instead, the genre becomes the self-conscious advocate of the mutually supporting economic and institutional means through which these beliefs and interests can attain a conspicuous value. We will thus be able to see how the national tale provides a radically secular analog to Coleridge's writing on the national church; it therefore provides an illuminating interlude in our discussions before we turn to Wordsworth's radically secularized view of the church itself. Now it is significant that, among other nation-centered fictions, the *Irish* national tale participated in a particularly controversial political discussion: namely, the one surrounding the Anglo-Irish Union of 1800. As I explained in chapter 1, Ireland looked like a perfect example of that worrisome *imperium in imperio* that could unsettle British national stability. Edgeworth's version of the Irish national tale could in fact heighten a reader's awareness of the asymmetrical beliefs and alliances that might impair a successful union – at the same time that it could also eventually assuage anxieties over Union by representing it in a way that would not eliminate Ireland's sense of its own difference.

The conventions of the Irish national tale – arguably solidified by Morgan's *Wild Irish Girl* – help to reveal this logic. According to these conventions, an Irish Protestant "absentee" landlord or the son of that landlord (usually descended from the Anglo-Irish stock that settled in Ireland under Cromwell), living in England, returns to Ireland for the purposes of renewing his claim on his property and restoring his reputation among the Catholic peasantry. A series of tangled adventures ensues, involving a series of mutual misunderstandings between the ignorant landowner and the native Irish, nevertheless culminating in a final reconciliation: often a marriage between the landowner and/or son and a woman who is in some way connected with Ireland's ancient past. What is less remarked upon by critics, but what I would argue is a crucial characteristic of these novels, is the way that Edgeworth's writing reorganizes prejudice. Rather than taking different backgrounds as the occasion for mutual exclusion – for each side to persist in opposing the other – her writing makes the differences between groups more visible precisely because of their prior inclusion within the larger entity of Britain. An expanding social and discursive entity, Britain might even be said to maximize opportunities for disagreement or difference to emerge.

This account departs in significant ways from the critical perspectives that depend on seeing Edgeworth's writing – and the national tale generally – as an argument on behalf of one national (or imperial) culture or another. Neither advocates of revolutionary nativism nor of patriarchal domination – the alternatives most frequently offered by these perspectives – Edgeworth's versions of the national tale make a case for a patriotism by assimilation.[18] To frame the priorities of Edgeworth's work in this way is to grant the instrumental, indeed vital, function of an expanding British economy in her writing: with the defense of which Morgan's Blackacre finds in the "philosophy of politics" that "sounds very well in an Edinburgh Review." For Edgeworth, the fictional structure of the national tale defines national character in a way that asserts the equally fictive resourcefulness of a British national economy: a structure of commercial relations that might ultimately encompass and provide distinction for the numerous different territories within its reach.

In *The Wealth of Nations* (1776), required reading in the Edgeworth household, Adam Smith provides a helpful gloss on the technique of the national tale when he describes the capacities of the economy to act not merely as an instrument of human will but as a more constructive source of "order and good government, and with them, the liberty and security of individuals."[19] Long after Smith and Edgeworth, Marx summarizes this mode of thought – and brings to mind the rhetoric of the national tale itself – when he describes the transformative effects of this new "order" of commercial relations; for its various and diverse participants, the capitalist economy "alters the social role they play in relation to one another" such that "the former believer becomes a creditor, and turns from religion to jurisprudence."[20] Like Smith, who thought the economy might encourage adherents of a "thousand small sects" to act with "philosophical good temper and moderation," Marx sees the economy as a technology that subordinates belief to economic obligation.[21] It must be said, of course, that Marx eventually comes to see economic exchange as a deadening of social value – a "purely formal" relationship between persons that must be restored to an original wholeness by being reconnected to a "family relationship with its naturally evolved division of labour."[22] But it is possible to see how Edgeworth's fiction – through the means of literary form – elaborates the relationship between individuals and their "purely formal" economic roles somewhat differently, and thus carries Smith's enthusiasm for the inclusiveness of the market in a different direction. In her handling, the sphere of economic transactions does not merely flatten out value or obscure differences between territories; it provides a much more potent resource for patterning distinctions that may not otherwise be visible. Edgeworth's tales and novels are thus *tolerant* fictions, that is, not because they suppress belief or advocate it. Instead, they imagine a way for beliefs to be registered according to the alliances and obligations accumulated in a network of commercial transactions: transactions that both embrace all beliefs and provide a new context in which those beliefs can be understood.

PRIVACY AND PREJUDICE: THE ECONOMY OF *HARRINGTON*

Edgeworth's *Harrington*, published in 1817 along with *Ormond*, explicitly promotes the cause of religious toleration, and shows how economic relations uphold this commitment. At the same time, moreover, the novel's commitment to toleration requires a coordinating ambivalence towards, or at least suspicion about, national self-determination – an ambivalence or suspicion that, we shall see, lies at the heart of the Irish national tale. *Harrington*, as the preface by Richard Lovell Edgeworth announces, was written explicitly in response to charges that Edgeworth's earlier novel *The Absentee* displayed "illiberal" attitudes towards its Jewish characters, and I will return to the relationship between the two novels at a later moment in this chapter. For now, though, we must notice that *Harrington*

confidently announces that the work has been written for an audience
that already accepts the demise of prejudice – or, to be precise, the demise
of prejudice as a guide for social policy. People of "enlightened days"
have rejected prejudices "universally believed by the English nation, and
[which] had furnished more than one of our kings with pretexts for ex-
tortions and massacres."[23] Edgeworth points, that is, not merely towards
the alteration of personal dispositions towards prejudice, but towards a
relation between prejudice and government – the extent to which the
former might serve as a "pretext" for determining the latter.

The source of such prejudice in *Harrington*'s initial pages is young
Harrington's nurse, Fowler, whose education of her charge consists
largely of telling him anti-Semitic stories: stories about Jews who conduct
secret sacrifices and make pork from the flesh of the children victimized
by their "midnight abominations" (*Harrington*, 4–5). Such stories are not
told merely for the purposes of creating prejudice; they are in fact designed as a way of scaring Harrington into compliance with the rules
of the household – to go to bed, for example, before Simon the Jew
(according to one bizarre threat) captures him and stuffs him in his bag.
But the effect of those stories is to make the meaning of his actions depend less on the good or evil attending upon the actions than on the
inherent evil of another person, and the contrasting inherent goodness
in himself. Furthermore, the stories encourage a blindness towards the
significance of public action in more general terms. Harrington's prejudice – like Fowler's – comes to look like a weird form of private language:
by scripting persons in advance of their public actions, prejudice offers
a "pretext" for reading the social world that continually writes off specific classes of persons outside the immediate household as inherently
disabling sources of terror to the self.

If Fowler's prejudices look like a private language, though, the point
of the novel is that such prejudices, backed up by political and economic
power, govern the policy of the family, Harrington's social class, and
the nation itself. Harrington continually finds himself surrounded on all
sides by reinforcements for his prejudice; his mother and father, joined by
Mowbray – Harrington's aristocratic school friend – surround him with
anti-Semitic sentiment that proves useful for cementing social bonds.
This negative sentiment – a "presentiment" (to use Edgeworth's word)
or predisposition towards Jews – seems "natural and proper" precisely
because it comes from within the home and retains the household's
aura of sanctity (178,46). And Harrington's father makes prejudice seem
like a politically valuable sentiment by insidiously weaving it into his

political designs. According to him, a man who gives in to the demands for religious toleration is a "Miss Molly" (27,41). The proper acquisition of heterosexual English manliness requires a personal contempt for, and a political exclusion of, Jews; and his policy gains support from a popular outcry against supporters of the "Jew Bill" who are said to be against England's national religion and thus against England itself (24).

Social relations, according to this logic, might be built entirely upon pretext or presentiment: they might be built solely upon a pregoverned set of associations that maps private on to public, and thereby fixes the identities of social actors in advance of their actions. Perhaps it goes almost without saying that such pretexts and presentiments rely upon a variety of utterly *mistaken* views of individuals; but the plot that eventually unfolds suggests that the antidote to this socially instrumental form of prejudice cannot be obtained merely by appreciating who people really are. In the most comprehensive account of Edgeworth's novel to date, Michael Ragussis reads *Harrington* as the means through which "stereotypes could be inspected and perhaps overturned." For Ragussis, Edgeworth's novel is "a demystification of the origins of prejudice and racial terror, whose secrets will be exposed . . . once we see the human cause behind an apparently inexplicable phenomenon."[24] But I think that *Harrington*'s interest in the economy leads towards a different conclusion. The logic of presentiment or pretext is shown to be both damaging *and* inaccurate, while the market economy acquires a contrasting importance in the novel's sequence of events: the economy continually provides a kind of text – rather than a pretext – for reading the effects of individual actions. *Harrington*'s tolerant vantage point comes about by recommending a new structure of *relations* between characters rather than more rational and demystifying beliefs that characters, or readers of the novel, might adopt. Because it emphasizes character as the effect of economic relations rather than pretextual dispositions, the economy continually provides Edgeworth's characters with the opportunity for tolerance insofar as they participate in the activities of the market. Against Mr. Harrington's model of intolerant English manliness, the novel sets up the marketplace as a system that produces alternative and interrelated values; the vitalizing means through which the beliefs, presentiments, or predispositions of characters can be registered in an exchangeable and conspicuous form.

This is why the alliance between Jews and the marketplace in *Harrington* does not merely acquiesce to age-old associations between Jews and usurous practices; an adherence to the laws of the market continually looks like the mark of tolerance just as a resistance looks like the mark of intolerance. When Berenice, daughter of Montenero the Jew, accompanies Harrington to the Mint and to the Bank, the two feel joined to each other out of mutual respect for nothing more and nothing less than the economy itself: in the Bank (in Harrington's words) is "the spirit of order operating like predestination, compelling the will of man to act necessarily and continually with all the precision of mechanism. I had beheld human creatures, called clerks, turned nearly into arithmetical machines. At the Mint I had seen the power of invention converting machines almost into men" (243–44). The Bank is less significant for creating or managing uniform currency – there is no mention of currency at all – than for producing interfunctioning social roles. The economy generates newly minted categories of persons – "clerks" that act like "machines." But mechanism is so far from being hostile to humanity that it seems like humans themselves. Even more interesting, however, is a complicated series of events in the novel that revolves around the "credit" of individuals and business enterprises. Anti-popery and anti-Jewish mobs become associated with a run on the banks, so that a hostility to toleration coincides with a desire to remove money from circulation. Mr. Harrington himself loses all of his money but maintains his character through his "credit" with the bank; his son helps protect Montenero and his collection of paintings – saving Montenero's "life" and "character" – from the intolerant mob; Montenero in turn withdraws money (using his paintings as credit) in order to support a friend of Mr. Harrington (429). The attenuated series of equivalences (Montenero=paintings=money=Mr. Harrington) implies an equation between objects – paintings and money – that do not resemble each other; the equivalences, furthermore, provide a link of agreement between persons who radically and dramatically differ. In another instance, the Jewish jeweller Manessa is wrongly accused by the Mowbrays of having stolen one of the Mowbray family jewels; after Lady Mowbray destroys the "credit" of the jeweller by privately spreading rumors about Manessa's crime, Harrington restores the lost credit by finding the real thief – who turns out to be Harrington's old nurse, Fowler. With breathtaking precision, Edgeworth makes the restored symmetry of economic relations coincide with the removal of the destructive effects of prejudice.

At the novel's end, Harrington is finally prepared to marry Berenice Montenero, but this is only after Montenero reveals that his daughter is Protestant rather than Jewish. Such a troubling resolution would appear to satisfy Mr. Harrington – who had previously insisted that Berenice convert – by conceding to his intolerant feelings. But the novel also wishes to make the concession to his feelings into a private, and therefore publicly irrelevant, matter. The logic of credit and debt underwriting their relations, Jews and Christians turn out to be most significant to each other – *outside* the family, at least – as persons of business rather than adherents of specific codes of belief. *Harrington* thus attempts to imagine an opportunity of tolerance and also a limit to it that becomes visible at the level of private or domestic choice.

Edgeworth's novel of toleration bears some marks – like the plot of courtship and marriage – of conventional domestic fiction, but *Harrington* regards the economy from a vantage point that differs substantially from that which we find in her own domestic novels. Edgeworth's *Belinda* (1801), perhaps taking its cue from Fanny Burney's *Evelina* (1778), tells the tale of a woman whose relations with men in public life are characterized by the profound congruency between that public and a marketplace. Women are displayed for marriage in the same way that commodities are displayed in a storefront; to play the alternately exhilarating and threatening game of courtship is thus to become commodified and to become aware of the commodification of others. Negotiating the hazardous world of false appearances, Belinda learns to style herself appropriately for the market while adroitly reading the commodified characters of others – no easy task, according to her friend Lady Anne, who warns her that "men have it in their power to assume the appearance of every thing that is amiable and estimable, and women have scarcely any opportunities of detecting the counterfeit."[25]

Even this brief account suffices to show how Edgeworth's domestic fictions organize an epistemology of character that both solicits and frustrates questions about accuracy: a person's external features, like commodities and financial instruments, can both represent and misrepresent the truth of an individual's psychological and monetary resources.[26] In a somewhat different way, as we have seen, *Harrington* portrays the economy as an even more productive resource for social life – and for individual identity itself. When Etienne Dumont, French translator of Bentham and correspondent of the Edgeworths, writes to Richard Lovell Edgeworth about the value of "la mode" – the world of fashion – we see an account that differs from the strategies of Edgeworth's domestic novels even while it helps to illuminate the logic of *Harrington*.[27] Fashion, Dumont writes, is "une espèce de pendule en d'encirque que régle les mouvements . . . Si la mode ne désidoit pas, chacun suivoit ses goûts et ses caprices d'une manière souvent incommode pour les autres. Ce petit code prévient la petite anarchie. Il facilite les communications sociales."[28] Dumont paradoxically takes fashion – the realm of values most distant from the value of human labor and supposedly the most wildly unpredictable – and makes it into a kind of regulatory device. Fashion strikes him as a fictive system of communication that relaxes its demand on complete agreement: an agreement which, if sought out independently by the individual participants in the market, would only lead to anarchy and mutual incomprehension. Such a tautological suggestion – that commodities make life commodious – is taken up in *Harrington*, where the market offers up a code that prevents anarchy and that facilitates "communications sociales." The retreat from the market can only confirm the world of presentiment and prejudice: an attempt to hold fast to a private and idiosyncractic system of values. By the end of the novel, that system of values no longer has any social legitimacy – a point most palpably made by the way that Fowler, the intolerant nurse, is convicted for her crime and sentenced to transportation to America.

If it is possible to view Edgeworth's foregrounding of the tolerant functions of the economy as part of a pattern of thinking characteristic of political economists such as Adam Smith, it is also possible to see how her writing builds upon and accentuates a specific possibility latent in that pattern of thinking. For Edgeworth – and for Dumont – a market economy does not simply cover up real virtues with false ones; it offers a "petit code" of socially animating effects, an opportunity at once to individualize and organize, separate and aggregate. This is the technique of *Harrington*, and I have lingered over a discussion of this tale of tolerance and intolerance in order to suggest the relevance of its logic for our understanding of Edgeworth's renditions of the national tale. Closer in their logic to *Harrington* than to her domestic fiction's suspicion of extra-domestic economies, the national tales view a British marketplace less frequently as a means of dissimulating or misrepresenting personal identity (as in her domestic fiction) than a means of achieving or generating it. Character, then – specifically Irish national character – becomes visible precisely by virtue of its integration within the capacious and expanding boundaries of the British economy and British secular institutions.

ENNUI AND THE NATION-EFFECT

My discussion of *Harrington* suggests that it bears an important resemblance to the Gothic novel rather than traditional domestic fiction, at least insofar as the novel deals directly with an intolerant nationalism and imagines an alternative form of social organization that is less specifically built around the uniformity of belief. We might find a parallel to *Harrington*'s Gothicism in Lady Morgan's *The Missionary* (1811) – in which the romance plot between Luxima and the Missionary is frustrated by the intrusions of religious prejudice and Inquisitorial cruelty.[29] And it turns out, in fact, that both works resist an identification with intolerant forms of nationalism in a way that is characteristic of the national tale itself. At one level, the complex disposition of Edgeworth's national tales towards conventional sources of national definition could be observed in the way that the Ireland of her novels – particularly Dublin – frequently emerges as a place that is barely distinct from England. In *Ennui*, the Dublin hotels are like their London counterparts only *more* elegant; the hero enthusiastically talks of buildings "which my prejudices could scarcely believe to be Irish" (*Ennui*, 169,70). *The Absentee*'s hero in a similar vein finds – again, in Dublin – "a spirit of improvement, a desire for knowledge, and a taste for science and literature . . ."[30] According to yet another character's ungainly but typical view of Dublin and its "vicinity," "the accommodations, and every thing of that nature now, is vastly put-up-able with" (95). In both novels, the urban center thus offers the hope of eventual improvement and development that is achieved through conformity with English standards.

There is another layer of complexity in Edgeworth's representations of Ireland, however, that is more worthy of notice. Her fiction does not only portray Ireland as a region characterized by familiar or unfamiliar beliefs. It also attends to the social *organization* of belief within Ireland – the extent to which institutional contexts make beliefs and cultural affiliations into occasions for inclusion and recognition. The agent M'Leod on Lord Glenthorn's estate in *Ennui* speaks from the perspective of the national tale itself when he claims that "religion is the great difficulty in Ireland," while also praising the virtues of secular institutions and their specific treatment of belief (216). He advertises Ireland as a place whose promise as a nation can be found in tolerant institutions where "the highest offices of the state are open to talents and perseverance" (304). "We make no difference between protestants and catholics," he says, in the spirit of Lancaster and Bentham; "we have always admitted both into our school" (216). In *The Absentee*, Edgeworth continues the campaign begun in *Ennui* by showing how the worthy agent Mr. Burke "tried to make all his neighbors live comfortably together" by encouraging "little services and good offices." Like Glenthorn's agent, Burke oversees a school where an observer can find "protestants and catholics sitting on the same benches, learning from the same books, and speaking to one another with the same

cordial familiarity" (*The Absentee*, 133–4). Although it may be tempting
to see Mr. Burke as a sign of Edgeworth's approval of Edmund Burke,
my discussion of Burke's confessional politics in chapter 1 should provide
some caution against reading his work as a guide to an author who was
so obviously ambivalent – as the details I have been discussing show –
about the role of religious belief in social institutions. (Edmund Burke's
tolerant position towards Catholics in Ireland was clearly acceptable to
Edgeworth, but his views on established religion were clearly different
from her own.)[31]

I am suggesting that this aspect of Edgeworth's version of the national
tale – frequently ignored by critics of the novels – is equally, if not more,
important than the genre's more celebrated devotion to the peculiarities
of local custom. For it is precisely this aspect of her novels that suggests
how interested they actually are in the capacity of liberal communities – in coordination with the functions of the economy – to shape environments where the difference between Catholic and Protestant would
make "no difference" as a requirement for institutional membership and
participation. In the agent Burke's words, moreover, we hear the echo
of the Edgeworths' fully secularized ambitions for their own writing that
I mentioned earlier in this chapter: children in these schools learn from
"the same books" just as the Edgeworths imagined that persons in all
parts of Britain would be reading the same work – works such as *Practical
Education* and Maria Edgeworth's novels.

The specific scenes and settings that I have been describing so far point
us towards a more fundamental logic at work in both novels. *Ennui*, for
example, is less concerned with the expression or repression of nationalist sympathies than with the way beliefs and allegiances gain articulation
by means of inclusion in a larger context of institutional and economic
arrangements. Ireland in this novel emerges most clearly not as a self-
determining nation but as a *nation-effect*: it is a nation only because it is
articulated through economic and institutional networks extending beyond it.[32] This is accomplished (as it is in the later *Harrington*) by exploring
the profound identification between property ownership and prejudice,
and by representing the market economy as a socially constructive pressure: a pressure that submits the authority of this identification to a new
regime of organization and redefinition.

Set during the Irish uprisings of 1798, the novel has as its hero
and first-person narrator the petulant and coddled Lord Glenthorn,
Irish-born son (supposedly) of an Anglo-Irish lord. Heir to estates in
England and Ireland, the young lord loses his money by gaming and

overspending, marries a woman for her fortune, and then loses her to the agent on his estate, Captain Crawley, who runs away with her. After a surprise encounter with his former Irish nurse, Ellinor, Glenthorn returns to his estate, Castle Glenthorn, in Ireland. There, he is brought under the reforming influence of his Scottish agent, Mr. M'Leod, who – in addition to his other services – helps the lord put down a rebellion of the United Irishmen. Glenthorn escapes this revolution only to experience it in another way. Ellinor – hoping to excite Glenthorn's sympathy after learning that her son Ody has joined the rebels and has been imprisoned – informs the lord that he was "changed" at birth: he is her son, and Christy O'Donaghue (Glenthorn's foster-brother, previously known as one of Ellinor's sons) is the real Lord Glenthorn. Glenthorn eventually surrenders his property to Christy O'Donaghue and returns to London to become a lawyer – both a "gentleman" and a "plodding man of business." After his training, he sets off again for Ireland, where he soon learns from M'Leod that the new proprietor of Castle Glenthorn has let it become a "melancholy and disgusting . . . scene of waste, riot, and intemperance" (317). He eventually marries the Anglo-Irish Cecilia Delamere – the heiress by law to the Glenthorn estate – but Christy gives the estate back to Glenthorn after the castle is accidentally burned down by Christy's son. Glenthorn, now "active and happy," proceeds to rebuild the castle that is now lawfully his.

From its initial pages, the novel makes Glenthorn into a representative of the general problem of absentee landlords who own estates in Ireland but live in England, earning income from their properties while also neglecting them. Heir to estates in England and "in one of the remote maritime counties of Ireland," Glenthorn suffers from a disease that afflicts members of London's fashionable society: the disease of "*ennui*," the symptoms of which are identified as "Frequent fits of fidgeting, yawning, and stretching, with a constant restlessness of mind and body." He experiences "an aversion to the place I was in, or the thing I was doing, or rather to that which was passing before my eyes, for I was never doing any thing; I had an utter abhorrence and an incapacity of voluntary action" (*Ennui*, 144–45).

Now Glenthorn's description of *ennui* as a malady of the upper classes – particularly of landed property owners – is crucial. Property owners are not merely afflicted by laziness or *in*action; they suffer from a diseased logic of action. This logic allows property to permit both action and the circumscription of action – action, in other words, and an "aversion" to action. And it is in this sense that *Ennui* makes even clearer the implied relation between property and prejudice at issue in *Harrington* and central to the Gothic novel. In *Ennui*, property and prejudice mutually enforce each other with extraordinary persistence. Prejudice looks like property itself, for Glenthorn receives prejudices against the Irish and Scottish that are handed down within the family from one generation to the next (145,181). Property, likewise, regularly assists prejudice; owning land allows him to regulate social contacts according to his predispositions – a tactic demonstrated by his scrupulous avoidance of "strangers" and "common people" who might have occasion to visit his estate (145).

Owning property, then, makes action look less like action and more like a simple extension of prejudicial disposition. Conversely, the world of strangers and common people intrudes in *Ennui* as a reminder of the menacing "business" of property ownership: a business that is beyond the reach of personal disposition. Glenthorn does everything he can to fend off the claims of the "business of various sorts which required my attention" (146). "I will give no account" (147), in fact, might very well be the appropriate motto for Glenthorn – and for all of Edgeworth's absentee landlords. Such a refusal of accountability is what leads the young lord to brush aside the responsibilities of owning property ("papers were to be signed, and lands were to be let") and entrust the management of that property to his servile and flattering friend, Captain Crawley. Crawley, the young lord imagines, will take care of his finances: he will "stand between me and the shadow of trouble," a standing-in for Glenthorn that takes on a bawdier meaning when Crawley stands in as Lady Glenthorn's lover (146). If the world of business transactions could be conceived as a world that gives a person a shadow, Glenthorn's *ennui* thus manifests itself as an attempt to blind himself to it. The point here is not only that the landlord overconsumes – which is the point of Swift's satire of the English cannibalizing the Irish in his "Modest Proposal" – but also that his private whim, in fact, can never allow business from becoming a matter of public record. We are thus told how newspapers take note of his "entertainments, equipages, and extravagance"; how footmen calculate the cost of his flowers; how "admirers of folly" count the numbers of candles burned in his house (146–47).

A crucial turn in the plot of the novel works a substantial change upon Glenthorn's understanding of his own actions. His old Irish nurse Ellinor appears on his English estate (just as his *ennui* has nearly driven him to suicide) and throws her arms lovingly around his horse; the horse throws its rider, Glenthorn is injured, and Ellinor nurses him back to health. The sequence of events may be most significant for Ellinor because she is finally reunited with the man who we eventually learn is her son; it may therefore help to establish the priority of a natural relationship between mother and son over the artificial attachments that Glenthorn has cultivated in his frivolous and indolent aristocratic way of life. But from another point of view – one that Glenthorn himself adopts – this sequence of events establishes a feeling of obligation that is far more general, for the young lord comes to take account of himself as a person acting upon – and acted upon by – other persons who are not (he thinks) necessarily related to him.

Edgeworth's footnote to the scene quotes from Sir John Davies's *A Discoverie of the True Causes why Ireland was never entirely subdued . . . until . . . James I* (1612, reprinted 1761), and uses the work to call attention to the culturally solidifying practice of fostering in Ireland – a privilege of foster-parents over "natural" parents that emphasizes the bonds of "sept" or "*clan*" over the bonds of family. Even though we will later learn that Ellinor is a "natural" mother, Edgeworth suggests by means of the note that the scene demonstrates the power of artificial rather than natural attachment, the power of communal feeling over blood relation. But what is surely even more provocative than this initial step beyond the family is that Glenthorn's "gratitude" emerges even in the absence of sectarian attachment. The text, that is, more consistently emphasizes Ellinor's strangeness (Crawley calls her the "Irish witch" [157]) rather than her familiarity. Glenthorn's gratitude emerges despite his account of her "vulgarity" and his "prejudice against the tone in which she spoke" – in short, despite his prejudice against her Irishness (157). The relationship that this encounter confirms could hardly be described as a relationship based upon sympathy. Instead, the incident demonstrates Glenthorn's pointed demotion of sympathy and initiates a whole series of occasions in which he proceeds to regard himself as a social being whose personal property and private dispositions eventuate in unforseen and unintended obligations.

At this point, then, Glenthorn begins to re-evaluate a range of relationships by acknowledging the "consequences" of both his actions and his neglected actions. When his steward informs him that Lady Glenthorn is about to leave him for Mr. Crawley, Glenthorn comes to blame himself for her actions: "with the consequences of my neglect I now reproached myself in vain," he reports, and he confronts his wife with her infidelity only by blaming himself (163). Even towards the end of the novel, Glenthorn learns of his former wife's death, but continues to pay her debts as if he could be held accountable for them (314).

Accepting consequences – even the consequences that he did not directly cause himself – leads Glenthorn, paradoxically, to feel "suddenly inspired with energy," to lose *ennui*, and gain a sense of self that he did not have before (164). The logic of responsibility eventually extends beyond the immediate confines of Glenthorn's domestic space to his estates in Ireland, making his personal responsibility look like a version of national policy. Personal conduct allegorizes the national: Glenthorn's return to Ireland is a way of ridding himself of a "tormenting establishment": a household full of servants turned masters, and a household that is – like the British religious establishment – "tormenting" to Irish Catholics (169).

But Glenthorn's conduct is striking not only for its ways of imagining the individual as a social model but also for its ways of confirming the validity of economic relations that continually bring to life the "consequences" of owning property. Viewing Castle Glenthorn for the first time, Glenthorn says, "gave me an idea of my own consequence beyond any thing which I had ever felt in England" (178). Although the sight of his cheering servants reminds him of "feudal times," he is more consistently reminded of the damaging effects of his negligent stewardship that persist despite the warm welcome he receives. His tenants proceed to confront him not merely with "homage" but with demands that make him aware of his own "power and consequence" and that rob him of his former "privacy and leisure" (178–83). And he eventually admits that "the feeling of benevolence is a greater pleasure than the possession of *barouches*, and horses, and castles, and parks – even greater than the possession of power" (188). Rather than describing himself as a feudal lord, Glenthorn at last regards himself as if he were "the King of Prussia." He does not resemble a feudal monarch, that is, but one of the most famous bureaucratic monarchs of the eighteenth century – later celebrated by Hegel for protecting the rights of peasants from corrupt lawyers and aristocrats – who "wanted to regulate all the mouse-traps in his dominions" (184).[33]

DELEGATED AGENCY AND THE BUSINESS OF MINUTE DETAIL

These initial alterations in Glenthorn's conduct and self-description – which might be understood under the heading of what Bernard Williams calls "agent-regret" (a feeling of responsibility for an injury without empirical grounds for believing one has caused it) – inaugurate a more extensive restructuring of accountability that in turn offers a resolution to the problem of ancient prejudice.[34] Glenthorn continues to re-evaluate his agency in new terms, ultimately questioning the status of the land-lord's agent, Mr. M'Leod. And it is this questioning that discloses the Irish national tale's profound philosophical interest in the relations between landlord and agent. According to the traditional structure of delegated agency, the landlord chooses an agent who will not only act in his place but act as a buffer for the landlord. The delegated agent relieves the landlord of the responsibility for dealing with problems that emerge in relation to his property. Simply put, he limits liability.[35] And in *Ennui*, this structure of delegation emerges quite clearly as the unique prerogative of the landowner, because it is yet one more way in which ownership per-mits the landlord's intentional circumscription of his own agency solely with reference to his own feelings, desires, and beliefs.

This prerogative also turns out to be deeply problematic, and Glenthorn eventually comes to work against the delegated, preadjudi-cated – in a word, prejudiced – version of agency, in which the meaning of action extends from the landlord's private construction and delegation of that action. As if to restructure the relationship between absentee and delegated agent, then, Glenthorn's agent-regret powerfully takes shape as a kind of agent-extension. Glenthorn's altering perspective as a landlord brings him to regard M'Leod's agent-functions with a distinctive eager-ness which corresponds to his increasing sense of consequence. The man who had no taste for "business" now recounts how he enthusiastically takes on M'Leod's functions:

As if I had been all my life used to look into my own affairs, [I] sat down to inspect the papers, and, incredible as it may appear, I went through the whole at a sitting, without a single yawn; and, for a man who never before had looked into an account, I understood the nature of debtor and creditor wonderfully well. (183–84)

Looking at personal affairs as economic affairs, Glenthorn learns, does not amount to adopting a more moral attitude or code of belief with which to guide his actions; it amounts to recognizing the attenuated relationship between moral or religious prejudices and economic effects. Part of the lesson that Glenthorn must learn, then, is that ownership can be a kind of action: a point made most compelling by the way that the agent M'Leod (the novel's ardent spokesman for Adam Smith) regularly alerts the landlord to the effects of ownership in terms of the actions that ownership entails or permits. Attending to those effects shows how these actions might be incorrectly judged if one were to judge actions only according to the landlord's pretexts or motives. Giving away money and signing longer leases, for example, at first seem to Glenthorn like demonstrations of benevolence until M'Leod explains that such actions (while benevolent according to the customary beliefs of landlords) may not actually lead to beneficial results. Renting land at longer leases turns out to look beneficial only until one sees how tenants "rack" portions of their rented land to "wretched under-tenants" (190). The agent M'Leod thus encourages a new view of agency itself: an agency that is not merely delegated according to prejudice but extended and given new meaning through the interanimating effects of other economic actions.

To take stock of this attenuated relation between belief and economic action is indeed (returning to Marx's formulation) to see how the believer becomes a creditor – or a debtor. The significance of this structure of debit and credit in the national tale, though, is not to be found merely in its substitution of abstract terms for more organic local ones, but in its capacity to raise the value of the local to a new level of significance. First of all, Glenthorn's attention to business makes him aware of how absentee property owners seem oddly drained of character: when he visits the Ormsby Villa, he "could scarcely . . . discern any individual marks of distinction" (202). The estate is filled with people of "no consequence and of no marked character," while they are at the same time part of a private and prejudicial sect: the same characterless women are comically "worshipped" by other property-owning "votaries" (222–23).

Second, the same attention to business makes him cognizant of the significance of "a perplexing multiplicity of minute insignificant details" that arise as a result of that business (184). And it is precisely this level of attention that makes previously invisible persons and objects surface with enhanced vitality. The assembly of Catholic creditors confronting Glenthorn enforces the sense that a structure of economic accountability has *made* them visible. Similarly, Glenthorn's relations with the laborers building a cottage that he has commissioned to be built for Ellinor furnish the very means for defining the specificity of that labor. The significance of labor is not limited to Glenthorn's ability to purchase it, for the transaction actually enhances the articulation of a local culture's specific textures. From "funerals and holidays" and local "habits" to "delays and difficulties" (188) specific to Ireland, the locality of the local takes on a new and decidedly public distinction through the process of economic negotiation.

The land that was once defined purely by ownership, an ownership that permitted the luxury of governing according to prejudice, thus becomes property that is relational and therefore represented through the literal activity of mapping. Glenthorn's territory becomes defined not merely as personal property but as an agglomeration of "above a hundred towns" (185). By contrast, the English Lord Craiglethorpe, friend of the Ormsbys and "full of English prejudices against Ireland and everything Irish," expresses those prejudices through his indifference to the contours of his own territory and of Ireland in general (209). Lazily delegating the task of surveying to his assistant, Mr. Gabbitt, Craiglethorpe plans to write "a book, a great book, upon Ireland," and Lady Geraldine satirizes his slipshod "means of acquiring information," which consist only of "posting from one great man's house to another." "What," she wonders, "can he see or know of the manners of any rank of people but of the class of gentry, which in England and Ireland is much the same?" (210–11).

The character of Devereux – the other writer in the novel – provides a direct contrast to Craiglethorpe. Devereux, a poet, demonstrates superiority of character through territory itself: his knowledge of territories speaks in his favor because that knowledge consists of an appreciation for the relation between territories. Explaining a "subterraneous way" or "cavern" between Castle Glenthorn and a neighboring abbey is the poet's analogy to Glenthorn's own new understanding of the significance of his property in terms of its interrelationship with other property and persons (218). The poet looks as though he might be an ideal property owner, while the property owner looks as though he might be an ideal poet. This convergence implies a connection between the management of writing and the management of property; it therefore comes as no surprise that the Edgeworths, in an 1807 review of John Carr's travel narrative *The Stranger in Ireland* (1805), repeatedly associate the book's lack of attention to the complex interrelations between territories in Ireland with its own poor organization as a text. The book's shortcomings are not to be found in its inaccurate observations but in its poor design. Its lack of a "table of contents" will "rather mislead than direct"; equally misleading "heads to chapters" simply reinforce a prejudicial view of Ireland as a strange and unmappable territory.[36]

I will return later in this chapter to the more specific issue of how Edgeworth's analogies between the management of property and the management of composition can be brought to bear on a more general understanding of her formal aims in the genre of the national tale. For now, though, we should also see that the novel's treatment of the economy plays an important role in shaping the plot of Glenthorn's discovery of his real parentage, his surrender of property, his rise to success as a man

of business, and his marriage to Cecilia Delamere. Learning that he is the
son of an Irish Catholic peasant rather than a Protestant landlord shows
Glenthorn that his social origins are entirely different from what he –
and everyone else – had imagined them to be. But far more important
than this exposure of the truth of his origins is the way that the narrative
continually undercuts the inherent significance of those origins and thus
the inherent significance of any change in them. In a sense, Glenthorn
has already been "changed" by the economic interactions that I have
been describing, and this takes temporal and logical precedence over the
change in accounts of birth. Glenthorn has already come to understand
that his own character is defined less in terms of the ownership of property
than in terms of the engagement of that property in an economy of debt
and credit.

The force of this earlier change registers at one level in the narrative's refusal to abide by its own unfolding of empirical fact. The name
"Christy O'Donaghue" never seems to stick to Lord Glenthorn, and the
novel (Glenthorn's own narration, that is) continues to refer to him as
the lord that he no longer is. The economic relations in the novel have
repeatedly suggested that Glenthorn has now come to understand himself as "Glenthorn" because of a realm of economic effects beyond any
personal account of either biological or customary validity. There are
still more palpable ways in which the narrative undercuts the apparent
importance of mistaken identity, though. Even when Glenthorn learns
that he is not the "real" lord (Ellinor tells him about a scar on the fore-
head of the young lord – a scar that Christy has and Glenthorn does not),
the significance of those origins is far from obvious. Very little in the way
of happy family reunions happens in this tale, for example, and Ellinor
dies soon after the outing of the truth – as if the existence of a secure
lineage needed to be smudged out as soon as it is established (289).[37] And
when Glenthorn gives his property and inheritance to Christy, he does
so in violation of a principle of law that naturalizes ownership through
possession. Possession, he knows, is "nine-tenths of the law" (279), but
he pursues an unnatural course of action by returning the property to
Christy, who does not even expect to get it back. The unnatural but
utterly consistent reasoning behind this choice is that Glenthorn, rather
than paying homage to his natural origins, returns the property mainly
because he feels a sense of responsibility for "committing injustice" that
he must correct by returning the property (279). Glenthorn's conduct
here is nothing other than gentlemanly, but being a gentleman is enabled by economic transactions. The difference between a lord and a
gentleman, Christy says, is that "any man . . . may be made a lord; but

a gentleman, a man must make himself" (290); Glenthorn thus seems to demonstrate Lord Y —'s claim that "we are the artificers of our own fortune" (303).

At the same time, however, the hero's actions are assisted actions, revealing precisely how much his character depends upon a realm of intertwined legal and economic relationships that are not entirely the result of individual effort. Lord Y — asserts that Glenthorn has a "claim" on his title, even after the truth of his birth has been revealed, because his "real character" in fact resides in public record and widespread reputation which he had previously ignored (296). Glenthorn's success in his career thus has less to do with his individual qualities and more to do with the mechanisms of trade that allow him to "distinguish [himself] among men" (305); he continually benefits from "gentlemen of the bar" who, he says, "honored me with particular attention" (306). The career of law itself commands his attention precisely because it emphasizes relations between persons rather than persons and their property in isolation, and it therefore provides an analogy for Devereux's career in poetry. The Benthamite Glenthorn becomes an expert at "indexing and common-placing," lending a more legible form or "plan" to the law's "endless maze" (306).

If Glenthorn's integration into the world of business seems to take precedence over distinguishing himself in the eyes of Cecilia Delamere – his future wife and heiress by law of the Glenthorn estate – it is because the marriage plot in *Ennui* (as in *Harrington*) precipitates from the logic of economy itself. The union of Glenthorn and Cecilia, that is, has less to do with romantic attachment than with their prior integration into a logic of accountability. Cecilia will not even think of Glenthorn as a suitor until his reputation as a profligate is cleared: until she can be sure that his poor financial position has changed according to public record, so that he is "the reverse of what he is reported to be" (300). Still more important, Glenthorn's marriage to Cecilia – which allows him to own vast amounts of property again – contributes to an expansion of financial obligation: he acquires not only property itself, in other words, but new occasions to manage and take account of it in a system of credit and debt.

FASHIONING UNION: *THE ABSENTEE*

Representing the rise in fortunes of Glenthorn is Edgeworth's way of representing the rise in fortunes of Ireland itself. With its significant revisions of the interconnected logics of inalienable property and prejudicial agency, *Ennui* implies that the rule of pre-economic sentiment and pre-economic ownership is itself the cause of the 1798 rebellion. *Ennui* offers the mechanisms of the market – the obligations incurred through debt and credit, deprivation and compensation – as the way to facilitate the absentee landlord's reconciliation with his Irish property and Irish people. While overcoming the damaging effects of reciprocal prejudices, the market also provides Ireland with unusually vivid marks of cultural distinction. This response to the problem of asymmetrical belief is particularly instructive as a way of understanding *The Absentee*, as well. This novel, however, takes Ireland *after* the 1800 Union as its setting, and thus accentuates the paradoxes explored in *Ennui*. *The Absentee* represents Union as a combined political and economic accomplishment that does not suppress Irish distinction as much as it embellishes and fortifies it. The novel follows the fortunes of the young Lord Colambre, whose adventures begin with his discovery of the precarious financial position of his parents, Lord and Lady Clonbrony. The Clonbronys, landlords of estates in Ireland who are residing in London, do their best to evade the clutches of their Jewish creditor, Mr. Mordecai; meanwhile, however, their estates in Ireland fall into decay under the increasing power of the Clonbronys' corrupt agents: the "upper" agent, Nicholas Garraghty, and the "lower" agent, Garraghty's brother Dennis. Colambre extricates himself from his mother's plans to have him marry the English Miss Broadhurst because of his love for Grace Nugent, ostensibly the daughter of Lord Colambre's (Irish) Uncle Nugent. His more pressing business, though, is not with romance but with finance: he travels to Ireland "to become acquainted with it – because it is the country in which my father's property lies, and from which we draw our subsistence" (*The Absentee*, 73).

While in Ireland, Colambre learns that a significant portion of his father's property is being administered not only unprofitably but inhumanely; he sees at first hand how the greed of the agents has resulted in dilapidated estates peopled by a starving and sometimes homeless Catholic peasantry. Eventually, he is able to keep his father from signing over complete control of his property to the Garraghtys, and instead urges him to put Mr. Burke, Clonbrony's more successful and humane agent, in charge. There is yet one more bit of unpleasantness that Colambre finds in Ireland, however: he hears a rumor about a scandal in the Nugent family past – of which not even Grace herself is aware. Colambre thinks that Grace's mother was a Reynolds who married his uncle, but the scheming Lady Dashfort – eager to have Colambre marry her daughter – tells him that Grace's mother was actually a profligate Catholic, Miss St. Omar, who bore the illegitimate daughter of a Captain Reynolds and took his name to avoid scandal. With the help of his friends Count O'Halloran and Sir James Brooke, Colambre finds that this story is actually only partly correct. The Count was given a marriage certificate by Reynolds; he in turn entrusted the document to a neglectful bureaucrat who left it among his papers. Sir James helps Colambre find it, and they are eventually able to track down Grace's grandfather in England and establish that she is indeed a legitimate daughter of old Mr. Reynolds's son and Mrs. Reynolds—formerly Miss St. Omar. By the end of the novel, Grace's legitimacy has been confirmed. Both her reputation and her fortune make her a perfect match for Colambre, and the Clonbronys return to their estates in Ireland.

In one way, political "union" in this novel achieves metaphorical expression through the marital union of Colambre and Grace, a woman mysteriously linked to Ireland's ancient past. Few critics have ignored the marriage metaphor and what they understand to be its political instrumentality.[38] But readers have often tended to pay less attention to the novel's sing-songy closing phrase—contained in a letter from an Irish tenant on one of Colambre's family's estates to his brother: "you see it's growing to be the fashion not to be an Absentee" (266). And this is only a symptom of the more general lack of critical attention to the complex relationship between local alliances and the alliances forged in the marketplace. This is the marketplace that makes the local into a fashion—or, to put it another way, that fashions the local—and thus the letter hints at the important ways in which the union of Britain and Ireland is a union forged through economic relations that extend beyond the more private and consensual union of Colambre and Grace.

To see the force of this account of union is to see why *The Absentee*—like *Ennui*—is not a novel that is simply about religious or national prejudice. It is about how the intertwined terms of property and prejudice are subsumed and ultimately defined by a logic of economic exchange in which the meanings of property and prejudice accrue according to their positions within a more dynamic and inclusive set of market relations. There are two versions of union in this novel that correspond to these different logics, and both compete to define marital union. For the Clonbronys, anxiously insinuating themselves into London's aristocratic circles, union is accomplished through the exclusion of alien beliefs and cultural markings—an exclusion corresponding with the logic of confessional uniformity that I have described in previous chapters. Lady Clonbrony's relations with other people make her try to purge Irishness from herself; as one observer reports at the beginning of the novel, she struggles to "look, speak, move, breathe, like an Englishwoman" (2). Her conformity, along with her accompanying prejudices towards the Irish "confusion of ranks" and "predominance of vulgarity," make her into a tireless defender of English cultural orthodoxy, upholding Lady Dashfort's maxim, "Whoever does not conform, and swear allegiance too, we shall keep out of the English pale" (82,100). A convert to "the pale" herself, she continually attempts to pass along her prejudices to her son – prejudices that comport with her efforts beyond the family to comply with and assert a uniformity in taste. Coupled with her efforts to stifle "*Iricism*" in herself and in those around her, her dabbles with Oriental decoration in her home – a Turkish tent, an "Alhambra," and a pagoda – make her into a comic version of a Christian missionary (27). Her bric-à-brac functions as a demonstration of traditional British domination of the East *and* Ireland (the association between the "Oriental" and the "Irish" having been cemented in works from William Collins to Thomas Moore and Lord Byron) that is rendered absurd as she marches her flock of party guests through her gaudy temples, preaching her doctrine of "the correct, and appropriate, and . . . picturesque" (37).

The prejudices that typify Protestant Anglo-Irish landlords – described as a kind of religious fanaticism called "*Londonomania*" – receive support from property ownership and the kind of "union" that aggrandizes property ownership. Lady Clonbrony's ambitions to increase her family's holdings of property are rhetorically linked to religious uniformity. They constitute a "doctrine" that she "had repeated for years so often and so dogmatically, that she conceived it to be incontrovertible, and of as full force as any law of the land, or as any moral or religious obligation" (43). A still more powerful logical link between property and religious prejudice arises, though; the attempt to enlarge the family's "consequence" through property ownership requires the Clonbronys to remove themselves from the consequences of owning property and govern according to prejudice (42). "Consequence," in Lady Clonbrony's sense of the word, has nothing to do with relations and only with possession of an "establishment" without obligations, an "independence" for individual and family without external support (19). Lord Clonbrony, while asserting more affection than his wife for his native country, nevertheless sees his estates merely as sources of personal subsistence: "If people would but, as they ought, stay in their own country, live on their own estates, and kill their own mutton, money need never be wanting" (21).

Lord Colambre's parents thus not only have prejudices; they prejudicially imagine their property to be separable from the "business" of its social "consequence." When Lady Clonbrony asserts her prejudices against the "*Iricism*" of the Nugent name, those prejudices emerge in the context of her refusal to acknowledge her family's financial affairs: "I know nothing of affairs – ladies of a certain rank seldom do, you know" (16). Colambre's adventures over the course of the narrative, then, do not consist merely of an attempt to change or correct his own or his family's beliefs about the Irish; he alters his diposition towards the social meanings of those beliefs and the social meanings of his property, both of which have legible effects on others. Sir James Brooke admonishes Colambre to "judge better by the conduct of people towards others than by their manner towards ourselves," and Colambre essentially adopts this advice as a recommendation to attend to the consequences of his family's actions (99). He thus feels a version of Glenthorn's agent-regret and subsequent agent-extension when he gets wind of his father's imperiled financial situation. Traveling around his father's estates in Ireland *incognito*, Colambre hides his identity as a curious but crucial way of understanding who he is by occupying his own shadow: his hidden identity allows him to view the activities of his father's delegated agents and acquire a sense of his family's consequence as economic agents in spite of their powers to delegate. He thus proceeds to shoulder the "blame" (145) that is due to his family by acknowledging the expansiveness of this altered logic of agency: he becomes the "eye or hand over the [landlord's] agent" (154).

The impact of this economic accountability cannot emerge in complete clarity until we realize how fully it conditions the relationship between Grace and Lord Colambre. For it would be quite plausible to argue that Grace and Colambre are not as much in love with each other as they are with the economy. Even though Grace is finally revealed to be the heiress of the Reynolds family fortune, the most important element of her characterization throughout the novel comes into view with Lady Clonbrony's complaint that Grace "often talks to me of embarrassments and economy" (16). At first, Grace appears to be destitute, and her financial position as one who feels the embarrassment of debt is her most crucial characteristic: her lack of a fortune makes her "distressed" and "anxious" because she feels indebtedness to the Clonbrony family for all of their kindness to her (16).

Christopher Ricks, in his discussion of Keats, suggestively labels embarrassment as a public-oriented – and decidedly English – emotion, and *The Absentee* arguably makes embarrassment not merely into an emotion but into a distinctive mark of a character's participation in the marketplace.[39] This makes embarrassment accompany the features of agent-regret and agent-extension that I have been using throughout this discussion; embarrassment regularly leads characters to regret actions and provide compensation for damages. The emotion that Grace and Colambre show most often, it turns out, is embarrassment rather than love: a feeling – also called "shame" – brought on by "debts," "distresses," and "difficulties" (16,20,60). The end of the novel, in fact, does not even represent the marriage of Grace and Colambre; it continues to assert the more important presence of the "wide circle" of society that is "peculiarly subject to the influence and example of a great resident Irish proprietor" (261). Larry Brady's letter reports on the couple's arrival on the family estate: "when they got out [of the carriage], they did'nt go shut themselves up in the great drawing-room, but went straight out to the *tir*ass, to satisfy the eyes and hearts that followed them" (263). Framing the conclusion to Grace and Colambre's courtship in this manner is Edgeworth's way of making the more public logic of indebtedness overtake domestic attachment. The affective union – affirmed by a similarity in presentiment, belief, or temperament – turns out to be less important than the economic union that circumscribes and regulates personal attachment.

The further point that must be made about *The Absentee* is that the economic union regulating this attachment – and all of the debts, distresses, and difficulties incurred within it – is the novel's way of assimilating, but also rearticulating, personal beliefs and prejudices. The embarrassment felt as a consequence of immersion in those transactions does, after all, have its color: red. And this is precisely what is behind Edgeworth's resourceful and pervasive punning on the word "pale." The "pale" to which Lady Dashfort refers – the pale that protects the integrity of (English, Protestant) belief and property – finds its analogy in the paleness or lack of distinction in certain characters that correlates with their lack of embarrassment. On the most physical level, land ownership is inconsistent with blushing: "you don't see young men of fashion here [in London] blushing about nothing," says Lady Clonbrony to Colambre. Yet again: "it's a great disadvantage to a young man of a certain rank to blush" (196). The absentee's pale skin corresponds with other related ways of talking about finances; the physical, in other words, is fiscal. Lord Clonbrony, while once a "great person in Dublin," is now "a mere cipher in London" (22). The absentee landlord's practice of spending without accountability – without "talking of embarrassments" – is spending with a "*carte blanche*" (17).

By contrast, Colambre's reddened complexion ("as if he had been out hunting for . . . three hours") – his embarassed blush and susceptibility to being "put . . . to the blush" – is the subject of repeated comment (195,243). Grace, moreover, continually shows herself to be part of an economy of credit and debt that gives identity its "tincture." She has a "tincture of Irish pride" (17); she is "blooming" when she expresses her indebtedness to Lady Clonbrony by caring for her during one of her many nervous fits (41).[40] But beyond this metaphorical register, *The Absentee* makes the economy into the very means through which Ireland receives its coloring – through which Ireland, in other words, emerges as a nation-effect. The Clonbronys' neglect of "affairs" is perfectly compatible with their attempts to imitate fashionable London entertainment – which are actually *un*fashionable and objects of public ridicule and contempt (35). When the discussion at a party given by Lady St. James turns to the subject of "Irish commodities and Ireland," Lady Clonbrony does her best to devalue both, while Lady Oranmore responds by taking up "the defence of Ireland with much warmth and energy"; the party guests admire the "honest zeal" with which she "abided by her country, and defended it against unjust aspersions and affected execrations." The inclusion of Lady Oranmore in the London social world thus demonstrates what Lady Clonbrony is slow to learn: "it was not necessary to deny her country to be received in any company in England" (59).

The Absentee in fact consistently shows that the economic relations between England and Ireland do not demand a suppression of Irishness but in fact enhance and facilitate its expression. Perhaps the greatest advocate of Irish commodities is the Irish Count O'Halloran, a quintessential Irish "gentleman" of the kind that Colambre hopes to be (127). O'Halloran's home overflows with objects of "Irish manufacture" from the count's handmade fishing flies to Irish sweetmeats (120–21). Irish "ortolans," a native bird, are served at his table, and a footnote advertises to the reader that the birds of Ireland are as fashionable as those in Paris: "these birds are worthy of being transmitted a great way to market; for ortolans, it is well known, are brought from France to supply the markets of London" (121). When the Clonbronys return to their estate in Ireland, moreover, they return to a family seat by burning the old furniture and redecorating it with Grace's assistance. In keeping with Lady Clonbrony's intentions to "set the fashion" in Ireland, the drawing-room is "new hung," Larry Brady's letter observes, and the chairs are covered with "velvet white as snow, and shaded over with natural flowers by miss Nugent" (202,266).

That Irishness might attain a distinctive value in an English economy explains the peculiar way in which the novel both raises and resolves concerns about Grace's questionable lineage. The rumor that Colambre hears about Grace – about her mother's illicit connection with Captain Reynolds – worries Colambre in part because it raises the specter of a disruptive sexuality that may in fact erupt in Grace herself. But what also worries him is the secrecy of Grace's birth: a secrecy that taps into the potent conventions of the Gothic novel by associating Grace and her mother – in various ways – with the privacy and invisibility of monastic institutions. The Nugent name itself is conspicuously Irish Catholic; by the 1820s, Lord Nugent had presented a petition on behalf of Irish Catholics to the British parliament.[41] The Nugents, moreover, are rumored to have been "connected with . . . the St. Omars" (110), which constructs a series of Gothic associations with Catholic subversion. Grace's own mother, a "St. Omar," was raised in a "convent" (226); "St. Omer" refers to a site in northern France of a Jesuit College commonly thought to be a wellspring of Catholic activity in England and Ireland. In Elizabeth Inchbald's *A Simple Story* (1791), the Catholic priest Dorriforth is "bred at St. Omer's," and Edmund Burke was said to have been educated there as well.[42]

Clearing Grace Nugent's name consists of making a private sexual liaison into something more public (a correction, as I mentioned earlier, of a neglectful bureaucrat): the public record of marriage that makes Grace Nugent into the legitimate daughter of Captain Reynolds. But what is most interesting about this turn of events is the way that the characters in the novel persist in seeing things, in a sense, as they are not; they (as well as she) assert Grace's connection to an Irish Catholic cultural heritage, a connection that is convenient but purely artificial. As in *Ennui*, establishing true parentage oddly requires that the parent be removed from the scene in order to deflate the force of biological connection. Although old Mr. Reynolds (Grace's grandfather) does not die, he assures Lord Colambre that "he would not see her if she went to him" (257). Grace, moreover, retains the very tincture of Irishness that would seem to be slightly inappropriate. She continues, after all, to be called "Grace Nugent"; this is not merely out of respect for her adoptive father, Colambre's Uncle Nugent, but because the name has become doubly significant for its "*Iricism*" and for its currency in the public mind. The name "Grace Nugent" in fact seems to signal her own sense of public relation itself – "I cannot bring myself to think that [the Colambres and Nugents] are not my relations, and that I am nothing to them," she claims (257). And this notion receives continual reinforcement from characters who use her name in order to show that she is something, rather than "nothing," to them. Mrs. Petito (Lady Clonbrony's former servant) and Larry Brady continue to call her Grace Nugent even on the last page of the novel. The accumulated associations between Grace and Ireland receive additional emphasis when the blind harper O'Neil sings Torlough Carolan's famous song, "Gracey Nugent" (264), a composition in Gaelic that was translated in numerous forms throughout the nineteenth century, including a prose translation in Morgan's *The Wild Irish Girl*.[43] The song's particular appropriateness in the context of the novel derives both from its emblematic connection with Irish culture and from its popular reception beyond Ireland: it functions as an appropriate sign of "*Iricism*" because it is translated and made valuable by works such as Morgan's novel.

I have left out any discussion of one very important character from the novel, Mr. Mordecai, the Jewish coachmaker and the Clonbrony's creditor. From the vantage point that I have been taking, Mordecai's role is perplexing, since his function is apparently to sponsor a system of debt and credit, even while the novel does not allow him to reap the rewards of that system. It is Mordecai, after all, who makes the Clonbrony family's debt visible to Colambre, and thus Mordecai who might be said to set the privileged logic of accountability in motion in the early pages of the novel. Two observations seem necessary in order to describe Mordecai's position in *The Absentee*: a position that, while troubling, is nevertheless utterly consistent with Edgeworth's thinking. First, his role as a Jew is to suffer from prejudices that the novel's logic associates with a specific – and retrograde – economic relationship. When Colambre first settles Mr. Berryl's finances with him, Mordecai treats the young lord to what he thinks are "approved Hibernian modes of doing business" which consist of suggestions to "*compromise*" and "*split the difference.*" Attempting to speak to Lord Colambre in tones of "familiarity," to settle a deal privately – "Between ourselves," he says – Mordecai shows how he is caught in the absentee's economic idiom (11). He works, in other words, within the landlord's prejudicial logic that makes a correspondence in personal sympathies and beliefs into the requirement for social inclusion, just as much as it makes a lack of correspondence into justification for exclusion. Mordecai's social opportunities, then, are limited to his shaky attempts to gain "familiarity" with the absentee landlords (in a way that imitates the Clonbrony's attempts to make themselves familiar with London nobility). His painful exclusion comes as a result, simply but profoundly, of his

Jewishness: a lack of correspondence that is continually made socially relevant by those who have the power to exclude him from their circle of familiars.

The second observation to be made about Mordecai relates to the exchange of letters between Rachel Mordecai Lazarus, a Jewish woman from North Carolina, and Edgeworth: this brings us back to the impetus for writing *Harrington* that I mentioned earlier. Lazarus shrewdly criticizes *The Absentee*'s unfavorable portrayal of Mordecai even though Edgeworth shows "justice and liberality" in her portrayal of other characters. Edgeworth responds in one way through *Harrington*, which (with *Ormond*) she sends to Lazarus for her opinion. *Harrington* does not in any sense reverse the logic of economic inclusion but simply extends it. It works as both a satisfying and an unsatisfying response to the problem of religious prejudice, since it manages to elevate the economy as a system that accommodates differences in belief and ethnicity while reasserting the persistence – perhaps the ineradicability – of personal prejudices. It is hardly surprising that Lazarus, while approving of the novel's effectiveness in "asserting the cause of toleration," still upbraids Edgeworth for making Berenice into a Christian rather than a "Jewess"; Lazarus can therefore only assume that Edgeworth approves of, and even identifies with, Mr. Harrington's personal prejudice.[44]

However convincing Lazarus's critique of *Harrington* may be, Edgeworth's other way of responding to her correspondent's complaints in fact reapplies the logic that she had put to work in the novels. She makes the Edgeworth household itself imitate and involve itself in the logic of a tolerant economy. Edgeworth writes to Lazarus, for instance, about her brother's involvement in a village school "for poor and rich where children of all religious persuasions are instructed together and live and learn to be good and happy." Like the good agents in her novels, her brother makes it a principle "never to interfere with the religious opinions of those who come to his school." The school, which puts particular emphasis on instruction in "calculation" for the purposes of "making bargains, estimates, etc.," gains Lazarus's approval since it seems to her like a system that will help "render merit the only criterion for bestowing friendship or preference."[45] The correspondence between Lazarus and Edgeworth continues to concentrate on a mutual appreciation for the tolerant logic of political economy, as Lazarus criticizes the oppressive policies of an otherwise "enlightened" British government in Ireland, or as Edgeworth praises liberal writers in *The Edinburgh Review* such as Brougham and Jeffrey. The Edgeworth–Lazarus correspondence follows the reasoning of *Harrington*, which (even in its imperfect solution) could imagine toleration principally through the extension of economic accountability that does not eradicate prejudicial belief as much as it rearticulates its public meaning.

The logic that I have been ascribing to Edgeworth's fiction, it could be argued still further, applies to the formal innovations typical of the Irish national tale: its production of a sense of difference generated from the economy of English language. To turn in this direction is to bring us back to the important functions of a figure such as Devereux in *Ennui*, who establishes a crucial connection between the writing of literature and the systematic social relations that precipitate from the economy. *The Absentee*'s version of this figure is to be found in Sir James Brooke, who – although not a poet – is perhaps the novel's most conspicuous *reader* and critic of popular "representations and misrepresentations of Ireland"; he is also the most apt reader of character as it is revealed in the "conduct of people towards others" (99).[46]

These author-figures argue on behalf of the more pervasive strategies of the national tales themselves, which employ the English language as a means of providing distinction to deviations from English which are both accessible and different. In these novels, the purpose of the "standard" English language rests on the extent to which it can be conscripted for the purposes of rearticulating belief as a *textual* effect. Not merely a normalization of difference (as John Guillory describes standard English usage), the "standard" could be seen as a way of making local belief or custom legible within the discursive framework of fiction and thus curiously dependent upon that framework for its own distinction.[47] To put it another way, Ireland can be apprehended in Edgeworth's fiction through a linguistic effect that accompanies and supports the economic production and accentuation of national distinction.

It is more than a mere coincidence, then, that local dialect in Edgeworth's fiction is frequently connected to economic circumstances and conditions – to consumption, production, buying, selling, saving, wasting. In Edgeworth's celebrated Glossary to *Castle Rackrent*, the very first note calls the reader's attention to the dating of Thady's narrative as "Monday Morning," a "prejudice," the Glossary explains, that is worthy of note because "all the intermediate days, between the making of such speeches and the ensuing Monday, are wasted" (*Castle Rackrent*, 123). A following note on Irish funeral practices explains that "the time spent in attending funerals may be safely valued at half a million to the Irish nation; the Editor thinks that double that sum would not be too high an estimate" (126). The Glossary thus explains one expression after another by translating a local Irish "prejudice" into systematic economic terms.

Ennui and *The Absentee*, in a similar fashion, make dialect and cultural difference emerge in all of their distinctness in specific economic contexts. While Glenthorn hears a series of economic demands that his tenants make upon him, he simultaneously attends to a new and particularized idiom: a "language so figurative, and tones so new to my English ears, that, with my utmost patience and strained attention, I could comprehend but a very small portion of what was said to me" (*Ennui*, 182). When the text of Glenthorn's narrative admits words such as *racked* and *mearing* into the context of the novel's standard English, the true purposes of the standard emerge: not as a suppression or normalization of Irish cultural and linguistic difference, but as a way of insisting upon its distinction by demanding the "patience" and "attention" of the reader.

The Absentee follows the lead of *Ennui* in its rendering of Irish local color as an effect of economic inclusion. Lady Clonbrony's tendency to imagine that Union demands conformity, for example, results in her social exclusion and also in a legible textual effect: her language is virtually unreadable. Lady Clonbrony speaks a language that attempts to assert its inclusion within the "pale" by conforming to the patterns and pronunciations of English as it is spoken in London; but this level of conformity only leads her to "caricatur[e] English pronunciation" (*The Absentee*, 5). She not only makes herself the brunt of jokes from the very beginning of the novel, but also robs herself of the ability to speak. As linguistic equivalents of pagodas and Turkish tents, her overdecorated jumble of attempts to cover up an accent (which Edgeworth designates with italics) mangle both individual words and grammatical connections. At Lady St. James's dinner, Lady Clonbrony's abuse of Ireland is reduced to mere noise (making her similar to Coleridge's portrayal of Warburton with his "potent abracadabra"): she can only speak by "repeating the same exclamations" (59). In contrast, the Irish Lady Oranmore – who does nothing to "deny her country" and does everything to defend its commodities – is said to converse with "warmth and energy" and "eloquence" (59).

The Absentee raises the particularity of Irish linguistic practice to a new level of value: while landlords assume a new responsibility towards their tenants and their economic agreements, they – just like us, as readers – dedicate an unprecedented attention to "*Iricism*." Colambre's attention to his family's tenantry makes him aware of a local economy which is defined in its own private or semi-private terms; and this continually exposes a new and attractively sectarian vocabulary. In one instance,

Colambre is told the definition of "*potsheen*," which denotes "the little whiskey that's made in the private still or pot" (144). Or, in yet another, he learns the meaning of the word "*tally*": "the way the labourers do keep the account of the day's work with the overseer, the bailiff; a notch for every day the bailiff makes on his stick, and the labourer the like on his stick, to tally" (150). Just as the novel's private economic terms become translated into the language of public accountability, the narrative's context of "standard" English makes a distinctively Irish expression seem valuable because publicly visible and translatable.

SCOTT, TOLERATION, AND THE NATIONAL TALE

Edgeworth's novels turn out to give us a picture of the national tale that looks somewhat different from the one treasured by some of her nineteenth-century readers. If Yeats had imagined the literature of Ireland as an instance of an autistic nation talking to "herself" (an image oddly resembling Lady Clonbrony), Edgeworth's work depicts an Ireland that speaks only when it is in the midst of conversation with others. However poorly her national tales fit with Yeats's definition, they fit more easily into Morgan's way of imagining the national tale as a highly problematic expression of nationalist sentiment. They provide perhaps the clearest example of how the national tale is *both* about the beliefs and sentiments that make persons feel attached to territories *and* about the "philosophy of politics" to be found in the "Edinburgh Review" ridiculed by Morgan's sheriff.

It is precisely this double-vision of the national tale, I would argue, that must be appreciated in relation to the novels of Scott, to which I want to turn my attention in the last pages of this chapter. We discover the value of the national tale's legacy for Scott not in its celebration of discrete nations or local peoples, but in its attention to institutions that organized and managed British people in different ways at different times. Revisiting Scott's historical novels with this altered sense of the impact of the "national" in the national tale provides a different perspective from Lukács's account of Scott in *The Historical Novel*, and from those critics who have been influenced by that account. Lukács provides a genealogy privileging the historical novel insofar as it represents the totality of national life: Scott's writing stands above the "second and third-rate writers" (including Radcliffe) for one reason: it is "keenly observant of the real facts of social development."[48] In his account, this social development can in turn be read as the accumulated details of personal interests and feelings; Lukács's practice of "historical humanism" accumulates support from character sketches of Scott's "prosaic" and "average" heroes – heroes that show how historical movements are carried out from "below" by common people rather than "above" by aristocrats and monarchs.[49] This account emphasizes the authority of psychology, manners, and customs in a way that has also been powerfully re-examined by Alexander Welsh and Judith Wilt; but it cannot fully appreciate the specific structures of social institutions with a comparable historical rigor.[50] It cannot, that is, account for the ways in which those characters (with contending psychologies, manners, and customs) are organized under differing modes of government. Although Lukács celebrates Scott's rendering of Jeanie Deans's "narrow Puritan and Scottish peasant traits" in *The Heart of Midlothian* (1818), for example, he is unable to establish any link between Scott's interest in representing narrow prejudice and his interest in representing the altering and highly contested social meaning of narrow prejudice under the auspices of British mechanisms of government.[51] A more accurate – and truly historical – reading of Scott's historical fictions would lead us to understand the way that Scott does not merely represent personal prejudices; he represents the differing levels of authority that prejudice assumes under the auspices of different institutional structures.

To embark on this line of argument is to acknowledge that in Scottish novels such as *Waverly* (1814) or *Old Mortality* (1816), characters negotiate with each other's religious or political alliances but also negotiate and debate the shifting sets of institutional protocols that allow their beliefs and alliances to be organized and articulated in different ways. *Waverly* is thus sprinkled with conversations about tensions between clerical lenience and a more constraining dedication to justice and the public good; after Edmund's arrest, Major Melville argues for adhering to the strict code of law to prevent a "gross injustice to the community," while the clergyman, Mr. Morton, urges a pardon on the basis of Edmund's "youth, misled by the wild visions of chivalry and imaginary loyalty" (chapter 32). Prince Charles, a "hero of romance," draws still further on Waverly's visions of chivalry and imaginary loyalty, and the novel continually dramatizes a struggle between the sentimental attachments to particular localities and the social obligations attached to membership in the larger entity of Britain: an entity whose very tolerance and permissiveness requires new, unfamiliar, and discomfiting obligations from its members. In *Old Mortality*, Henry Morton is accused of excessive sympathy with Presbyterian fanatics at the same time that he is accused by the

Presbyterians themselves of a slavish adherence to the laws of the state. Morton's simultaneous generosity and indifference make him, in Scott's logic, a perfect advocate for the tolerant British state. With his pleas for "general justice," for only "moderate" demands by the Presbyterians for whom he fights (chapter 27), or for "free exercise" of religion without rebelling against the government (chapter 28), he becomes the spokesman for the dubious project of liberal government, which aims to "tolerate all forms of religion which were consistent with the safety of the state" and at the same time – according to the Presbyterians – inflicts "a rape upon the chastity of the church" (chapter 37).

And in *The Heart of Midlothian* (1818), the novel that Lukács repeatedly singles out for its mastery of "psychological and moral contrast," we find that Scott's novel, rather than merely displaying contrasts in personal psychology and morality, takes a greater interest in the degree to which the altering legal and institutional mechanisms of the modern state reconfigure the social impact of the beliefs and customs that typify specific regions.[52] Jeanie Deans is able to intervene on her sister Effie's behalf against the law that would convict Effie of child murder if no witness came forward to testify to her giving birth. The 1690 statute throughout the novel emblematizes the rule of British law over Scotland; but the very possibility for the law to be reversed by Jeanie's appeal to the Duke of Argyle and then to the Queen depends upon Jeanie's respect for it. Conversely, the Queen's ability to act on Jeanie's behalf does nothing to "annu[l] the Act of Parliament" (chapter 37); the family is to be relocated to Roseneath, the "occasional residence" of the Earls and Dukes of Argyle, technically "beyond the bounds of ordinary law and civilization" (chapter 42).

Going outside the boundaries of ordinary law is, in many senses, a perfection of the secular state, however. The Duke of Argyle is (like Reuben Butler, who becomes Jeanie's husband) one of the novel's premier spokespersons for the tolerant state. Jeanie's father continually complains about "the quiet and indifferent manner in which King William's government slurred over the errors of the times" and "passed an act of oblivion even to those who had been its persecutors, and bestowed on many of them titles, favours, and employments" (chapter 18). And the Duke not only supports but profits by this new system of government; his influence with the Queen makes him into a model of assimilation at the same time that he asserts the interests of Scotland. His family seat at Roseneath is less an embodiment of Scottish national character than of a perfected form of liberal government. Reuben, with his liberal or

"Erastian" attitudes about religion, his "loosening of the reins of discipline," and his avoidance of "points of controversy" – practices that put him at odds with David Deans – is made pastor of the church at Knocktarlitie (chapter 47); and the Duke shows himself to be an "enthusiast equally in agriculture and in benevolence" rather than an enthusiast for any specific religion (chapter 42).

Critics such as Ina Ferris and Fiona Robertson have convincingly contrasted Scott's methods with modes of writing practiced by Radcliffe, Edgeworth, and Morgan: writers whose tales of sensation or sentimental national attachment were supposedly rejected by Scott and his sympathetic critics, in order to construct and solidify the more objective, masculine, and learned features of the historical novel.[53] I am arguing, however, that we need to see how the novels by these female writers were neither simply sensational nor endorsements of national sentiment but investigations of the secular organization of sentiment: an investigation carried on in Scott's fiction. To be sure, Scott's writing differs from the work of such writers as Edgeworth and Morgan by taking the whole of the British nation as his subject, and by showing the differences and struggles within that nation. But this is less a reversal than a development of thought that can already be found in the Irish national tale itself: a brand of fiction that shows how crucial the British nation, its institutions, and its economic structure might be for articulating Ireland's sense of its own differences and struggles.

CHAPTER 5

Wordsworth and "the frame of social being"

THE CONSTITUTIONS OF BELIEF

Imagine a procession, William Wordsworth asked his friend John Scott in a letter of 1816, in which Lord Holland and members of the political "opposition" walk through a series of British monuments. "Give them credit for feeling the utmost and best that they are capable of feeling in connection with these venerable and sacred places, and say frankly whether you would be at all satisfied with the result." Like the badgering narrators so familiar from his own poetry, Wordsworth is not satisfied to pose the question only once. He continues to ask it – but in slightly different ways. Presented with a view of an "English landscape diversified with spires and church towers and hamlets," would Holland and his cohorts have "a becoming reverence of the English character?" And finally: "Do they value as they ought – and even as their opponents do – the constitution of the country, in Church and State?"[1]

It may seem unlikely that any of Wordsworth's correspondents in 1816 could have doubted what his response might have been to such questions. After all, this was the author of *The Excursion* (1814), the nine-book epic poem swelling with praise for the constitution of the country in church and state. His patriotic verse appeared in *The Champion*, later to be collected in his 1807 *Poems in Two Volumes* as "Sonnets Dedicated to Liberty," and in future editions as "Poems Dedicated to National Independence and Liberty." His letters – by this date – had doggedly denounced Brougham, Jeffrey, Romilly, Holland, and other adversaries whom Wordsworth considered to be slaves of the "manufacturing spirit" and "the calculating understanding."[2] Such influences, he charged, were quickly dissolving the nation's "moral cement" or "moral basis" which had been held together by its traditional "habits and prejudices."[3] The later honors that he would accumulate – an honorary degree from Oxford in 1839 and the Poet Laureateship in 1843 – further proved that

Wordsworth had become nothing less than a national icon of social conformity. Or at least it seemed that way to conservatives such as John Keble, one of the leading forces behind the Oxford Movement, who declared that the poet's work had long provided the very "moral basis" and "cement" of which Wordsworth spoke. Those readers could turn to him, Keble said in his Crewian Oration at Oxford, "who sincerely desire to understand and feel that secret harmonious intimacy which exists between honourable Poverty, and the severer Muses, sublime Philosophy, yea, even our most holy Religion."[4]

Wordsworth's needling questions to Scott, then, might seem to have an obvious answer. But maybe they seem a bit less obvious when we look back upon the teasing ambiguity of the questions themselves. What kind of "feeling" is Wordsworth talking about? What kind of "value"? How would a landscape reveal a "reverence of the English character": is "character" in the landscape, or is it in the person who views it? Does "reverence of" mean "reverence *within*," or "reverence *for*"? What we begin to discover in the letter is that Wordsworth emphasizes the need for "feeling," for "reverence," and for "value," – analogous terms that help to charge a public with the duty to adhere to a prescribed "character." But the precise *content* of that character – how it might be described in terms of specific beliefs or dispositions – is very far from clear. The point I wish to make at the outset is not that the letter is simply flawed in its lack of psychological detail. My point is that the letter assumes a strategic position in relation to belief (as a source of feeling, reverence, and value): a position defined, at least in part, by an ultimately revealing obscurity.

To put the matter another way, I want to suggest that the indecision on the subject of prejudicial belief is the result of a certain kind of decision. This is a decision – a decision about indecision – visible even in Wordsworth's most eloquent poetic defenses of the established Anglican Church as the nation's "moral basis." In this chapter, I want to develop a contrast between the insistent secular logic of the national tale – a genre that honors and articulates local beliefs without necessarily adopting any of them – and Wordsworth's more overt support of the Anglican establishment. Here, we will see how Wordsworth confirms the importance that Coleridge attached to the church in British national life. But we will also see that, like Coleridge, Wordsworth understood the church less as a body of beliefs than as an accommodation and articulation of vastly dissimilar orientations; and thus his work does not so much oppose Edgeworth's as complement it. For Wordsworth, that is, the power of establishment consists in its seemingly endless capacity for accommodation, and this power takes poetic shape as a church so infinitely capacious that it is ultimately indistinguishable – or barely distinguishable – from nature itself. While Coleridge imagines the church as organic – a structuring of all structures – Wordsworth literalizes or empiricizes that organicism to make the most natural religion into an instance of national religion.

My inquiry begins with *The Excursion*, the notorious poem in which the defense of the establishment made it a bible for nineteenth-century Anglicans and mere bombast for less sympathetic readers in Wordsworth's day and in our own. I will argue that this poem, while in one sense a defense of religious establishment, nevertheless imagines a specific *kind* of establishment that is not as conventional as either the work's supporters or detractors have portrayed it to be. Indeed, *The Excursion* would be more accurately understood as a poetic reconstitution of religious establishment and the social body shaped and maintained by it. Religious establishment is less significant for enforcing doctrinal conformity than for organizing the movements of national and imperial populations in the absence of that conformity. Rather than eliminating dissent, the national church absorbs, encloses, and directs it; as a result, the poem's culminating moments of "communion" or spiritual "renovation" are best described as *social* rather than spiritual.[5] The fitful spiritual odyssey of *The Excursion*'s recalcitrant skeptic known as "the Solitary" – while continually providing occasions for him to register his dissent from conventional religious beliefs – yields the inescapable truth that even dissent from those beliefs borrows its force from the auspices of Britain's church-guided "powers of civil polity" (9.415).

Reading *The Excursion* this way will lead us to look both backwards and forwards in Wordsworth's career to see something new in his poetic interest in ecclesiastical institutions generally and Britain's national church in particular. The reading I put forward of *The Excursion*'s defense of establishment, a defense that is actually a redescription of its aims, will help us to read Wordsworth's earlier dissent from the social authority of the church in a way that revises familiar accounts of that dissent. The explicit critique of established religion in book 3 of *The Prelude* (which provides one of my central examples) displays sympathies with the counter-institutional arguments of religious dissenters at Cambridge and beyond. But book 3 also envisions an *institutional placement* for dissent in a hypothetical "sanctuary for our country's youth."[6] This is a hypothetical establishment, in other words, that serves as the very condition for Wordsworth's dissent from the conventional practices and power structures of the Anglican church. What is merely a presumed establishment in this part of *The Prelude* becomes the more explicit and visible subject matter of Wordsworth's later additions to the poem in book 6, just as it is the subject matter of *The Excursion*. I end this chapter by briefly looking ahead to Wordsworth's later defenses of the church in *The Ecclesiastical Sonnets* and other later poems: works that continue to defend establishment, but with a paradoxical representational strategy that helps to secure an increasingly forceful alliance between religious establishment and poetry. The church, although visible, is now diffused in the landscape. Consigning the church's physical structure to near extinction is, curiously, Wordsworth's final statement on its power rather than its weakness. It is as pervasive as the ground on which he stands; like poetry itself – as Wordsworth would have us see it – it is the most basic condition of social life.

The claims that I make reassess the importance of Wordsworth's associations, later in his life, with the Oxford or Tractarian Movement – a movement primarily known for its opposition to the "fashionable liberality" and latitudinarian tendencies in the Anglican church.[7] Wordsworth did indeed cultivate relations with some of the leading figures in this movement, and Stephen Gill has discussed the great extent to which the likes of Frederick William Faber became influential admirers of the poet's work. It was reportedly at his urging that Wordsworth added poems to the *Ecclesiastical Sonnets* "in order," Faber wrote, "to do more justice to the Papal Church for the services which she actually did render to Christianity and humanity in the middle ages."[8] Beyond any direct influence, figures in the movement such as Keble (whom Faber introduced to Wordsworth) continually claimed Wordsworth as an ally in their causes. Newman, who would eventually convert to Catholicism, credited the poet with inducing the "great progress of the religious mind of our church to something deeper and purer than satisfied the last century."[9]

The argument that I pursue in this chapter, however, suggests that Wordsworth's connections with the Oxford Movement – connections that were both the product of his efforts and the efforts of others – might not provide the most reliable way to describe his poetic vision of Britain's religious establishment. My method is not to retouch the biographical or historical record by clarifying Wordsworth's actual religious sympathies. Instead, I wish to give an account of how Wordsworth's poetry treats religious sympathy itself: an aim that leads me to draw into question not only the claims about Wordsworth and the Oxford Movement but the broader critical tendency (especially amongst critics in the late twentieth century) to evaluate the meaning of his poetry in terms of its relation to some comprehensive political or religious doctrine – either radical or conservative.

This tendency has frequently emerged as a rebuttal to the kind of view that Matthew Arnold adopted in his efforts to construct an opposition between religious and political doctrine and Wordsworth's great poetry. The very reasoning behind the Tractarian enthusiasm for Wordsworth led Arnold to issue his enduring, perenially cited judgments on the poet's later work, which he dubbed the "inferior work" or "obstructio[n]" that followed his "golden prime."[10] We can still hear echoes of this view in Harold Bloom's criticism of the late Wordsworth's "dogma" and "dogmatic orthodoxy," leading to a poetic "decline" vividly described as "the heavy frost that encrusted a spirit endowed by Nature with a vitality nearly the equal of Blake's."[11] The more general claim supporting this aesthetic critique – that Wordsworth brings his later poetry into the service of a system of ideas that is not uniquely or naturally his own – has outlived the more narrow practice of aesthetic evaluation in order to inform a whole range of oppositions between private and public, the poetry of the individual mind and the poetry of religious or political interests. M. H. Abrams takes the poetry of *The Prelude* and the "Prospectus" to *The Recluse* to be a "secularized form of devotional experience," an internalization and privatization of religion that allows the poet's mind to take over "the prerogatives of deity," while Wordsworth's later poetry effectively reverses these priorities.[12] His later writing moves – in Kenneth Johnston's formulation – "from a naturalistic, individualistic view of imagination to a social, institutional one."[13]

There are at least two significant ways in which both deconstructive and historicist critics have tended to respond to the opposition between these two Wordsworths (private poet and public dogmatist), both perspectives aiming to demystify what they regard as the overtly humanist pieties on which the opposition seems to rest. In one particularly influential account, Paul de Man shows how the kind of Wordsworthian humanism championed by Arnold depends upon a species of linguistic mystification at least as potent as any religion. The transcendent purposes of Wordsworth's poetry are merely "evasions" of the disarticulating power of "sheer language." "The work of Wordsworth is moral or religious," de Man concludes, "only on the level of a surface which it prohibits us from finding."[14] For many historicist critics, the moral or religious ground of poetry may be as illusory as de Man suggests, but such an illusion can be cleared away by appealing to a less mystified political or religious viewpoint that the poet either masks or more openly expresses. In Marjorie Levinson's account of "Tintern Abbey," for example (a reading whose vocabulary is particularly rich for my purposes here), the "doctrinal dimension" of the poem reveals itself as a Protestantizing privilege of "private, spontaneous worship" that amounts to a "suppression of the social."[15] Thomas Pfau, responding to Levinson's reading and related versions of it, clarifies this "doctrinal dimension" of Wordsworth's poetry as a contribution to a discourse of taste typical of middle-class radicals anxious to assert social authority and cultural competence.[16] Pfau sharpens the new historical picture by reinterpreting "suppression" as self-conscious positioning, but his account competes with a number of other refined attempts to locate Wordsworth's poetry within a range of precise political or religious standpoints. To James Chandler, Wordsworth is a Burkean Whig; to Robert Griffin, he is – even early in life – a High-Church Tory (a position that, as Peter Manning shows, led to discomfiting contradictions); to Richard Brantley and Robert Ryan, he is an advocate of a more "humane" low church Anglicanism.[17]

Obviously I am compressing these viewpoints considerably, but my aim is to respond to the general impulse in recent criticism to counter the apparent mystifications of Arnoldian humanism by working in one of two directions: either understanding Wordsworth's poetry as the site of an utterly inaccessible consciousness occluded by the formal operations of language, or understanding it as a mystified claim to human community beyond which can be located deeper class-based or political affiliations. Although both critical directions may seem to apply considerable pressure to Wordsworth's transcendent humanism, there is still a surprising result: for they confirm the assumptions of humanist accounts in a more covert way by viewing poetry as either the denial (in deconstruction) or confirmation (in historicism) of a real, affective human community. What I will be arguing throughout this chapter is that Wordsworth's writing cannot, in fact, be understood entirely in terms of its alliance or lack of alliance with narrowly defined beliefs or interests. This is because his writing takes a somewhat wider view of what personal orientations *mean* in the context of British public institutions. Wordsworth's endorsement of the Anglican church is not a dogmatic attempt to exclude or endorse specific beliefs – whether radical or conservative; it is instead an attempt to imagine a new way for adherents of contending doctrines to be socialized in relation to each other. Thus even in his latest and most fervent embrace of established religion, Wordsworth endorses the church as a possibility for relentless ordering, an institutional omnipresence that would give a verbal shape and extend its social purview to those who previously seemed furthest from the reaches of traditional ecclesiastial authority.

PLACING BELIEF IN *THE EXCURSION*

To account for Wordsworth's strategies is to investigate a way of thinking about belief that permeates virtually every statement he makes about religion in his letters and prose works. Even when he talks with the greatest openness about the value of Anglican orthodoxy, it is difficult for him to talk about that value as a set of coherent doctrines that might serve as the occasion for regulation or exclusion. It may be true that his account of the Anglican church appears to agree with Edmund Burke's when he claims that the religious establishment is "a fundamental part of our constitution," because it is "the most effectual and main support of religious toleration."[18] There are, however, crucial distinctions to be made that should make us suspicious of Chandler's attempts to make Burke and Wordsworth look the same.[19] In Burke's account, the Protestant church is tolerant because of Protestant*ism*'s tolerant set of specific beliefs and prejudices that are valid only because they are embedded in traditions that predate personal memory. Such prejudices – while they may provide the basis for tolerance – also require a thoroughly problematic level of conformity, since they are the basis of a collective psychology that continually needs to ratify itself by adhering to a collective psychology in the national past.[20]

Wordsworth's account is somewhat different in its reluctance to see establishment as an institution characterized by any clearly defined body of beliefs or prejudices, showing us how the admiring lines on Burke's defense of "social ties / Endeared by Custom" (7.527–28) is more ambivalent than the celebrated lines added to *The Prelude* in 1832 might suggest. While his sister Dorothy announces to a friend that the Wordsworths have become "regular churchgoers" by 1807, William grumbles in a letter to Sir George Beaumont about a "very injudicious" village parson whose sermons unleash abuse (which Wordsworth comically imitates) on the "hadversaries to Christianity and Henemies of the Gospel.'"[21] As a regular communicant, it seems, he cannot understand himself – or others – as part of a traditional model of Anglican communion. Although Wordsworth's extensive note on the Reverend Robert Walker in his *Sonnets on the River Duddon* (1820) does indeed describe the purity of the clergyman's "moral precepts," he declines even here to specify what they are. Instead, he praises Walker's "management" of daily "affairs" and ceaseless "industry" – praise that echoes the lines on Walker in *The Excursion* (7.310–39).[22] Elsewhere, he considers education to be "for the honour of God," but a school should nevertheless do everything it can to avoid "subtle distinctions in points of doctrine, and . . . facts in scripture history."[23] The church, in order to accommodate "the wants of a shifting and still-increasing population," needs to keep "clear of intolerance and injustice" (*WPr* III:256). For Burke, the church is a "wise architect" for the state: a superintending consciousness that needs to replicate its beliefs through the legitimating mechanisms of oaths and tests. For Wordsworth, the church ends up looking less like an architect than like architecture itself: not a body of beliefs but a body that gives structure to beliefs, whatever they might be.[24]

Perhaps this last formulation brings us somewhat closer to the terms in which Wordsworth introduced his project of *The Recluse* in his preface to *The Excursion* in 1814. The preface provides a celebrated "allusion" to the whole of his large-scale poetic project (the never-finished *Recluse* of which *The Excursion* was a part) as a "gothic church."[25] The allusion certainly shows just how much Wordsworth might have been thinking about the relation between poems and churches (following in the tradition of George Herbert, also an inspiration for the *Ecclesiastical Sonnets*); but what we cannot help noticing about the allusion is the significance of the church not as a place for a specific kind of worship but as a set of interrelated architectural elements.[26] He likens, for instance, the "biographical" or "preparatory" poem now known as *The Prelude* to an "antechapel," other parts of the work to the "body" of the church, and still others to "little cells, oratories, and sepulchral recesses." *The Recluse* as a whole, then, looks like a church because the structure creates a sense of inherence: the opportunity to regard those parts in a new context that lends them the sense of being "properly arranged."[27]

While it may not be possible to see the preface to the poem as a key to *The Excursion* itself, it at least emphasizes a grammar of spatial relationships that is crucial in a work where there is no part of the British empire that does not appear to count as one of the religious establishment's far-flung cells, oratories, or sepulchral recesses. In fact, the Church of England, as *The Excursion* imagines it, is nothing other than the mappable totality of British dominions; it is less an emblem of uniformity than an ensemble of visible and coordinated social movements. The title begins to make this apparent at the most general level. "Excursion" resonates with military associations (an "issuing forth" of soldiers for obtaining territory) and thus with the organizational operations of a state. But the term also coincides and creates a productive tension with the impulse towards *excursus* or digression ("a progression beyond fixed limits," "a deviation from custom, rule, or propriety").[28] The logic of the title's oscillation between order and digression, furthermore, finds its way into the sweep of nine books of poetry that are both occasions for religious and moral argument (what Wordsworth calls in the preface the "dramatic" mode of the work) and *locations* of argument that organize or frame those dramatic encounters within a scheme of geographical relations. Belief, that is, becomes subjected to a spatial rule with very much the same kind of cartographic rigor that Franco Moretti ascribes more exclusively to the development of the nineteenth-century novel.[29] The "haunts" of the Wanderer and the Solitary tie spirit to space, states of mind to the grammar of geography: a grammar emphasized by threading these haunts of the poem together as we move from the local "moorland" of book 1 to the "Imperial Realm" of book 9. We can easily see why Wordsworth was as interested in the topic of William Pasley's *Essay on the Military Policy and Institutions of the British Empire* (1811) – also read and admired by the Edgeworths – as he was in religion, regarding the "labours of the statesman" to be similar to those of "a mighty Poet when he is determining the proportions and march of a Poem."[30]

This general account only begins to suggest to us something unusual about the way that the poem constructs the role of the church in imperial Britain. A brief synopsis helps us to see still more. *The Excursion* begins with a meeting between two figures, the Poet or "Author" (the narrator of the entire poem) and the "Wanderer," in book 1, where the Wanderer tells the poet the tale of Margaret and Robert (the revised form of the unpublished *Ruined Cottage*). In book 2, the Wanderer and the Poet encounter the "Solitary," who – after once pursuing the twinned causes of "Christ and civil liberty" with revolutionary "zeal" – has "forfeited all hope in human nature" now that the "glory of the times" has "fad[ed] away" (2.227–315). The challenge of the rest of the poem is to correct his "despondency" (as the title to book 4 calls it) or "the golden fruit / Of self-esteem" (as the Solitary himself calls it [2.489]). With the aid of the "Pastor," the Solitary is ushered towards a tentative "renovation" within the social act of "communion" in the ninth and final book. The degree to which this communion has ministered to his "enfeebled Power," his "wounded spirit," and "erring notions" is left to the author's "future labours" (9.783–96). There were, of course, no future labours on the subject of the Solitary.

That the Solitary is led towards a spiritual communion that is only tentative or unachieved indicates two very significant and seemingly incompatible directions in the poem. In one respect, *The Excursion* could be understood as the narrative of the Solitary's interrupted conversion to the normative spiritual values of the community. The Solitary's biography, sketched by the Wanderer for the Poet in book 2, plays out as the tale of broken social bonds based upon faith in God, family, and country: the Wanderer "trace[s] the change" of how the Solitary gave up his service as "Chaplain to a military troop / Cheered by the Highland bagpipe" (2.175–6), and how he "broke faith" with the ancestral bonds of community (2.246–48) to become "dissevered from mankind" (2.732). The Poet's own telling of the Solitary's further progress (through the tutelage of the Wanderer and the Pastor) would likewise appear to be a reverse mirror-image of that change, a restoration of broken faith. The end of the poem looks forward to future accounts of that process, the process through which "erring notions were reformed" (9.790).

As a whole, then, the poem raises a question that Geoffrey Hartman summarizes as follows: can the Solitary's mind be restored to health? And if *The Excursion* is finally unable to answer the question, it at least affirms the logic that makes it seem like a valid question in the first place. For Hartman, the affirmation of spiritual growth and the halt that Wordsworth puts to it may be evidence of the author's own laudable skepticism: "Wordsworth is honest enough not to resolve the question."[31] But if Wordsworth leaves the Solitary's spiritual reformation open to question, he does not cast as much suspicion on the poem's locus of spiritual authority bent on reforming him. Not only a poem about lost and (potentially) recovered faith, this is – according to many of its readers – a poem about the social role of faith within a larger community that demands conformity to a certain *kind* of faith. This second dimension is most certainly what led to those opinions of *The Excursion* that have tended to be more quotable than the poem itself: Byron's claim that "*The Excursion*" was "writ in a manner which is my aversion," Jeffrey's complaints about the work's "tissue of moral and devotional ravings," or Hazlitt's charge (speaking of the Wanderer and presumably of Wordsworth himself) that "we are talked to death by an arrogant old proser and buried in a heap of the most perilous stuff and the most dusty philosophy."[32] It is this dimension of the work, moreover, that prompts Hartman to complain about its divided aims: "the poem, instead of keeping to the dilemma of the Solitary, becomes on occasion a defense of the Established Church."[33] If Hartman essentially suggests that Wordsworth's "honest" irresolution about faith is betrayed by a more *dis*honest devotion to Anglican orthodoxy, more recent critics have developed this account into still sharper insights into Wordsworth's ideology. To Alan Richardson, the poem endorses a "reactionary and hegemonic language" pressed into the service of "disciplinary" and "nationalistic" social strategies; to Celeste Langan, the poem exposes the ideological contradictions within those strategies, for the Solitary is a "defaulted citizen" unable to conform to the spiritual "cure" exacted by the Wanderer, Poet, and Pastor.[34]

The advantage of these recent accounts, to be sure, is that they see Wordsworth's imagined institution of the church not merely as an aesthetic flaw but as a focus of substantial and urgent creative energy. By doing so, however, they represent the church as an agent of conformity in terms that are far more extreme – and less problematic and interesting – than Wordsworth's own. The Solitary is not merely subjected to the process of spiritual renovation for the purposes of achieving an oppressive or "reactionary" uniformity; he is – and we are – gradually brought to an understanding of how he was already renovated, already a participant in the community that he had apparently resisted. *The Excursion* thus depicts the movement from solitude to community as a movement that does not involve a change in consciousness – as required by a church that demands religious conversion – as much as it involves a redescription of consciousness within a pattern of social affiliation that treats disagreement as a kind of agreement, dissent from community as a kind of community in itself.

It would hardly be worth arguing, from this perspective, that *The Excursion* is anything but a defense of established religion; indeed, part of what I want to contend is that we must instead recognize the pervasiveness of that institution throughout the poem as the very breath of social life. This is why the church so frequently becomes the subject of extravagant encomium in this poem, and – although such passages have not won the hearts of today's readers – neither their frequency nor their specific characteristics should go unnoticed. Book 5, for instance, spares no eloquence in its praise of the "sacred pile" of the Pastor's church, which inspires the Poet with "a great coolness ... that seemed to strike / The heart, in concert with that temperate awe / And natural reverence which the place inspired" (5.141–44). The Poet's "Address" to the established church in book 6, moreover, speaks of how "English hearts" on "swelling hills" and "spacious plains" can

> perceive
> What in those holy structures ye possess
> Of ornamental interest, and the charm
> Of pious sentiment diffused afar,
> And human charity, and social love. (6.125–29)

These descriptions of churches, in fact, are more unusual and interesting than they might initially seem to those who wish to see poetry about churches as inherently conservative or narrowly ideological. Observing the "sacred pile" makes the Poet dissolve into the "coolness" of air (taking inspiration so literally that it looks like nothing other than wind); "temperate awe" similarly ambiguates the boundary between the speaker's attitude and the surrounding climate. In the following quotation, "pious sentiment" is "diffused" as if sentiment were on the verge of becoming less a quality of mind than a feature of landscape or pattern of weather. The praise for the church, these passages suggest, does not amount to an attempt to secure any articles of faith: belief is inspired by the view of a church, but both structure and state of mind dissolve in landscape and atmosphere.

These and other passages convinced many of Wordsworth's contemporaries – whose responses differed significantly from those of Byron, Jeffrey, or Hazlitt – that *The Excursion*'s defense of establishment was not in any clear sense the defense of religion that they expected it to be. Coleridge, who had many years earlier judged Wordsworth to be "at least, a *Semi*-atheist," wrote to Wordsworth that the poem had failed to achieve a "manifest scheme of redemption."[35] Evangelical readers criticized Wordsworth's "failure to emphasize the distinctive doctrines of a saving faith."[36] And in his *Recreations of Christopher North*, collected from a series of articles published in *Blackwood's*, John Wilson wrote disapprovingly of *The Excursion* as an example of sacred poetry, for it avoids all mention of "Christian Revelation" and "Christian Faith": the poem "Speaks nobly of cathedrals, and ministers, and so forth, reverendly adorning the land" yet there is no "religion preached in those cathedrals and ministers, and chanted in prayer to the pealing organ . . . "[37]

I will return, somewhat later in this chapter, to *The Excursion*'s puzzling images of churches – and others like them that form a dominant topos in the later work – in order to show why (for Wordsworth) they make a great deal of sense. For the ambiguity regarding where the lines of belief and the institutional organization of belief begin and end, in fact, constitutes an important aspect of Wordsworth's account of the ecclesiastical institution itself. But we can approach these images (and the institution they purportedly celebrate) more effectively if we return – first by looking more closely at the figure of the Solitary – to the problem in *The Excursion* that has continually troubled or intrigued critics of the poem. Why is it a work that both praises the established church, while also taking an equal (if not greater) interest in a refusal, or inability, of individuals (such as the Solitary) to conform? We will see that the question can be addressed by recognizing how the poem depicts the reform of dissenting figures not as a reform of dissent itself but a re-formed *relationship* between dissent and religious establishment.

THE DILEMMA OF THE SOLITARY AND THE SOCIABILITY OF DISSENT

Perhaps the most energetic opposition to conventional notions of religious establishment in *The Excursion* comes from the smugly skeptical Solitary himself: for him, religion is both a cause and an emblem of false conformity in social life. The forced conformity to rituals, oaths, and other conventional observances makes public life into a kind of theater where the officially sanctified representation of persons serves only as the deceptive covering for more sinister interests. In one of his most extended articulations of this position (which could be seen as a sardonic rewriting of the "blessed Babe" passage from *The Prelude*, in which the child, "gather[ing] passion from his mother's eye," is made one with Nature's "gravitation" and "filial bond" [2.237–80]), the Solitary views the theater of society as so thoroughly encompassing that it coincides with birth:

> Mark the babe
> Not long accustomed to this breathing world;
> One that hath barely learned to shape a smile,
> Though yet irrational of soul, to grasp
> With tiny finger – to let fall a tear;
> And, as the heavy cloud of sleep dissolves,
> To stretch his limbs, bemocking, as might seem,
> The outward functions of intelligent man;
> A grave proficient in amusive feats
> Of puppetry, that from the lap declare
> His expectations, and announce his claims
> To that inheritance which millions rue
> That they were ever born to!   (5.261–73)

In the Solitary's reading, the infant babe does not merely learn how to think and act; he learns how to cover up his thoughts through dissimulation. By asserting a necessary disjunction between thinking and doing, between intention (the child's expectations) and action (his declaration or announcement), the Solitary aims to show that a child's social pedagogy consists of learning to treat actions as objects to be manipulated by his intentions: socialization is nothing other than hypocrisy.

The general commentary on the falsity of social interaction quickly moves into the more specific indictment of religious ritual that gives falsehood its social legitimacy. The Solitary thus continues with this account of the infant's baptism:

> In due time
> A day of solemn ceremonial comes;
> When they, who for this Minor hold in trust
> Rights that transcend the loftiest heritage
> Of mere humanity, present their Charge,
> For this occasion daintily adorned,
> At the baptismal font. And when the pure
> And consecrating element hath cleansed
> The original stain, the child is there received
> Into the second ark, Christ's church, with trust
> That he, from wrath redeemed, therein shall float
> Over the billows of this troublesome world
> To the fair land of everlasting life.   (5.273–85)

The "ceremonial" (colored by the commentary that preceded it) is a puppet-like manipulation of the child that can only confirm a child's "mockery" of society's thoroughly empty "outward functions": functions that pompously presume to have "cleansed" the infant of an "original stain" that is itself a product of empty and hypocritical religious discourse. This is a ritual made by humans, the Solitary shows, who falsely imagine that they can transcend humanity itself. It is only with a degree of irony, then, that "trust" is invoked as a way of describing the ceremonies of an essentially hypocritical institution; the "redemption" to be achieved is likewise a salvation from heavenly wrath that only thinly disguises the earthly wrath of humans who manipulate ceremony to their advantage. The Solitary continues by describing how this institution sponsors a whole language of social interaction that depends upon dissimulation:

> Corrupt affections, covetous desires,
> Are all renounced; high as the thought of man
> Can carry virtue, virtue is professed;
> A dedication made, a promise given
> For due provision to control and guide,
> And unremitting progress to ensure
> In holiness and truth.   (5.286–92)

The Solitary's insight consists in his ability to observe the sheer hypocrisy of renouncing, by way of a "profession" or "promise," corrupt affections and covetous desires in advance of even having them. By pointing out the church's own structure of false profession, false dedication, false promise – the passive constructions ("are . . . renounced," "is professed," and so on) making the performance seem particularly hollow – the Solitary gives a kind of explanation for his breaking faith with society. Society's own faith is already broken with itself.

In the critique of false conformity, we hear the voices of Godwin, Frend, or Dyer (among others), figures I mentioned in chapter 1 with whom Wordsworth was associated in the 1790s.[38] And thus the importance of the Solitary's position on church ritual derives not only from the force of its own logic – a logic that it shares with the similar opposition to ritual in the "Immortality" Ode – but also from its recognizable affiliation with the discourse of Protestant Dissent: a discourse that (as the Wanderer informs the poet) devoted itself to "The cause of Christ and civil liberty, / As one, and moving to one glorious end" (2.221–22). What, then, is the larger poetic purpose of the Solitary's powerful rejection of established religion: a position that once may have seemed attractive to Wordsworth himself – according to Nicholas Roe's account of the poet's relations with these radical Dissenters – at a certain point in his career?[39]

Perhaps, in keeping with some of the more comprehensive accounts of the poem by William Galperin, Alison Hickey, and Celeste Langan, we could see the Solitary's presence as a constant reminder of the contradictions and contingencies lurking beneath the poem's attempt to provide a spiritual "therapy" that repeatedly falls short of actual human need.[40] Rather than see the Solitary as a radically destabilizing force in the poem, though – as a herald of a "failure of a . . . romantic or secularized imagination," as Galperin puts it[41] – I would suggest that this figure occupies a central position in the context of Wordsworth's efforts to redefine an establishment with more inclusive and expansive contours. Surely there is no better place to begin observing this logic than the Solitary's own monologue that I cited above. What is in fact most remarkable about this passage is that the Solitary's account of the infant babe exerts a disturbing pressure on the very logic of social dissimulation that he wishes to produce. While the notion of dissimulation tends to rely upon a disjunction between belief and the public declaration of belief, the passage actually blurs such a disjunction precisely because the infant, "irrational of soul," has a consciousness that is only barely locatable – or perhaps not locatable at all. The Solitary, then, may make a particularly strong case from the point of view of the infant's mental reservation: the infant's private consciousness either mocks or dissimulates from a sanctified region of intentionality. But the passage also troubles that account by suggesting that the privacy of this consciousness emerges as the effect of the very social discourse – emblematized and supported by the church – that poses as the target of the Solitary's critique. Rather than showing the child as an opponent of this discourse, the Solitary's argument more convincingly, albeit indirectly, implies that the institutions of society provide a far more vital and indispensable source of self-description. Despite his opposition to ritual, the Solitary inadvertently exalts it as the inheritance that "millions rue that they were ever born to": the opportunity and burden that is social discourse itself.

What I am approaching here might have some relation to Pierre Bourdieu's account of ritual as an instance of *doxa*: a uniform exchange that marks and facilitates relations between the members of a "habitus." Bourdieu might help us to see how Wordsworth imagines ritual as the "medium between the group and itself," for it "*signifies* to someone what his identity is, but in a way that both expresses it to him and imposes it on him by expressing it in front of everyone." But if we can see how Bourdieu's account of the habitus eventually rests upon the conviction that "the belief of everyone, which pre-exists ritual, is the condition for the effectiveness of ritual," we can also see that Wordsworth's version of established religion's social and discursive function is related but also quite different.[42] For the passage essentially suggests that ritual, far from requiring specific beliefs, might be of value precisely because it enables social contact in the absence of shared belief.

This point comes across in a more extended episode when we first encounter the Solitary in book 2, in which the Solitary's position of dissent and resistance seems conspicuously dependent upon the social institution from which he supposedly removes himself. The Wanderer leads the Poet to the haunt of the Solitary, the "lonely and lost" figure residing in the "urn-like" vale. After the Poet hears the "brief communication" of the Solitary's biography rehearsed by the Wanderer (2.163–315), the two hear a "funeral dirge" sung by a "band" of "rustic persons" (2.386–87) which they assume to be a dirge for the Solitary himself. Their surmise seems to be confirmed when they find a bedraggled "Novel of Voltaire, / His famous Optimist" (2.443–44) buried, "left and forgotten" (2.425), amid the "baby-houses" – lending "help to raise / One of those petty structures" (2.435–46) – that have been built by children in a "cool recess" (2.415). But suddenly the very subject of their conversation appears:

"Behold the man whom he [the Wanderer] had fancied dead!" (2.497).

The sequence of events in this scene reflects back in surprising ways on the shape of the Solitary's biography, with its wayward path from virtuous conformity to ill-spirited skepticism that now stands in need of moral and religious restoration. What characterizes the shape of the Solitary's biography – his breaking of social contract – is contradicted by this portion of the poem, where it is in fact suggested that the Solitary never lost society to begin with. Society cannot be lost because it cannot be found: it enables its own foundations. The Solitary, says the Wanderer, is one whom "no depth / Of privacy is deep enough to hide" (2.471–72): a comment that expresses both the Solitary's desire to avoid society as well as the utter impossibility of achieving that desire. The repeated lesson that we learn from this episode is simply that there is no meaning for a state of mind – there is, in fact, no existence – that lies outside the network of social relations that is overseen and also constituted by ecclesiastical guidance. The Solitary is, first of all, not only "lonesome and lost" (2.333) but also a locatable figure: the characters in the poem collectively divert the Solitary from his own "nook" and thus from his own private belief – a "nook / That seemed for self-examination made; / Or, for confession, in the sinner's need, / Hidden from all men's view" (3.471–74). Although hidden from view, his "sweet Recess" (2.349) in the "urn-like vale," like a "sepulchral recess" in Wordsworth's description of the Gothic church in the preface to the poem, seems in its very seclusion to be an extension of church architecture. And when the Wanderer and Poet in book 2 mistakenly believe that the Solitary himself is dead, the mistake actually operates as a correction of the Solitary's deluded attempt to live outside establishment as a source of social order. The funeral ritual – which is actually preceded in book 2 by an "annual wake" accompanied by a "tabor and pipe" (2.121) – provides an occasion for the Solitary to be reminded of pervasive and inescapable communal practices: practices that convey the deeply social nature of the Solitary's separation from community.[43]

The lesson is made in another way in the same episode when we hear about how the children in the vale have constructed their "baby-houses" to incorporate Voltaire's *Candide* – dismissed by the Wanderer as "the dull product of a scoffer's pen, / Impure conceits discharging from a heart / Hardened by impious pride" (2.484–86). Calling attention to the children's constructions as "petty structures" – the Poet's words – may be Wordsworth's way of satirizing Voltaire, whose own structure of thinking seems by analogy to look conspicuously underdeveloped, childlike, or "petty." But we need not give up that observation entirely in order also to see how important the children are for incorporating the Solitary's reading material – just like the Solitary himself – into their society. The book by the "laughing Sage of France" – who is elsewhere taken to task for his "ridicule" of "confiding faith" (4.996,1006–9) – is "left and forgotten" like its owner. But the book also finds a new place in the children's miniature society: a society that easily accommodates dissent by making it seem like an integral part of social order. Voltaire's book has been "aptly disposed" within their architectural structures – "disposed" suggesting how the children have not merely thrown it out but placed it and reoriented it – along with "party-coloured earthenware" (dishes and pots that are not only multicolored but hint at divided political "party" [2.434–35]). And the children continue to act throughout this book as reminders of a social context that the Solitary has never escaped. When he finally appears before the Wanderer and the Poet, they find him, oddly, performing the functions of a chaplain, a counsellor to the children of the valley whose "task" it is to "comfort" them (2.506–511, 531–2). He thus fulfills the social role (as a chaplain to the regiment) that he had ostensibly refused.

RELIGION AS SOCIETY, SOCIETY AS RELIGION: FROM "THE WANDERER" TO THE "AUTHENTIC EPITAPHS"

The point of book 2, then, is not merely to characterize the Solitary as solitary: a figure who has broken society's "contracted bonds" (2.215). In fact, the more startling assertion to be conveyed here is that those bonds are not "contracted" in any way at all. They are not produced, that is, merely as a result of personal belief or preference that is declared and then withdrawn; the ever-present church establishment looks like a necessary anteriority, the mark of a sociability that insistently precedes itself.[44] The Solitary can even be said by this logic to participate in the rites of the church even when he seemingly refuses them. "Here you stand," the Wanderer tells the Solitary, "Adore, and worship, when you know it not; / Pious beyond the intention of your thought; / Devout above the meaning of your will" (4.1147–50). Religious establishment is less a reflection of collective belief than a social permeation and enclosure of belief – a state of affairs in which "worship" could be constituted in the absence of an individual's intention to worship, in which the constraints on membership in community could be so drastically reduced as to include those of different beliefs, or those who do not believe at all. It should not escape our notice that Wordsworth describes these lines, in a letter to Catherine Clarkson – attempting to explain the poem to Patty Smith, her Unitarian friend – as the Wanderer's effort to "remin[d] the Solitary of such religious feelings as cannot but exist in the minds of those who affect atheism."[45] Wordsworth thus powerfully relegates the question of personal belief or non-belief to what a person may "affect." The Wanderer is essentially affirming that the Solitary can be part of the religious community not by virtue of anyone's attempt to convert him, but by virtue of his inclusion in a pattern of communal actions – the precondition for his having a belief (or having a belief against belief), for making it known to others, and for making it known even to himself.

So far, I have only discussed the position of the Solitary in the poem, but the poet's mobilization of this figure – through which the private is shown to be already public, religious "self-examination" and "confession" already part of secular institutionality – affords considerable insight into the reasoning that informs Wordsworth's inclusion and alteration of an earlier piece of writing, *The Pedlar* of 1798, within the text of book 1 ("The Wanderer"). Both what is retained within the new context of *The Excursion* and what is added and revised in that context are crucial for the observations I want to make; for Wordsworth's adaptation of the biographical narrative of the Pedlar – later to become *The Excursion*'s Wanderer – rewrites earlier poetry by writing an ecclesiastical institution *into* that poetry. Writing the institution into poetry, however, does not eliminate the Wanderer's independence from conventional, orthodox belief; for "The Wanderer" depicts a religious establishment that in fact oversees and secures departures from established – that is, traditional – beliefs.

First, then, we should take note of how *The Pedlar* – identified by Wordsworth himself as semi-autobiographical – presents a view of the Pedlar as a child of nature. Crucial elements from the Pedlar's biography stay intact in *The Excursion*: like the Pedlar, who is "untaught" and "undisciplined," the Wanderer is a "lone Enthusiast" (*P* 261; *E* 1.348) with a "religion" that, in the Poet's words, "seemed . . . / Self-taught, as of a dreamer in the woods; / Who to the model of his own pure heart / Shaped his belief" (*E* 1.409–12).[46] As a child of nature, the Wanderer seeks out the solitude "in caves forlorn, / And 'mid the hollow depths of naked crags" (*P* 49–50; *E* 1.154–55) and other such places that also remind us of the poet's refuges in the first book of *The Prelude*. And the revision likewise works to trace the growth of the Wanderer's "active power" that is supposedly exercized independently of conventional social institutions. He has "small need of books" (*P* 58; *E* 1.163); he is "unwarped / By partial bondage" (*P* 270–71; *E* 1.357–58); after attempting to teach at a school in the adjoining village, the "wanderings of his thought" force him to "resign / A task he was unable to perform" (*P*229–34; *E*1.313–15).[47]

Second, however, we must also take note of how *The Excursion* frames the earlier poetry – and its resistance to conventional institutions – within the new context of religious establishment. In *The Pedlar*, the boy's "thanksgiving to the power / That made him" is rendered simply by "his mind," regardless of its specific "prayer and praise" (111–14). With some revision, Wordsworth incorporates the passage into *The Excursion* in this way: "No thanks he breathed, he proffered no request; / Rapt into still communion that transcends / The imperfect offices of prayer and praise, / His mind was a thanksgiving to the power / That made him; it was blessedness and love" (1.214–18). The changes that Wordsworth makes in the passage might appear to involve combining the words "communion" and "thanksgiving" to provide a more conventional direction to the young Wanderer's thoughts. But it would be more correct to say that the *un*conventionality of the Wanderer's spiritual credentials – the absence of "thanks," "request," or "imperfect offices of prayer and praise" – is itself relocated within the grammar of institutionality, of "communion" and "thanksgiving": an institutionality devoted not merely to religious uniformity but to a social coherence above and beyond uniformity.

Clearly the possibility of giving thanks without thanking (just like the Solitary's worshiping when he does not know it) is a possibility explicable within the domain of theology; that is, the boy's lack of thanks – as opposed to the "imperfect offices of prayer and praise" – can be treated as thanks (thanks that *are* perfect) through nothing other than Grace itself, as Calvin described it in his *Institutes*. But we must also realize that *The Excursion* continually appropriates the Providential perspective – what the Pastor much later in the poem calls "controlling Providence" (6.561) – for an institutional perspective. As if to appropriate Calvin's account of coaction, according to which sin or righteousness is both voluntary and necessary, individual and Providential, the Wanderer's anti-institutionalism is enabled and overseen by establishment itself.[48] The church can thus be described further on in the Pedlar/Wanderer's biography as the persistent, indeed inescapable, guide for the boy's own distance from institutional "bondage":

> The Scottish Church, both on himself and those
> With whom from childhood he grew up, had held
> The strong hand of her purity; and still
> Had watched him with an unrelenting eye.
> This he remembered in his riper age
> With gratitude, and reverential thoughts. (*E* 1.397–402)

Although the passage's privilege of the social and institutional over the natural has led certain commentators such as E. P. Thompson to lament this apparently conservative endorsement of religious orthodoxy, the more pervasive logic that I have been describing suggests that the "strong hand" and "unrelenting eye" of institutional guidance in fact underwrites the youth's freedom from church discipline.[49] As a child, *The Excursion*'s Poet asserts, the Wanderer was a member of the church's social group without knowing it: to use the Wanderer's own idiom, he was pious beyond the intention of his thought, devout above the meaning of his will. By remembering the agency of establishment with "gratitude" and "reverential thoughts," he is not remembering an early devotion to the church. He is instead remembering and revering something far more general: a memory of the coactiveness of individual assertion and institutional guidance.

But what is the function of this guidance, as Wordsworth sees it? Perhaps it is the collection of narratives or "authentic epitaphs" told by the Pastor about his flock in books 6 and 7 of the poem that initially reveals the most about how Wordsworth views the church as a thoroughly vitalizing resource of social definition for individual selves: the church as a point of reference, as Wordsworth puts it in the "Essay on Epitaphs" that appeared in a note attached to book 5, for the "concerns" of the "community of the living and the dead" (*WP*II:56). These narratives of persons, many of whom have died and lie in the churchyard where the Pastor speaks, can be appreciated in *The Excursion* first and foremost as versions of public records – accounts of human movement from birth to death that follow a logic of social inclusion far beyond the level of personal beliefs and private alliances. John Herman Merivale thus described *The Excursion* in *The Monthly Review* as a "poetical parish register."[50] This is not to say that the Pastor takes no notice of beliefs and alliances, for he in fact produces a veritable catalogue of personal virtues and vices. In the tale of unrequited love in book 6, for instance, the "simplicity of mind" with which the young man faces rejection by the "haughty maiden" is "a thing most sacred in the eye of Heaven" (6.178–79); the grave of Ellen is "a hallowed spot of earth / More holy in the sight of God or Man" because of her "religious tenderness of heart" (6.802–03,798). In contrast, the tale of the miser later in book 6 portrays a woman "vexed" by the "two passions" of "unremitting, avaricious thrift" and "a strange thraldom of maternal love" (6.709–10); Wilfred of Armathwaite, a figure described in book 6 whose biography quite clearly resembles the Solitary's, "rose in arms, and, braving / Divine displeasure, broke the marriage vow" (6.1092–93).

But these virtues and vices – if these are even the right terms for what is being described – can sometimes be confusing. Perhaps "an unremitting, avaricious thrift" seems quite obviously to be a sin. Nevertheless, the sin is not "avarice" but "thrift"; we feel the strain that the line makes (a strain felt through unremitting iambs) to force a differentiation between *this* thrift and other, more admirable, examples of thrift (the tale of the Quarryman and his wife, for example, from book 5 [670–837]). How "maternal love" could become a "thraldom" is more puzzling still, and seems only unsteadily partitioned from "a religious tenderness of heart." The point to be gathered from this realization, however, is not that such virtues and vices have no meaning. For even though it may well be true that the Pastor's records fail to offer any satisfying way to contradict the Solitary's suspicions that even the "best might of faith" cannot overcome "want and weakness" (5.360,439), the narratives are less significant for offering imitable or avoidable models of virtue than for exemplifying the breadth of religion's secular social awareness: a region of institutional observation that extends beyond any individual's adherence or non-adherence to virtuous or vicious beliefs.

It might be more accurate, in fact, to say that the Pastor's monologues – rather than cultivating proper moral or religious sentiment – take on the task of tracing or narrating an attenuated relation between belief and its effectiveness in natural or social environments. And it is this region of interdependent personal, social, and natural effects that constitutes, and is constituted by, pastoral observation. These are narratives, after all, that demonstrate how either virtuous or vicious states of mind inadequately empower individuals to submit either nature or other persons to their "mastery" (6.164). The outcome of a moral disposition or personal acquisition – of love (as in the case of the lover), of perseverance (in the case of the miner), of talent (in the story of the Prodigal) – never straightforwardly unfolds as the determination by that disposition or acquisition. Instead, each narrative unfolds as a tale of an impossible moral autonomy, a tale of necessary interdependency that is articulated through the

Pastor's unceasing accounts of how persons are "assisted" – either helped or hindered – by elements in nature or society (6.183). With an attention to how one person's resources (mental, erotic, financial) depend upon other resources – both natural and human – the Pastor articulates a complex network of "elements" that "preserve, and . . . restore" (6.184–5), a complex of afflictions that brings "injury" to the "mortal body" (6.1051–52).

Could it be that *The Excursion* at such moments elaborates precisely what Mitchell Dean has described as a "moral–political space" – in which wealth and poverty are not simply advantages and disadvantages but opportunities for the expanded activities of government to survey and manage populations?[51] Indeed, I think that it is on these terms that we can begin to discern the connection between the Wanderer's tale of Margaret, from book 1 of *The Excursion* ("The Wanderer"), and the "authentic epitaphs." Religion is most in evidence in *The Ruined Cottage* (and its revision) not as a sentimental doctrine that the Wanderer wishes to communicate to the Poet; it is a practice of observing a network of social dependencies – a practice that the poem ceaselessly identifies with a religious establishment's more secularized functions. It may be true, as David Simpson notes, that Wordsworth's revisions to *The Ruined Cottage* for its incorporation into *The Excursion* (especially in lines 1.934–40) emphasize Margaret's Christian fortitude, describing her ability to feel "The unbounded might of prayer" and to find "consolation" from a "soul / Fixed on the Cross."[52] The point I want to make is not that such revisions (and Simpson's comments on them) are unimportant, but that the wider context of *The Excursion* elaborates upon a *social* mission for religion that is not simply identical to spiritual consolation. We could, then, see *The Ruined Cottage* and its later incarnations in terms that differ substantially from Alan Liu's materialist account of the poem, which views it as a "fraudulent account of human poverty" and a "capitalization upon inhumanity."[53] What I have been suggesting is that the network of observed economic relations in the poem are not occlusions of humanity; they are precisely what make human suffering legible. Margaret's home, progressively decaying and opened to external elements, emerges as an object of poetic interest because it is already punctured by a collaborating poetic and social intrusion that accounts for the movement of resources (human and non-human) across the boundaries of the domestic environment. Such an intrusion finds expression in many ways, including a widened sense of family: Margaret treats the Pedlar with "a daughter's welcome"; the Pedlar reports to have "loved her / As my own child" (1.499–500). And this only begins to suggest how the permeable barrier of the household is the precondition for decline – Margaret's "sad reverse" (1.566) – to be rendered in a relentless pattern of economic effects. The Pedlar's narration, a discursive passage aligned with the "public way" (1.40,453) and "public roads" (1.387), thus turns out to be a strategy for constructing the movements or locations of labor, money, and material resources in and out of the household. The home and its garden repeatedly appear as a collection of "border lines," a "threshold," a "cottage window," a "grey line" (1.723,748,825,883) – poetic calibrations registering a ceaseless flow of persons and objects.

Wordsworth clearly identifies the tale of Margaret and the tale of the Solitary himself: Margaret's neglect of domestic duties, for example, parallels the Solitary's similar breaking of faith. But – to extend the argument I have been making – these characters are also identified in another way. Like the Solitary for whom "no depth of privacy is too deep to hide," for whom no breaking of bonds allows him to break from community, Margaret's domestic relationship – with all the moral and religious values attached to that relationship – is woven into a wider set of secular mechanisms of observation that gives suffering a distinctive texture captured in Wordsworth's verse. This treatment of the domestic space continues, moreover, in the Pastor's narratives. For if those narratives do little to exalt or recommend moral or religious beliefs, their true object of interest is in domestic relations that are more than objects of glorification or idealization; they are first and foremost an observed scheme of widely distributed, interdependent harms and benefits. In the story of Ellen, for example – a story explicitly connected by the Poet to the tale of Margaret (6.1060) – Ellen's employment in "domestic service" as a foster-mother reveals domesticity to be a place of competing and possibly defeating obligations, not merely the locus of sentimental value. Her service to the "pair, whose infant she was bound to nurse," is necessary for her domestic livelihood, even while her employers deprive her of "all communion with her own" (6.960–61). The tale represents the pathos of broken communion, while it also exposes the violence and inequality within the communion of the home, a place where "The ungentle mind can easily find means / To impose severe restraints and laws unjust" (6.954–55). This narrative can be connected to the account of Margaret and Robert in book 1, in other words, not just because it tells a tale of shared human suffering designed to strike a chord of sympathy in the listener. The home is also defined by its permeability: its susceptibility to observation from a position that connects the privacy of the domestic space to the "laws" of social space.

POETRY, POPULATIONS, AND THE PROVIDENTIAL STATE

The point that I am making here is that the Pastor's narratives, by equating religious community with an all-encompassing pattern of social interactions, depict religious community as a community that, by constituting the very possibility of social life, has no religious exterior. And this way of formulating the church's role is precisely what makes the poem translate its disposition towards belief into a still more general disposition towards populations. For in *The Excursion*, the need to move people's *beliefs* in one direction or another is subordinated to the need to move – and account for the movements of – *people*. If the earlier books of the poem presume a community beyond doctrinal agreement or disagreement, the following books interpret that insight to authorize the writing of poetry as the writing of populations, and thus confirm the church's capacity for potentially infinite accommodation. The Wanderer, the Solitary, and the Poet thus conduct their movement through the poem in a way that is best described not as a spiritual conversion but as a social one – or, better still, a conversion to society. The progress of the poem is a progress towards an increasing contextualization of its central figures within larger groups of persons that compose the pastoral "domain" (5.549,635; 6.95): a "domain" that enlarges throughout the remainder of the work. This makes book 5 not merely the book where the Pastor appears – the Pastor who holds "spiritual sway" over his people – but the book that moves away from the "spot," the "fixed centre of a troubled world" (5.15–16) towards "Fair dwellings, single, or in social knots" (5.88). Accompanied by the Pastor's discourse of "mild and social cheerfulness" (6.93), the characters in the poem are guided (by the Pastor) in larger groups of people: "singly," in "pairs," and finally a "company." They are progressively shown their relationship to wider patterns of social affiliation: a "neighbourhood," "country," or "society" at large – and finally the British empire (9.107,137).

The centerpiece of the last book of *The Excursion* is the miniature excursion (recalling the "excursion" to Mount Snowdon in book 13 of *The Prelude* [13.10–65]) to a "green hill's side" (*E* 9.570), an "elevated spot" (9.580), from which the company views a sunset: a moment of "unity sublime" (9.608), a "communion of uninjured minds" (9.784), leading to the Pastor's oration (the "vesper service" [9.755]) and the close of the poem. From one perspective, the "unity sublime" towards which this book leads is indeed a scene of idealized spiritual union. As if to foreground the significance of union on these terms, the progress towards it continually draws upon symbolic means to demonstrate the way that the psychologies and interests of particular individuals are combined or "blended" in that union. Each individual's observations, while a unique person's "property" (9.512), become part of a shared "spirit": "One spirit animating old and young" (9.526). And this shared spirit continues to preside over the company's procession to the "elevated spot" where all pause to view the prospect, "admiring quietly" (9.582), while sharing their "discoveries" (9.585). This culminates in the spectacle of the sunset: a vision of "unity sublime" and "prodigal communion" during which "particular interests were effaced / From every mind" (9.589–90).

Now this moment of religious communion actually follows another celebrated passage (one that Wordsworth planned for, but extracted from, *The Prelude*) that seems both to anticipate and trouble it: the "twofold image" of a ram reflected in a "deep pool." Both the ram, with its "imperial front," and the "shadowy counterpart" in the pool, "seemed centre of his own fair world, / Antipodes unconscious of each other, / Yet in partition, with their several spheres, / blended in perfect stillness, to our sight" (9.439–51). This scene, as it is glossed by the Pastor's wife (in manuscript version for *The Prelude*, by the poet himself), shows a perfect image of community – of union that preserves singleness. That community is achieved only through illusion, however – an illusion not only because it is a reflection of something real but because even the ram itself, as part of the "twofold image," has a hallucinatory quality – is testimony to the affecting transience of its potency. "Combinations so serene and bright," she comments, "Cannot be lasting in a world like ours, / Whose highest beauty . . . / Seems but a fleeting sunbeam's gift, whose peace / The sufferance only of a breath of air!" (9.468–73).

This gloss on the ram and its reflected image, insisting as it does on the fragility and instability of social coherence, is hardly suppressed in the poem; in fact, it tends to define, in a rather troubling way, the very nature of communion itself. The Lady's reading of the "twofold image," that is, echoes in the Solitary's grim reflections on the dying fire kindled on the shore of the "fair Isle" where the company has stopped for a "choice repast": the fire, now "deserted," "dying or dead," is an "emblem . . . / Of one day's pleasure, and all mortal joys!" (9.551–55). And if we could hardly expect anything more sanguine from the Solitary, we might be more surprised to find that the Pastor himself does not so much contradict this account of human communion as confirm it. During the communal vision of the sunset in which "particular interests / Were effaced from every mind," the Pastor's address to the "Eternal Spirit" or "universal God" clarifies that this is, indeed, only a "local transitory type / Of thy paternal splendours" (9.614–20). After the close of this address, the Poet offers little to cheer his audience, painting a scene of nearly complete darkness, where "No trace remained / Of those celestial splendours" and even "the star of eve / Was wanting"; the "inferior lights" in the sky are "too faint almost for sight" (9.759–63).

Although Alison Hickey's subtle reading of *The Excursion* points to such passages as confirmations that "solitude, separateness, and particularity are our usual lot"[54], it is nevertheless the case, I would argue, that they have their purpose in the poem's relentless assertion of community formed through the incorporation of the very disharmony that might be presumed to destroy it. For at the same time that book 9 produces an unachieved spiritual coherence, it also asserts a social coherence in the absence of spiritual agreement. Book 9, first of all, continually views individual experience – how persons might deviate from or commune with others – as if it were dependent upon a movement of a group that is larger and more inclusive than any individual's experience. The entire excursion to the "elevated spot" is crucial for asserting this logic, providing one more chance for Wordsworth to reflect upon the poem on the origin and progress of his powers – and to rewrite it as poetry about the experience of a group. When the group, at the suggestion of the Pastor's wife, occupies the "boat" that "lies moored / Under a sheltering tree" (9.425–6), and proceeds towards the "elevated spot," Wordsworth quite clearly calls upon scenes of solitary experience from *The Prelude*: this includes not only the Mount Snowdon episode – as I mentioned above – but also the stolen boat episode from book 1 (*Prelude*, 1.372–426). And *The Excursion* takes every opportunity to make these analogous experiences into experiences with more openly social, and not merely natural, surroundings. The Poet's recollection of youth becomes explicit in *The Excursion* when, taking the oars, he recalls when, "A Youth, I practised this delightful art; / Tossed on the waves alone, or 'mid a crew / Of joyous comrades" (9.486–88). The memory – with its ambiguating "or" that blurs solitude and society, the state of being "alone" and "mid a crew / Of joyous comrades" – may be symptomatic of *The Excursion*'s more pervasive way of writing society into poetry to create the impression that society had been there, or at least could have been there, all along. In the stolen boat episode from *The Prelude*, the young poet goes "alone into a Shepherd's Boat," as if to render the process of self-construction as a departure from society and its laws (*Prelude*, 1.373). But just as Wordsworth writes the poet's "private thoughts" and recollected "image of a mighty mind" from the Mount Snowdon passage as shared "discoveries" in

The Excursion (*E* 13.19,69), he also recasts book 1's "act of stealth and troubled pleasure" (*Prelude*, 1.388–89) in order to make the Pastor into a sign of an all-encompassing institutional guardianship. *The Excursion* rewrites the Shepherd as a Pastor, and the Pastor as a guardian of the boat's movement: his "hand," he says, guiding the "helm" (*E* 9.496). As "the shepherd of his flock" (5.101), the Pastor is not the object of injury but the representative of unrelenting protection.

Such revisions begin to suggest that the anterior social movement of the poem absorbs and directs the spiritual movement of the poem – and it might very well be said that this comes to define the very contours of the national church itself: the church is enlisted on "the wide waters" of empire, in the service of "the will, the instincts, and appointed needs / Of Britain" (9.375–77). Taking on the task of education, for example, the church ensures that "none, / However destitute, be left to droop / By timely culture unsustained" (9.303–5). Wordsworth's support for this "National System of Education" announced in the "argument" for book 9 – and explicitly connected to Andrew Bell's "marvellous facilities" for education in a note to the poem – is support for a "simple engine" for instruction under "an enlightened and conscientious government," capable of "universal application."[55] Even though Bell became closely associated with church schools against Lancaster's more secularized educational plans, we see that Wordsworth praises Bell primarily in agreement with Bell's own description of his school system: rather than a tool for enforcing specific religious doctrines, it would produce "general order and harmony" while encouraging a "social disposition" among its students.[56] The Pastor's defense of the sustaining instructional role of "timely culture" likewise refers less to a uniform ideology than to a culture of cultures; for in each instance, he identifies the church not with the task of conversion to save souls, but with the task of insuring a national and imperial population from suffering incurred by all manner of "obstructions" in the "course" of human life – "such objects as oppress / Our active powers" (9.71,114,130–31). Whereas the pathetic narratives make oppression and obstruction into the occasion for ceaseless observation, the Pastor at this point shows how the very visibility of benefits and harms in those narratives comports with the larger social mission of the church. This is a mission understood as a compensation for the pain and suffering in private life: the church establishment is a "solemn institution" designed to "guard against the shocks, / The fluctuation and decay of things" (5.998–999). And thus book 9 offers a vision – to complement the pathetic narratives – of the established church's goal to save individuals from "absolute neglect" and "unremitting toil" (9.97–98): establishment becomes a source of universal remittance.

Wordsworth, having described a community in the absence of doctrinal compatibility, beyond any intention to commune, makes Britain's ecclesiastical institution into the very condition for secularization itself. While there is little reason for us to question the far-reaching imperial ambitions of Wordsworth's poem, moreover, it is also crucial for us to see that *The Excursion* has a curious way of relieving the church of its goal of religious conversion; the members of the national and imperial community are *already* converted, already included in Wordsworth's Providential state. To put it yet another way, the poem disaggregates religion from government by relieving the state from the task of enforcing doctrinal conformity, but – in another sense – it *re*aggregates religion with government. Religion in *The Excursion* thus becomes a kind of government with greatly enlarged functions that in turn help to exalt British government itself as a kind of religion.

Wordsworth constructs his vision for the church in a way that in fact informs a whole range of interconnecting arguments during his own day – arguments that on the one hand invested government with a new level of providential authority and on the other hand outlined increasingly secularized functions for the church. In *Illustrations of Divine Government* (1816) – read and praised by Wordsworth – Thomas Southwood Smith imagined God himself as a supreme Benthamite governor whose primary design towards man is "to make him happy" and to reduce pain.[57] Smith, friend and admirer of Bentham, continually pursued a project in his numerous reports on health and sanitation to endow all institutions of government with a profoundly expanded mission: national health was not to be effected by proper morals or virtuous conduct, but by the proper institutional constructions that framed and guided people's movements. Richard Yates, in *The Basis of National Welfare* (1817), arguing from a different position, redefined the function of the church itself – which he deemed necessary not for individual salvation, but for "the only sure and permanent BASIS OF NATIONAL WELFARE." It would ideally increase its "beneficial and protecting influence" devoted to the statistical evaluation and organization of populations regardless of specific beliefs: established religion would relocate its functions from the politicized spirituality of conventional theocracy to the spiritualized policy of the secular state.[58]

The logic of these arguments, moreover, informed a whole range of institutional practices. The expanding and secularizing of the practices of religious groups, as Thomas Laqueur describes in his account of the

"Sunday School Movement," came to serve as a model for large-scale firms and the liberal state.[59] Practices of government, likewise, asserted an increasingly intimate connection with the specific social effectiveness of belief. The religious census of 1851 aimed to record the church attendance of all religious groups; ministers from hundreds of parishes participated in what Ian Hacking calls "the evolving British system of official statistics."[60] The official recording of marriages, births, and deaths outside the Anglican communion, moreover – a practice enacted in *The Excursion*'s "poetical parish register" – would be expanded throughout the nineteenth century.[61]

THE PRELUDE'S HYPOTHETICAL ESTABLISHMENT AND THE "FRAME OF SOCIAL BEING"

I will eventually want to explain how it is that this extensive mission for the established church coheres with Wordsworth's images of the church dissolving into landscape or thin air: images that appear in *The Excursion* and continually reappear in the poetry written and revised throughout the rest of his career. Before moving forward to those later defenses of established religion, however, I first want to suggest that *The Excursion*'s account of the church's virtually limitless tolerance is actually not far from the *opposition* to establishment that Wordsworth voices in *The Prelude*, on which I have so far commented only intermittently. In my discussion of *The Excursion*, I have suggested that Wordsworth's "rewriting" of the poetry in *The Prelude* – the "blessed Babe" passage, or the stolen boat episode – involves writing society into the later poem. That account requires some development, however. For even the most explicit dissent from established religion in *The Prelude* is dissent from a certain *kind* of existing religious establishment. This dissent must itself be situated within a hypothetical establishment, as if a revised version of religious establishment could finally be invoked as the poet's ally against religious uniformity.

This is certainly not to draw attention away from Wordsworth's earnest claims in *The Prelude* to have resisted the regimes of conventional education – much in the manner of the Pedlar's biography that I discussed earlier. This is a resistance that clearly makes poetic fitness into the inverse of institutional fitness, or so it would seem. Book 3's review of the contents of books 1 and 2 concludes that the youthful poet's "rambling like the wind" and "ranging like a fowl of the air," render him "ill tutored" for the "captivity" of university life (*Prelude*, 3.359–63). Such an

inversion of conventional scholastic credentials to prove poetic credentials extends into the mode of opposition that is particularly crucial for my
claims here: the poet's resistance to the confessional norms of Anglican
worship that regulate Cambridge's university life. Anglican conformity,
supported with oaths, tests, and compulsory chapel attendance, is likened
to "the witless shepherd who would drive his flock / With serious repetition to a pool / Of which 'tis plain to sight they never taste" (3.416–18).
"A weight must surely hang on days begun / And ended in worst mockery," he continues; followed with an admonition to "Ye Presidents and
Deans" to "Be wise" and "to your bells / Give seasonable rest, for 'tis
a sound / Hollow as ever vexed the tranquil air" (3.419–23). Like *The
Excursion*'s Solitary, Wordsworth sees in church ritual only a "mockery"
of religion composed from the "hollow" sounds of ritual that only vex
the purer sounds of nature.

The opposition to conventional worship in book 3, of course, provides a particularly concentrated airing of *The Prelude*'s more general
opposition to institutional conformity, thus asserting the value of "confessional" poetry against the political instrumentality of religious confession, as Frank D. McConnell has argued.[62] Indeed, book 3's address to
Coleridge – "And here, O friend, have I retraced my life / Up to an emi-
nence" (3.169–70) – sets the "Tale" telling the "glory of my youth" against
"outward things / Done visibly for other minds – words, signs, / Symbols
or actions" (3.174–76). The poet's own words, signs, symbols, or actions,
it is implied, must be taken as more sincere representations than the
hollow sounds of the bells associated with the purely theatrical, meaningless performance of church worship. If the problem of church worship
is that it provides a vivid example of how persons might not have beliefs but might have beliefs made for them, Wordsworth's point at this
moment is that *his* words, signs, symbols, and actions are evidence of a
more true or genuine belief. The poet can compensate for the mental
extortion of Anglican ritual by rejecting the "outward things" in favor
of the inward mind and its creation of a self-made world: "I had a world
about me – 'twas my own, / I made it; for it only lived to me, / And to
the God who looked into my mind" (3.142–44). This internal world
continually finds figurative expression as an opposing counterpart to
conventional ritual: the poet makes false religious community yield to
"community with highest truth" (3.120); the hollow tolling of bells in
college chapels gives way to the poet's "god-like hours" in which he feels
the "majestic sway we have / As natural beings in the strength of Nature"
(3.192–94).

This might be the very kind of explanation that would move us onward from book 3 to similar ways in which the poem represents established religion in book 7: the "comely bachelor" ascending his pulpit after "a toilette of two hours" with his hypocritical "seraphic glance" to the heavens. One of London's many "grave follies" and "public shows," the comely bachelor shows Wordsworth yet another instance of London's confused world of theatrical representations (7.544–49) – an instance powerful enough for Wordsworth to retain even in his revisions to the poem, so that it followed (only with slight modification) immediately upon the passage added in 1832 praising the "Genius of Burke." Still more, this logic of poetic dissent coincides with what critics frequently understand to be the poem's criticism of institutionalized authority on a broader scale, its pervasive tensions between internal and external worlds in Cambridge, London, and Revolutionary France.[63]

There is something else at stake in Wordsworth's opposition to established religion besides asserting the truth or sincerity of personal belief, however. Wordsworth's curious but illuminating gesture, first of all, is to make any mere rebellion against institutional conformity in book 3 coincide with conformity itself, as if to imply that repression and pure expression are complementary rather than contradictory. Routinely inflecting his account of the academic world with the rhetoric of religious politics, Wordsworth thus sets himself at a distance both from those "loyal students faithful to their books" *and* from "hardy recusants" (3.62–3), as if loyalty and disloyalty are equally objectionable. But if this is so – if both conformity and nonconformity seem equally problematic – it is only because Wordsworth seeks in *The Prelude* to define another kind of establishment, an establishment providing a purely hypothetical enclosure for the very position of dissent articulated throughout the rest of the book. This is a kind of tolerant establishment emerging in the lines immediately following the admonition to the university's "Presidents and Deans," that I quoted earlier. The passage represents the technology of confession as "officious doings" that "bring disgrace / On the plain steeples of our English Church, / Whose worship, 'mid remotest village trees, / Suffers for this" (3.418–21). Wordsworth thus makes *The Prelude* assign an imagined existence to the church which is separable from its actual practices at Cambridge. And the most significant aspect of this view of the church – a view that shows how Wordsworth anticipated similar accounts in *The Excursion* and beyond – is that the "English Church," although certainly idealized, is concretely described as a part of the landscape: a collection of steeples among "village trees." Even the "worship" to which the passage alludes seems oddly removed from personal expression (there are no people performing the worship). "Worship" looks as if it can be located in the structure of the church itself; the steeples make their own worship.

To be sure, nothing better characterizes *The Prelude*'s hypothetical church establishment than its crucial location in – even its confusion with – a landscape. Consider, for example, this passage in which Wordsworth reports that, amid the confessional conformity of Cambridge,

> Yet I could shape
> The image of a place which – soothed and lulled
> As I had been, trained up in paradise
> Among sweet garlands and delightful sounds,
> Accustomed in my loneliness to walk
> With Nature magisterially – yet I
> Methinks could shape the image of a place
> Which with its aspect should have bent me down
> To instantaneous service, should at once
> Have made me pay to science and to arts
> And written lore, acknowledged my liege lord,
> A homage frankly offered up like that
> Which I had paid to Nature.   (3.380–92)

The relationship that Wordsworth develops here between nature and institution does not involve an opposition between one and the other; nor does it involve merely naturalizing an institution so that the traditional will seem natural. In contrast to the moralized landscapes of a poem such as William Cowper's *The Task* (1785), where nature reinforces conventional "piety and sacred truth, and virtue," Wordsworth calls upon nature as a place where there are no requirements on belief; the very absence of an institutionalized belief makes it seem like the most appropriate model for the institution itself.[64] The "ideal academic environment" (as the Norton edition footnotes this description) deliberately blurs the distinction between institutional and natural environments to such an extent that book 3's further accounts of its imagined institutions look like nothing other than nature itself:

> a sanctuary for our country's youth
> With such a spirit in it as might be
> Protection for itself, a virgin grove,
> Primaeval in its purity and depth –
> Where, though the shades were filled with chearfulness,
> Nor indigent of songs warbled from crowds
> In under-coverts, yet the countenance

Of the whole place should wear a stamp of awe –
A habitation sober and demure
For ruminating creatures, a domain
For quiet things to wander in, a haunt
In which the heron might delight to feed
By the shy rivers, and the pelican
Upon the cypress-spire in lonely thought
Might sit and sun himself.   (3.440–54)

The "sanctuary for our country's youth," as Wordsworth plans it, is not a place where worship – or "awe" – is exacted or enforced, since the "stamp of awe" is worn by nature – "the virgin grove" – itself. In many respects, the passage reflects Wordsworth's strategic practice throughout *The Prelude* of importing a vocabulary of church discipline to describe natural surroundings: in book 1, for example, nature is described as a "ministry" (1.494) that provides the poet a "sanctuary" (1.527); the poet's "spirit" is "clothed in priestly robe" for "holy services" (1.60–63). What I am arguing, however, is that this combination of terms, while it may seem to sanctify nature with traditional religious figures to create a version of natural supernaturalism, strives towards an institutional level of commentary that is most visible in the passages that I have been examining. For what is crucial here is that the socializing power of the church is being affirmed precisely against institutional conformity: its real power is to be discerned in its ability to serve as the hypothetical institutional landscape that gives shape to the poet's own non-conforming self-portraiture.

Wordsworth's hypothetical institutions in book 3, I think, help us to see the corresponding significance of the church as a "frame of social being" (6.427) as he describes it in the passage on the Convent of Chartreuse added in 1816–19 to the sixth book of the poem. To Wordsworth, revisiting his passage on the Chartreuse from the *Descriptive Sketches* (1793) which was reworked once again in the unfinished *Tuft of Primroses* (composed in 1808), the convent is a "sacred mansion" (*Prelude*, 6.423); its religious order has been expelled by zealous revolutionaries – an act which Wordsworth reports here but never actually saw – who are scolded for their "impious work" by nature: "stay, stay your sacrilegious hands" (6.430, 433). Recalling how his "heart responded," the poet adds his own plea to nature's: "spare / These courts of mystery, where a step advanced / Between the portals of the shadowy rocks / Leaves far behind life's treacherous vanities" (6.450–53). There is a crucial conflict in the poet's allegiances here, however. For the very request to spare the convent is made under the influence of the poet's "conflicting passions" that lead him also to pay

homage to "the patriot's zeal," to "new-born Liberty," to "Justice," and
to the revolutionaries' "mighty projects" (6.441–3).

This conflict adds a significant amount of complexity to the clearly
defined moralizing of the *Descriptive Sketches*, with its unambiguous characterizations of the convent, now profaned by French "blasphemy,"
as the guardian of a religious "Power" that holds "Reason" in check
(*Descriptive Sketches*, 54,55,59). While the convent in *The Prelude* symbolizes
a certain kind of retreat from social "vanities," it nevertheless affirms a
specific kind of social organization that the revolutionaries have rejected.
This passage does not take issue with the beliefs of the revolutionaries –
their "patriot's zeal" – as much as it opposes the revolutionary treatment
of belief (as Wordsworth understands it) in a more general sense. Jean-
Joseph Mounier's *On the Influence Attributed to Philosophers, Free-Masons, and
to the Illuminati on the Revolution in France* (1801) – reviewed in the first issue
of *The Edinburgh Review* – argued that "a man is not criminal, if, remaining obedient to the laws, he delivers his opinion in a public discussion,
without obliging others to conform to it." According to Mounier, the
English fear of French philosophy amounted to an unjust criminalization
of opinion; but he also included the French revolutionaries themselves
among those who regarded not only the expression but the mere possession of dissenting beliefs as justification for exclusion or punishment.
The very term "Jacobin," Mounier explained, derives from a "convent
of religious persons denominated *Jacobins*," who "put to death without
pity those who opposed their opinions."[65] The logic of Mounier's analysis applies to Wordsworth's view here: Wordsworth finds that he can
support the convent as a "frame of social being" while *also* registering his
own seemingly unorthodox "patriot's zeal." But this is only because of
the way that religious community, in the poet's vision of it, frames zealous
opinion. In the French revolutionaries' actions, Wordsworth discerns a
zeal that has been exercized by finding criminality in dissenting belief; the
revolutionaries have thus proceeded to "expel / The blameless inmates"
(6.425–26) with whom they disagree. Wordsworth sees a subversion of
the "frame of social being" that is not simply a subversion of proper
religious belief but a subversion of tolerant social organization itself.

ESTABLISHMENT, TOLERATION, AND THE INSTITUTION OF POETRY

The counter-confessional logic of Wordsworth's imagined institution –
an opposition to institutional conformity generated within the institution
of the church – helps us to see how the hypothetical establishment of

The Prelude's book 3 might be related to opinions about *actual* religious establishments that emerge as the subject of later revisions to book 6 that I have just discussed, and the subject of *The Excursion*. By the time *The Excursion* was published, moreover, the logic of institutions comes to be defined in Wordsworth's mind as a logic of the poetry that both describes and identifies with those institutions. I turn to these powerfully connected and tirelessly developed institutional and poetic rationales in the remaining pages of this chapter.

The kind of reasoning that led Wordsworth to see established religion as an inclusion of dissent also led him to proclaim a very specific, but by no means straightforward, relationship between his poetry and the religious beliefs of its readers. In the "Essay, Supplemental to the Preface" of 1815, he remarks on the "affinities between religion and poetry" – echoing accounts such as Robert's Lowth's in his *Lectures on the Sacred Poetry of the Hebrews* (1753).[66] At the same time, however, he suggests in no uncertain terms that "pious and devout" readers of poetry promote the "distortion" of poetry itself (*WPr* III:65–66). Wordsworth's slightly altered quotation from the Chartreuse passage in the "Essay" ("– Past and future, are the wings / On whose support, harmoniously conjoined, / Moves the great Spirit of human knowledge –") shows how closely he connected the pious distortions of religious readers with the "impious work" of the revolutionaries, and the work of poetry with the convent's "courts of mystery."[67] Religious readers distort because they require poems to carry religious "truths": "Attaching so much importance to the truths which interest them, they are prone to overrate the Authors by whom these truths are expressed and enforced." On the one hand, these readers may ascribe a power to poetry that is actually their own power, an imposition of their own beliefs. "They come prepared to impart so much passion to the Poet's language," the "Essay" charges, "that they remain unconscious how little, in fact, they receive from it." On the other hand, the religious reader may suppose that poetry is an attempt to impose a belief that is either agreeable or disagreeable: she may deny herself enjoyment by condemning "opinions touching upon religion" because "religious faith is to him who holds it so momentous a thing, and error appears to be attended with such tremendous consequences." If the religious reader misjudges poetry, according to the logic of the "Essay," religious poetry is likewise liable to be misjudged. "We shall find that no poetry," Wordsworth adds, "has been more subject to distortion, than that species the argument and scope of which is religious; and no lovers of the art have gone further astray than the pious and the devout" (III:65).

These considerable efforts to delineate the hazards of religious belief and religious poetry add an intriguing complexity to Wordsworth's more celebrated claim in this work that "every Author, as far as he is great and at the same time *original*, has had the task of *creating* the taste by which he is to be enjoyed" (III:80).[68] For it seems as if the very problem with the adherents of religious beliefs is that they insist upon the importance of establishing a correspondence between the reader's and the author's beliefs: a believer either wants to enforce beliefs by writing religious poetry, or wants to enforce those beliefs by reading poetry according to their prejudices. But this area of tension only serves to point out how Wordsworth's emphasis on shared taste is actually an emphasis on poetry as a way of sharing in the absence of more comprehensive agreement; the only way to create shared taste is to abandon the quest for shared beliefs. The "Essay," after all, never argues against specific beliefs or against the specific readings that might be proposed by adherents of those beliefs. Indeed, even when he locates "excesses" in certain religious "sects," it is quite simply because they assume, with "calculating understanding," that poetry has calculating designs upon them, or that poetry must reflect their own calculating designs. With a religion that is only "cold and formal," the sects Wordsworth mentions make the form of the poem into a demand for uniformity so strong that the only "consequences" assumed to be felt by that poem consist in the poem's agreement or disagreement with a prejudice seeking privately to generate its own sense of consequence. Wordsworth thus lowers the importance of sectarian belief in the very process of raising the issue of sectarianism, for he eventually claims to observe virtually *all* ways of reading his poetry – "the love, the admiration, the indifference, the slight, the aversion, and even the contempt" – as "proofs for the present time that I have not laboured in vain" (III:80). The sense of common experience and shared taste that comes from reading his poetry derives simply from its having been read.

It seems, then, as if Wordsworth's "Essay" takes a view of poetry that is as tolerant as the institution of the church as it was defended from *The Prelude* to *The Excursion* – insofar as it explains poetry as a perspective on beliefs that is more accommodating than the beliefs themselves. But if this is true, how could Wordsworth reconcile such notions to the collection of poems first published in 1822 as *Ecclesiastical Sketches* and then expanded in later years as *Ecclesiastical Sonnets in Series*? If the precise character and extent of Wordsworth's commitment to the Anglican establishment had seemed at all questionable to the reviewers of *The Excursion*, the *Sonnets* – whether derided or admired – appeared to express their sympathies with conventional Anglican orthodoxy much more clearly. John Wilson, one of only a few admiring reviewers, declared, "It is thus that Christianity, and great establishments for the preservation of its doctrines pure and unsullied, ought to be thought of in the meditative mind of genius."[69] Today's critics, following suit, have come to the plausible conclusion that the sonnets confirm the author's affiliation with the Oxford Movement and his embrace of conservative political and religious doctrines more generally.[70] And the author's own testimony would seem to support such judgments: the Fenwick note on the sonnets defends his praise of Laud's "aims to restore the ritual practices" in the church – praise that is pronounced "long before the Oxford Tract movement."[71] In the prefatory letter to the work, Wordsworth claims an alliance with another celebrated defense of established religion, Southey's *Book of the Church*: "my Friend, Mr. Southey, was engaged with similar views in writing a concise History of the Church *in* England." And he further bolsters his work's conservative politics by announcing the sonnets as a response to the liberal cause of toleration: "The Catholic Question, which was agitated in Parliament about that time," inspires the poet to write on "certain points in the Ecclesiastical History of our Country" which "might advantageously be presented to view in verse."[72]

Exactly how writing sonnets on ecclesiastical history can offer an answer to the "Catholic Question" is not directly explained here. And, although it may seem as though Wordsworth's mere support for the church would place him amongst the opponents of Catholic emancipation that I discussed in chapter 1, the fuzzy logic in the introductory letter might encourage us to note other ambiguities regarding their commitment to religious orthodoxy in the comments by Wordsworth's reviewers and by the author himself. By the time that Christopher Wordsworth's *Memoirs of William Wordsworth* were published in 1851, a review of the work in *The Gentleman's Magazine* reported on the nephew's attempt to make his famous uncle seem like a conservative supporter of the "faith of Oxford" by "burden[ing]" the *Memoirs* "with long extracts from obsolete pamphlets by his uncle about Cintra . . . and the Catholic claims": an attempt that the reviewer dismissed as "singularly lame and impotent" and lacking any support in Wordsworth's poetry.[73] In relation to the *Ecclesiastical Sonnets* more particularly, it should be noted that reviewers who either praised or criticized the work recognized it as a conspicuously weak advocate for Anglican ideology.[74] Even Wilson's review saw the work as poetically, rather than politically, effective: the product of a "meditative mind of genius." Wordsworth's own comments are also revealing. I suggested in chapter 2 that Southey's *Book of the Church* may not simply be conservative propaganda – it may actually yield insights into the Gothic novel's logic of toleration. But Wordsworth imagines himself going even a step beyond Southey; for the poet's italicization in his description of Southey's ostensibly analogous work – a "History of the Church *in* England" – turns, yet again, on a similar attempt to establish the priority of his poetry (an ecclesiastical history *of* England – an appropriation and modification of Bede's *Ecclesiastical History of the English People* [731]) over a more specific defense of coherent religious interests. Southey's account is made to seem like a subdivision of his own larger project; Wordsworth's subject is not merely the history of "the Church" but the history of *ecclesia* according to its most basic definition: *government* more generally as it operates through the particular instances of church government. "Ecclesiastical" as a descriptive term for "sonnets," moreover, implies that the sonnets do not simply take *ecclesia* as a *subject* for representation. Indeed, the work itself is offered as a kind of *poetic ecclesia*: a governing perspective on or over the interests associated with the powers of contending churches.

If this is true, it is still hard for any reader to ignore the way that the sonnet series represents Britain's ecclesiastical history as nothing other than a history of conflict: a history in which the authority of the church has been purchased through hostility and violence towards adherents of systems of belief inimical to the Anglican church. The sonnets often seem to offer an answer to the "Catholic Question," for example, by quite clearly depicting Catholicism as a source of danger to national unity, as a dominating tyrant or "proud Arbitress" (1.36).[75] Catholicism is not the only enemy to social order, however, for the proliferation of sects is said to lead to civil "strife" which threatens to destroy the church's "golden mean" (3.11). The translation of the Bible, while initially seeming a "Transcendent Boon" for Protestants, nevertheless incites divisions owing to "bigotry" and "passions" which "spread like plagues" and cause "thousands wild" to "tread the Offering / Beneath their feet, detested and defiled" (2.29).

Now on the one hand, the sonnets are able to exercise a profound opposition to both Catholic and Protestant forms of dissent because dissent is associated with destabilizing forces of delusion and disordered fancy. The sonnet on "Transubstantiation" (2.11) thus represents Catholicism as the product of disordered minds: "dim association" leads to "awe and supernatural horror," and "all the people bow their heads, like reeds / To

a soft breeze, in lowly adoration." St. Dunstan, who provides numerous
opportunities for derision in Southey's history, appears in another sonnet
as a mastermind capable of "moulding the credulous people to his will,"
so that in his figure is "presignified, / The might of spiritual sway" (1.28).
Analogous terms apply to Dissenting sects in a sonnet bearing the title
"Distractions": "sects are formed, and split / With morbid restlessness."
A sect is an outcome of an "ecstatic fit" which "spreads wide" throughout
the nation (2.41).

   From a somewhat different point of view, though, the sonnets do not
merely oppose themselves to beliefs but to belief's political instrumentality: the tendency of belief to take some form of more destructive "spiritual sway." The sonnets thus construe dissent as dangerous insofar as
it imperils the very "frame of social being" – to use *The Prelude*'s idiom –
itself. This logic of the church establishment, and poetry's relation to that
establishment, is perhaps most visible in the sonnet on the "Monastery
of old Bangor" (1.12):

> *The oppression of the tumult – wrath and scorn –*
> *The tribulation – and the gleaming blades –*
> Such is the impetuous spirit that pervades
> The song of Taliesin; – Ours shall mourn
> The *unarmed* Host who by their prayers would turn
> The sword from Bangor's walls, and guard the store
> Of Aboriginal and Roman lore,
> And Christian monuments, that now must burn
> To senseless ashes. Mark! How all things swerve
> From their known course, or vanish like a dream;
> Another language spreads from coast to coast;
> Only perchance some melancholy Stream
> And some indignant Hills old names preserve,
> When laws, and creeds, and people all are lost!

Wordsworth's poem draws on three texts that provide accounts of
Ethelforth's attack (sanctioned by Augustine) on the monastery at
Bangor, occupied by Welsh troops under the leadership of Brocmail:
Sharon Turner's, Taliesin's – as translated by Sharon Turner – and
Bede's. What is significant about all of these accounts, in Wordsworth's
appropriation of them, is that they champion or deride one side or the
other according to their prejudices: Bede's account in the *Ecclesiastical
History* chastises the "faithless Britons" (who refused to abide by
Augustine's demands for religious conformity);[76] Taliesin's account,
quoted in Turner's *The History of the Anglo-Saxons from the Earliest Period*

to the *Norman Conquest* (1820), sides with "Brocvail of Powys, who loved my muse"; Turner comments in a note on the passage that "it is not likely that a rude Anglo-Saxon warrior would take any care to preserve British MSS."[77] Turner's account, even while it proclaims the rudeness of the Anglo-Saxon Ethelforth, is particularly crucial for Wordsworth because it draws attention to what the poet regards as the true accomplishment of religious establishment: its preservation of British manuscripts: "Aboriginal and Roman lore, / And Christian monuments, that now must burn / To senseless ashes." The monastery, in Wordsworth's way of thinking, does not merely defend ancient prejudices (through St. Dunstan's art of "presignif[ying]" in sonnet 1.28); indeed, the "lore" of which he speaks is something more inclusive – the very possibility of knowledge that will "vanish like a dream." That we are meant to see the sonnet on these terms – a defense of establishment as a defense *against* prejudicial belief – seems quite clear in Wordsworth's own commentary on the sonnet. After quoting from Bede's *Ecclesiastical History* and its account of the destroyed library in the monastery at Bangor, he notes: "The account Bede gives of this remarkable event, suggests a most striking warning against National and Religious prejudices." And if Wordsworth's note makes the destruction of the library seem like the ultimate expression of destructive contending prejudices, the poem furthers this notion by adopting a noticeably tolerant, contrasting position for poetry itself. The strategy of italicized quotation in the first two lines shows how Wordsworth has preserved a kind of "lore" captured in Taliesin's own perspective – a perspective that celebrates the Welsh side against Ethelforth. Taliesin's "impetuous spirit" is significant not only for identifying national and religious prejudice but also for exemplifying that prejudice: a national and religious prejudice that is the widely acknowledged territory of Bardic utterance.[78] Both Bede and Turner, moreover, uphold their own prejudices in their retellings of the event. The poem seeks to absolve itself of a similar charge by declining to take up one side of a rivalry between beliefs (the poem and the note to the poem reject attachment to either side) and by asserting the value of the monastery as sponsor of a discourse that is the very condition for the articulation of those beliefs as preserved "lore."

The sonnets continue to assert the importance of the church as secular government, and to ally poetry itself with that government. I must repeat here, as I have said elsewhere in this chapter, that I do not by any means wish to deny or suppress Wordsworth's passionate support for the church itself; I am arguing that he could not support the church without

simultaneously rejecting religious uniformity. The sonnet on "An Inter-
dict" (1.36) is particularly forceful in its ways of imagining the church –
just as it was imagined in *The Excursion* – simply as the public foundation
of civil life. The Pope's punishment for King John's refusal to allow
Stephen Langton (appointed Archbishop of Canterbury in 1207) is to
close the "gates of every sacred place," and thus apparently to deprive a
people of society itself: "Bells are dumb; / Ditches are graves – funereal
rites denied; / And in the churchyard he must take his bride / Who dares
be wedded." Beyond the level of individual poems, furthermore, these
sonnets achieve a counterpoint between the Bardic defense of national
and religious prejudice and the Wordsworthian enclosure of prejudice
at the level of the structure of the sonnet series itself. The explicit reference to "series" in the revised title for the work – first taking on the
name *Ecclesiastical Sonnets in Series* in 1837 – had a special significance for
Wordsworth. In a letter to Sharp on the sonnets, he remarks upon the
"one obvious disadvantage" of the work, which was its dependence upon
historical details that might "enslav[e] the fancy."[79] The possibility that
the sonnets might seem to require an armature of prior knowledge finds
an antidote in the serial structure of the work, as the note to the *Sonnets*
explains: "for the convenience of passing from one point of the subject to
another without shocks of abruptness, this work has taken the shape of a
series of Sonnets." In an attempt to forestall the kind of objection that he
anticipates in the letter to Sharp, that is, Wordsworth suggests that the
individual sonnets should be read as a complete poem; if it is, the reader
will presumably be drawn into a structure that emphasizes a poetic form
of "convenience." "Convenience" turns out to be Wordsworth's method
for establishing his poetic structure as an organization of all specifically
religious modes of convening to which "convenience" is etymologically
related: conventions, conventicles, convents. The reader, moreover, will
encounter the "pictures" in each poem as if they were a complete work
"in a form of stanza to which there is no objection but one that bears
upon the Poet only – its difficulty."[80] By drawing attention to form over
historical fact, "series" over "pictures," Wordsworth avoids enslaving the
fancy to history and the Bardic national interests that might be associated
with it. He directs attention away from the prior attachments of fancy to
fact and towards the "difficulty" of the poem itself – a series of sonnets
treated as a series of connected stanzas. Enslavement gives way to the
organized labor of writing and reading.[81]

By the time that Wordsworth was writing the latest additions to the
Ecclesiastical Sonnets, his way of characterizing the church quite clearly

shows why he could provide this kind of poetic support for it. The sonnets added to the series anatomize ecclesiastical functions first and foremost as public functions: the church's role, for example, in marriages (3.26), care for the sick (3.28), and funerals (3.31). Even those functions that seem to involve a conformity in belief seem instantly to dissolve the specificity of that belief. The sonnet on "Catechizing" (3.22), for example, is more about flowers than about people; the sonnet on "Conversion" (1.17) makes the voice of Christian priests into a "voice / Heard near fresh streams."[82] This brings us to yet another important way of characterizing *the* church – the Church of England – through images of individual churches: images clearly related to those I mentioned earlier in my discussion of *The Excursion*. The *Ecclesiastical Sonnets* continually describe churches as structures embedded in the landscape, and a speaker and / or worshiper whose consciousness is equally indistinct: either dissolving into atmosphere or absorbed into the church's structure. The prefatory letter to the *Ecclesiastical Sonnets*, in fact, describes a picturesque walk as the initial inspiration for the sonnets themselves – a walk, yielding "cherishing influences," with Sir George Beaumont in 1820 "through different parts of his estate, with a view to fix upon the site of a new church which he intended to erect."[83] And the sonnets continue this logic by representing church establishment in terms of progressively less constraining forms of architectural circumscription: to such an extent that churches come into view as the most hazily defined structures – sometimes ruins, sometimes barely visible spires – amid their natural surroundings. In one instance, Wordsworth likens a church establishment to a panorama of "Spires" and "Steeple-towers" (3.17) that are barely distinguishable in the landscape. In another, the "clouds of incense" that "veiled the rood" resemble "a pine-tree dimly viewed / Through Alpine vapours" (3.40).[84]

Wordsworth, we now see, has traveled from poetry about persons in landscapes with hypothetical churches (in early parts of *The Prelude*) to poetry about churches in landscapes with hypothetical persons in the shape of natural imagery: brambles, birds, and wild animals. The latter is a poetic practice that Wordsworth would never relinquish for the rest of his life. His series of poetic Tours – in 1820, 1833, and 1837 – make churches into landmarks, points on an itinerary that (akin to words in a sentence or stanzas in a poem) move the speaker on to further opportunities to feel nature's cherishing influences. In "The Pass of Kirkstone" (1820), the church is identified with a road: not a place of worship, but a "guide" through a landscape that gives "the rich bounties of constraint." Poems such as "Devotional Incitements" (1835) make flowers into censers and birds into the singers of "unwearied canticles" – the kind of logic that informs *The White Doe of Rylstone* (1815) with its equation between a saintly Doe and the "consecrated Maid" Emily Norton. The complex of images in such poems is indeed different from the writing in *The Prelude*, in "Tintern Abbey," or in other earlier works. But what I have been suggesting is that the interest in the potentially dissenting subject in Wordsworth's earlier poetry (or, at least a subject distanced from institutional interference) is consistent with the accommodation of that subject into the very institutional frame that is the more explicit focus of representation in this later poetry: a "frame of social being" that requires no more oaths of allegiance or sacramental tests than nature itself. Conversely, the later poetry is not merely an orthodox repression of heterodox belief; for the frame of the institution – blending, like belief, into landscape – is imagined as that which is only natural to all persons, no matter what their beliefs might be. Established religion is represented as "natural," though, not because it demonstrates a loss of confidence in human relations (the deconstructive argument), and not because it mystifies those relations (the historicist argument).[85] It is natural because it is omnipresent. The social relations overseen and constructed by the Wordsworthian *ecclesia* are as fundamental to the self as the self's actual or potential refusal to yield to them.

CHAPTER 6

"Consecrated fancy": *Byron and Keats*

ORPHAN OF THE HEART: *CHILDE HAROLD'S PILGRIMAGE*

In the previous two chapters, I have been arguing that the national tale finds a common ground with Wordsworth's poetry because of their shared commitments to secular institutions as a vital support of local distinction. In the national tale, the nation becomes apprehensible as a nation within a realm of extra-national relations; in Wordsworth's poetry, the Solitary – as model for, rather than an exception to, communal membership – gains distinction as a Solitary precisely because of his inclusion and recognition within the reach of the church establishment. These strategies are indeed truly different. The national tale arrives at a way of treating belief that departs in substantial ways from Wordsworth's ever-present religious establishment that presides over his poetry just as it presides over the nation, while Edgeworth consigns religion to near invisibility. But these strategies comment on each other even while they differ. For if Wordsworth sees religion as a kind of secular government, Edgeworth sees the mutually supporting mechanisms of the economy and secular institutions as a kind of religion: or, at least, as a source of vitality and security that recovers the functions of religion's most ancient forms.

To emphasize the complementarity of these two views is to emphasize what Bentham had understood as the ultimate goal of the secular organs of state, which would not merely oppose themselves to religion but in fact recover what he considered to be religion's most basic function as the all-encompassing source of social organization. At the same time, this exalted form of secular government would submit religion itself – indeed, all forms of religion – to its rule, organizing and overseeing the operations of consensual groups of believers within the state's increasingly tolerant choreography. The complementary work of the national tale's aggressive secularism and Wordsworth's fervent but paradoxical religiosity, I should also emphasize once again, continues a fascination with – and fictional solution for – religious conflict that had been explicitly thematized in the Gothic novel. This chapter shows how Byron and Keats even more openly gravitate towards the anxieties and terrors generated in the Gothic in order to shape their works as poetic responses to political debate. Critics such as Martin Aske and Philip Martin have already taken note of how these writers rely upon the Gothic for numinous or sensational effects; Byron and Keats, they argue, indulge in the titillating and shocking effects of the Gothic that were highly marketable – especially with an expanding audience of female readers.[1] I describe the poetry I study here, however – primarily Byron's *Childe Harold's Pilgrimage* (1813–18), Keats's *The Eve of St. Agnes* and *Lamia* (1820) – as "Gothic" in a different way. These are poems that continually involve explicitly destructive or dangerous dramas of belief: for Byron, wars of religion repeatedly involve a struggle between rival beliefs that can only be resolved by eliminating one group of believers in favor of another. Keats's poetry, rather than showing beliefs as utterly irreconcilable, depicts dramas of belief and incredulity in which his protagonists or speakers – even if they are warned about the hazards of believing – seem only too willing to accommodate themselves to the designs and stratagems of others.

Furthermore, these invocations of the Gothic dynamics of belief, although they provide a striking exposure of the violent effects of either adhering or refusing to adhere to a specific set of beliefs, ultimately express a confidence in poetry's status as a tolerant regulation of the religious, and anti-religious, prejudices that they portray. Poetry becomes a substitute for religion, in a sense, but not because it advocates new beliefs or sentiments. Rather, it relieves itself of the need to enforce belief and thus expands its appeal to a wider range of readers. Byron, then, comes to resist the political power of religious belief with all the energy of the enlightened *philosophes*, while also opposing his work to the bigotry of the *philosophes* themselves. If *Childe Harold* "is a *poem*," he writes, it will "surmount" the "obstacles" of "angry poets and prejudices."[2] For Keats, the crucial gesture in *The Fall of Hyperion* (1820) – to maneuver his poetic project in relation to the dreams of the "fanatic" and the worship of the superstitious "savage" – is only a late configuration of his ongoing attempt to construct poetry that solicits beliefs without being confined to the purposes of either manipulating – or being manipulated by – those beliefs.[3] *The Fall* speaks for the way that the other poems in the 1820 volume *Lamia, Isabella, The Eve of St. Agnes, and Other Poems* make poetry aspire to function as an alternative to religious belief, a "spell of words" saving "imagination" from "the sable charm / And dumb enchantment" precisely because it is *written* and survives the adherents of specific beliefs (*The Fall*, 9–11). The poet's status is secured not because of the authority of his convictions, but because he has "Trac'd upon vellum or wild Indian leaf / The Shadows of melodious utterance" (5–6).

To address the politics and poetics of religious belief in Byron's writing is to embark on a discussion at once integral and remote from previous accounts of his work. Studies of Byron frequently address either his careful and sincere consideration of a variety of religious doctrines, or his atheistic or skeptical rejection of all religious doctrines. James Kennedy's *Conversations With Lord Byron* (1830) assures readers that Byron did not engage in "any real critique of Christianity" and was in fact a man of strong religious principles; even Byron himself claimed on numerous occasions to "incline" himself "very much to the Catholic doctrines."[4] More recent critics have continued to view Byron's poetry in similar terms. Robert Ryan, for example, makes a case for his divided commitments between Deism and Calvinism, which are less important for providing adequate religious doctrines than for demonstrating Byron's respect for the "transcendent mystery of the divine."[5] Bernard Beatty's somewhat broader reading of Byron's religious commitments understands his "sense of immediate given life" as proof that he was "always in some sense a religious poet."[6]

Critics more frequently contend, however, that Byron's apparent interest in religious beliefs contributes to an ironic commentary on belief from a far more skeptical point of view. Opposing himself to all forms of political and religious "cant" and to all "systems" of thought whatsoever, Byron scoffs at canons of taste early in his career in *English Bards and Scotch Reviewers* and keeps up an attack on false beliefs by "holding up the nothingness of life" against vain "speculation" in *Don Juan*.[7] His shifty claims to be a Deist, a Catholic, or a Calvinist, or at any moment to "turn Musselman,"[8] strike many readers as criticisms or parodies of religious faith rather than sincere expressions of conviction. According to one view, this skepticism conveys a commitment to human values that is more general than any religion. Byron's poetry is thus said to devote itself to "the strange creature man" through a "respect for actuality and a respect for the integrity of the individual."[9] If the skeptical Byron might seem to replicate the religious Byron with his humanist doctrine, Jerome McGann's *The Romantic Ideology* finds a value in Byron's poetry not because it represents a system of enlightened values, but because its "immediacy" and attention to "concrete particulars" make it more faithful and responsive to human relations than any religion or secular humanism that critics have previously attributed to him.[10] But if McGann's account aims to correct the abstractions of the secular humanist's account, it is nevertheless true that the very attempt to freight "immediacy" and "concrete particulars" with political or ethical weight – the attempt, that is, to make materiality seem like an argument against ideology – is not as far from the humanist account as it might wish itself to be. McGann's account of Byron's particularism is not far, that is, from Beatty's Christian account of Byron's "sense of immediate given life" that makes him a "religious poet."

To proceed with the argument I want to make about Byron is not to delineate his viewpoint on a human condition, and not even to make a claim about his "nihilism" (that is, a personal philosophical perspective on the meaninglessness of all systems).[11] It is, however, to argue that Byron's resistance to the legitimacy of religious (or quasi-religious) systems of belief is also a resistance to a more rational perspective on belief that would merely seek to cure religion of its illusions. Byron's work stages the violent drama of contending beliefs in order to assert an alternative status for poetry: a discourse that both avoids the logic of confessional uniformity and that seeks thereby to ensure an even more secure level of authority.

Childe Harold's Pilgrimage provides a rich illustration of this poetic positioning because of the way it might seem at first to contradict it. It is a poem that continually attracted criticism from reviewers for its lack of moral purpose, and for which Byron was prodded by John Murray and Robert Charles Dallas to form his poem into a work that would be less offensive to "customers among the *Orthodox*."[12] What those suggestions tend to obscure, however, is that *Childe Harold* does not merely adopt beliefs that are amoral or un-Christian; it instead seeks to designate a place for itself as poetry in relation to beliefs more generally. Byron's strategy in this poem can be illuminated by understanding it as a distinctive poetic solution to the violence that he addresses in his parliamentary speech on the Catholic claims of 1812, where religion emerges in his argument both as a troubling source of warfare and bloodshed and as the ultimate object or focus of political emancipation. The speech makes established religion seem not only cruel but disorganized, and advocates toleration precisely because it yields enhanced order and security.[13] He continually remarks upon the victimization of Irish Catholics by British Protestants: "If it must be called an Union, it is the union of the shark with his prey; the spoiler swallows up his victim, and thus they become one and indivisible."[14] To argue against this victimization, Byron quotes from chapter 10 of William Paley's *The Principles of Moral and Political Philosophy* of 1785 ("Of Religious Establishments and of Toleration"): "I perceive no reason why men of different religious persuasions should not sit upon the same bench, deliberate in the same council, or fight in the same ranks, as well as men of various religious opinion upon any controverted topic of natural history, philosophy, or ethics" (*BPr*, 38). Here – in a spirit similar to that of Edgeworth's *Absentee* or Bentham's *Chrestomathia* – Byron shows sympathy for such views by arguing for Catholic emancipation both as a liberation of Catholics and as an ordering of individuals of different faiths in the activities of the state. Paley's claim suggests that political, military, and educational institutions are themselves sources of social order that can accommodate adherents of different beliefs; Byron's clever advocacy of the Catholic claims follows suit by repeatedly making forced conformity look like a source of disorder, and the toleration of nonconformity look like a source of contrasting stability. The union of the shark with its prey thus creates a unity – "one and indivisible" – but with a violence built into its structure. Adherents of Protestant ascendancy in Ireland, using their "catechism" to heap abuse upon the "damnable idolatry of Catholics," are analogized to "cannibals," and their schools to "dunghills, where the viper of intolerance deposits her young, that when their teeth are cut and their poison is mature, they may issue forth, filthy and venomous, to sting the Catholic" (*BPr*, 37–38). The Protestant church, because it limits the freedom of Catholics, imitates the dangerous thing that it seeks to eliminate. By contrast, Byron characterizes the toleration of nonconformity as a relief of internal "distress" and a security against the power of Napoleon – an argument for internal unity through disharmony that should remind of Coleridge's similar claims as I discussed them in chapter 3. The "extension of freedom" allows for a greater "benefit of strength" and increased "patriotism"; he claims that "Ireland has done much" for the British nation, and forecasts that it "will do more" if freedoms are extended to it (*BPr*, 33,43,40).

Childe Harold is consistent with the aims of the parliamentary speech, I would argue, not because it provides any models for a tolerant society, but because it provides a specific poetic solution to the religious violence that it represents – a strategy that makes the poem's relation to the Gothic (he acknowledges Radcliffe's influence in stanza 17 of canto 4) explicit.[15] The struggle between systems of belief for a mutually exclusive "omnipotence" (4.93) only leads to ruins or scenes of destruction – ruins

and scenes of destruction that are in turn viewed as the very subject of
the poet's meditations. What is crucial about Byron's alliance between
poetry and the ruins of belief, moreover, is that these ruins – ruins of
religious monuments that are also monumentalized ruins – turn out to
be the only source of articulation for any belief, and thus the object of
the poet's aspirations for preserving his own work. *Childe Harold* makes
the survival of the meaning of a belief depend upon the decay of its
self-determining power.

Although I have already suggested that the object of this discussion
is not to labor over Byron's allegiances to particular systems of belief,
we cannot in fact overlook the frequency with which *Childe Harold* does
indeed seem to invoke an opposition between superstition and true or
right belief. It might very well be said that Byron's poetic persona, for example, allies itself with an obligation to embrace the cause of enlightened
knowledge and thus oppose all forms of delusion. Byron thus separates
"Foul Superstition" from "true worship's gold" (2.44); his project is to
"ponder boldly," searching for the "truth"; for "'tis a base / Abandon-
ment of reason to resign / Our right of thought – our last and only
place / Of refuge" (4.127).[16] His entire political and poetic program for
recovering the lost glory of ancient civilizations and ancient liberty, in
fact, might seem to rest precisely upon such polarities between reason
and unreason.

Certainly this level of opposition might lead us to support the kinds
of claims that readers have made about the poem's overt interests in
recovering a value of the human – the "sense of immediate given life"
that is obscured by oppressive systems of belief. But Byron mobilizes
religious belief in this poem not merely to distinguish between false and
true belief, or between illusion and disillusion. He goes to considerable
lengths, after all, to distance himself from what he calls the "*skeptical
bigotry*" of the historians and philosophers of the Enlightenment – Gibbon
and, more crucially, Voltaire.[17] Gibbon, all "fire and fickleness," devotes
himself only to "laying all things prone, – / Now to o'erthrow a fool, and
now to shake a throne" (3.106), and Voltaire fares no better: his work is
a "weapon with an edge severe, / Sapping a solemn creed with solemn
sneer" (3.107). Even though *Childe Harold* would seem to oppose itself to
imprisoning and enslaving systems of belief, moreover, it actually extols
Italy in canto 4 as a source of religious authority: "Parent of our religion!
Whom the wide / Nations have knelt to for the keys of heaven" (4.47).
In another instance, Rome is said to be a "city of the soul" and "Lone
mother of dead empires," to whom turn "the orphans of the heart" (4.78).

The contrast between this account and the *Historical Illustrations of the Fourth Canto of "Childe Harold"* (1818), written by his friend and traveling companion John Cam Hobhouse, further illuminates Byron's strategy. Certainly Hobhouse's own support for religious toleration (he is particularly well known for his unsuccessful bid to have Parliament review Jewish disabilities in 1820) shows a common ground between the poet and the radical politician.[18] But Hobhouse's notes routinely offer up a more straightforwardly enlightened wisdom culled from the pages of such works as Drummond's *Academical Questions* (1805), upholding the cause of "truth" over enslaving bigotry and prejudice (*BP*II:257). While Byron enthusiastically describes the "vast and wondrous dome" of St. Peter's as an "eternal ark of worship undefiled," Hobhouse interjects a characteristically contrary line of reasoning (*Childe Harold*, 4.153–54). Halting at stanza 154, Hobhouse alerts the reader to Catholic defilement within the wondrous dome that Byron describes: to the "ferocious superstition" of "flagellation," whose "tumultuous sound of blows" interrupts and destroys Hobhouse's pleasure. Hobhouse's prose, as Malcolm Kelsall observes, "is being used to foster controversy in a way the verse is not."[19] Catholicism appears to Hobhouse as an intolerable lag in the "progress of reason," and shows the author that "a considerable portion of all societies, in times the most civilized as well as the most ignorant, is always ready to adopt the most unnatural belief, and the most revolting practices."[20]

Byron's praise for the eternal, undefiled ark of worship, while distanced from Hobhouse's enlightened critique of religion, does not exactly embrace a religion in any familiar sense, either. Indeed, Rome functions as a parent figure but as a parent of dead empires, and consequently as a parent who is actually an estranged parent to "orphans of the heart," children who are not beneficiaries of the parent's sympathies. (The last, unfinished, canto of *Don Juan* describes "orphans of the heart" as "such as are not doomed to lose / Their tender parents in their budding days, / But merely their parental tenderness" [17.1].) Rome offers a religious heritage that is appropriate as much for its interruption and discontinuity – a discontinuity in sympathy – as for its continuity. The ancient city does not stand for a particular religion as much as it stands for something more general: a symbol of all cultural symbol-making.

The reason why Byron can come to value St. Peter's, furthermore (similar to the reason why Keats can value his Grecian urn as a "Foster child of silence and slow time"), is because he is *not* merely a participant in its customary modes of worship. Whereas Hobhouse draws attention to an intolerable asymmetry between the unnatural beliefs of Catholics and his own (more natural) reason, Byron finds a poetic value in the "wondrous dome" only because religious *beliefs* are not shared but instead are obscured, by likening the structure of St. Peter's – in Wordsworthian fashion – to the natural beauty of alps, clouds, and ocean (*Childe Harold*, 4.155–56). This poetic resolution seems to work adequately enough in the poem as long as religion can seem only like an unrecoverable part of history, or at least can be removed to a comfortable historical distance. The poem, at such a moment, promises a separation between public memorial and obscured public memory. But this strategy would hardly seem adequate in a poem that makes unresolved contentions between adherents of different beliefs part of the present: contentions that routinely involve violently incompatible claims on persons and property. That is, the treatment of belief in this poem frequently coincides with violent acts of appropriation that can only be followed by other similarly violent acts on behalf of other systems of belief. The property of the nation becomes a version of private property held by the adherents of a specific community of believers, and thus the history of the nation can be summed up – as it so frequently is in this poem – as identical to the history of religions struggling for social omnipotence. One national religion succeeds another: "slave succeed to slave" (2.77) for "religions take their turn: / 'Twas Jove's – 'tis Mahomet's – and other creeds / Will rise with other years, till man shall learn / Vainly his incense soars, his victim bleeds; / Poor child of Doubt and Death, whose hope is built on reeds" (2.3).

Byron attached a note to these lines I have just quoted (and the six stanzas following it) from the second canto (stanzas 3 through 9) – a note sent to Dallas but never published – that most clearly relates *Childe Harold* to the parliamentary speech I discussed earlier. The note condemns the "age of bigotry" in which "the puritan and the priest have changed places, and the wretched catholic is visited with the 'sins of his fathers'"; it thus glosses the lines as if they referred not only to intolerance abroad but to intolerance in Britain, where the machinery of political exclusion repeats the "sins" of which the Catholics are accused.[21] There is a sense in which the idea of succession – a "wretched interchange of wrong for wrong" in a "contentious world" (*Childe Harold*, 3.69) – leads Byron to distil a moral lesson from this wretched interchange and convey it to the intolerant. We hear him grasping for "the moral of all human tales" with sermonizing gestures that come perhaps too easily – "hope is built on reeds," or "'tis thus the mighty falls" (4.107). To fall is to lose a sense of "common joy": a common joy that Byron's verse sacramental-izes and sentimentalizes by associating it with sacred objects violated by profane interests – a "rifled urn," for example, or a "violated mound" (2.90).

Perhaps such gestures provide a sheen of humanized virtues that in turn announces the poem's kinship with Spenserian romance. But if the program of "militant Protestant chivalry" in Spenserian romance en-lists combat in support of a religious and moral purpose, the contending religious beliefs in *Childe Harold* cannot achieve this form of resolution and instead continually erode the force of their own self-determining articulation.[22] The very fervor and violence with which beliefs are con-veyed curiously coincide with their silence or illegibility as personal ex-pressions of belief, as if the object of the poem were to hasten present beliefs into obsolescence. The narrator's meditations on the temple of Jupiter Olympus in canto 2 – "Here let me sit upon this massy stone, / The marble column's yet unshaken base" (2.10) – make this particularly clear. The columns of the temple offer an occasion for Byron to distin-guish between poetic and religious interest: the columns are objects of the poet's contemplation and yet they are "proud pillars" that "claim no passing sigh, / Unmoved the Moslem sit, the light Greek carols by"(2.10). The violently opposed Moslems and Christians have no interest in the ruins compared to the interest demonstrated by the poet. To be sure, Byron's aim here is to rouse "fair Greece" to defend itself from British plunder – "The last, the worst, dull spoiler" Lord Elgin (2.11); Britain is the latest in the line of succession ("Even the gods must yield – religions take their turn"[2.3]) mentioned only a few stanzas earlier. But Byron strangely rouses national spirit on behalf of its own decay, as if that spirit might reach its greatest satisfaction by being transformed into ruin. The problem with the unmoved Moslem and the caroling Greek, after all, is not that they have *not* pressed the monument in the service of their beliefs, in order to make monuments convey a particular body of public memory. The problem is that they have not joined the poet's own brand of allegiance, which can be attracted by the temple's columns precisely *because* of their decay. Such ruins are not the representatives of any living and animating beliefs but examples of "mouldering shrines" that are the homes of "shrinking Gods" (2.15). While Greece is a "relic of departed worth" (2.63), a land suffering from "lost gods and godlike men" (2.85), this depletion of "worth" (on the scale of human virtue or heroism) makes it appropriate from the vantage point of poetic worth. "Though fallen," Greece is "still great" (2.73).

RELIGIOUS RUIN, POETIC SURVIVAL; OR, WHY THE ONLY
GOOD NATION IS A DEAD ONE

Byron's embrace of a Greek nationalist cause and his passionate call to the "true born patriot" to join him in it oddly and problematically confront his embrace of a Romantic disposition towards belief (2.73). National spirit encounters a series of contending claims upon the "nation" that can be resolved only by embracing the demise of, or distance from, the very beliefs that are the source of contention over national definition. This logic, paradoxical as it may be, helps to illuminate related works that emerged after the publication of the first and second cantos of *Childe Harold*. The *Hebrew Melodies* (1815) show their sympathies for the emancipation of Jews by invoking scenes of loss, destruction, and deprivation as the appropriate objects of poetic contemplation ("The Vision of Belshazzar," "On the Day of the Destruction of Jerusalem by Titus," "By the Rivers of Babylon We Sat Down and Wept," "The Destruction of Sennacherib"). Nationalism can be most fully realized by eliminating all possibility for a national *possession*.

Byron's "Turkish Tales," the poetic enterprises that were inspired by the first two cantos of *Childe Harold* (Murray encouraged Byron to write tales with an "oriental" flavor), similarly depict intertwined religious and nationalist sentiment that is relentlessly linked to a chilling panorama of silence, alienation, destruction, and decay.[23] In *The Corsair* (1814), for example, one of the hero's distinguishing marks is his denial that his beliefs can redeem the destructive effects of his actions. On the one hand, these tales represent contentions between incommensurable beliefs – Turk and Greek, Moslem and Christian, Crescent and Cross – as powerful sources of social organization *and* as sheer artifice. The most fervent religious beliefs only appear as empty rituals to which Seyd conforms while quaffing "Forbidden draughts" (*The Corsair*, 2.32); religion is costume or bric-à-brac, a "saintly garb" (2.144) that Conrad casts off to deal his "demon death-blow" (2.151). On the other hand, however, the hero's aim is not merely to oppose the artificiality of religion with a purer form of belief, human "compassion" (2.227), or self-interest. Rather, Conrad's heroism is most clearly conveyed through his insistence on the inability of any belief to account for, or excuse him from, his crime: "Things light or lovely in their acted time" become "to stern reflection each a crime" (2.351–52). Rather than a paragon of heroic or aristocratic virtue, that is, the paradigmatic hero of the "Turkish Tales" is most striking because he embraces a responsibility for the violent, destructive effects of sectarian struggle that no religious or humanized doctrine can purify. The strategy of the "Turkish Tales" thus differs from the way that Southey's *Thalaba the Destroyer* (1801) makes the Islamic hero into a spokesman for Christian virtue, just as it differs from the way that Thomas Moore's *Lallah Rookh* (1817) maintains a consistently skeptical relationship to religious irrationality and imposture.[24] Neither an endorsement of religious principles nor an acceptance of more rational philosophical principles, Byron's "Turkish Tales" find a resolution to contentions between Christian and Moslem, Greek and Turk only by submitting the self-enclosed, self-adjudicating structures of belief to a scene of ruin. Even though Byron dedicates *The Corsair* to Moore – and thus allies himself with Moore's overt comparisons between Greek and Irish nationalism, Turkish and British oppression – the "Turkish Tales" do not champion a particular nationalist cause as much as they champion accommodation: a universal accommodation achieved by representing universal defeat.

To return to *Childe Harold*, then: the logic I have been tracing suggests that the poem does not merely keep a cautious distance from religious and national alliances, nor does it merely endorse such alliances – alternatives adopted by various critics of Byron's work. Richard C. Sha, on the one hand, argues that *Childe Harold* displays Byron's "ambivalence towards monuments" and their "ephemerality"; Anne Janowitz's even more radical claim is that Byron's rejection of heroic and nationalistic ambition drives him into a "dangerous" embrace of this ephemerality that imperils the very integrity of poetry. Vincent Newey, on the other hand, suggests that "*Childe Harold* ironizes, while remaining dependent upon, never relinquishing, a teleology of fulfillment for the poem, for pilgrimage, and for the life of man as well."[25] And Jerome Christensen categorizes the fourth canto in particular as a monumental triumph of British cultural hegemony; Italian ruins are an imagined imperial acquisition.[26] What I am arguing is that Byron endorses neither a skeptical perspective nor a metaphysical, imperializing perspective. Rather, serialized religious violence permits Byron to reach a poetic solution to violence itself, a solution to be found by assiduously locating the possibility for expression in the process of mouldering and decay.

Indeed, this is precisely why Byron adopts an unusual way of characterizing political and military strength: a demand for internal conformity that reverses itself as a more profound weakness. The third canto associates Napoleon – a rich resource for the author's poetic self-perception – with the league of "madmen who have made men mad / By their contagion; Conquerors and Kings, / Founders of sects and systems, to whom add / Sophists, Bards, Statesmen, all unquiet things / Which stir too strongly the soul's secret springs" (*Childe Harold*, 3.43). The founders of sects and systems are at once too powerful and yet powerless, for theirs is a kind of power that "eats into itself, and rusts ingloriously" (3.44). Byron's point is not simply to show how all power corrupts: the more interesting aim of these lines is to make religious or political uniformity (in keeping with the claims of the parliamentary speech) necessarily divide and disorganize itself. By contrast, poetry can be claimed as a discourse whose very expansiveness – and its indifference to moral corruption – is precisely what saves it from corruption.

Although self-determination, whether personal or national, repeatedly appears self-defeating, Byron's ultimate strategy is to offer sites of poetic contemplation that are appropriate only insofar as they are undetermined as the property of any specific believer or believers. The poet-narrator can call "lovely Spain" a "romantic land" not because it glorifies any specific national consciousness but because of its resistance to exclusive possession, its status as "land" rather than property. The lack of propertied enclosure, that is, provides an opportunity for poetic enclosure. It is on such sites as a river – the "Dark Guadiana," in his account of the Battle of Albuera – that Byron focuses his verse, since it provides an occasion for him both to invoke religious conflict and to set it at bay:

> But ere the mingling bounds have far been pass'd
> Dark Guadiana rolls his power along
> In sullen billows, murmuring and vast,
> So noted ancient roundelays among.
> Whilome upon his banks did legions throng
> Of Moor and knight, in mailed splendour drest:
> Here ceas'd the swift their race, here sunk the strong;
> The Paynim turban and the Christian crest
> Mix'd on the bleeding stream, by floating hosts oppress'd.
>
> (1.34)

Or, at an earlier moment in his account of the Convent of "our 'Lady's house of woe,'" Byron indulges in a series of typically Gothic descriptions: of monks with their "little relics," of "impious men" punished for their beliefs, and of the hermit Honorius, hoping "to merit Heaven by making earth a Hell."[27] He then moves on to focus on the "crags" where "rude-carved crosses near the path" are "memorials frail of murderous wrath":

> For wheresoe'er the shrieking victim hath
> Pour'd forth his blood beneath the assassin's knife

> Some hand erects a cross of mouldering lath;
> And grove and glen with thousand such are rife
> Throughout this purple land, where law secures not life.
>
> (1.21)

Surely Peter Manning is correct to observe that Byron's narrative method in the Albuera stanzas (1.34–44) requires and achieves a safe distance from the violence it represents. But we could still add to this account that Byron does not merely repress or deny human sympathy as a psychological defense, as Manning suggests.[28] Rather, the Gothicism of Byron's "Gothic gore" (1.35) described in the Albuera stanzas, in the account of the crosses, and in similarly "Gothic" moments elsewhere in the poem, is to be discerned in the way that Byron offers a distinctive poetic solution to the very problem of serialized religious violence that results in destruction and bloodshed. The Gothic gore in these stanzas derives from an unresolved – and unresolvable – contention among beliefs, and Byron makes land itself seem as if it could act as a rejoinder to that contention. Belief seems like a merely artificial imposition on landscape with an "impious hand" (1.15). But land, along with the very beliefs imposed upon it, can finally be described in terms so rigorously material that materiality – the ebb and flow of nature's accidental forces, unattached to any personal claims upon or about those forces – seems utterly resistant to any imposition of consciousness. Crest and turban, lost in the "bleeding stream," are of poetic interest precisely *because* they have been unleashed from their informing consciousnesses. Even the very acts of representing beliefs seem to be absorbed among, to the point of disappearing within, nature's processes: the crosses being placed in the landscape are already "mouldering" as if belief needed to deteriorate at the moment of its articulation.

But the complete extent of Byron's treatment of belief in this poem can be observed in the way that mouldering belief seems both utterly material and yet more than material. Nature is composed of mute objects; yet, more than an assortment of mute objects, nature functions as a matrix of more formal points of convergence for incommensurable prejudices. Asymmetry looks symmetrical. This is why the landscapes of *Childe Harold* end up offering, through their very materiality, an antidote to their status as material exposed to the possession of, and determination by, a unique human consciousness. The Dark Guadiana in stanza 34 of canto 1 is the site of "mix'd" pressures of belief, pressures that are both resisted and preserved in nature's mixing of religious representations – as if the mingling turban and crest, just like the "bleeding stream," demonstrated through metonymic means a metonymy constructed by nature itself. The image of the Dark Guadiana, furthermore, shows how crucial it is for Byron to affiliate his poetry with these natural processes, since nature appears to have performed the double gesture of erasing belief and procuring its legibility in a new form.

The contrast I have been examining, between sectarian prejudice and Byron's "Romantic" poetic organization of prejudice, ultimately contributes to *Childe Harold*'s construction of the figure of the poet; the poet, just like the territory of the nation, becomes the object of political and religious prejudice. Dante and Boccaccio, for example, are "proscribed" bards – and proscription assumes a profound resonance for Byron precisely because it identifies the writer as outlaw. This identification takes hold not because of the writer's intention to betray the rule of law but because the writer is one who is *written out* of the law by the force of prejudicial exclusion (by "factions" and "the hyaena bigot's wrong" [4.57, 58]): by the desire – just like Napoleon's – to preserve orthodox social and poetic entities from internal corruption and disharmony. Dante and Boccaccio acquire a significance for Byron for a very different but surprising reason. If their poetry has outlasted bigotry and factionalism, this endurance is celebrated as if the damage done to these authors during their lives and after their deaths could be counted as a certain kind of honor. Destruction and ruin offer an unusual poetic rebuke to bigotry and factionalism, since Byron strangely reveres the tragic effects of reciprocal bigotry. The poet-narrator's worship of these writers with a "reverent tread" in the "mausoleums of the Muse" (4.60) is a worship of poets that can be secured only because the worship is attached to the ruins of beliefs (both the author's and his proscribers) that outlast any agent that would argue for their authority.

Whether celebrating national monuments in architecture or poetry, *Childe Harold*'s tolerant poetic imperative requires it to engage in a sustained merger between monumental human constructions and the accidents of nature and history. Nature acquires its own monumentality, and mouldering monuments achieve their monumentality by becoming unpropertied nature. For Byron, then, "Santa Croce's precincts" house "Ashes which make it holier, dust which is / Even in itself an immortality" (4.54), a curious reversal in which a church does not sanctify ashes but ashes sanctify a church because of the muteness of the bones enshrined there. At this stanza, Byron's own note pays a somewhat eccentric but revealing homage to Madame De Staël, author of *Corinne, or Italy* (1807), "whose eloquence was poured over the illustrious ashes, and whose voice is now as mute as those she sung" (*BP*II:235). Crucial as De Staël's text is to *Childe Harold* (like Byron's poem, her novel is steeped in the tradition of the Gothic), the distinction between the works is striking at this point. In *Corinne*, the eponymous hero's visit to Santa Croce makes her feel alienated from the priests who are praying for the dead, and the tombs only make her feel the weight of loneliness without "stimulus." She wishes instead for a heroic recovery of her former "talents" after losing all hope of marrying Oswald.[29] Byron, however, oddly celebrates and yearns for the death that Corinne desires to transcend. In the note, in fact, there is no mention of "De Staël" but only "Corinna," as if the writer's life could only be found in the text that survives after death. Death, in fact, is more than an unfortunate and disappointing reality; it is *necessary* for the survival of the author's writing, since it is the way for her work to continue to attract the attention of readers and thus attract interest beyond the narrower prejudices ("the fear, the flattery, and the envy"[*BP*II:235]) of her contemporaries. In Byron's stanza itself, the bodily remains of the poets emerge as a strange source of vitality. The "bones" are not only bones but bones with names attached; their immortality as mere bodily matter depends upon their status as more than matter and attached to a sequence of names that are part of common cultural currency: "Angelo's, Alfieri's bones . . . / The starry Galileo . . . / Machiavelli's earth" (*Childe Harold*, 4.54). The cultural currency of these names, in turn, hinges upon Galileo's identification with the stars and Machiavelli with the earth, as if personal names are not merely personal but the very means of knowing the world and the universe. Like a möbius strip, the stanza makes the monumental into natural into monumental into natural: alternatives that ultimately seem less like alternatives than like necessary descriptions of each other. The dust is monumental nature, or a natural monument; by the same token, Italy's attraction for the poet's imagination can be assured rather than threatened by its ruin: its "decay," Byron writes, is "impregnate with divinity" (4.55). The poet's way of exalting decay rather than the survival of his voice, I think, helps us to see why it is that Byron – identifying himself with the poetic figures of Dante and Boccaccio – in fact forces ruin upon himself: he associates his own poetry with the "wreck" of Rome, now become a "shrine" that is "divinely desolate" (4.131). Embracing poetry as a ruin means shutting off the avenue of poetry as sympathy ("I seek no sympathies" [4.10]). But the absence of sympathy is felt neither as a tragic loss nor as a poetic defect; it is a poetic gain because of its distance from the logic of sectarian sympathy which the poem both names and seeks to avoid.

KEATS, POETIC OATHS, AND VULGAR SUPERSTITIONS

Byron, I have been arguing, makes prejudices survive only within the realm of a poetic articulation that depends upon the demise and redirection of their self-determining power. This perspective on belief – one framed as a poetic perspective on a political problem of religious intolerance – may indeed seem to be a rather odd solution to that political problem, since it seems to represent the deaths of adherents of contending beliefs in order to accommodate them. At the same time, however, Byron's verse pursues this strategy precisely in order to procure a specific status for poetry's relationship to present readers: verse that views the pressures of belief as deadened – or at least curtailed – in a reader's encounter with the poem. Byron shows the reader how the poem is her destiny.[30]

To state the case more contentiously, I would argue that the claims for poetic authority in *Childe Harold* are self-consciously articulated against the self-determining authority of beliefs – as if the poem were striving to become the antithesis of poetry as a "commonplace" with an appeal to "common truth" or "common sense," as John Guillory describes the project of eighteenth-century didactic and pastoral verse.[31] It is this logic that I want to locate in Keats's poetry, as well: poetry that has frequently been described in connection with religion or with religious belief, but only recently in connection with the politics of religion. To turn to Keats's writing is, to be sure, an abrupt shift from Byron's resistance to aligning his poetry with religious beliefs to Keats's contrasting attempts to forge such an alliance by casting his lyric speakers and starring characters as the most fervent worshipers and hoodwinked believers. Beyond this difference, however, lies an even more profound compatibility. For the acts of worship that seem central to Keats's poetic enterprise are, I would argue, crucially fashioned as the very means through which poetry might both avoid enforcing belief and thereby signal its own strength and durability.

If most critics of Byron have been more comfortable fitting him into the tradition of philosophical skepticism, it has been far more common for generations of influential readers – from Joseph Severn in Keats's day to David Perkins in our own – to understand the poet's work as a kind of religion serving as the proper object of disinterested devotion. Keats's work supposedly replaces doctrines of religion (doctrines either corrupt or missing in the real world) with a doctrine of what M. H. Abrams terms "agnostic humanism."[32] The New Critical account of

Keats makes his poetry seem like the articulation of a particularly refined level of human sympathy, but the very idea of an "agnostic humanism" may simply beg the question as to how humans are to be defined in order to experience Keatsian humanism. Although willing to accept the fundamental logic of the New Critical accounts, readers in recent years have been more inclined to see Keats's general commitment to human "sympathetic" or "empathetic" levels of response as a disguised form of class interest: a class interest that is merely repeated and endorsed rather than recognized and analyzed by sympathetic formalist critics. For Jerome McGann, the poetry in Keats's 1820 volume can be most fruitfully viewed as a denial of the social conditions that are at once invisible in the artefact of the poem and yet appreciable *as* a denial because of the conditions of production and reception.[33] Marjorie Levinson, adopting a somewhat different view of the poems, interprets Keats as a much more highly self-conscious participant in the nervously mobile middle class of Regency Britain. Taking her cue from the stinging reviews by his contemporaries, Levinson ingeniously reads the contemporary outrage over the poet's aesthetic fraudulence and sexual immaturity as the truth of Keats's poetic self-allegorization. "Escapism" becomes "project": the fetishistic beauty of his verse reflects its "marginal, longing relation to the legitimate bourgeoisie . . . of his day"; his "adolescence," "literariness," "stylistic suspensions," and "pronounced reflexiveness" are symptoms of the writer's precarious middle-class status, "between the Truth of the working class and the Beauty of the leisure class."[34]

I will discuss Levinson's normalizing vocabulary through which "working class" can be equated with truth at a later moment; let it suffice to say for now that McGann's and Levinson's accounts (and those that have been influenced by theirs) offer their most acute correction of the New Critical readings primarily by showing how poetry stands in relation to a previously unacknowledged truth of specific motives and interests.[35] Other critics have still more recently suggested that Keats's poems take their shape from an entirely different set of interests, however. Readers such as Paul Hamilton discern a far more subversive slant in Keatsian aestheticism than Levinson's account allows: for him, "aesthetic success" is itself subversive, for it "calls into question the universals of which art is the acceptable expression and legitimating front."[36] And work by Jeffrey Cox and Nicholas Roe, still more relevant for the discussion I am pursuing, portrays Keats as an opponent of a whole range of political and religious orthodoxies. Cox sees Keats as a "political" poet whose 1817 volume adopts a particularly iconoclastic view towards the way that

Wordsworth comes to the "service of traditional religion and finally of traditional political power as well."[37] Roe argues even more broadly that from *Endymion* to "To Autumn," we can find a poet adopting, at various points in his career, a "radical skepticism and republicanism," a "jacobin potential" achieved through what Roe keenly observes as a "complex of oppositional values." Expanding on Robert Ryan's insightful account of Keats's political and religious radicalism, Roe's detailed study of Keats's education – including his schooling at the Dissenting Enfield Academy under the tutelage of John Clarke, where Keats might have been exposed to the ideas of Dyer and Frend (although there is little evidence to suggest that he read their work) – suggests how well schooled Keats may have been in radical thought.[38]

The subject of Keats's education and political connections, now very well-worn, is interesting to me for reasons that differ from those offered by critics who have seen the poet's affiliations with Dissent as an index to his radical political leanings. As intriguing as those affiliations may be, I have been arguing so far in this book that the Dissenting intellectual milieu did not only argue on behalf of the political validity of their own beliefs; they also frequently argued for a different relation between institutions of government and the beliefs of the persons who were superintended by them. Understanding Keats's poetry, similarly, requires that we acknowledge not merely his identification with a specific kind of religious or political belief, but his negotiation of belief more generally. That negotiation is handled differently in different poems. In his "Lines on Seeing a Lock of Milton's Hair," a poem written in 1818 but not published until 1838, Keats cleverly represents Milton as a member of a religious orthodoxy from which the speaker is conspicuously removed. To make a "burnt sacrifice of verse / And melody," to Keats's mind, is only a "mad endeavor" (9–10,6); he instead comes up with something more modest: a "Delian oath," through which the poet vows to "Leave to an after time / Hymning and harmony / Of thee, and of thy works, and of thy life" (25–27,18). Such an oath, echoing Milton's wish in *The Reason of Church Government* (1642) to "leave something so written to after-times, as they should not willingly let it die," at once validates the poem as an act of political and religious faith and simultaneously reveals the poem's (and the poet's) exclusion from a system of normative beliefs that he hopes, at some point, to acquire.[39] This oath is "Delian" – that is, to Delos, the birthplace of Apollo – and thus his alliances are made to seem conspicuously regressive in relation to Milton's Christianity. If Milton's "Nativity" Ode had made classical gods yield to the Judeo-Christian

God, Keats equates his poetic immaturity with a doctrinal immaturity, and the poem itself as an example of a "childish fashion," which will someday be "vanish'd from [his] rhyme" (22–23). Keats's pre-Christian, polytheistic religious immaturity must be overcome in order to be the mature English poet: a poet who follows the logic of the Nativity Ode, ending up as part of a Christian church that sings of Milton, his works, and his life.

Keats thus drafts his *gradus ad parnassum* not in relation to Milton the political poet – Milton the spokesman for an English republican discourse – but Milton the mature Christian poet; he sees himself as a poet whose ability to go on in his vocation depends upon living up to Milton's Christian standard.[40] The point, of course, is not biographical but formal: it is not that Keats actually feels that he must become a Christian or that he is not one to begin with, but that writing good poetry is *like* adopting a new set of beliefs. This, however, is only one poetic response that Keats frames in relation to religious belief. For if it seems in this poem as if poetry functions for him as a proper Christian religion to which he must conform, there is a very different way to approach religious belief in other works: one that makes poetry seem like the purest rejection of the very logic of poetic commitment proposed by the Milton "Lines." Keats's 1818 letter to Reynolds on "the chamber of maiden thought" and "the grand march of intellect" suggests that Milton's religious affiliations – to the "remaining Dogmas and superstitions" in Protestantism following freedom from "the Inquisition and burning in Smithfield" – do not guarantee his authority as much as they compromise it.[41] Milton, in this letter, is disabled as a poet insofar as his intellect is blinded by false beliefs. And in "Written in Disgust of Vulgar Superstition" (1816), a poem written earlier than either the Milton "Lines" but not published until Houghton's 1876 edition of Keats's poetry, Keats treats established religion with a contempt that looks very much like a poetic requirement. The speaker invokes established religion as an enemy to his own vision of enlightened poetic greatness. The "church bells" that summon people to prayers and the "sermon's horrid sound" show how "the mind of man is closely bound / In some black spell," for organized religion "tears" him from things of greater value and greater pleasure: "fireside joys, and Lydian airs, / And converse high of those with glory crown'd" (1–8). The poet can only vaguely hope that, in some uncertain future, "fresh flowers will grow / And many glories of immortal stamp" (13–14).

Read in the light of this sonnet, the Milton "Lines" would seem conspicuously "vulgar" and hypocritical expressions, but the "Lines," written after the sonnet, might also be understood as a sober correction of it. Would it be possible, therefore, to see the "Lines" as Keats's capitulation to a more properly Miltonic poetic authority – or at least a desire to commit himself to acquiring that authority? Perhaps. But it might be less convincing to see the poems as illustrations of a development from dissent to orthodoxy than as logically symmetrical alliances with opposing beliefs – alliances that seem particularly significant because they are written up as failed acquisitions of poetic voice. Keats is thinking about a correspondence between poetry and belief – either an acceptance of the coercive terms of collective belief (in "Lines"), or a refusal of collective belief by some stronger sense of personal belief or conviction (in "Vulgar Superstition").[42] But the acceptance or refusal of common beliefs yields a problematic result. What is problematic is not the status of these works for us as readers of the poems, but the status of these works for Keats as a poet, who openly displays a self-conscious lack of poetic conviction inversely proportionate to the strength of religious – or anti-religious – conviction. These are poems that in fact seem only to collapse under pressures from contending beliefs: on the one hand, the Milton "Lines" devote themselves to a religious orthodoxy that jeopardizes the value of the very poetry that lends religion its support; on the other hand, "Vulgar Superstition" makes an opposition to establishment seem either chilled or emptied by its own vigor.

SEEMING AND BELIEVING: THE GOTHIC MUSE AND *THE EVE OF ST. AGNES*

So far I have been describing works that seem designed for poetic implosion, and Keats refrains from publishing them as if to confirm that their strength of personal conviction makes them inadequate as publishable poems. The dynamics of religious inclusion and exclusion, of acceptance and refusal, continue to be addressed in Keats's writing. I want to argue, however, that still other works – including those in the 1820 volume of poems – suggest that one of his primary preoccupations as a writer was not merely to espouse one set of contending beliefs or another (orthodox or heterodox, Miltonic, or anti-Miltonic) but to frame poetic projects that were responses to contending beliefs more generally.

This is what connects Keats's writing to the logic of toleration – a logic that likewise connects it to the Gothic novel; and it is hardly surprising, from this vantage point, that the Gothic is never very far from Keats's mind when he discusses the poetry that would be contained in the *Lamia* volume. Writing to his brother George and sister-in-law Georgiana Keats in 1819, he comments on the poems he had recently written – "the Pot of Basil, St. Agnes Eve, and . . . a little thing called the Eve of St. Mark" – as works with "fine Mother Radcliff [*sic*] names." The remark may not seem terribly interesting if it we take it as a remark *only* about the names of his poems and the names or characters in Radcliffe's novels. Perhaps what is more intriguing is the way the letter points us towards Keats's and Radcliffe's shared interests in religious terror, in the *politics* of religious belief that Keats continues to address in the letter. The observation about the names of poems, in fact, quickly leads to an extended account of the consecration of a chapel; and this shows how the more profound political logic of the Gothic – not merely its names – occupies Keats's mind. The letter continues, first by recounting a trip by chaise to a chapel "built by Mr. Way, a great Jew converter, who in that line has spent one hundred thousand pounds," and it goes on to speak directly of the consecration of the chapel, which was "crammed with clergy." "I begin to hate parsons," Keats writes,

they did not make me love them that day when I saw them in their proper colours. A parson is a Lamb in a drawing-room, and a Lion in a vestry. The notions of Society will not permit a parson to give way to his temper in any shape – So he festers in himself – his features get a peculiar, diabolical, self-sufficient, iron stupid expression. He is continually acting – his mind is against every man, and every man's mind is against him – He is a hypocrite to the Believer and a coward to the unbeliever – He must be either a knave or an idiot – and there is no man so much to be pitied as an idiot parson. The soldier who is cheated into an Esprit du Corps by a red coat, a band, and colours, for the purpose of nothing, is not half so pitiable as the parson who is led by the nose by the Bench of Bishops and is smothered in absurdities – a poor necessary subaltern of the church.[43]

The letter is especially relevant for my discussion, I think, because of its easy shift from the subject of the Gothic to the subject of the dynamics of belief: dynamics of belief that are as important in the writing of this poet as they are in the Gothic novels of "Mother Radliff." The parson, and the logic of conversion with which he is associated, attracts Keats's attention within a discussion of his poetry not only because of the "absurdities" of church doctrine, but because of the structure of church authority that makes belief into the basis for political unity. The parson is a "poor necessary subaltern of the church," one who is "led by the nose" rather than thinking for himself; and he must likewise try to make subalterns out of his audience of believers and unbelievers. In one sense, the parson – with his mind against every man, and every man's mind against him – seems to disrupt the ideal sympathy of political community. But in another sense his very demand for sympathetic conformity – his attempt to make minds like each other – is precisely what puts his mind against his audience's. His lack of sympathy with the audience is the effect of his attempt to achieve it; and he ends up sundering that audience into the superstitious converted – those to whom he is a "knave" – and the excluded unbeliever who regards his attempts to convert as utterly meaningless – and for whom the parson is only an "idiot" or "coward." Like Byron's analogy between England and Ireland and the "shark and its prey," Keats makes the politics of religious conformity look both oppressive *and* disorderly, tyrannical *and* chaotic.

What we see in this letter, furthermore, is that Keats sets up the relationship between audience and parson in the same way that he sets up the relationship between himself and the authority of established religion in the poems that I discussed earlier. If the Milton "Lines" configure Keats as the poet who must identify himself with Milton's religion, the letter implies that the poet must become the superstitious worshipper to the poetic "knave" that is Milton. Likewise, the perspective adopted by "Vulgar Superstition" makes established religion into an object of contempt or ridicule, corresponding with the unbeliever who regards the parson as an idiot or coward. That Keats's subject in his letter is not merely the practice of a religious establishment but the practice of poetry, moreover, is to be discerned not only in the parallelism that I have just described but in the way that the letter proceeds. For Keats goes on – continuing the letter several days later – to describe the influence of the literary reviews as if they were a version of religious establishment: "These Reviews... are getting more powerful, especially the Quarterly – they are like a superstition which the more it prostrates the Crowd and the longer it continues the more powerful it becomes just in proportion to their increasing weakness." Maybe Keats seems to fear the reviews because of their ability to enforce public superstition – to perpetuate false opinions. This, at any rate, is the way we might read the comment if "their" in "their increasing weakness" is meant to refer to "Crowd." But he may instead (or also) mean to have "their" refer to "Reviews," thus implying that their strength is also their weakness. For they are weak precisely to the extent that they attempt to enforce beliefs about the works under consideration, attempting to command conformity that will necessarily divide the audience it seeks to unify.[44]

The letters elsewhere show Keats to be an avid reader of radical anti-establishment – in fact, anti-religious – propaganda. He reports regularly on his reading of Hazlitt's attacks on the established church in *The Examiner* in 1817, Horace Smith's "Nehemiah Muggs, an Exposure of the Methodists," Reynolds's "two very capital articles" in *The Yellow Dwarf* on "Popular Preachers," to name just a few examples.[45] Keats's 1819 letter might easily be compared with Horace Smith's "Nehemiah Muggs," a satirical portrait of a trader-turned-preacher, whose "unconverted congregation" greets his sententious doctrines of abstinence with laughter and contempt.[46] But what I have been trying to show is that Keats's letter may have been less interested in satirizing a specific set of religious beliefs and practices, and more interested in articulating an uneasiness with *any* attempt that his poetry might make to align itself with, or argue for, such beliefs and practices. This is because – as Keats sees it – the discourse that aims to gain religious or political adherents (or adherents on behalf of a specific literary taste) seems, in its very exertion of power, to secure its own weakness.

The letter mobilizes a hostility to belief, or, more accurately, it asserts a priority of poetry over belief, that might indirectly define Keats's poetic project itself. If the parson's discourse divides its audience by trying to convert it, his poetry's power is demonstrated by rejecting such a need for conversion, thus shoring up poetic authority by relinquishing a logic of confessional authority. I would argue that this way of understanding his poetic mission sheds a new light on what Keats refers to when he famously remarks upon "the grand march of the intellect" in the letter I mentioned earlier: Keats's way of distinguishing between Milton's dogmatic Protestantism and Wordsworth's ability to "think into the human heart" (KL1:282). In 1828, in fact, Lord Eldon chose the phrase "the march of intellect" as a synonym for "liberality," a socially disruptive force – as he saw it – bent upon "uprooting" the alliance of church and state, "the foundations of all that constituted the happiness and glory of this country."[47] It is this mission – one that participates in the march of intellect not merely as an adoption of rational beliefs but as a controversial political and poetic disposition towards belief – that informs *The Eve of St. Agnes* and reveals its profound connections to the Gothic novel. Here, Keats constructs a poem rich with psychological struggle, in which Madeline's superstitions fall prey to the manipulation of objects and images that compel belief and enable Porphyro's pursuit of private desires and interests. Yet the poem invokes those struggles precisely in order to ensure its own status as a more potent fiction – resistant to the superstitions of the believer and the doubts of the unbeliever – that self-consciously solicits and manages pressures of belief.

Although the reader's attention might plausibly focus on Madeline's ritual as the center of the poem, it is still the case that *The Eve of St. Agnes* encourages an experience of reading that does not immediately permit a reliable rational viewpoint from which we can observe such beliefs or rituals. Rather, Keats crowds the poem with a whole range – let us call it a string – of incommensurable beliefs and prejudices, a world in which the romantic liaison between Madeline and Porphyro both violates and mirrors prejudicial ties of kinship. The house of Madeline's family teems with "barbarian hordes, / Hyena foemen, and hot-blooded lords / Whose very dogs would execrations howl / Against his lineage" (85–88); the revelling crowd surrounds Madeline with a drama of conflicting private passions – a "throng'd resort / Of whisperers in anger, or in sport" and "looks of love, defiance, hate, and scorn" (67–69). Meanwhile, the nurse tells Porphyro of the "dwarfish Hildebrand" who curses "thee and thine, both house and land" and of the "old Lord Maurice" who presumably utters a similar curse which she will not repeat (100–3).

Madeline's ritual – through which, according to legend, "Young virgins might have visions of delight, / And soft adorings from their loves receive / Upon the honey'd middle of the night" (47–49) – looks like an escape from these prejudices: indeed, the object of the superstitious ritual is to gain access to an experience produced neither by herself nor her family but by a supernatural source. At the same time, however, the poem keeps reminding us that the ritual, while designed to tap into the supernatural authority of a realm beyond the pressures of individual or collective consciousness, nevertheless remains dependent upon them. Madeline's preparations for her vision engage her in a denial of the world of sensations that is, after all, an imperfect denial: the music is not unheard but "scarcely heard," she does not "hee[d]" the object of sight but she nevertheless sees "many a sweeping train / Pass by" (57–59). Half in the world of her own (and other people's) prejudices, her ritual is only a half-escape from them; she seeks a place beyond the influence of prejudicial beliefs, even while she falls under their influence.[48]

The point would seem to be only further reinforced by making every escape from prejudice seem like a renewal of its forces. Ritual and worship are routinely unmasked as instruments of specific personal desires and interests. Porphyro, for example, appears to have his own ritual to attend to – imploring "All saints to give him sight of Madeline, / But for one moment in the tedious hours, / That he might gaze and worship all unseen; / Perchance speak, kneel, touch, kiss – in sooth such things have been" (78–81). The archly turned alexandrine, though, provides a reminder of – and distance from – the rituals of Spenserian romance. "In sooth such things have been" at once points to the genre of romance – where tales of men worshiping women have been told – and at the same time insinuates that such a notion is *only* the product of romance and a merely artful way of disguising other (sexual) motives. Porphyro thus becomes the superstitious idolator of Madeline's body; but – to use the terminology of Keats's letter – he turns out to be the hypocritical "knave" for Madeline's superstitious worship; his worship becomes only the first step towards making her yield to his personal desire. Porphyro's worship simply provides the means of empowering one consciousness over another, leading Madeline to become "lost" in his "heart." His promises, couched in the vocabulary of romance – "Say, may I be for aye thy vassal blest? / Thy beauty's shield, heart-shap'd and vermeil dyed?" (335–36) – are designed to compel a belief from Madeline that he will actually care for her after raping her, a belief that would be as subject to doubt as any of Madeline's other superstitions.

Belief, Michel de Certeau observes, "occurs between the recognition of an alterity and the establishment of a contract." It is thus central as a support of "expectancies," systems of belief linking "present behaviour to a future that escapes them."[49] It is precisely this instrumental quality that *The Eve of St. Agnes* attaches to belief, at the same time that it reveals terms such as "contract" and "expectancies" to be occasions for relations between persons to emerge as asymmetrical, unstable, or unequal. If Madeline's beliefs are engaged in planning for a future that escapes her, that is, such beliefs are continually shown to be subject to the manipulations of Porphyro, who has his own beliefs in what that future might be. Planning for one's future means losing one's "heart" in – and to – another. But if the poem draws attention on the one hand to the way that an adherence to specific kinds of beliefs (beliefs in rituals, family integrity, personal integrity) might be manipulated by arts of illusion, it also draws attention to itself as a superior and in fact indispensable art of illusion – a "piece of consecrated fancy," as one reviewer put it, upon which other arts of illusion are shown to depend.[50]

To understand the poem on these terms is, first of all, to draw attention to the apparent sponsor of religious illusions, the beadsman telling his rosary in the first stanza of the poem (1–9). Marjorie Levinson has one way of explaining the centrality of this figure; for her, the beadsman "willfully restricts his freedom of feeling," practicing a perversely aestheticized renunciation of satisfying experience that stands for Keats's poetic practice more broadly.[51] Levinson's analysis seems persuasive for isolating the beadsman as a surrogate figure for the poet (and the rosary an "unusually concentrated emblem of the telling style of 'St. Agnes'"), but her reading too quickly resorts to a vocabulary of repression and denial, too easily banks upon a "we" with a normative "expressiveness," "consciousness," or "ego-life" that acts as critical leverage against Keats's supposedly perverse renunciation.[52] Does not this reading also neglect the very specific status of the beadsman (distinct, say, from a parson) that makes him so compelling for Keats? Just as in Scott's *The Antiquary*, the beadsman in this poem is both a purveyor of blessings and an object of others' blessings, both a donor and recipient of charity; he can thus demonstrate the poem's own status in between, rather than merely a restriction of, specific sympathies. To say still more, the beads themselves may be most significant here not because they are the instrument of a repressive system of beliefs ("severed," as Levinson suggests, from the "real" or from "natural ends"); they are the very means through which a belief might gain expression.[53] Keats's beadsman practices both an archaic and thoroughly modern secular form of sympathy beyond all religious sympathy. For at the same time that the beads in *The Eve of St. Agnes* are linked to specific persons and a specific regime of power with its private beliefs and interests, they are also beads that provide an enclosed structure of interrelationships and hierarchies that therefore provide direction to a believer. The rosary's meaning is not derived from the persons for whom the prayers are made; the prayers derive from the connections within the circular arrangement of the beads themselves.

The beadsman and rosary at the beginning of the poem only begin to show us how Keats takes advantage of a whole range of images that seem to lead a double life: images that are both moved by prejudice while all the more compellingly imagined as frames for, and limits upon, prejudice. On the one hand, then, the poem continues to invoke religion within the dynamics of power: religion and religious ritual are merely deceptive coverings that, as Angela says, allow men to "murder upon holy days" (119), or that make Porphyro into an "impious" worshiper, parroting oaths ("by all saints I swear," "O may I ne'er find grace / When my weak voice shall whisper its last prayer," "believe me by these tears," and so on) even while breaking them (145–50). Porphyro's oaths insist upon the force of intention but also upon the fragility of such intention – since the body that swears insists upon its evanescence and anticipates its death.

On the other hand, even while vows and oaths are represented as both fervent and fragile, a whole series of artificial surfaces accumulate depth and resonance precisely because of their artifice. This holds true for the way that "The sculptured dead on each side seem to freeze, / Imprisoned in black, purgatorial rails; / Knights, ladies, praying in dumb orat'ries, / He passeth by; and his weak spirit fails / To think how they may ache in icy hoods and mails" (14–18). The stanza keeps drawing attention to the way that the beadsman imputes a life to the sculpture that it does not have – as if to demonstrate the workings of superstition. But the sculpture is not merely the product of belief; indeed, it elicits or shapes belief in such a powerful way that it appears to drain the beadsman of his own "spirit." Indeed, the stanza so rigorously pursues the dependence of consciousness on its being drained or emptied into art that it in fact makes it unclear who (the beadsman or the poem's narrator) believes that the sculpture "seemed to freeze." And by these means the poem immediately takes on *for itself* the capacity it assigns to the rosary and to the "sculptured dead": the capacity to solicit a range of different consciousnesses into a framework of possibilities that is not limited by the beliefs or dispositions held by an observer or reader.

Richard Moran's philosophical account of metaphor is particularly helpful here, since his view of the "framing effect" of metaphor – denoted by the realm of seeming in Keats's second stanza – suggests that metaphor "does not just sum up the beliefs that led to it; it is meant to amplify and focus them, bringing them into contact with others." Metaphor, Moran further asserts, thus has a way of "changing someone's mind" that does not involve "changing his or her beliefs."[54] Perhaps this account of "framing" – an account that makes metaphor resemble a rosary – indicates the way that *The Eve of St. Agnes*, while it shows individual characters framing each other, also exerts a more powerful and pervasive framing effect of its own. The celebrated stanzas that so lushly describe Madeline's ritual further illustrate this point, for they both gesture to conflicts between contending alliances but also powerfully assert the metaphorical operations of the poem itself as a new formation of alliance:

> A casement high and triple-arch'd there was
> All garlanded with carven imag'ries
> Of fruits, and flowers, and bunches of knot-grass,
> And diamonded with panes of quaint device,
> Innumerable of stains and splendid dyes,

As are the tiger-moth's deep-damask'd wings;
And in the midst, 'mong thousand heraldries,
And twilight saints, and dim emblazonings,
A shielded scutcheon blush'd with blood of queens and kings.

Full on this casement shone the wintry moon,
And threw warm gules on Madeline's fair breast,
As down she knelt for heaven's grace and boon;
Rose-bloom fell on her hands, together prest,
And on her silver cross soft amethyst,
And on her hair a glory, like a saint:
She seem'd a splendid angel, newly drest,
Save wings, for heaven:–Porphyro grew faint:
She knelt, so pure a thing, so free from mortal taint.   (208–25)

These lines assign a specific political instrumentality attached to color
(not far removed from the Jew converter's chapel): one that enlists "innumerable stains and dyes" in the formation of an allegiance to the
sanctified region of the family. The escutcheon's red line represents a
blood line or affiliation between families, and thus stands both as a mark
of inclusion (the joining of two lines of decent) and as a mark of general
exclusion – a sign used to denote the primacy of private family alliances.
But such images – with their own iconic functions – are brought into a
surprising connection with each other and with the framing "casement."
Keats goes so far as to reverse the priority of window and frame: working
from the outside inward, the stanza at first captures the attention with
its account of decorative "imageries" that are poetically privileged above
the heraldic "device[s]," as if to represent the poem's own privilege as
a framing of the contending Gothic devices of exclusion and inclusion.
The panes of glass, furthermore, are described in an intriguing reversal
of priority as if they decorated the casement (the casement is "diamonded
with" the panes) rather than the other way around. The poem manipulates these heraldries, moreover, in order to absorb them into its own
framing effects, the play of light and color making Madeline seem like a
"splendid angel." While Madeline prays *to* a saint, we are also told that
she is *like* a saint herself, and this builds upon the earlier suggestion that
she is "all akin / To spirits of the air, and visions wide" (201–2). This
is a kinship with sainthood, a likeness to saintliness, continually delin-
eated as a metaphorical reworking of kinship achieved through the play
of light and color. It is not, in other words, the result of Porphyro's belief that she is a saint, any more than it is the result of her intentions
to make herself into one: the assertion of kinship with the saints in fact

directs our attention to the poem's own claims to produce a new canon of saints freed from both traditional kinships established through blood and belief.

This rearrangement of alliances and "device[s]" within the text of the poem helps to explain precisely why it is that *The Eve of St. Agnes* routinely frames belief as if it were captured within the act of reading. Metaphor is put to use as a way of drawing attention to the work's own refocusing of belief, its proclamation of a new-found advantage in its status not merely as a belief but as a text about which beliefs may be formed. Porphyro looks upon Angela – as she tells him of Madeline's ritual – "like puzzled urchin on an aged crone / Who keepeth clos'd a wond'rous riddle-book, / As spectacled she sits in chimney nook" (129–31); Madeline is "asleep in legends old" (135); her soul is "Blissfully haven'd both from joy and pain; / Clasp'd like a missal where swart Paynims pray" (240–41). And it is perhaps the ambiguity in the last analogy that emblematizes all of the other examples: "clasp'd" could mean "closed," or it could mean "held" (held open *or* closed); the "missal" – which could be either an instrument of conversion or the paynim's own book of devotion – is unattached to any particular *kind* of worship. It thus simply asserts the fact of reading – a reading to which the poem itself aspires – without reference to religious boundaries.

Still more, though, this account also helps us to see how Porphyro occupies a position that potentially disturbs Keats's project even while that disturbance is managed in a thoroughly poetic fashion. Porphyro attempts to become the object of Madeline's beliefs: he attempts to fulfill the expectations that are part of her superstitious ritual, fitting himself to the image in her mind. Romance, for Porphyro, is deception, a way of connecting a false religious validity to natural desire. He is "no rude infidel" but her "famished pilgrim" or her "eremite"; he claims her to be his "miracle" so that she will see him as hers (277,339,342). Porphyro's fitting himself to Madeline's mind in order to make her believe in him – his attempt to make himself conform to her expectations and beliefs, culminating with the heap of sumptuous "delicates" laid out beside her bed – emerges at the level of psychological intrigue, the devotions of one person based upon the falsely or misleadingly sworn devotions of another. And if Porphyro's language of romance is merely an instrument of deception, Keats's own romance might begin to seem like a similarly deceptive enterprise.

But there is another role for romance in Keats's poem: one that further demonstrates the way that Keats's version of Spenserian romance seeks to manage and order belief in such a way as to reorient the "ideological functions of Romaunt" that Manning ascribes to Byron's stance in relation to Spenser in *Childe Harold*. Like Byron's, this is a reoriented version of romance simultaneously weakened as a vehicle of Christian ideology and strengthened as poetic fiction.[55] In the last three stanzas of the poem, Keats makes the shift from Porphyro's vows – "I will not rob thy nest / Saving of thy sweet self"; "O'er the southern moors I have a home for thee" (340–41,351) – to third-person narration. The gesture at once removes narration from dissimulating or misleading vows while at the same time indulging a language of romance that makes people seem like simulacra: "They glide, like phantoms, into the wide hall; / Like phantoms, to the iron porch, they glide" (361–62). The rhetoric of romance then intensifies in the last stanza:

> And they are gone: ay, ages long ago
> These lovers fled away into the storm.
> That night the Baron dreamt of many a woe,
> And all his warrior-guests, with shade and form
> Of witch, and demon, and large coffin worm,
> Were long be-nightmar'd. Angela the old
> Died palsy-twitch'd, with meagre face deform;
> The Beadsman, after thousand aves told,
> For aye unsought for slept among his ashes cold.   (370–78)

The shift towards this more self-consciously fictional mode at the poem's end helps us, I think, to see how it is that Keats has engaged the fictionality of *The Eve of St. Agnes* within the service of a discourse that is not merely confined to the sphere of irrational or dissimulating beliefs. Romance instead emerges as a far more vitalizing force behind its assertions: romance is Keats's rosary.

The point that I am making can be approached first of all by observing that the last stanza contains at least one crucial ambiguity: are the benightmared guests themselves in the shape of "witch, and demon, and large coffin worm," or are those shapes the stuff of their nightmares? This confusion between what we are to take as "imagined" and what we are to take as "real," between what people dream and what they are, shows how the lines have raised the level of supposedly irrational superstitions to a disconcerting level of authority, the poem indulging in the fantasies that it had represented as the possessions of individual consciousnesses that were misled by such fantasies. Second, however, this indulgence does less to discredit the fictionality of the poem's perspective than to point our attention towards the authority of the poem's fictive constructions and towards our own dependence upon them. In the penultimate stanza, the repetition of "like phantoms" at once accentuates the fictionality of the poem's perspective and yet also encourages us to view the repeated literary figure as the very condition – the ground, so to speak – for understanding a sequence of events. The last stanza, moreover, contains a rapidly narrated sequence of events implying that the first element in the sequence – the elopement of Madeline and Porphyro – might be the proximate cause of the following elements: the Baron's dreams, the guest's nightmares, the death of Angela and the beadsman. But it operates as a proximate cause (one critic calls that cause a "fact" about the poem), rather than sheer accident, only because of the proximity afforded by the stanza itself that *creates* the sense of cause.[56]

To put it another way, romance is not the repression of real causality in Keats's poem; it *is* causality. And this final stanza helps us to realize something about the relation between the poem's fictions and its appeal to the senses that was present from the very first lines. The first stanza of *The Eve of St. Agnes* might be distinguished from the last because of the way that it engages the "telling" of the poem (at first) within an empirical project: conveying the sensation of extreme cold through the images of the cold owl, the limping hare, the silent flock. The beadsman's "telling" of his beads, furthermore, might appear as a contrasting denial of human need (as Levinson argues) because his "telling" looks like a kind of fictional text helping him to suppress those needs. What is crucial here, however, is that the empirical project can be accomplished by constructing an animal need that can only be ascertained through the enterprise of a poetic construction. Need becomes visible here precisely by means of an artifice that takes an apparently self-sufficient animal world – Bataille writes, "the animal is in the world like water in water" – and postulates an insufficiency within that sufficiency.[57] If the beadsman might seem to suppress need through fictional – that is, religious or superstitious – desire, need can in fact only be ascertained thanks to the access to it provided by poetic figures. Romance, rather than a denial of actual needs with superstitious or irrational beliefs, acquires the more precious resource for conceiving need itself.

LAMIA, A POEM FOR THE NON-ELECT

What I have been arguing so far is that *The Eve of St. Agnes* is a quintessentially "Gothic" poem, and that its Gothicism derives from its impulse to relegate beliefs to a position of dependency on the vitalizing artifice of the poem. I think that this helps us to see why it is that the "Ode to Psyche" (1820) is an ode that rejects a collective psyche – Psyche is without altar, virgin choir, shrine, or conventional instruments of worship – while endorsing a thoroughly individualized form of worship: "Yes, I will be thy priest, and build a fane / In some untrodden region of my mind." But Keats's strategy is also to institutionalize this same internal movement: the mind is to be externalized as Psyche, the mind / goddess to be worshipped. The brain, moreover, does not simply house personal belief or devotion; it turns itself into architecture – a "fane" with a "rosy sanctuary" with a "bright torch" and "casement ope at night, / To let the warm Love in" (50–65).

Lamia, also in the 1820 volume of poems, might seem to offer a contrasting position. To many critics, at least, Keats's poem – about a serpent-turned-woman who seduces Lycius, the young students of Corinth's resident skeptic Apollonius – dramatizes the author's mounting anxieties about the legitimacy of his "rosy sanctuary" when faced with the demands and pressures of the outside world.[58] Apparently identifying poetry itself with a superstition vulnerable to the stern eye of reason, *Lamia* has seemed to critics such as Jack Stillinger to be a poem depicting the dangerous forces of the imagination, embodied in the figure of the serpent woman who manipulates Lycius's beliefs.[59] She is able to "clear his soul of doubt"[60] and prevent the intrusion of "but a moment's thought" (2.39).

Such readings are certainly supported by Lamia's deceptiveness; she seduces Lycius by concealing her origins – "by playing woman's part" (1.337) – and by evading his "close inquiry" into her reasons for wanting to avoid any encounter with the skeptical Apollonius (2.103). We are continually reminded, furthermore, of the fragility of these charms: of how Lycius has retreated from "the busy world of more incredulous" (1.397), or the "noisy world almost forsworn" (2.33). He continues to speak as if plagued by the knowledge that his experience is only the stuff of "sweet dreams" (1.377), a view that is seemingly confirmed by the poem's ending.

The pressure of doubt arises in this poem with particular starkness because of the shift from the opening episode in part 1 – where Hermes gives the "snake" Lamia a "woman's form" (1.120) in exchange for allowing Hermes to behold his "guarded nymph" (1.125) – to the busy world of Corinth. This exchange between Hermes and Lamia is crucially untainted by such doubt (there is no distance between imagined and real, fiction and fact, since "dreams of Gods" are "Real" [1.127]), and thus typified by a perfect contractual symmetry. The shift away from this private exchange to Corinth is a shift to a more public ("busy") world and a more "incredulous" world, as if the very presence of society entailed both the production of false appearances and the threat of having falsity exposed by an incredulous audience. The movement from Crete to Corinth is not only a movement from "myth" to "history" (as Daniel Watkins suggests) but also from a mythical world to a world of hypocritical self-mythologizing.[61]

It might be possible to argue that this deliberate foregrounding of credulity and incredulity reflects Keats's thoughts about his own poetry and its inability to withstand an inquiry into its commitments to addressing the concerns of his own busy world. But by making Keats seem like a poet who has put too much faith into his own false constructions we perhaps neglect the way that the poem does not merely take sides with faith or doubt, but takes an even more embracing view of the poem's relation to those positions. Indeed, *Lamia* raises the issue of believing and not believing – or believing something ostensibly more rational – precisely in order to relegate those beliefs to a position that is subordinate to the poem.

While Lamia's deceptive constructions (the house, the wedding feast) seem to be apt analogies to the poet's own fanciful constructions, we must also realize that the poem makes those apparent deceptions appear to be even more solid than the very persons who might either believe or disbelieve in them. Lycius, for example, seems to diminish in size ("he shrank closer") and dissolve like a dream just as much as Lamia herself when they encounter Apollonius: "Why does your tender palm dissolve in dew?" she asks him (1.370). When he presses Lamia to agree to a public marriage, his "passion, cruel grown" seems "fierce and sanguinous," but only for a man on the verge of losing the empirical sensations that would seem to ground his doubts: he is described as "senseless" (2.147), one "whose brow had no dark veins to swell" (2.77). Even Apollonius, while he seeks to penetrate beyond Lamia's deceptions, repeatedly appears to be less substantial than they are. When Lamia and Lycius see Apollonius in the street, he seems so strangely apparitional that Lamia must ask Lycius who he is: not because she cannot match the face to the name, but because he is invisible to her. She cannot "bring to mind / His features" even when he is apparently within their view (1.372–73). As much as Lycius may chide himself for living in "sweet dreams," Apollonius is a "ghost of folly," practicing "proud-heart sophistries, / Unlawful magic, and enticing lies," perhaps with no greater claim to reality or truth than Lamia (1.377,2.285–86).

Surely we cannot ignore the fact that, at the same moment I have just discussed, Lycius does not hide himself from Apollonius; he blinds himself to him. His wish is not to avoid being seen but to avoid seeing himself being seen: "Wherefore did you blind / Yourself from his quick eyes?" Lamia asks (1.373–74). This blinding might appear to be a blinding to the set of empirically oriented beliefs that Apollonius brings to bear upon the world: Lycius chooses, in other words, to believe rather than see – and thus the act of self-blinding could be said to confirm that Lamia's "spell" is merely a denial of the world of sense. But it could be the case instead that this moment reflects not merely a wish to blind one's self to seeing, but a wish to avoid the mutually exclusive alternatives of seeing and believing: the alternatives between which Apollonius, and Lycius himself, seem to waver. And it could also be the case that Keats, accepting the role of Lycius here, has similarly blinded himself – in a rather appealing way – to those alternatives.

This possibility is further entertained in *Lamia*'s manner of setting up a distinction between seeing and believing (between ocular evidence and belief beyond or without evidence) while also making the two seem like versions of each other, and making the poem adopt a resistance to those alternatives. On the one hand, *Lamia* continually invokes seeing as a threat because seeing means seeing through representations with a gaze that reveals their falsity – Apollonius's "eye" is "Like a sharp spear . . . / Keen, cruel, perceant, stinging" (2.299–301). On the other hand, this seeing looks like a set of prejudices that guides seeing. Certainly the ambiguous characterization of Apollonius – his discerning eyes are also "demon eyes" (2.289) – may cause us to question the validity of his perceptive powers. Still more, though, the very occasions that arise to expose Lamia's falsity – occasions that look like public exposures – turn out also, or instead, to demonstrate the force of privately generated prejudice. Lycius's demand upon Lamia to consent to a public wedding, that is, may demonstrate the importance of marriage as a public display, but this public display strangely turns into a process of legitimation through private alliances. While Lamia might seem to urge Lycius to "change his purpose" (2.69) in order to shield the falsity of her charms from discovery, the wedding exposes not merely her falsity but her lack of purely conventional signs of legitimacy. The skeptical concerns about her reality or unreality thus coincide with, and are reinforced by, a policy of social exclusion. The "holy rite" of marriage only exposes how Lamia is an alien in the community of Corinth, without friends and family: "'I have no friends . . . no not one; / My presence in

wide Corinth hardly known'" (2.92–93); and later: "this fair unknown /
Had not a friend" (2.110–11). She is an alien, furthermore, whose lack
of friends or family translates into a lack of shared worship or ritual
that reminds us of the goddess without a shrine in the "Psyche" ode:
"'My parents' bones are in their dusty urns / Sepulchred, where no kindled incense burns, / Seeing all their luckless race are dead, save me'"
(2.94–96).[62]

This lack of friend and family, of shared ritual, brings into further relief
the importance of the marriage ceremony (obviously Keats is recalling
its function in Coleridge's "The Rime of the Ancyent Marinere" [1798])
as a celebration of shared experience: a collection of rituals that are the
result of "custom" and common memory (2.106). Lamia's charm (like
charm of the Mariner's "strange power of speech") is inseparable from
its novelty, its distance from received customs and traditions. It cannot
be "remember'd . . . from childhood" (2.153) any more than it can coincide with the remembered principles of Apollonius's "cold philosophy"
(2.230). Apollonius, moreover, may look upon the "secret bowers" with a
penetrating "eye severe" (2.157), but his ability to discern depends upon
the operation of prejudice. What he sees, Keats takes time to emphasize, is what he believes beforehand: "'twas just as he foresaw" (2.162).
Philosophy's potent threat derives not from its superior claim to reason
or from its privileged access to reality. The threat derives exclusively
from its resemblance to a system of shared values or beliefs that allows
one not to have believing guided by seeing but to have seeing guided
by foreseeing: by values that both mark a specific community and that
exclude participation within it.

Another way of putting this is that doubt in *Lamia* comes to seem like
an exertion of censorship. Keats, in fact, comments on the blasphemous
libel trial of "Carlisle [*sic*] the Bookseller," publisher of "deistical pamphlets . . . Tom Payne [*sic*] and many other works held in superstitious
horror" in a letter that also comments on the prejudices of reviewers
towards his poetry. While the reviewers create the "mire of a bad reputation" against him (as if Carlile were in the position of Keats who is
in the position of Lamia), Keats continues by speculating on the ability
of *Lamia* to "take hold of people in some way." This is to be achieved
not by securing any sense of agreement in beliefs or tastes amongst his
audience, but by providing "either pleasant or unpleasant sensation," for
"what they want is a sensation of some sort."[63] The poem's self-conscious
response to the prejudices adopted by a public appear within the poem
itself, moreover. For Lamia's charm turns out to resemble a truly novel

recombination of religious imagery and ritual:

> Of wealthy lustre was the banquet-room,
> Fill'd with pervading brilliance and perfume:
> Before each lucid pannel fuming stood
> A censer fed with myrrh and spiced wood,
> Each by a sacred tripod held aloft,
> Whose slender feet wide-swerv'd upon the soft
> Wool-woofed carpets: fifty wreaths of smoke
> From fifty censers their light voyage took
> To the high roof, still mimick'd as they rose
> Along the mirror'd walls by twin-clouds odorous.
> Twelve sphered tables, by silk seats insphered,
> High as the level of a man's breast rear'd
> On libbard's paws, upheld the heavy gold
> Of cups and goblets, and the store thrice told
> Of Ceres' horn and, in huge vessels, wine
> Come from the gloomy tun with merry shine.
> Thus loaded with a feast the tables stood,
> Each shrining in the midst the image of a God.
>
> (2.173–90)

This "mighty cost and blaze of wealth" (2.198) might signify Lamia's –
and perhaps Keats's – imperializing imagination. It is not simply the
exertion of power that is at issue here, however, but a specific vantage
point on traditional religions. Keats has shown earlier in the second book
that his poem rejects traditional notions of love that are "hard for the
non-elect to understand," and it might be said that Lamia's own composition at this moment is likewise suited for the non-elect reader (2.6). The
heroic couplets remind us not only of its Augustan predecessors; the imperfect rhyme ("stood" / "God") combined with the specific collection
of images plundered from Eastern religions can be nothing other than
Keats's rumination on and stylistic imitation of the successful "Turkish
Tales." Lamia's conjuring here – just as in Byron's Tales – is insistently
secular, a decidedly literary conjuring that renders up religion for public
observation, anatomization, and consumption. What renders Lamia a
subject of suspicion in the poem, then, is not merely her falsity but her
controversial, cosmopolitan disposition towards belief. The culminating
example of Lamia's tutelage, the wedding feast, makes her seem like
a graduate of "Cupid's college" (1.197) that directly conflicts with the
teachings of Lycius's tutor. Earlier in the poem, she continually displays
all the marks of secular instruction and its emphasis on the classification
of knowledge (she can "unperplex bliss from its neighbour pain / Define
their pettish limits, and estrange / Their points of contact, and swift

counterchange" [1.192–94]; her "dreams" in the "serpent prison house" are dreams that constitute a version of a mythological Pantheon from "Elysium" to "Pluto's gardens" [1.206–12]). The instruments of ritual in the passage above become significant not because of their individual functions in ritual, but because they have been removed from their customary functions in religious ritual and reassembled within the new space of the banquet – a space that produces an encyclopedic disposition towards ritual. This is a disposition emphasizing not merely a specific belief, but something more fundamental: ritualization itself.

What is significant about this encyclopedic collecting of images, I think, is that it de-emphasizes the relation between those collected images and specific systems of beliefs that might ratify them, while it simultaneously endows this collection with more durability than those beliefs. Keats conveys this durability in yet another way, disclosed through the note he attaches to the poem. The note, directing us to *The Anatomy of Melancholy*, emphasizes how Burton's version of the story – adapted from Philostratus's *de Vita Apollonii* – clarifies that when Lamia "saw herself descried . . . she, plate, house, and all that was in it, vanished in an instant."[64] The purpose of recounting this version of the story is twofold. First, it draws our attention more acutely towards the way that Keats's own version makes it far less clear that the objects Lamia creates have disappeared – they have not "withered" or "vanished" at the "potency" of Apollonius's gaze in the same way that Lamia herself has. In fact, Lycius expires on the "high couch," a piece of furniture that Apollonius treats as unreal, but that the poem (colluding with Lamia) encourages us to treat as real – along with the "marriage robe" (2.309–11). These are, at least, fictional entities so acceptable – perhaps essential – to the reader that critics seldom take note of this strategy. Other critics mistakenly claim that the objects have disappeared, inadvertently reinforcing the sense that Lamia's banquet furnishes a ground of figures from which other figures are (falsely) said to vanish.[65] To put it another way, the fictionality of the dreamworld seems, even to the wariest of readers, conspicuously resistant to any effort to treat it as a lie that must be converted into a truth. There is also a second point to Keats's note, however – a point about poetry's relation to belief more generally. With its emphasis on *Lamia*'s literary lineage (a lineage that substitutes for Lamia's uncertain lineage in the poem), the note establishes that Philostratus's fiction has neither withered nor vanished from the pressure of doubt. Keats works a correction upon the tale in order to emphasize a correlation between the lingering charms of Lamia's banquet and the lingering charm of Philostratus's narrative. His refusal to represent the vanishing of

Lamia's work pays tribute to the tale's ability to withstand the efforts of contending beliefs to undo its power.

We can now see exactly how it is that both Byron and Keats respond to *The Excursion* – to which I will return once again at the end of my concluding chapter in order to make more comprehensive claims about the relationship between the poem's detractors and the poem itself. For now, however, it will suffice to show that Wordsworth's exploration of pagan mythology and ancient religions more generally is not so much contradicted but confirmed in the writing that I have discussed in this chapter. In *The Excursion*, the Wanderer elaborates a particularly tolerant vantage point on pagan ritual. In book 4 (631–887), he repeatedly solicits the power of the imagination in one sense as an occult and idolatrous power: the "Chaldean Shepherds" that look on "the polar star, as on a guide / And guardian of their course" or "The lively Grecian" that "Could find commodious place for every God" show how "The imaginative faculty was lord / Of observations natural" (4.694–721). Pagan worship, from this perspective, is a false hierarchy of values attached to objects of the senses that are merely objects in a world of multiple objects. In another sense, however, such "illusions" become "outward ministers / Of inward conscience": a "standard," a "measure and a rule" that guides belief and action, rather than a projection of private disposition (4.834, 836–37,816,808). The operations of occult ritual serve to "exalt / The forms of Nature, and enlarge her powers" (4.845–46), a phrasing that shows how the elaboration of the church-guided British state in book 9 does not simply exclude the logic of pagan ritual but in fact appropriates its functions in order to "exalt" and "enlarge" the powers of the state.

The poetic disposition towards belief that I have been describing in Keats's writing aspires to a similar poetic culture of religious cultures, an occultation of the poem itself as a more capacious framework that both solicits the power of contending beliefs and yet outlasts them. One of *The Excursion*'s few admirers – he thought it one of "three things to rejoice at in this Age" – Keats appropriates Wordsworth's terms for understanding myth both as an illusion *and* as a sustaining language beyond illusion; poetry is continually described in his letters as if it were the Chaldean's guiding star.[66] Shakespeare thus appears as a "presider," a "High Power" giving him "support" during "years of...momentous Labour."[67] And Keats views his own poetic ambitions as an attempt to make his work act as a presider to other readers, his *Endymion* striving – in what is most likely a reference to *The Excursion* – to attain the status of the "Polar star of Poetry." In general he aspires to produce a "system of Salvation," a "system of Soul-making" that is the "Parent of all the more palpable and personal schemes of Redemption among the Zoroastrians the Christians and the Hindoos."[68] The endurance of mythology is thus appropriated in the poems I have been discussing as the source of poetic toleration precisely because of its historical endurance (the Latin *tolerare* meaning both "to endure" through time and "to tolerate" or "to put up with"). The very point of mythology, it could be said, is that its sustained power – its ability to gather the interest of author and reader – cannot be explained by an adherence to a *belief* in the gods of mythology.[69] The only belief required is a belief in the constructedness of myth – or, a belief in mythologizing. Certainly this is the thought behind Coleridge's dreams of producing a "true Pantheon of Heathen mythology...for the use of Schools, & young Artists."[70] Keats, from his appropriation of mythological renderings from "I Stood Tip-Toe Upon a Little Hill" and *Endymion*'s "Hymn to Pan" to the "Ode to Psyche" and *Lamia*, does not merely take myth as a subject for poetry; he investigates the precise degree to which the very notion of "myth" itself is poetic.

In canto 3 of *Childe Harold*, Byron even more explicitly responds to *The Excursion* when he likens Childe Harold to "the Chaldean" who "could watch the stars, / Till he had peopled them with beings bright / As their own beams; and earth and earthborn jars, / And human frailties, were forgotten quite" (3.14). (Although critics point out the Wordsworthian tone of the third canto, they most frequently refer to the influence of "Tintern Abbey," encouraged by Byron's own praise for the *Lyrical Ballads* and acknowledgment of Wordsworth's influence on *Childe Harold*.)[71] Byron's stanza may seem to cut against the grain of *The Excursion*, since the hero of the poem in fact cannot simply forget human frailty: "this clay will sink / Its spark immortal, envying it the light / To which it mounts, as if to break the link / That keeps us from yon heaven which woos us to its brink" (3.14). *Childe Harold* would thus seem to prepare the way for a more extensive satire of Wordsworthian idealism in *Don Juan*. But what I have argued about *The Excursion* is that Wordsworth is interested in religion insofar as it permits the inclusion even of the most skeptical of perspectives. By the same token, Byron's stanza, while it deflates the Chaldean's fanciful personifications, nevertheless winds up affirming their value. For "clay" is not simply equated with the remembrance of frailty; it is "envying" the "light" to which the "spark immortal" aspires, and it thus depends upon the poetic (personifying) "link" between human and divine at the "brink" of heaven – even in the process of opposing it.

CHAPTER 7

Conclusion: the Inquisitorial stage

DON CARLOS AND THE AESTHETICS OF PERSECUTION

The Inquisition *on stage*; the Inquisition *as a stage* to be succeeded, indeed overruled, by a new regime that is both represented on stage and inhabited off stage by the reader or audience: this is the logic that governs the dramatic works I investigate in this concluding chapter. To bring my previous discussions to a close in this way is to look both backwards and forwards. We return full circle now to the Gothic novel – to the mechanisms through which the Gothic surveyed, enclosed, and regulated the terrors of confessional uniformity. But we also add a new dimension to that discussion by expanding the implications of Godwin's striking way of representing the enclosure of confessional uniformity as a new source of terror in *Mandeville*. The hero's plight, as we saw in chapter 1, is to experience the loss of any sense of profound opposition that might derive from his religious or political dissent. Political membership is no longer characterized by a communion of beliefs that must exclude other conflicting beliefs, but by a more capacious Providential state whose triumphant authority achieves its most sublime expression precisely by relinquishing its demand for doctrinal agreement.

In the dramas that I discuss in this chapter, writers showed the continuing currency of the Gothic's politics of religion while capitalizing on the convergence between the theatrical techniques of confessional authority (its practices of oath- and test-taking, its numerous celebrations and rituals of conformity) and the conventions of theater itself.[1] Lord John Russell's *Don Carlos* (1822), Shelley's *The Cenci* (1819), and Byron's *Cain* (1821) – a more disguised Inquisitorial drama – allowed an audience to view the technology of confessional government, and conscripted that audience within the drama's regulation of it. A great deal of recent criticism of Romantic drama has centered on the issue of theatricality and performance, and in this conclusion I both intersect with and depart from many of these arguments. Although postmodern interpretation in the work of critics such as Carlson and Jewett has tended to privilege a view of Romantic theater as a demonstration of theatricality or performativity, I am in fact suggesting that works I group together under the name of "the Inquisitorial stage" sought to expose the theatrical basis for theocratic regimes of government to a new level of scrutiny.[2] Theater, that is, became one of the strongest nineteenth-century advocates for the breakdown of the confessional state's theatrical politics; it became the means through which a British audience (of readers or playgoers) could attempt to solidify its position of liberal tolerance.

Although *Don Carlos; or, Persecution* is probably the least known of the works I discuss here – and is also the latest, having appeared in 1822 – it provides a useful way of demonstrating how dramatic representations of Inquisitorial authority took a typically liberal position with respect to religious belief that inflects the other works that I discuss.[3] *Don Carlos*, among all these works, is undoubtedly the most open about its political leanings: Russell dedicates the drama to Lord Holland (one of the most celebrated reformers of the day), and further proves the work's liberal credentials by referring with approval to articles in *The Monthly Magazine* of 1822 that further supported the play's politics, and pays homage to the account of Don Carlos in Juan Antonio Llorente's *Critical History of the Inquisition in Spain* (1817–18). The network of texts to which Russell alludes is significant, for the Inquisition presented a powerful array of images for writers to call upon well into the nineteenth century as a way of mobilizing liberal positions in political discussion. As Edward Peters has argued, the Inquisition could serve as a literary touchstone for writers who wished to represent an archetypal form of injustice, to such an extent that Inquisition scenes seemed "obligatory" in the Gothic novel.[4] The writers I study here were clearly influenced by this literary tradition established in works ranging from Schiller's frequently read plays *Die Rauber* (1781), *Die Geisterseher* (1789), and his own *Don Carlos* (1787) to the Gothic novel in Britain.[5]

And there were even more specific reasons why the Inquisition might have become a popular subject of literary representation. The Inquisition was not strictly a literary topos but had seemingly approached rather dangerously close to British shores. In 1816, Samuel Romilly presented for the audience of the House of Commons an extensive account of Inquisition-style persecutions against Protestants in France extending from the years before the Revolution to the present. Under Napoleon, he reported, Protestants suffered torture that was "not of the ordinary kind"; and he went on to provide details of women "scourged in a most brutal manner" with "small pieces of iron and small nails . . . by which these people were torn," and a man who was "literally . . . cut into pieces with axes and broad swords."[6] Still more, the Spanish Inquisition, not abolished until 1834, served as a popular focus for political propagandizing. Thomas Clarke's *History of Intolerance* (1820–23), for example, contrasted "liberal maxims of legislation" in Britain with the "pestiferous policy of intolerance" in the Spanish Inquisition; John Stockdale, publisher of Shelley's Gothic novel *St. Irvyne; or, The Rosicrucian* (1811), published his *History of the Inquisitions, From Their Origins to the Present Time* in the same year.[7] Other accounts were readily available in translation, including (to name just a few) D. Antonio Puigblanch's *The Inquisition Unmasked*, translated by William Warton in 1820, Lavallée's *History of the Inquisition*, and Llorente's *Critical History*.

The Inquisition functioned not merely as an object of fear, however. In fact, it would be more correct to say that it provided an opportunity for a liberal press to look at the continent and distance itself from "that diabolical ordeal . . . that uniformly tampered with the lives and liberties of millions of the human race."[8] What the interest in the Inquisition shows – in popular journalism and in parliamentary debate – is that the Inquisition had come to function as a testing ground for political liberals to articulate their positions. Persecution by groups abroad seemed to require stern opposition at home; but persecution also challenged British authors to assert, or campaign for, the superior tolerance of British government itself – even towards potentially dangerous or intolerant groups. A British mode of governing needed to distance itself from the technologies of the Inquisition both abroad *and* at home. In the theatrical spectacle of Inquisitorial politics, writers could meet the ultimate challenge of toleration: to observe and oppose intolerance precisely by performing the complex task of breaking down the conventions of confessional government that had traditionally excluded or eliminated the presence of seemingly hostile political opposition.

We hardly need to consult Russell's sources in order to discern the political logic at work in *Don Carlos* and its representations of the Inquisition. The Inquisition, as Russell represents it here in its sixteenth-century context, is thoroughly dedicated to maintaining the status of traditional beliefs while also contradictorily extirpating traditional beliefs. Its demand for the uniformity of traditional belief, that is, requires simultaneously that it break the bonds of traditional belief for a whole range of the nation's subjects. "Familiar custom" amongst Moslems, for example, must be "purged out by fire" (3–4); the persecution of Flemish Protestants is the backdrop for much of the drama. In contrast, Don Carlos – the play's spokesman for liberal toleration – routinely displays his sympathies with the heretics (he is a heretic and blasphemer himself) who supposedly endanger the kingdom. The hero openly acknowledges these sympathies, embracing rather than suppressing his reputation as an outlawed believer, as if his choice of religious sympathy could be counted as one of his most compelling political credentials. At the same time, the play's multiple schemers (including the Grand Inquisitor Valdez, Don Carlos's duplicitous friend Don Luis, and the jealous Leonora) skillfully conflate the hero's religious infidelity with both political and sexual infidelity; they accuse him of an adulterous relationship with his stepmother the Queen, and of hatching radical political plots against the King.

Two interesting features of Don Carlos's speeches need to be emphasized. First, he is the play's most determined advocate of greater tolerance. One reviewer of the play asserted that it "seldom makes us weep for individuals; though it makes us glow, and sigh, for *principles*," and Don Carlos himself makes this particularly apparent by routinely speaking like a parliamentary crusader.[9] He provides ample defense of his liberal principles based upon his dedication to Bible-reading; studying it "alone and unassisted," he deems it the "best and dearest gift / That man can give to man" (41). He continually champions independent judgment on all matters of faith – "the Calvinist, the Greek, the Indian Brahmin, / Proclaims his dogma true" (66) – and he is particularly controversial in the court because of his lenience towards the Flemish rebels.

Second, however, Don Carlos is not merely the advocate of freedom but the advocate of a more *secure* social order that can be brought about through toleration itself. As I suggested earlier, his sympathy with heretics is actually combined with a keen sense of political obligation. Although he willingly admits to having broken the oath he has taken at the *auto-da-fé*, he combines his contempt for oath-taking with an extremely powerful loyalty and respect for social harmony. Religious intolerance, he asserts (echoing Russell's comments in parliament that I mentioned in chapter 1), only produces disorder; the Inquisition only encourages the dishonesty that it supposedly attempts remove. "A forced conversion is a forced deceit," he argues, and it only reveals its own "want of faith" by forcing false declarations from others; he continues to argue that those who are tortured will only acquire "new strength, / New temper, from the fire of persecution" (67).

If Russell's hero points to the disorder that proceeds from confessional government, he just as fervently expresses his commitment to a social order that is both tolerant and well managed. Russell's *Essay on the History of the English Constitution* (1865) claimed that freedom of speech and the press was not only desirable from the standpoint of personal interest but "also beneficial to the community at large."[10] Don Carlos, likewise, continually frames his commitment to tolerant government in terms of an increased sense of social solidarity and public responsibility to the "collected millions, / The people of two hemispheres, who . . . / . . . will take their hue / Of joy or sorrow from my smile or frown" (29). His objection to persecution extends his desire for efficient government, reflected in his suggestion to his father that unrest in Flanders could be staved off most effectively by withdrawing military force and instead granting the people "their privilege . . . / To worship God in their own simple form." To follow this method would be to exercise a "kindness" that is "more politic than force"; "Rebellion's hydra-head will straight be crushed, / Or of itself fall off" (42–43).

THE CENCI AND THE RULES OF ENLIGHTENED ART

Staging the Inquisition, in Russell's drama, means staging not only the injustice of confessional authority – the way that the political operations of confessional regimes oppress adherents of nonconforming beliefs – but also its failure, its inability to secure order. This level of disorder is recognized by a character in the play, Don Carlos himself, who is – in the end – the object of persecution. But this disorder is also observed by the audience, who (like the reader in the prefaces of Radcliffe's Gothic novels) is placed in the privileged position of observing the constitutive inadequacies of confessional government. Still more, this audience presumably recognizes the kind of government that Don Carlos imagines as the ideally British government that is both tolerant and well ordered: the government, in other words, for which Russell himself so tirelessly campaigned.

Even though the accusation against the drama's dedication to principles over characters may have been correct, Russell's drama helps us, with all of its starkness, to understand the intertwined political and dramatic stakes of Inquisitorial authority in Romantic drama. The Inquisitorial stage – the dramatic representation of the Inquisition and the treatment of Inquisition as a historical "stage" to be succeeded by a new logic of social order – operates according to a coherent logic at work in other dramas of the period. From Wordsworth's *Borderers* (1797) and Coleridge's *Osorio* (1797) to Henry Hart Milman's *Fazio* (1818) and Keats's and Charles Brown's *Otho the Great* (written in 1819–20), the self-enclosing logic of confessional authority is routinely set up to be viewed either on stage or in the text in the process of its collapse. If the Renaissance stage could be distinguished for the way it enacts or performs the problematic and unstable dependence of political authority on oaths and confessions (as Steven Mullaney has so persuasively argued), the Inquisitorial stage in British Romanticism did not merely demonstrate this condition of dependence but more clearly displayed its inadequacy.[11] The works I am discussing displayed the mechanisms of confessional authority at work on stage (either actual or in the mind of the reader of "closet" drama): mechanisms that could be submitted to a stunning collapse before the eyes of the reader or viewer. Toleration therefore becomes discursively accessible in these works – as in Russell's play – as a defeat of the *political* mechanisms of religious oath- and test-taking, and as a palpable defeat of the generic mechanisms of theater (or, at least, theatricality) itself.

Russell's *Don Carlos* helps us to see how a far better-known work such as *The Cenci* is inappropriately considered by critics who view it as an autonomous investigation of the aesthetic, philosophical, or linguistic concerns specific to the work of the individual poet rather than a participant in a widely shared practice of putting Inquisitorial authority on stage. *The Cenci* is thus a play that anticipates the logic of Russell's drama: it theatrically represents a tyrannical *and* disorderly confessional authority that must itself be enclosed and regulated by a counter-confessional rule of law. It differs substantially from Russell's drama, however. At least *Don Carlos* provides the reader or viewer with a certain level of comfort by permitting her to identify with the hero's vision of a tolerant social order – a vision that is conveniently spoken of but not realized – so that its specific effects can remain hidden. In *The Cenci*, however, Shelley represents both the oppressiveness of confessional authority *and* the tragic dimensions of a secular authority that succeeds it.

Shelley efficiently summarizes the events of the play in his preface: a preface thoroughly reminiscent of the Gothic novel in its framing of the drama as a public exposure of Inquisitorial cruelty. In brief, it is the story of Beatrice Cenci, who is raped by her father and then plots with her mother-in-law, her brother, and her lover "to murder their common tyrant." The crime is discovered; despite their "earnest prayers" to the Pope to intervene, the accomplices in the father's murder are put to death.[12] Aside from sketching the outlines of the "fearful and monstrous" story of the Cenci family, the play's introductory material conveys an overriding concern with the issue of "tolerance" and "toleration." Shelley's dedication to Hunt, which precedes the preface, immediately touches on that issue by writing of Hunt, "One more gentle, honourable, innocent, and brave; one of more exalted toleration for all who do and think evil, and yet himself more free from evil . . . I never knew" (238). Shelley would have had ample reason to cast Hunt as a champion of toleration; his letters from Italy acknowledge receipt of *The Examiner* and praise Hunt's articles and excerpts on the established church (including selections from Bentham's *Church of Englandism*).

Whereas Hunt in the dedication is described as an ideally tolerant individual, Beatrice in the preface is drawn as a counter-example to Hunt: one who might have been more tolerant than she actually was by resisting vengeance upon the father who tortured her. "The fit return to make to the most enormous injuries," we are instructed, "is kindness and forbearance, and a resolution to convert the injurer from his dark passions by peace and love" (240). Shelley's judgment on Beatrice and what course of action she might have taken (returning rape with "peace and love") must surely strike most of today's readers as either naive or misogynistic. Some critics have been able to explain such a perspective by pointing to the way Shelley expects the play's spectator to be split between sympathy and censure, or by schematizing the structure of the work as an opposition between expediency (we sympathize with her immediate need) and morality (we do not sympathize with her moral standards).[13] But if Shelley has on the one hand raised Beatrice's specific moral or religious leanings as a problem, there is yet another sense in which the drama undercuts the force of such a claim. Even if Shelley has made tolerance look like a personal quality that Beatrice as a character has neglected, the drama is perhaps even more striking for the way in which it represents toleration as a legal rather than as a moral or religious issue, and for the way that it represents Beatrice as a tragic victim of the toleration that she might have espoused but has apparently forsworn.

By the time that *The Cenci* was published, the audience for the drama would have already experienced the latest installments of Britain's political Inquisitions. In October 1819, two months after the work was completed, Richard Carlile was charged with blasphemous libel for his publication of Paine's *The Age of Reason* and Elihu Palmer's *Principles of Nature*; he was fined £500 and sentenced to a three-year prison term. The intimate tie between the drama's representations of the Inquisition and these events was hardly lost on Shelley, who would clearly have seen such events as the culmination of a logic of political authority at work in his own drama. He asked Charles Ollier, his publisher, to send a copy of *The Cenci* (and *Prometheus Unbound*) to Southey, writing in a letter to his fellow poet that "the opinion of the ruling party to which you have attached yourself always exacts, contumeliously receives, and never reciprocates, toleration." And Shelley conveys in the same letter that he sees himself as a victim of Southey's intolerant judgments on his well-publicized unChristian behavior, including his blasphemous publications, his scandalous treatment of his first wife Harriet and their children, and his affair with Mary Godwin – by now his second wife.[14] (By this time, moreover, Harriet's father had obtained an order from Eldon, Lord Chancellor, to deprive Shelley of parental rights to his children with Harriet, citing *Queen Mab* and other publications as proof of his unsuitability as a father.)

Such details serve to show that, if the Inquisition served Russell's political aims, it touched on the still more intimate ways in which Shelley viewed his own domestic affairs. The same could be said of Byron, who in 1819 saw Hobhouse imprisoned in Newgate for publishing a radical pamphlet, and in 1820 saw the Guiccioli family suspected of "liberal principles," the "Governing party" threatening to "shut Madame Guiccioli [Byron's lover] up in a *Convent*."[15] These latter adventures, to which Byron refers in another letter to Augusta Leigh as his "*romance*," reveal the mutually supporting forces of the Catholic church and traditional structures of the family that form the Gothic background for the writing of *Cain*.[16] But the biographical details only add to the still broader political and aesthetic aims of Shelley's and Byron's dramas. *The Cenci*, as Shelley put it in a letter to Thomas Medwin, was "addressed to a Protestant people" that was supposedly more tolerant than the Inquisitorial politics represented in the play; at the same time, the British audience could see similar (Protestant) Inquisition scenes playing out in their own courts. The letter thus speaks for the undeniable urgency that Shelley attached to the manner in which the play solicits an ongoing vigilance against the logic of Inquisitorial politics. But the more intriguing feature of *The Cenci* is that Shelley makes even the political solution to Inquisitorial politics unleash a whole range of effects that are at least as terrifying as the Inquisition itself.[17]

Shelley explains in the preface that Catholicism "pervades intensely the whole frame of society"; it is not contained, governed, or framed, but is itself the container, the governor, or frame for society (240). And by putting it in these terms, he emphasizes the centrality of confessional government in the play that is to follow: a confessional government that is as much a characteristic of the English government of Shelley's day as it is of the sixteenth-century Italian regime depicted in the work. The early acts of the drama represent characters mobilizing a language saturated with the rhetoric of confessional authority; Beatrice and her father seem like mirror images of each other both because of their crimes and also because of their ability to justify them or cover them up with claims of divine authority. Cenci, we learn in the first lines, pursues his criminal actions not in spite of papal authority but because of it: "That matter of the murder is hushed up / If you consent to yield his Holiness / Your fief that lies beyond the Pincian gate" (1.1.1–3). He pursues his criminal actions because the Pope releases him from punishment in return for property. Throughout the play, leading up to his death, Cenci is both tyrant and pious "Anchorite" (1.3.4), offering "prayer" and "supplication" (1.3.24,26); his charges against his wife's "blaspheming" make him look like a perfect paragon of religious conformity (2.2.162).

All of this seems appropriate enough, given Shelley's life-long opposition to Christianity, his personal skepticism towards all things religious. Yet what perplexes many critics of the play is Beatrice's own repetition of that vocabulary. She only too willingly summons her own "piety to God" to justify her crime (3.1.387); she glosses the killing of Cenci not as the work of her own mind, but as the "hell within him" that God has "extinguish[ed]"(4.3.34). Those who assist Beatrice in killing her father, moreover, only encourage these justifications – she is "God's angel" (5.1.43) – and claim their mission to be a "high and holy deed" (4.3.35). Jerrold Hogle has attempted to untangle the curious doubling in speech of Beatrice and Cenci, victim and assailant, by pointing to the way in which it reveals an "ideological" doubling: as Hogle would have it, Beatrice turns out to be an accomplice not only in the murder of Cenci, but in her own rape, since her own language reinforces the system of patriarchy that made her a victim in the first place.[18] Hogle is quite right to point out the similarity in rhetorics, but the insistence on the mutual reinforcement of ideologies blurs the extent to which the drama more consistently holds up ideology – in far more comprehensive terms – for a rigorous examination of its social purposes. The similarity to be noted between Beatrice's and Cenci's appeals to God crucially conveys the problem of confessional government – with all of its appeals to religious agreement – itself. Or, to put it another way, the purpose of doubling Cenci's speech with Beatrice's is not merely to show how Beatrice's speech parrots her father's patriarchal ideology, but ultimately to make an even more profound point about the relationship between government and either religious or political ideologies more generally.

True to the spirit of Bentham and other tolerant reformers, then, Shelley has his characters demonstrate the workings of confessional oath-taking by showing both the social persuasiveness *and* the utter falsity of religious rhetoric – the disjunction between an utterance and an actual belief, between the claim to religious motive and an actual religious motive. Cenci cloaks his crimes with false confessions of faith; Beatrice strikes us as equally suspicious in her attempt to legitimate her crime on the basis of appeals to divine authority. (Indeed, as Michael Kohler has pointed out, the unreliability of testimony in the play makes it difficult to discern the very nature of Cenci's crime against Beatrice.)[19] Still more important, though, is the way that the drama ultimately overturns its own initial privileging of motives. For the very attempt to insist upon the importance of such motives is accompanied by the countermovement of the drama's plot, which makes them seem increasingly irrelevant. After Cenci has been killed by Marzio and Olimpio, the killers hired by Beatrice, little time elapses before the crime is discovered and Beatrice is convicted – but not before it is first revealed that Cenci was to be arrested and put to death by "unforbidden means" (4.4.29). Simply put, Beatrice is convicted of a criminal action that would have been a legal action had it been conducted under the auspices of the state.

It is at this moment that the drama abruptly reaches a turning point in its logic; the theocratic structure which has authorized Cenci's crimes quite suddenly and inexplicably convicts him of criminal action. Surprising as the moment may be, it thoroughly complies with the logic of the Gothic novel's similar reversals of confessional authority (it is an inverse mirror-image of *Mandeville*, a novel in which the hero is the victim of an offense judged to be legal). And it is at this moment, furthermore, that the drama begins its relentless elaboration of a legal machinery that counterpoints the supposed integrity of Beatrice's motives for her crime. To be sure, her speech continues its extra-legal appeals to divinity in ways that compellingly register a demand for sympathy. "[I]f some circumstance / should rise in accusation," she assures her stepmother Lucretia,

> we can blind
> Suspicion with such cheap astonishment,
> Or overbear it with such guiltless pride,
> As murderers cannot feign. The deed is done,
> And what may follow now regards not me.
> I am as universal as the light;
> Free as the earth-surrounding air; as firm
> As the world's centre. (4.4.42–50)

Perhaps no other lines speak so strongly on behalf of Beatrice's claim to an innocence antecedent to action and its attendant consequences (all "circumstance," or "what may follow"). And the imagery of radiance – "I am universal as the light" – is confirmed by Beatrice's subsequent assurance that the body is such a transparent medium between intention and effect that the "truth of things" will be "written on a brow of guilelessness" (5.1.82–83).

Yet we read or hear such lines only to observe at the same time that the workings of justice are not held in any similar state of awe. In fact, for all of the ways that Cenci appeals to the sympathy of the church in his oaths and prayers, and for all of the ways that Beatrice conveys the symmetry between her will and God's, the drama works decisively to discount the meaning of such confessions. To put it another way, it works by theatrical means to discount the theatricality of confession itself, and it is this logic to which Shelley referred, perhaps, in his account of the drama's "rules of enlightened art" in a letter to Thomas Medwin: rules that stand in a distinct tension with Beatrice's enlightened claims to "universal . . . light."[20] And it thus offers a remedy within drama for what Shelley regarded as the "inefficacy of the existing religious no less than political systems for restraining and guiding mankind."[21] Beatrice's claim, it turns out, is undermined by the brilliantly glowing evidence of the murder: the "gold-inwoven robe" that, "shining bright" under the "glimmering moon," leads the officers of justice to her accomplice Marzio. And in a similar fashion, the innocence she proclaims to be written on her brow is contradicted by the note written to her from Orsino and found on Marzio's person; the note points to her as a correspondent and thus to her participation in the crime.

Time after time, her attempts to excuse herself only look like self-incrimination. "My lords," she addresses her accusers,

> if by my nature I had been
> So stern, as to have planned the crime alleged
>   . . . do you think
> I should have left this two edged instrument
> Of my misdeed; this man, this bloody knife
> With my own name engraven on the heft,
> Lying unsheathed amid' a world of foes,
> For my own death?   (5.2.93–101)

Beatrice has suddenly described her "nature" differently: not, this time, as guileless and innocent, but with a surfeit of cunning that might have led her to cover up evidence of her guilt. But this is actually less interesting for its shiftiness than for the way that the drama subordinates her "nature" (her established character, her state of mind) to the very "circumstance" that she earlier viewed to be separable from her internal being. Regardless of how she may appeal to God, to the purity of her beliefs, her guilt is determined by her murderous action. When Beatrice tells the Judge that the murder of Cenci is a crime that "is or is not what men call a crime, / Which either I have done or have not done" (5.3.85–86), she does not merely equivocate but confirms her own self-doubling: her claim to moral or extra-legal innocence, and her claim to consequential or legal guilt.

A detour into another seldom-discussed Inquisitorial drama of the period by Henry Hart Milman can add some depth to the point that I am making. Milman, admired by both Shelley and Byron, was author of numerous theological works and the Biblical dramatic poem *The Fall of Jerusalem* (1820);[22] the author's *Fazio: A Tragedy in Five Acts* (1818) was particularly interesting to Shelley, who attended the play and (according to Peacock) drew on the character of Bianca for the character of Beatrice in his own work.[23] It is surprising that critics usually do no more than mention the mere fact that Shelley saw this play.[24] Milman's extraordinarily popular drama has overdecorated speeches but a simple plot that might at least begin to reveal what it offered to Shelley. Finding his wealthy neighbor Bartolo murdered, Fazio hides the body, steals his money, and becomes a wealthy Florentine philanderer. Meanwhile, his wife Bianca stays at home listening to gossip about her husband's carousing with her ambitious and mean-spirited rival Aldabella. Once she gets wind of the Duke's suspicions about Bartolo's death, she vengefully helps to have her husband convicted – not only of theft but of a murder that he did not commit, even though all circumstantial evidence indicates his guilt. Though anguished over her own motives for bringing him before the law, neither her repentance nor her claim to know her husband's innocence can remove the Duke's sentence of death. Milman's play shows Shelley, I think, a thrilling example of a hero victimized by the "irrevocable breath of justice" that "wavers not" in its operations.[25] Bianca's violation of her supposedly sacred duty to her husband (matrimony referred to throughout the play as an act of "solemn faith" pledged in the "church of God"[31]) makes her an enemy to the thoroughly hypocritical sanctity of the family. But when the Duke announces that Bianca's compliance with the law "Will chronicle thee, woman, to all ages / In human guilt a portent and an era" (37), he at once refers to her violation of the family's sacred authority and to her participation within a new regime or new "era" – a new stage – of legal responsibility. Bianca finds herself enclosed within the secular auspices of the law – "Fine laws! rare laws! most equitable laws!" she cries – which overcome the cruelty of the family's hypocritically sanctified space with laws that are just as cruel, precisely insofar as they are equitable (53).

Bianca's offense to the sanctity of the family – an offense conscripted within the secular operations of law which in turn render Bianca the law's victim – makes her a fitting model for Beatrice. More exactly, it is Bianca's legal predicament, rather than Bianca herself, that must have fascinated Shelley. The very legal means that *The Cenci* puts into motion in order to overcome the relentless displays of religious hypocrisy simultaneously make Beatrice into a conspicuous victim of its protective operations: a victim whose religious temperament and moral integrity have been drained of all self-determining authority. *The Cenci* is obviously a tragedy, then, but it is also a record of the transformation of Beatrice from the subject of a confessional or Inquisitorial regime to the subject – paradoxical though this may seem – of a tolerant one. As an example of the confessional subject, Beatrice is deprived of any public identity – she is "barred from all society" (1.1.46); as a member of the tolerant regime represented at the end of the drama, Beatrice achieves a recognizably public identity – the public identity and distinction of a parricide. While Beatrice had previously suffered from her own invisibility to public view, her crime makes her public and makes her subject to a general law for parricides: "Parricide grows so rife," the Cardinal explains, "That soon . . . the young / Will strangle us all, dozing in our chairs" (5.4.20–22). Many readers of Shelley's work have found *The Cenci* appropriate for the aims of historical criticism in a way that his more "abstract" or "idealistic" works, such as *Prometheus Unbound*, are not.[26] But what we can now see about *The Cenci* is that its politics are not opposed to Shelley's aesthetic abstractions – any more than the aesthetic abstractions in *Prometheus Unbound*, as I argued in chapter 1, are simply opposed to politics. *The Cenci* represents a politics through abstraction, by showing the acquisition of a public identity – under the auspices of criminal law – to be separable from particular moral or religious beliefs and expressions of those beliefs.

CAIN, BLASPHEMY, AND THE INVENTION OF MURDER

The Cenci shows an act of aggression against the oppressiveness and criminality of church-sponsored patriarchal authority – an act of aggression that is consequently dealt with by an extra-religious rule of law that captures all characters within its code – thus enacting, albeit in tragic form, the kind of social order to which Russell's *Don Carlos* gives voice. It is precisely this set of literary interests that I wish to maintain in the foreground as a way of discussing *Cain*'s participation within the work of putting the Inquisition on stage. Byron's drama, of course, does not literally represent the "Inquisition," but I believe that its attention to the politics of religion indicates its logical compatibility with the compositions that I have been discussing so far. I want to claim that *Cain* represents a Providential authority that thoroughly overturns the logic of confessional authority; Byron's angelic bureaucracy, in this work, performs the functions of the secular state.

There are certainly other dramas of Byron's that perhaps fit more obviously into the paradigm of the Inquisitorial stage that I am describing. Certainly *Manfred* (1817), with its hero's rejection of the Abbott's attempts to reconcile him to the "true church" (3.1.51), is relevant to my line of discussion; *Werner* (1822), to cite another example, shows a typically Gothic collusion between church and state to be a mutual protection of status and violence. But I turn to *Cain* because of its less obvious but perhaps more intriguing exploration of these themes. With its well-known story from Genesis, it both adds and subtracts from the Biblical text in order to investigate what Byron called "the politics of Paradise"; the author's subject is not only religion but the political mobilization of religious belief.[27] *Cain* is explicitly set up as a blaspheming rebel, an outcast from the spiritual center of the human community, whose ultimate expression of rage is his violence against his brother – a violence which, he insists, only accidentally results in fratricide. Cain's punishment for his crime is not death but life with an ever-present mark: on the one hand, a mark of his crime, and on the other hand, a mark of the ever-present and vigilant protection of God. This, in the logic of the Inquisitorial stage, is nothing other than the power of the state itself.

Commentators on Byron's drama have frequently seen Cain as yet another one of the author's Satanic surrogates for himself; I want to acknowledge the importance of such arguments while also showing that Byron frames his drama more particularly as an investigation of the social (rather than merely religious or moral) meaning of Satanism, skepticism, or any of the other beliefs ascribed to Cain or Byron. By 1821, the year John Murray published *Cain*, the literary press of the day had assembled a devilish picture of the author. Robert Southey in his preface to his *A Vision of Judgement* (1821) enrolled Byron in the "Satanic School" of writers, whose works "breathe the spirit of Belial in the lascivious parts" and display a "Satanic spirit of pride and audacious impiety."[28] Others levied more personal charges against him, proclaiming him an "infidel," a "libertine of the most dangerous description," capable of "rivet[ing] the attention of both sexes."[29]

Cain only reinforced this notion of Byron as a Satanic figure – a view continued in the opinions of modern critics of the work.[30] Byron's contemporary readers saw his drama as an instance or instrument of criminality, but not because it sympathetically portrayed a murderer; the play was guilty of blasphemy. (The character Cain, in fact, could frequently be seen as a figure whose emblematic crime was blasphemy rather than murder; Thomas Woolston, during his trial for blasphemous libel in 1729, cast himself as a Cain figure whose crime had caused him to forfeit his rights as an Englishman.[31]) John Matthews wrote in *Blackwood's* that the entire drama "may very properly be called a literary *devil*, not only because Lucifer himself is a leading character of the drama, but that it is perhaps of all the effusions of the satanic school, the best entitled to that distinction."[32] And legions of critics came to similar conclusions about *Cain*'s / Byron's blasphemies in the tumult of pamphlets, sermons, and reviews that flared immediately after the publication of the work and continued for over a decade afterwards.

What is clear is that critics, while concerned with Byron's personal deviance from religious norms, were also concerned with the implications of that deviation for social stability; objections to *Cain* surfaced because the drama violated a canon of established beliefs that formed the basis of civil society.[33] Critics thus upheld the illustrious defenders of Britain's established church and the various oaths and tests which kept it intact; and they employed a charge of blasphemy against Byron that had already been applied to the likes of Carlile, Cobbett, and Hone. The reviewer for *The British Critic*, for example, was able to generalize to say that Byron "has now for many years past never published any work in which he has not directly or indirectly denounced Christianity, 'the religion of the country,' as a system of superstition, and as the fruitful source of innumerable ills."[34] *Cain* above all his other works struck readers as particularly offensive: a reviewer in *The Investigator* leagued himself with the Society for the Suppression of Vice in an effort to accuse many writers of the day, including Byron and Shelley, of "outrages of all decency and decorum," which violated English "morality" and "manners." Byron the infidel takes the "blessing of the church and converts it to a curse."[35] The Reverend Henry John Todd, alias "Oxoniensis," author of *A Remonstrance*

Addressed to Mr. John Murray, Respecting a Recent Publication (1822), claimed that Byron's work would damage "religion, morality, and law," and that the "blasphemous impieties . . . may mislead the ignorant, unsettle the wavering, or confirm the hardened skeptic in his misbelief."[36]

The aim of Byron's detractors may have been to create both a canon and a nation cleansed of heterodoxy. But this aim – which viewed public order as the exclusive claim of orthodoxy to the ownership of property – was supported by a contradictory line of legal reasoning. The reports of the work's impropriety only encouraged booksellers to pirate the work in cheaper volumes, and the commentary surrounding it further increased as Murray employed Counsellor Lancelot Shadwell to apply to the Court of Chancery for a restraint against the publisher Benbow's pirated edition. Eldon, however, refused to grant such an injunction, arguing that the right to personal property could not be claimed in a blasphemous work (a reasoning also used in the refusal to grant Southey an injunction to stop the pirating of *Wat Tyler* in 1817). Eldon's decision points towards the disabling quandary built into the confessional state's logic: a logic that showed not only the intolerance of blasphemy law but also its inefficiency. The charge of blasphemy not only deprived authors and printers of the ability to obtain copyright protection but also substantially weakened the very government that suppressed works as blasphemous by encouraging increasingly intractable publications of the supposedly suppressed work. As one writer in *The Quarterly Review* commented on this reasoning, works "circulated without restriction *because* it was supposed their tendency might be injurious to the best interests of society."[37] The commitment to the uniformity of belief within the territory of the law (the commitment, that is, to Protestantism's exclusive right to property in the text), in other words, had led to the unsettling promulgation of those works outside the boundaries of legal protection. Thus the controversy surrounding *Cain* demonstrated the logic at work in the Inquisitorial dramas themselves, which revealed the intolerance *and* the disorder of confessional regimes.

Now if Byron's adversaries were concerned primarily with the disharmony of *Cain* and other works with the prevailing moral sentiments of Britons, their view of what makes up a society was not entirely at odds with views about the social value of religious agreement that get an airing in the drama itself. Cain's story from Genesis 4 is significant not only as the story of a rebellion against God – as critics have tended to emphasize by revealing the contention between God's demand for conformity and Cain's desire for an epistemological "truth" that is offered by the temptations of Lucifer. More than this, *Cain* appropriates the Biblical text in order to revise it radically. Cain not only rejects the word of God but rejects a specific social value of religious belief: while opposing God's will, his opposition turns out to be thoroughly consistent with God's government.

Byron's reference to Warburton's *Divine Legation of Moses* in his preface to the drama is crucial for pointing out the structure of the play. *Cain* is, first of all, a "Mystery," and critics who have given any attention to the term tend to point to Byron's simple explanation of it in his letters as a tragedy on a Biblical subject. But Byron refers to Warburton partly because of Warburton's own emphasis on religious mysteries, the "Nature and End" of which were to "teach the Doctrine of a Future State" and thereby inculcate a "virtuous life" (*Cain*, 156–57); he thus alludes to Warburton's continued emphasis on the uses of religion – and the text of religious mysteries – for the purposes of enforcing social conformity. There is added twist, though. Warburton's *Divine Legation*, as the preface explains, argues that the Old Testament provides no examples of any such doctrine of a "Future State"; it is thus necessary to regard the New Testament as the completion of the Old Testament in order to enforce the Bible's didactic value. Byron's strange maneuver in *Cain* is to introduce discussion and evidence of a future state at the same time that it ambiguates the moral lesson or encouragement of virtuous action in the present that a future state is supposed to offer. If Warburton uses the New Testament as the correction of the Old Testament, Byron turns to the Old Testament story of Cain as a correction of Warburton's account.

The context of Warburton's *Divine Legation* is helpful, I think, because it focuses our attention on the way that *Cain* explicitly concentrates on its hero as a rebel against the word of God and also, and more forcefully, against a social order that is constructed around the word of God. It is primarily this social aspect of religion that Byron stresses; religion does not consist only of a human's relationship with God but of one human's relationship with others. It is a source of communal cohesion that Cain acutely feels, for example, with Abel's "earnest prayer" that is "wrought" upon him, and by his own reluctant "promise" to Adah to participate in their rituals. Adah, whom Byron designed to be (like Abel) "as pious as possible," accuses Lucifer, moreover, not merely of stoking the flames of her husband's skepticism but of breaking the bonds of sympathy between persons, addressing him as "thou that steppest between heart and heart" (1.1.346).[38]

This intense demand for sympathy at least explains how appropriate it is that in Lucifer Cain finds a suitable comrade: one who encourages and shares his own thirst for knowledge. There is something odd about Cain's apparent resistance to established codes of faith and greater sympathy with Lucifer, though. Cain may find more sympathy in Lucifer, who provides a new form of companionship because he shares Cain's ways of thinking. But this improved form of sympathetic interaction is also oddly emptied of life. Cain's voyage to the underworld reveals an ideal community of perfected beings, on the one hand, unlike his own earthly community: a realm, as Byron puts it in a letter, of "beings endowed with a higher intelligence than man, but totally unlike him in form, and with much greater strength of mind and person."[39] On the other hand, however, what Lucifer calls the realm of death – even though it is "peopled" – is populated with persons without relationships, because it is radically unclear what is a person and what is a world or place inhabited by persons. The "dim worlds" are "peopled" but are also like people, or at least living organisms, "swelling into palpable immensity / Of matter"; by the same token, the "matter" that looks like people seems "made for life to dwell on, / Rather than life itself" (2.2.1–11). Lucifer's world is filled with people but also strangely unpopulated, because these are persons without (or with very unclear) relations to each other; Cain's world has few people but feels strangely full, since its tiny community (the world keeps looking "small and smaller" [2.2.35]) has already evolved an intricate system of interpersonal relationships.

What Cain ultimately realizes, moreover, is that these relationships do not demand sympathy as much as they provide an even more vital sense of community and individual identity that persists even when sympathy is denied. Although Cain in one sense seems like the adversary of human society and its normalizing social codes, he nevertheless continually re-gards that society as a necessary curse. We thus find Cain asserting an especially powerful sense of dependency between himself and others: "What should I be without [Adah]?" he asks (2.2.309). He loves his sister precisely because he might not even be a self without her: Adah, he says, "makes my feelings more endurable" (2.2.320–21).

Cain's way of valuing Adah's presence suggests that even though he does not actually share the sympathies of those who surround him (con-formity must be "wrought" from him), his feelings of separation and alienation are "endurable," oddly enough, because of the presence of those who incited them in the first place. To put it another way, the very humanity of the human world palpably consists in its ability to relieve persons of the burdens of sharing – perhaps even having – human feeling. There are other more striking ways in which *Cain* shows this to be true. Byron consistently and comically represents Lucifer as a more or less comfortable participant in the fallen world; even though Adah blames him for his intrusion into the family's stability, she still makes him seem like a mere nuisance rather than a source of moral or religious evil, a *bon vivant* who whisks Cain away from his everyday duties for jaunts in other realms.

In a still more important way, the permissiveness of the fallen world is exposed by the way that Cain, while first cast as an arch-rebel against the communal beliefs that supposedly structure the world's social relations, learns that his rebellion against society is quintessentially social. The play ultimately represents the triumph of a secular society in which beliefs have ceased to act as the means of social cohesion. This point is reinforced with Byron's peculiar liberties with the text of the Bible – liberties that some detractors took as evidence that he had not read the scripture carefully enough, but that actually reveal his attention to the varying degrees of connection between Cain's beliefs and his actions. The drama makes it clear that Cain had all the rules of faith plainly laid out before him, since he is informed by both Lucifer and Abel that only the sacrifice of animals is pleasing to God. Verse 5 of Genesis 4 reads that "unto Cain and his offering [the Lord] had not respect. And Cain was very wroth, and his countenance fell."[40] Byron's emendation suggests that Cain had enough knowledge to make his sacrifice more pleasing, but did not: he could foresee God's disapproval and chose to avoid it.

This refusal to participate in communal ritual might seem to make Cain's subversion all the more pronounced, but it is crucial that his killing of Abel provides a striking point of contrast. This is a crime against a person rather than any code of belief, and it is also a crime that Byron carefully sets up as an accident: an interpretation that also takes some liberty with Genesis 4, in the laconic account of the eighth verse, "Cain rose up against Abel his brother, and slew him." Byron's Cain repeatedly pleads that his blow was not a murderous one: "I smote / Too fiercely, but not fatally . . . / . . . 'twas a blow / And but a blow" (3.1.326–31). And the play is quite insistent, furthermore, upon the impossibility of Cain's even knowing the existence of death. He stands by in wonderment asking, "Is silence death? / No; he will wake; then let me watch by him. / Life cannot be so slight, as to be quench'd / Thus quickly!" (3.1.349–52). Although Cain may have been the first murderer – still more, the first to witness the death of another human – Francis Jeffrey quibbles with Byron's logic here, for, as he sees it, "the young family of mankind had, long ere this, been quite familiar with *the death of animals* – some of whom Abel was in the habit of offering up as sacrifices; – so that it is not quite conceivable that they should be so much at a loss to conjecture what Death was."[41] Byron's insistence upon Cain's blindness to the consequences of his actions, however, is more crucial than Jeffrey's commentary on the author's "mistake" would suggest. It underscores the extent to which the meaning of Cain's actions is severed from any intent to commit a crime. The significance of Byron's logic lies not only in the fact that Cain did not mean to strike a blow as hard as he did, but also that he could not have intended that blow to mean the death that it comes to mean for the "young family of mankind."

But the real purpose of framing Cain's murder of Abel as an accident is not to excuse Cain from his guilt. Rather, it is to insist upon his guilt – even with its lack of grounding in his actual intent to commit murder – as a convenient artifice that everyone, even Cain himself, comes to accept. Cain's guilt, however, is also accompanied by leniency, since – following the text of Genesis – he is also provided with a "mark" on his "brow" that provides "Exemption from such deeds as thou hast done" (3.1.498–99). This exemption contrasts sharply with the heap of curses that Eve casts upon him: "May all the curses / Of life be on him! and his agonies / Drive him forth o'er the wilderness, like us / From Eden, till his children do by him / As he did by his brother!" (3.1.421–25). The purpose of this contrast is to show, on the one hand, how Cain has been driven out of the confessional community of the family: Eve sees Cain's crime as a punishment that should repeat the expulsion from Paradise, driving Cain further and further away from the sacred bonds of human community that have been constructed after the Fall. Cain's actual punishment, on the other hand, removes him from the family but acknowledges him as a member of a wider human society; it imposes upon him a painful mark but also a mark that is the sign of Providential protection extending far beyond the family's precincts.

I am suggesting here that Byron's drama occupies a place on the Romantic Inquisitorial stage by representing Providential authority in the manner of a perfected secular authority. If I were reading *Cain* in absolute isolation from other compatible texts of the period, I might be accused of imposing an allegorical interpretation upon Byron's work. But I think that its association with other dramas of the period reveals that the mark of Cain is thoroughly consistent with the operations of secular government as they are depicted in the other dramas I discuss here. And there is still more to add. *The Vision of Judgment* (1822), Byron's response to Southey's *A Vision of Judgment* depicting the soul of George III being received into heaven, takes aim against Southey with a strategy that is comparable to *Cain*'s. Byron's *Vision*, published in the first issue of *The Liberal* in 1822, takes aim not merely against the conventional morality that Southey's poem represents, but against the very structuring of the religious and moral foundations of the state.

The preface to Byron's *Vision* points to "the gross flattery, the dull impudence, the renegado intolerance, and impious cant" of Southey's work, and keenly shows the hypocrisy of Southey's accusations against the "Satanic" school of poets, following the publication of *Wat Tyler* that so clearly showed Southey's earlier sympathies with supposedly more radical political causes. Byron's poem at first glance seems to respond to Southey's changes in radical political principles by touting Byron's own medium of satire as the more consistently radical posture. The poem, that is, reveals its author as the poet of greater honesty or sincerity in conveying his true heterodox principles – as he implies later in the preface. But there is still something else at stake here; Byron's further claim to treat the supernatural personages in the poem "more tolerantly" leads us to the work's peculiar way of treating political and moral values. The poetic response to Southey, I think, goes beyond a satire of the earlier *Vision*'s hypocritical opinions – even though Byron's speaker continually draws attention to his own daringly blasphemous beliefs, or to his deviation from Church of England "catechism," both of which presumably cut through Southey's hypocrisy with brutal honesty.[42] The more unsettling and ingenious gesture of *The Vision of Judgment* is to represent the same heavenly hierarchy of Southey's *Vision* but on different terms: Byron construes heaven as a court of law where the emphasis on formal processes or procedures is able comically to blur, confuse, or render ineffectual the conventional distinctions between moral, religious, or political doctrines.[43]

Southey's poem is preoccupied with moral oppositions between the "holier virtue," espoused by "Souls of the Good" in the heavens, and "rabid fanatics" like Robespierre and Danton, those with "evil thoughts" and "blasphemous rage." It is a poem, furthermore, that clearly announces itself as prejudicial since he portrays the king as *pre-judged*. Although a "vision of judgment," the title is a misnomer. George III does not in fact need to be judged, since Southey poetically renders him as a "reverend form" with a "heaven-directed" face in advance of any judgment.[44] Byron's cosmogony, however, is utterly indistinguishable from an earthly bureaucracy; his poem is more *Bleak House* than *Divine Comedy*. Clogged with angelic clerks and haggling lawyers, heaven in this *Vision* submits abstract distinctions in doctrine to the formal procedures of legal debate. None of the pathos and oppositional energy of Milton's characterizations – neither Satan's melancholy grandeur, nor Michael's forbidding majesty – is to be found here. Michael peacefully negotiates with Satan with a "civil aspect" and "mutual politeness" before the gates of heaven (33,35). Satan, furthermore, is a lawyer meticulously presenting his case on "a point of form" (64) for George III's punishment. Heaven and Hell are not opposed to each other as potent symbols of Good and Evil as they are in Southey's work; they are cooperating entities in a single working apparatus distributing rewards and punishments. These are distributed not according to the evil or good of a person's "intentions" – since kings have repeatedly "paved hell with their good intentions" – but, with utilitarian spirit, according to the damages that they have brought upon subject populations.[45] "His doom depends upon his deeds," Michael says, and the damages are minutely accounted for in the ledgers kept by St. Peter and his attendant angelic clerks (37). This record constitutes the basis for Satan's case – the intolerance and oppression of the king's reign – and thus the battle over the king's soul rests entirely upon a matter of accounting rather than a fundamental opposition in moral or religious value. The poem's narrator, furthermore, is not of the devil's party, but of the barrister's: "not one am I / Of those who think damnation better still"; he recommends instead "circumscribing, with some restriction, / The eternity of hell's hot jurisdiction"(13), as if Heaven and Hell were part of a peacefully functioning entity that could be reformed from within.

The further impact of this reasoning crystallizes with Southey's appearance in the poem. What characterizes Southey is not merely the fact that he has changed his opinions; his *Vision* is an epideictic exercise (in contrast to Byron's forensic or legal exercise) seeking to unify followers of religious and political causes. Writing "praises of a regicide" and "praises of all kings whatever," advocating "republics far and wide" as well as "pantisocracy . . . a scheme less moral than 'twas clever," Southey's verse has poetic value only insofar as it attempts to endorse one prejudicial system of values or another in order to gather specific audiences of purchasers and reviewers (97,99). Southey is rendered ridiculous in *The Vision of Judgment*, then, but it is crucial to see precisely why. Neither Heaven nor Christianity is rendered ridiculous. Southey is ridiculous because the apparent occasion for his praise – the heavenly hierarchy to which he appeals – only has contempt for it. Indeed, Southey's religious bigotry is decidedly at odds with the Providential felicific calculus represented in Byron's poem.

Southey's punishment, of course, is to be knocked down from the gates of Heaven by St. Peter, ultimately winding up in his "lake"; his bathetic works sink while the poet himself (still filled with air) rises to the surface to continue his writing. He thus returns to the place that is the home of the poetic sectarians – as Byron describes the Lake poets in *Don Juan* (which associates Wordsworth with "Joanna Southcote's Shiloh and her sect" and pokes fun at the Lake poets' "conversion" to a conservative political "creed," cultivated "by dint of long seclusion" and "continued fusion / Of one another's minds" [*Don Juan*, 3.95, Dedication 5]).[46] *The Vision* exercises its furthest satirical reach in its portrayal of heaven's bureaucratic operations that are indifferent to Southey's fervent yet uncomprehending religious praise. And it could thus be argued that Byron cunningly extends the logic of *Cain* in *The Vision of Judgment* by making Southey into a would-be Abel who offers a supposedly proper sacrifice of verse – only to have it rejected precisely because of its stultifying efforts to adhere to, and gain adherents to, a specific religious and political code of propriety.

For all of this breathtaking mockery, *The Vision* is not entirely a rejection of the poetic strategies of the Lake poets; it is in fact a further development of those strategies. If Byron could characterize Southey merely as a conservative ideologue, this was at the expense of accounting for Southey's somewhat more complex and interesting project – as I described it in chapter 2 – to redefine the church itself as a guarantee of secular public order. It could be argued that, if Southey returns to the lakes in *The Vision*, Byron is not far behind him. Still more intriguing, however, is Byron's relationship to Wordsworth's *Excursion* and to Wordsworth's later work more generally. Byron found cause to complain about the length of Wordsworth's poem as well as its obscurity – "a sample from the vasty version / Of his new system to perplex the sages" (*Don Juan*, Dedication, 4). But the energy of this opposition perhaps obscures the compatibility between Wordsworth's poetic vision and that of Byron and other second-generation Romantic writers. Scholars have seldom needed to look beyond the dismissive attitudes towards Wordsworth's religious orthodoxy (found in other works such as Shelley's ingenious *Peter Bell the Third*) in order to determine the reactions of these writers to the later Wordsworth; even Keats, one of *The Excursion*'s few outspoken admirers, is deemed by most critics to have adopted a more antagonistic stance towards the work than his comments would suggest.[47] Having made a somewhat different argument about *The Excursion*, however – an argument that challenges conventional views about its adherence to traditional Anglicanism – I would contend that we can detect a somewhat different trajectory from that poem's intertwined social and literary projects to the works that I have been discussing in the last two chapters. Byron's *Cain* sets up a typical figure of the Romantic rebel. But he is "typically" Romantic because his rebellion is, crucially, a social one; his opposition to religious observances is itself observed and accommodated by an exacting but permissive Providential authority. In this sense, Byron has not rejected *The Excursion*; he has made Cain into his Solitary – a figure included within the auspices of Providential protection despite his rejection of conventional orthodox beliefs. His *Don Juan*, trading "lakes" for "oceans," furthermore, repeats rather than rejects the movement of *The Excursion*, which extends its view to the "wide waters" and "new communities / On every shore" across the globe (*Excursion*, 9.375,379–80). To reject Wordsworth's apparent religious orthodoxy, in other words, is actually to confirm Wordsworth's own revisions of the church's social mission.

Have we not, then, arrived at a new account of Romanticism and the "secular" – a new account of a jointly achieved literary and institutional ambition? This account can only make us think – amidst a whole range of arguments that unproblematically fuses romanticism and religion, poetry and belief – that the specific *negotiation* of belief has been lost to contemporary scholarly examination. While it has been common enough for critics to make Romantic writing seem like either a noble or naïve embrace of beliefs – whether Christian, heterodox, or atheistic – we must now feel as though such trends in scholarship continue to follow a line of thought made popular in the late nineteenth century. The assumption that the literary imagination either conflicts or complies with the elaboration of modern institutions – the conviction that writing can be viewed according to a polarity between a resistant creativity and a mechanical rationality – is an interpretive paradigm inherited from sources (surprising though the combination may seem) ranging from Arnold's *Culture and Anarchy* (1869) to Nietzsche's *The Genealogy of Morals* (1887). This is an interpretive paradigm from which we have not yet extricated ourselves. Perhaps this is attributable to our own desire to generate new academic pieties leveled against what we perceive to be unyielding institutional orthodoxies, but we must acknowledge this view as a product of our own limited vision rather than an actual claim that can justly be attributed to a wide spectrum of late eighteenth- and early nineteenth-century writers.

One way of viewing the common trends in scholarship that I am mentioning would be to see them merely as mistaken positions that I am now correcting. Another more interesting way would be to see them as already enclosed within, and accounted for, the Romantic disposition towards belief described in this book. Beginning with the Gothic novel, which makes religious heterodoxy seem like the basis for an ideal institutional subjectivity, we discover a way of imagining a form for the secular state that in fact cultivates resistance within itself. The still further development of this view makes Wordsworth's account of the church a fulfillment of the Coleridgean idea of a national church – an anti-institutional institution – even while it remains thoroughly compatible with the radically secular economies of Edgeworth's fiction. Byron gleefully rejects all three of these writers in canto 1 of *Don Juan* – Wordsworth, Coleridge, and Edgeworth – as adherents of well-worn, outmoded religious and metaphysical doctrines. But he makes his comic image of the heavens in *The Vision of Judgment* into a perfect example of secular government – a perfect example, that is, of the disposition towards belief adopted by the very writers he purports to reject. This feeling of separation within community – a separation from communal feeling that is itself communal – is, I have been arguing, a Romantic invention. The ongoing project adopted by these writers is to imagine and support a social order in which the deepest feelings of communal belonging – such feelings ranging from pleasure to sheer terror – might be inspired, paradoxically, by minimizing the importance of having one's feelings shared.

Notes

INTRODUCTION

1. I would suggest, in fact, that Martha Nussbaum's version of "cosmopolitanism" is an example of how constraining some ideas of liberalism (what John Rawls would identify as "comprehensive" theories) can be. See Nussbaum, "Patriotism and Cosmopolitanism," in *For Love of Country: Debating the Limits of Patriotism*, ed. Joshua Cohen (Boston: Beacon Press, 1996), 3–17.

2. My use of the term "religious toleration" is aptly explained by Jerome Schneewind: "A society that is religiously tolerant is one in which the religious beliefs, or rejection of religion, of the citizen are not allowed to affect their [*sic*] legal right to live, marry, raise children, worship, pursue careers, own property, make contracts, participate in politics, and engage in all the other activities normally open to citizens in that society." See Schneewind, "Bayle, Locke, and the Concept of Toleration," in *Philosophy, Religion, and the Question of Intolerance*, ed. Mehdi Aminazavi and David Ambuel (Albany: State University of New York Press, 1997), 4.

3. Jeremy Bentham, *Chrestomathia*, ed. M. J. Smith and W. H. Burston (Oxford: Clarendon Press, 1983), 121.

4. William Wordsworth, *The Excursion* 9 415. All references to the poems are from *The Poetical Works of William Wordsworth*, 5 vols., ed. Ernest de Selincourt and Helen Darbishire (Oxford: Oxford University Press, 1940–49).

5. Gauri Viswanathan usefully sums up the specific but also profound importance of religious belief in British culture by stating that " 'Belief' can . . . be defined against the backdrop of nineteenth-century social history as a reference not to doctrinal authority but to the aspirations, understandings, expectations, needs, imagination, and goals that constitute the self-definition of people, the very content of which is denied or suppressed in the construction of their legal or social identity." See Viswanathan, *Outside the Fold: Conversion, Modernity, and Belief* (Princeton: Princeton University Press, 1998), 52–53.

6. Stanley Fish, *The Trouble With Principle* (Cambridge, MA: Harvard University Press, 1999); Kirstie M. McClure, "Difference, Diversity, and the Limits of Toleration," *Political Theory* 18 (August 1990): 361–91; Robert C. Post, "Cultural Heterogeneity and Law: Pornography, Blasphemy, and the First

Amendment," *California Law Review* 76 (1988): 297–335; Michael Sandel, "Judgemental Toleration," in *Natural Law, Liberalism, and Morality*, ed. Robert P. George (Oxford: Clarendon Press, 1996), 107–11; Charles Taylor, "Atomism," in *Philosophy and the Human Sciences: Philosophical Papers* (Cambridge: Cambridge University Press, 1985), 187–210.

7. McClure, "The Limits of Toleration," 380; Fish, *The Trouble With Principle*, 158.

8. Julie Ellison, *Cato's Tears and the Making of Anglo-American Emotion* (Chicago: University of Chicago Press, 1999); William Jewett, *Fatal Autonomy: Romantic Drama and the Rhetoric of Agency* (Ithaca: Cornell University Press, 1997); Celeste Langan, *Romantic Vagrancy: Wordsworth and the Simulation of Freedom* (Cambridge: Cambridge University Press, 1995).

9. When used alone without a modifier, I follow scholarly tradition in using "dissent" to mean "Protestant dissent." When uncapitalized, "dissent" means simply "nonconformity." This more general meaning for "dissent" is historically relevant since even Catholics were occasionally referred to as "dissenters." See *Parliamentary History of England*, vol. xxviii (1798), col. 113.

10. M. H. Abrams, *Natural Supernaturalism: Tradition and Revolution in Romantic Literature* (New York: W. W. Norton, 1971), 65, 91; J. Hillis Miller, *The Disappearance of God: Five Nineteenth-Century Writers* (Cambridge, MA: Harvard University Press, 1963).

11. Robert Ryan, *The Romantic Reformation: Religious Politics in English Literature, 1789–1824* (Cambridge: Cambridge University Press, 1997); Martin Priestman, *Romantic Atheism: Poetry and Freethought, 1780–1830* (Cambridge: Cambridge University Press, 1999).

12. Kevin Gilmartin, *Print Politics: The Press and Radical Opposition in Early Nineteenth-Century England* (Cambridge: Cambridge University Press, 1996); Steven Goldsmith, *Unbuilding Jerusalem: Apocalypse and Romantic Representation* (Ithaca: Cornell University Press, 1993); Ian McCalman, *Radical Underworld: Prophets, Revolutionaries, and Pornographers in London, 1795–1840* (Cambridge: Cambridge University Press, 1988); Nicholas Roe, *Keats and the Culture of Dissent* (Oxford: Clarendon Press, 1997).

13. Kevin Binfield, "Demonology, Ethos, and Community in Cobbett and Shelley," in *Romanticism, Radicalism, and the Press*, ed. Stephen C. Behrendt (Detroit: Wayne State University Press, 1997), 157–69.

14. Saree Makdisi, *Romantic Imperialism: Universal Empire and the Culture of Modernity* (Cambridge: Cambridge University Press, 1998); Michael Ragussis, *Figures of Conversion: "The Jewish Question" & English National Identity* (Durham, NC: Duke University Press, 1995); Cannon Schmitt, *Alien Nation: Nineteenth-Century Gothic Fictions and English Nationality* (Philadelphia: University of Pennsylvania Press, 1997); Katie Trumpener, *Bardic Nationalism: The Romantic Novel and the British Empire* (Princeton: Princeton University Press, 1997).

15. Makdisi, *Romantic Imperialism*, 61.

16. Gerald Newman, *The Rise of English Nationalism: A Cultural History, 1720–1830* (New York: St. Martin's Press, 1987), 123, 161.

17. See E. P. Thompson, *Witness Against the Beast: William Blake and the Moral Law* (New York: New Press, 1993).

18. Edmund Burke, *Works of the Right Honourable Edmund Burke*, 16 vols. (London: C. and J. Rivington, 1826), v:79.

19. Samuel Taylor Coleridge to Charles Lloyd, 15 October: 1796, *Collected Letters of Samuel Taylor Coleridge*, ed. Earl Leslie Griggs, 6 vols. (Oxford: Oxford University Press, 1956–71), 1:240.

20. Coleridge, *Lay Sermons*, ed. R. J. White, vol. vi of *Collected Works of Samuel Taylor Coleridge* (Princeton: Princeton University Press, 1972), 197–99.

21. Coleridge, *On the Constitution of Church and State*, ed. John Colmer, vol. x of *Collected Works* (Princeton: Princeton University Press, 1976), 43.

22. Maria Edgeworth, *Castle Rackrent and Ennui*, ed. Marilyn Butler (Harmondsworth: Penguin, 1992), 146, 184.

23. Sir Walter Scott, *The Waverly Novels: Centenary Edition*, 25 vols. (Edinburgh: Adam and Charles Black, 1871), vol. vi, chapter 37.

24. Wordsworth, *The Prelude* (6.427), in *The Prelude: 1799, 1805, 1850* (New York: W. W. Norton, 1979). References to *The Prelude* are to the 1805 version, unless otherwise noted.

25. John Keats to George and Georgiana Keats, 19 February 1819, *The Letters of John Keats*, 2 vols., ed. Hyder Edward Rollins (Cambridge, MA: Harvard University Press, 1958), ii:62–63.

26. Lord Byron, *Childe Harold's Pilgrimage*, 2.15, vol. ii of *The Complete Poetical Works*, edited by Jerome McGann, 7 vols. (Oxford: Clarendon Press, 1980–93).

27. Lord John Russell, *Don Carlos; or, Persecution. A Tragedy, in Five Acts*, 2nd edn. (London: Longman, 1822), 42.

I ROMANTICISM AND THE WRITING OF TOLERATION

1. J. C. D. Clark, *English Society 1688–1832: Ideology, Social Structure, and Political Practice During the Ancien Regime* (Cambridge: Cambridge University Press, 1985).

2. *Hansard Parliamentary Debates*, 1st series, vol. xxxv (1800), cols. 351, 353.

3. G. Kitson Clark, *Churchmen and the Condition of England 1832–1885* (London: Methuen, 1973), 26.

4. In addition to J. C. D. Clark's work, relevant writing on British society and religious politics includes Linda Colley, *Britons: Forging the Nation 1707–1837* (New Haven: Yale University Press, 1992); Gerald Newman, *The Rise of English Nationalism*.

5. Aristotle, *The Basic Works of Aristotle*, ed. Richard McKeon (New York: Random House, 1941), 1277–82.

6. John Wilson, "Dr. Phillpotts and Mr. Lane on the Coronation Oath," *Blackwood's Edinburgh Magazine* 24 (July 1828): 9.

7. *Hansard*, 2nd series, vol. xx (1829); col. 223.

8. Robert Peel, quoted in Boyd Hilton, "The Ripening of Robert Peel," in *Public and Private Doctrine: Essays in British History Presented to Maurice Cowling*, ed. Michael Bentley (Cambridge: Cambridge University Press, 1993), 81.

9. Colley, *Britons*, 330.

10. Norman Sykes, *Church and State in England in the 18th Century* (1934; New York: Octagon, 1975), 267.

11. W. H. Wickwar, *The Struggle for The Freedom of the Press, 1819–1832* (London: George Allen and Unwin, 1928), 131.

12. Ursula Henriques, *Religious Toleration in England 1787–1833* (Toronto: University of Toronto Press, 1961), 79; J. C. D. Clark, *The Language of Liberty 1660–1832: Political Discourse and Social Dynamics in the Anglo-American World* (Cambridge: Cambridge University Press, 1994), 87–88, 95.

13. David Hempton, "Religion in British Society 1740–1790," *British Politics and Society from Walpole to Pitt 1742–1789*, ed. Jeremy Black (London: Macmillan, 1990), 201–64.

14. Leonard Levy, *Blasphemy: Verbal Offense Against the Sacred, from Moses to Salman Rushdie* (New York: Knopf, 1993), 429.

15. William Blackstone, *Commentaries on the Laws of England*, 4 vols. (1765–1769; Chicago: University of Chicago Press, 1979), IV:43.

16. Edmund Burke, *Works*, V:176. All further references to Burke's *Works* are noted parenthetically in the text by volume and page number.

17. See Burke's arguments against colonial administration in *Works*, XII:213–23, 323–25.

18. See Milton's defense of the freedom of the press based upon the ideal of the "true warfaring Christian" ("wayfaring Christian" in the first edition), as opposed to a "fugitive and cloistered virtue" in *Areopagitica*, in *Complete Poems and Major Prose*, ed. Merritt Y. Hughes (New York: Macmillan, 1985), 728.

19. Joseph Priestley, *Letters to the Right Honourable Edmund Burke, Occasioned by his Reflections on the Revolution in France* (Birmingham: Thomas Pearson, 1791), 63.

20. David Bromwich, *A Choice of Inheritance: Self and Community from Edmund Burke to Robert Frost* (Cambridge, MA: Harvard University Press, 1989), 43–78; James Chandler, *Wordsworth's Second Nature: A Study of Poetry and Politics* (Chicago: University of Chicago Press, 1984).

21. For an account of how an opposition to theory and abstraction could become a means of defining an asystematic British unity against French rationalist doctrines, see David Simpson, *Romanticism, Nationalism, and the Revolt Against Theory* (Chicago: University of Chicago Press, 1993).

22. These range from the canonical account of Alfred Cobban, *Edmund Burke and the Revolt Against the Eighteenth Century: A Study of the Political and Social Thinking of Burke, Wordsworth, Coleridge, and Southey* (1929; New York: Barnes and Noble, 1960), to more recent deconstructive accounts such as Tom Furniss's *Edmund Burke's Aesthetic Ideology* (Cambridge: Cambridge University Press, 1993).

23. Thomas Hobbes, *Leviathan*, ed. C. B. Macpherson (Harmondsworth: Penguin, 1968), 627–28.

24. William Warburton, *The Alliance Between Church and State, or, the Necessity and Equity of an Established Religion and a Test-Law Demonstrated* (London: Fletcher and Gyles, 1736), 32, 112.

25. Clark, *English Society*, 376.

26. W. H. Mallock, "The Logic of Toleration," *The Nineteenth Century* 5 (January 1879): 81.

27. On anti-Catholic propaganda in England, see Christopher Hill, *Antichrist in Seventeenth-Century England* (1971; London: Verso, 1990).

28. See Christopher Hill, "The English Revolution and Patriotism," in *Patriotism*, ed. Raphael Samuel, 3 vols. (London: Routledge, 1989), 1:158–68.

29. Henry Parnell, "Divided Allegiance of the Catholics," *The Edinburgh Review* 43 (November 1825): 152.

30. *Hansard*, 2nd series, vol. xx (1829); col. 1156.

31. Sydney Smith, "Ingram on Methodism," *The Edinburgh Review* 11 (January 1808): 386.

32. Robert Southey, "The Roman Catholic Question – Ireland," *The Quarterly Review* 38 (January 1828): 595, 570–71.

33. Francis Jeffrey, "Pamphlets on the Catholic Question," *The Edinburgh Review* 11 (October 1807): 126.

34. Henriques, *Religious Toleration*, 140–41.

35. Southey, "The Roman Catholic Question – Ireland," 578.

36. Henry Hart Milman, "Pulpit Eloquence," *The Quarterly Review* 29 (April 1823): 301.

37. Smith, "Ingram on Methodism," 341–62.

38. Milman, "Pulpit Eloquence," 305.

39. Southey, *The Life of Wesley and the Rise and Progress of Methodism*, 2 vols. (London: Oxford University Press, 1925), ii:91, i:1; Southey, "The Progress of Infidelity," *The Quarterly Review* 28 (January 1823): 493–94.

40. *Hansard*, 2nd series, vol. xix (1828): 126.

41. *Ibid.*, col. 120.

42. *Hansard*, 3rd series, vol. vii (1833), col. 224.

43. *Hansard*, 2nd series, xx (1829); col. 1158.

44. Protestant Dissenters were admitted, however, by special yearly indemnity acts that were able to mitigate the force of religious tests.

45. My account of legal history surrounding this issue is indebted to Joan Connell, *The Roman Catholic Church in England 1780–1850: A Study in Internal Politics* (Philadelphia: American Philosophical Society, 1984); Wendy Hinde, *Catholic Emancipation: A Shake to Men's Minds* (Oxford: Basil Blackwell, 1992); and G. I. T. Machin, *The Catholic Question in English Politics 1820–1830* (Oxford: Clarendon Press, 1964). On the activities of Dissenters in the movement for Repeal, see Richard Burgess Barlow, *Citizenship and Conscience* (Philadelphia: University of Pennsylvania Press, 1962).

46. Francis Jeffrey, "Pamphlets on the Catholic Question," 128.

47. For a recent example of this claim, see A. N. Wilson, *God's Funeral* (New York: Norton, 1999).

48. See John Wolffe, "Evangelicalism in Mid-nineteenth-century England," in *Patriotism*, ed. Samuel, 1:188–200.

49. Stephen Prickett, *Words and the Word: Language, Politics, and Biblical Interpretation* (Cambridge: Cambridge University Press, 1986), 99.

50. Alisdair MacIntyre, *Secularization and Moral Change* (London: Oxford University Press, 1967), 9, 18.

51. Keith Vivian Thomas, *Religion and the Decline of Magic* (New York: Scribner, 1971); Brian C. J. Singer, *Society, Theory, and the French Revolution: Studies in the Revolutionary Imaginary* (New York: St. Martin's Press, 1986).

52. Isaac Kramnick, *Republicanism and Bourgeois Radicalism* (Ithaca: Cornell University Press, 1990).

53. Joseph Priestley, *Letters*, 126–7.

54. Gauri Viswanathan, *Outside the Fold*, 16.

55. David Robinson, "The Catholic Question," *Blackwood's Edinburgh Magazine* 18 (July 1825): 13.

56. Patrick Brantlinger and Donald Ulin, "Policing Nomads: Discourse and Social Control in Early Victorian England," *Cultural Critique* (Fall 1993): 40.

57. John Rawls, "Justice as Fairness: Political not Metaphysical," *Philosophy and Public Affairs* 14 (Summer 1985): 225. See also, more generally, Rawls's *Political Liberalism* (New York: Columbia University Press, 1993).

58. For the standard account of the view I argue against, see C. B. Macpherson, *The Political Theory of Possessive Individualism: Hobbes to Locke* (Oxford: Oxford University Press, 1962), 194–262.

59. John Locke, *Two Treatises of Government*, ed. Peter Laslett (Cambridge: Cambridge University Press, 1960), 287. All further references to the *Treatises* are noted parenthetically in the text by page number.

60. J. G. A. Pocock thus misreads Locke (in order to dismiss his influence), claiming that he was susceptible to the "danger of making the individual, his rights, and his personality, anterior to the formation of civil society." See Pocock, *Virtue, Commerce, and History* (Cambridge: Cambridge University Press, 1985), 170.

61. Locke, *A Letter Concerning Toleration* (Buffalo: Prometheus Books, 1990), 19. All further references to this work are noted parenthetically in the text by page number.

62. I distinguish my account from James Tully's view of Locke's emphasis on inculcating humanized moral habits to replace religious beliefs in "Governing Conduct," in *Conscience and Casuistry in Early Modern Europe*, ed. Edmund Leites (Cambridge: Cambridge University Press, 1988), 12–71.

63. Locke made this substitution earlier in the argument: "The part of the magistrate is only to take care that the common wealth receive no prejudice, and that there be no injury done to any man, either in life or estate" (*Letter*, 48).

64. Although my argument bears some resemblance to Kirstie McClure's "Difference, Diversity, and the Limits of Toleration," my interest differs from her emphasis on Locke's account of the "epistemological grounds of state power" which depend upon the "factual" (380).

65. Philip Furneaux, *An Essay on Toleration* (London: T. Cadell, 1773), 1.

66. On the propensity in radical rhetoric for claims of truth, transparency, and free contract see James Epstein, *Radical Expression: Political Language, Ritual, and Symbol in England, 1790–1850* (Oxford: Oxford University Press, 1994).

67. Heather Glen, *Vision and Disenchantment: Blake's "Songs" and Wordsworth's "Lyrical Ballads"* (Cambridge: Cambridge University Press, 1983), 90.

68. William Cobbett, *A History of the Protestant Reformation in England and Ireland* (New York: Benziger Brothers, n.d.), 59.

69. Priestley, *Letters*, 128, 82.

70. Richard Price, *Political Writings*, ed. D. O. Thomas (Cambridge: Cambridge University Press, 1991), 4–5.

71. William Godwin, *Enquiry Concerning Political Justice* (Harmondsworth: Penguin, 1985), 570, 572.

72. *Hansard*, 2nd series, vol. XVIII (1828), col. 679.

73. Several writers on Romanticism and religion have discussed this particular line of argument. See Robert Ryan, *The Romantic Reformation*; Stephen Prickett, "The Religious Context," in *The Romantics*, ed. Stephen Prickett (New York: Holmes-Meier, 1981).

74. Joel Barlow, *Advice to the Privileged Orders*, in *The Political Writings of Joel Barlow* (1796; New York: Burt Franklin, 1971), 40.

75. Priestley, *Essay on the First Principles of Government*, in *Political Writings*, ed. Peter Miller (Cambridge: Cambridge University Press, 1993), 62. All further references to this work are noted parenthetically in the text by page number.

76. Barlow, *Advice*, 79.

77. William Frend, *Considerations on the Oaths Required by the University of Cambridge* (London: J. Deighton, 1787), 28.

78. George Dyer, *The Complaints of the Poor People of England* (1793; Oxford: Woodstock Books, 1990), 154, 177–83, 194–95.

79. My use of the term "social body" earlier in this argument, and my account of the "disaggregation" of religion and government, is inspired by Mary Poovey's *Making a Social Body: British Cultural Formation 1830–64* (Chicago: University of Chicago Press, 1995), 1–24. I mean to emphasize a shared set of concerns with this book, while also outlining a different account of them.

80. Priestley, *Letters*, 84.

81. David Hume, *Political Essays*, ed. Knud Haakonssen (Cambridge: Cambridge University Press, 1994), 109.

82. Jean Jacques Rousseau, *On Social Contract*, in *Rousseau's Political Writings*, ed. Alan Ritter (New York: Norton, 1988), 110, 108, 120, 150–51.

83. Barlow, *Advice*, 28.

84. John Stuart Mill, "On Liberty," in *On Liberty and Other Essays*, ed. John Gray (Oxford: Oxford University Press, 1991), 24, 49.

85. Robert Robinson, *Ecclesiastical Researches* (Cambridge: Francis Hodson, 1792), 203.

86. Isaac Taylor, *Fanaticism* (London: Holdsworth and Ball, 1833), 29, 76.

87. *Ibid.*, 120, 95, 116, 200.

88. Priestley, *An Address to Protestant Dissenters of All Denominations* (London, 1774; Boston: Thomas and John Fleet, 1774), 15.

89. Barlow, *Advice*, 38.

90. *Ibid.*, 74, 77, 134, 124.

91. Adam Smith, *The Theory of Moral Sentiments*, ed. D. D. Raphael and A. L. Macfie (Indianapolis: Liberty Classics, 1982), 185; Emile Durkheim, *The Division of Labor in Society*, trans. W. D. Halls, intr. Lewis A. Coser (New York: The Free Press, 1984) 17, 61.

92. Louis Althusser, *Lenin and Philosophy, and Other Essays*, trans. Ben Brewster (New York: Monthly Review Press, 1971); Herbert Marcuse, "Repressive Tolerance," in Robert Paul Wolff, Barrington Moore, Jr., and Herbert Marcuse, *A Critique of Pure Tolerance* (Boston: Beacon, 1965), 81–117.

93. Marilyn Butler, *Romantics, Rebels, and Reactionaries: English Literature and its Background, 1760–1830* (Oxford: Oxford University Press, 1981), 44.

94. Michel Foucault, *Discipline and Punish: The Birth of the Prison*, trans. Alan Sheridan (New York: Vintage, 1979), 242–43. The importance of Bentham in this context has been acknowledged in Frances Ferguson, "Pornography: The Theory," *Critical Inquiry* 21 (Spring 1995): 670–95.

95. On Bentham's writing on religion, see James E. Crimmins, *Secular Utilitarianism: Social Science and the Critique of Religion in the Thought of Jeremy Bentham* (Oxford: Clarendon Press, 1990).

96. Leigh and John Hunt, eds., *Mother church relieved by bleeding, or Vices and remedies: extracted from Jeremy Bentham's "Church of Englandism"* (London: Leigh and John Hunt, 1825).

97. Jeremy Bentham, *Church of Englandism and its Catechism Examined* (London: Effingham Wilson, 1818), xv–xvi.

98. *Ibid.*, xxi, 75.

99. Bentham Manuscripts, University College London, 6:30, 6:35.

100. Bentham, *Letters to the Conde Toreno on the Proposed Penal Code*, in *The Works of Jeremy Bentham*, 11 vols., ed. John Bowring (Edinburgh: William Tate, 1843), VIII:546. All further references to this edition are noted parenthetically in the text by volume and page number.

101. Levy, *Blasphemy*, 359.

102. The relationship between equality and mechanisms of security in Bentham's writing is explored in P. J. Kelly, *Utilitarianism and Distributive Justice: Jeremy Bentham and the Civil Law* (Oxford: Clarendon Press, 1990), 71–103.

103. Bentham Manuscripts, 6:149.

104. Michael Walzer, *On Toleration* (New Haven: Yale University Press, 1997), 25, 84.

105. Anna Laetitia Barbauld, *An Address to the Opposers of the Repeal of the Corporation and Test Acts* (London: J. Johnson, 1790), 16.

106. For one account of the relationship between citizenship and the "cult of sensibility," see Simon Schama, *Citizens: A Chronicle of the French Revolution* (New York: Alfred A. Knopf, 1989), 123–82.

107. Although Bentham is frequently known as an enemy of all fictions, he actually wished to emphasize a distinction between two *kinds* of fiction, the

"poetical" and "political": the fiction of the "lawyer and priest" and the functional fiction of politics that was the "coin of necessity." See C. K. Ogden, ed. *Bentham's Theory of Fictions* (New York: Harcourt Brace, 1932), 17–18.

108. On Bentham's view of the proper role for the church, see Bentham's papers on "Qualifications: Present Abstract Utility," Bentham Manuscripts, 6:40.

109. William Hazlitt, *The Spirit of the Age, or, Contemporary Portraits* (New York: Chelsea House, 1983), 8.

110. John Stuart Mill, *Mill on Bentham and Coleridge*, ed. F. R. Leavis (1950; Westport, CT: Greenwood Press, 1983), 43, 44, 79.

111. Bentham, *Chrestomathia*, 90. All further references to this work are noted parenthetically in the text by page number.

112. Hazlitt, *Spirit of the Age*, 5.

113. Bentham, *Chrestomathia*, table 2.

114. *Parliamentary History*, vol. xxviii (1798), cols. 391–92.

115. *Hansard*, 2nd series, vol. xix (1828), col. 157.

116. *Hansard*, 2nd series, vol. xxi (1829), col. 372; *Hansard*, 2nd series, vol. xix (1828), col. 392.

117. *Hansard*, 3rd series, vol. xxi (1834), col. 782.

118. *Parliamentary History* vol. xv (1753), col. 98.

119. Mill, *Mill on Bentham and Coleridge*, 95.

120. Edward Said, *The World, The Text, and the Critic* (Cambridge, MA: Harvard University Press, 1983), 35.

121. Clifford Siskin, *The Work of Writing: Literature and Social Change in Britain, 1700–1830* (Baltimore: Johns Hopkins University Press, 1998); James Chandler, *England in 1819: The Politics of Literary Culture and the Case of Romantic Historicism* (Chicago: University of Chicago Press, 1998), 31.

122. Tony Tanner, *Jane Austen* (Houndmills: Macmillan, 1986), 170.

123. Jane Austen, *Mansfield Park*, ed. Kathryn Sutherland (Harmondsworth: Penguin, 1996), 72. All further references to this work are noted parenthetically in the text by page number.

124. Alistair Duckworth, *The Improvement of the Estate: A Study of Jane Austen's Novels* (Baltimore: Johns Hopkins University Press, 1971), 35–80; Tanner, *Jane Austen*, 142–75.

125. Those critics who have examined the role of religion in the novel tend to view the church as a form of "religious orthodoxy" supporting Austen's conservative politics. Marilyn Butler, *Jane Austen and the War of Ideas* (Oxford: Clarendon Press, 1987), 225.

126. For a contrasting view of the domestic sphere as a source of value and security, see Katie Trumpener, *Bardic Nationalism*, 162–92.

127. Lionel Trilling, *The Opposing Self: Nine Essays in Criticism* (New York: Viking Press, 1950), 228.

128. My argument differs, then, from attempts to claim *Mansfield Park* as a radical critique of religious and political establishments – a "bitter parody of

conservative fiction," as described by Claudia Johnson, *Jane Austen: Women, Politics, and the Novel* (Chicago: University of Chicago Press, 1988), 96.

129. Timothy Clark, *Embodying Revolution: The Figure of the Poet in Shelley* (Oxford: Clarendon Press, 1989); Paul M. S. Dawson, *The Unacknowledged Legislator: Shelley and Politics* (Oxford: Clarendon Press, 1980).

130. Percy Bysshe Shelley, *Shelley's Poetry and Prose*, ed. Donald J. Reiman and Sharon B. Powers (New York: W. W. Norton, 1977), 132–36. All references to *Prometheus Unbound* are noted parenthetically in the text by act, scene, and line number. Further references to Shelley's poems are from the same edition.

131. Harold Bloom, *Shelley's Mythmaking* (Ithaca: Cornell University Press, 1969), 91–147.

132. For versions of this account, see Jerrold E. Hogle, *Shelley's Process: Radical Transference and the Development of His Major Works* (New York: Oxford University Press, 1988), 167–221; Tilottama Rajan, *The Supplement of Reading: Figures of Understanding in Romantic Theory and Practice* (Ithaca: Cornell University Press, 1990), 298–322.

133. Shelley to Thomas Love Peacock, 23–24 January 1819, *The Letters of Percy Bysshe Shelley*, ed. Frederick L. Jones, 2 vols. (Oxford: Clarendon Press, 1964), II:72.

134. Although I agree in some respects with Marlon Ross's account in "Shelley's Wayward Dream Poem: The Apprehending Reader in *Prometheus Unbound*," *Keats–Shelley Journal* 36 (1987): 110–33, I am departing from his general view of the work as a primarily psychological preparation for the poet's ideal community.

135. Shelley to Thomas Love Peacock, 23–24 January 1819, *Letters*, II:71.

136. Shelley to Leigh Hunt, 3 November 1819, *Letters* II:139.

137. Donald Reiman, "Wordsworth, Shelley, and the Romantic Inheritance," *Romanticism Past and Present* 5 (1981): 6.

2 "HOLY HYPOCRISY" AND THE RULE OF BELIEF: RADCLIFFE'S GOTHICS

1. Montague Summers, introduction to Charlotte Dacre, *Zofloya, or, the Moor* (London: Fortune Press, 1928), xvii.

2. For examples of these arguments, see David Durant, "Ann Radcliffe and the Conservative Gothic," *SEL* 22 (1982): 519–30; Robert Miles, "The Gothic Aesthetic: The Gothic as Discourse," *The Eighteenth Century* 32 (1991): 39–57; Ronald Paulson, *Representations of Revolution* (New Haven: Yale University Press, 1983), 215–47. Cannon Schmitt addresses issues and texts I discuss in this chapter in his *Alien Nation*, 21–46, but arrives at a conclusion that resembles these accounts.

3. As examples, see Freud's *Totem and Taboo* (New York: Norton, 1950); René Girard, *The Scapegoat* (Baltimore: Johns Hopkins University Press, 1986); Clifford Geertz, *The Interpretation of Cultures* (New York: Basic Books, 1973).

4. Irene Bostrom has provided a comprehensive view of the way that Gothic and historical fiction sided either for or against Catholic emancipation in "The Novel and Catholic Emancipation," *Studies in Romanticism* 2 (1963): 155–76.

5. *Hansard Parliamentary Debates*, 2nd series, vol. xix (1828), cols. 511–17.

6. J. M. Black, "The Catholic Threat and the British Press in the 1720s and 1730s," *Journal of Religious History* 12 (1983): 364–81; John Miller, *Religion in the Popular Prints 1600–1832* (Cambridge: Chadwyck-Healey, 1986).

7. William Empson, "The Last of the Catholic Question – Its Principle, History, and Effects," *The Edinburgh Review* 49 (March 1829): 218.

8. Hansard, 2nd series, vol. xx (1829), col. 905.

9. *Ibid.*, col. 235.

10. *Ibid.*, col. 604.

11. Gender is important in this instance, and in my account of the Gothic generally, insofar as it is associated with the position of women as preservers of religious value within the home. For a different account of women as readers of the Gothic, see Karen Swann, "Suffering and Sensation in *The Ruined Cottage*," *PMLA* 106 (January 1991): 83–95.

12. Scott Bennett, "Catholic Emancipation, The 'Quarterly Review,' and Britain's Constitutional Revolution," *Victorian Studies* 12 (1969): 293–95.

13. Robert Southey, *The Book of the Church*, 2 vols. (London: John Murray, 1824), 1:140. All further references to this work are noted parenthetically in the text by volume and page number.

14. David Zaret, "Religion, Science, and Printing in the Public Spheres in Seventeenth-Century England," in *Habermas and the Public Sphere*, ed. Craig Calhoun (Cambridge: MIT Press, 1992), 212–35.

15. *Hansard*, 1st series, vol. xxxv (1800), cols. 340, 372, 381, 383.

16. Richard Hurd, *Letters on Chivalry and Romance*, vols. CI–CII of *Augustan Reprint Series* (1762; Los Angeles: Augustan Reprint Society, 1963), 79–82. The point I am making might be seen as a development of Margaret Anne Doody's observation that the home in the Gothic novel is "wild and unsafe." See Doody, "Deserts, Ruins, and Troubled Waters: Female Dreams in Fiction and the Development of the Gothic," *Genre* 10 (1977): 567.

17. My discussion of the intersection of private and public bears some similarity to Jacques Donzelot's account of the state's government through the family in *The Policing of Families*, trans. Robert Hurley (New York: Random House, 1979).

18. William Watt, *Shilling Shockers of the Gothic School: A Study of Chapbook Gothic Romances* (Cambridge, MA: Harvard University Press, 1932), 18.

19. Horace Walpole, *The Castle of Otranto*, in *Three Gothic Novels*, ed. Peter Fairclough (Harmondsworth: Penguin, 1968), 61, 83–84.

20. Clara Reeve, *The Old English Baron*, ed. James Trainer (London: Oxford University Press, 1967), 105, 130, 131.

21. Walpole, *The Castle of Otranto*, 39–41.

22. Reeve, *The Old English Baron*, 6.

23. Although my terms are different, my thinking on these matters coincides loosely with Steven Knapp's *Literary Interest: The Limits of Anti-Formalism* (Cambridge, MA: Harvard University Press, 1993).
24. Mary Poovey, *A History of the Modern Fact: Problems of Knowledge in the Science of Wealth and Society* (Chicago: University of Chicago Press, 1998), 249–63.
25. Ann Radcliffe, *A Journey Made in the Summer of 1791 through Holland and the Northern Frontier of Germany, with a Return Down the Rhine: to which are added Observations During a Tour to the Lakes of Lancashire, Westmoreland, and Cumberland* (London: G. G. and J. Robinson, 1795), 389. All further references to this work are cited parenthetically in the text by page number.
26. See Walter Scott, "Mrs. Ann Radcliffe," in *The Lives of the Novelists* (Edinburgh, 1825).
27. As Alison Milbank observes in her helpful notes to the Oxford edition, Radcliffe's vague knowledge of Catholicism leads her to mistake a "friary" for a "convent" (Radcliffe, *A Sicilian Romance*, ed. Alison Milbank (Oxford: Oxford University Press, 1993), 201n). All further references to this work are noted parenthetically in the text by page number.
28. Radcliffe, *The Italian*, ed. Frank Garber (Oxford: Oxford University Press, 1968), 1–4. All further references to this work are noted parenthetically in the text by page number.
29. The Inquisition theme has been analyzed in Mark Hennelly, Jr., " 'The Slow Torture of Delay': Reading *The Italian*," *Studies in the Humanities* 13 (December 1986): 1–17. Hennelly's argument is that all characters, and the reader of the text, become implicated in the scenario of confession. Evidence has been supplied for Radcliffe's use of Philippus Van Limborch's *The History of the Inquisition* (1731) in John Thomson, "Ann Radcliffe's Use of Philippus Van Limborch's *The History of the Inqusition*," *English Language Notes* 18 (1980): 31–33.
30. See for example, Ian Duncan, *Modern Romance and Transformations of the Novel: The Gothic, Scott, Dickens* (Cambridge: Cambridge University Press, 1992); Durant, "Ann Radcliffe and the Conservative Gothic," 519–30; Caroline Gonda, *Reading Daughters' Fictions 1709–1834: Novels and Society from Manley to Edgeworth* (Cambridge: Cambridge University Press, 1996), 140–73.
31. Radcliffe, *The Castles of Athlin and Dunbayne: A Highland Story*, ed. Alison Milbank (Oxford: Oxford University Press, 1995), 3.
32. Radcliffe, *The Mysteries of Udolpho*, ed. Bonamy Dobrée (Oxford: Oxford University Press, 1966).
33. Eve Kosofsky Sedgwick, "The Character in the Veil: Imagery of the Surface in the Gothic Novel," *PMLA* 96 (1981): 255–70; Anne Williams, *Art of Darkness* (Chicago: University of Chicago Press, 1995).
34. Sedgwick, "The Character in the Veil," 261, 262.
35. Critics such as D. A. Miller, John Bender, and Franco Moretti have drawn attention to the ways in which eighteenth- and nineteenth-century fiction employs the third-person narrator as a device that either represents the

internalization of social "discipline" on characters (Miller) or the imposition of an utterly impersonal or imperializing vision (Bender, Moretti). Here, however, judicial procedure – neither psychological nor indifferently formal – provides a more vital formal resource for individual characters. See D. A. Miller, *The Novel and the Police* (Berkeley: University of California Press, 1988); John Bender. "Impersonal Violence: The Penetrating Gaze and the Field of Narration in *Caleb Williams*" in *Critical Reconstructions: The relationship of Fiction and life* (Stanford, CA: Stanford University Press, 1994), 11–126; Franco Moretti, *Signs Taken for Wonders: Essays in the Sociology of Literary Forms*, trans. Susan Fischer, David Forgoes, and David Miller (London: Verso, 1988), 83–108.

36. Michael Ignatieff, *A Just Measure of Pain: The Penitentiary in the Industrial Revolution* (New York: Columbia University Press, 1978), 18.

37. Radcliffe, *The Romance of the Forest*, ed. Chloe Chard (Oxford: Oxford University Press, 1986), 168. All further references to this work are noted parenthetically in the text by page number.

38. See, for example, Daniel Cottom, *The Civilized Imagination: A Study of Ann Radcliffe, Jane Austen, and Sir Walter Scott* (Cambridge: Cambridge University Press, 1985), 35–67.

39. William Godwin, *St. Leon: A Tale of the Sixteenth Century*, ed. Pamela Clemit (Oxford: Oxford University Press, 1994), 311.

40. William Godwin, *Mandeville*, ed. Pamela Clemit, vol. VI of *The Collected Novels and Memoirs of William Godwin* (London: William Pickering, 1992), 225. All further references to this work are noted parenthetically in the text by page number.

41. Percy Bysshe Shelley, review of William Godwin's *Mandeville*, in *Shelley's Prose or The Trumpet of a Prophecy*, ed. David Lee Clark (Albuquerque: University of New Mexico Press, 1954), 311.

3 COLERIDGE'S POLEMIC DIVINITY

1. Samuel Taylor Coleridge, *The Watchman*, ed. Lewis Patton, vol. II of *The Collected Works of Samuel Taylor Coleridge* (Princeton: Princeton University Press and London: Routledge and Kegan Paul, 1970), 9. All further references to this work are noted parenthetically by page number and abbreviated as *CW*, II.

2. Coleridge also discusses the connection between religion and print in the second of the *Lectures on Revealed Religion* and in *The Plot Discovered*, in *Lectures 1795 on Politics and Religion*, ed. Lewis Patton and Peter Mann, vol. I of *Collected Works* (1971), 137, 312. All further references to this work are noted parenthetically by page number and abbreviated as *CW* I.

3. See the "Prospectus," where Coleridge asserts that his Miscellany will "co-operate . . . with the WHIG CLUB in procuring a repeal of Lord Grenville's and Mr. Pitt's bills, now passed into laws" (*CW* II.5). The *Conciones*, moreover, describes the "Friends of Freedom" in terms of their opposition to the

Test and Corporation Acts, "that persecute by exclusion from the right of citizenship" (*CW* I:39).

4. Thomas McFarland, *Coleridge and the Pantheist Tradition* (Oxford: Oxford University Press, 1969); James D. Boulger, *Coleridge as Religious Thinker* (New Haven: Yale University Press, 1961). For a different view of this trajectory, see Jermoe Christensen, *Coleridge's Blessed Machine of Language* (Ithaca: Cornell University Press, 1981).

5. Nicholas Roe, *The Politics of Nature: Wordsworth and Some Contemporaries* (New York: St. Martin's Press, 1992); *Wordsworth and Coleridge: The Radical Years* (Oxford: Clarendon Press, 1988); Nigel Leask, *The Politics of the Imagination in Coleridge's Critical Thought* (London: Macmillan, 1988); John Morrow, *Coleridge's Political Thought: Property, Morality, and the Limits of Traditional Discourse* (London: Macmillan, 1990), 62.

6. Coleridge, *The Friend*, ed. Barbara E. Rooke, vol. IV of *Collected Works* (1969), I:232–33; Coleridge, *Lay Sermons*, ed. R. J. White, vol. VI of *Collected Works* (1972), 126–27. All further references to these works are noted parenthetically by page number and abbreviated as *CW* IV.1 and *CW* VI, respectively.

7. Coleridge, review of [M. G. Lewis], *The Monk*, in *Shorter Works and Fragments*, ed. H. J. Jackson and J. R. de J. Jackson, vol. XI of *Collected Works* (1995), XI.1:58.

8. I will concentrate my discussion on the *rifacciamento* (Coleridge's term) of *The Friend*, published in November 1818.

9. For this tradition of demonization of Catholic and Protestant institutionalized religion, see Christopher Hill, *Antichrist in Seventeenth-Century England* (1971; London: Verso, 1990).

10. The stance of *The Watchman* in the context of dissent was noted even at the time of its publication; John Colmer notes that Thelwall accused Coleridge of a too-narrow sectarianism in his newspaper, making it unpopular even for the democrats that ostensibly formed his audience. See Colmer, *Coleridge: Critic of Society* (Oxford: Clarendon Press, 1959), 43.

11. William Warburton, *The Divine Legation of Moses*, 4 vols. (1738–65; New York: Garland Press, 1978), I:VI,XX–XXI,XXIX.

12. Christensen, *Coleridge's Blessed Machine of Language*, 199.

13. On the tradition of enthusiasm in the eighteenth century – and its oxymoronic relation to personal regulation – see Shaun Irlam, *Elations: The Poetics of Enthusiasm in Eigtheenth-Century Britain* (Stanford: Stanford University Press, 1999).

14. On Hume's "doxa," the reliance on an untheorized, unsystematized set of beliefs and customs, see Jerome Christensen, *Practicing Enlightenment: Hume and the Formation of a Literary Career* (Madison: University of Wisconsin Press, 1987), 85–88.

15. William Hazlitt, *The Complete Works of William Hazlitt*, ed. P. P. Howe, 21 vols. (New York: A.M.S. Press, 1967), XVII:106.

16. R. J. White, introduction to *CW* 6.

17. Coleridge's discussion of "polemic divinity" is pursued elsewhere, including the *Logic*, ed. J. R. de J. Jackson, vol. XIII of *Collected Works* (1981), 150. See also Coleridge's approving comments in *The Friend* on the "books, pamphlets, and flying sheets" published during the interregnum, "during which all the possible forms of truth and error . . . bubbled up on the surface of the public mind, as in the ferment of a chaos" (IV.1:410). All further references to the *Logic* are noted parenthetically by page number and abbreviated a *CW* XIII.

18. Julie Carlson, *In the Theater of Romanticism: Coleridge, Nationalism, Women* (Cambridge: Cambridge University Press, 1994), 44; Jon Klancher, *The Making of English Reading Audiences 1790–1832* (Madison: University of Wisconsin Press, 1987), 165.

19. The same sentiment is to be found in a letter to T. G. Street of 22 March 1817, where Coleridge charges that the activities of radical journalists will lead to "the suspension of Freedom of all kind." *The Collected Letters*, IV:714. All further references to the letters are noted by volume and page number, and abbreviated as *CL*.

20. Coleridge to the Reverend John Edwards, 29 January 1796, *CL* I:79.

21. Coleridge to Lloyd, 15 October 1796, *CL* I:240. Coleridge expanded this statement in a March 1798 letter to his brother George: "I have snapped my squeaking baby-trumpet of Sedition & the fragments lie scattered in the lumber-room of Penitence. I wish to be a good man & a Christian – but no Whig, no Reformist, no Republican." Quoted in E. P. Thompson, "Disenchantment or Default? A Lay Sermon," in *Power and Consciousness*, ed. Conor Cruise O'Brien and William Dean Vanech (London: University of London Press, 1969), 153.

22. This appeal resembles other arguments in the work of William Wilberforce, Hannah More, Anna Laetitia Barbauld, Anne Yearsley, and others who argued against the slave trade. On the Christian dimension of the abolition movement, see David Turley, *The Culture of English Anti-Slavery, 1780–1860* (London: Routledge, 1991).

23. J. A. Appleyard, *Coleridge's Philosophy of Literature: The Development of a Concept of Poetry, 1791–1819* (Cambridge, MA: Harvard University Press, 1965), 59; John Colmer, *Coleridge: Critic of Society*, 31–50.

24. Isaac Kramnick, *Republicanism and Bourgeois Radicalism*.

25. Forest Pyle, *The Ideology of Imagination: Subject and Society in the Discourse of Romanticism* (Stanford: Stanford University Press, 1995), 48, 57. For a related view of the centrality of contradiction in Coleridge's thinking, see William H. Galperin, *The Return of the Visible in British Romanticism* (Baltimore: Johns Hopkins University Press, 1993), 156–204.

26. Christensen, *Coleridge's Blessed Machine of Language*; Julie Ellison, *Delicate Subjects: Romanticism, Gender, and the Ethics of Understanding* (Ithaca: Cornell University Press, 1990); Arden Reed, *Romantic Weather: The Climates of Coleridge and Baudelaire* (Hanover, NH: University Press of New England, 1983).

27. See Coleridge's defenses of such early poetry in the second *Lay Sermon* (*CW*VI:122n) and The *Friend* (*CW*IV.2:22n–26n).
28. Coleridge, "Fears in Solitude", lines 63–64, 78 in *Poetical Works*, ed. Ernest Hartley Coleridge (Oxford University Press, 1912). All further references to the poetry are from this edition and are noted parenthetically by line number.
29. Robert Southey, *Joan of Arc, an Epic Poem* (Bristol: Joseph Cottle, and London: J. Robinson, 1796), 4:280, 286.
30. For a contrasting account of Coleridge's individualist turn in "Fears"; see Karl Kroeber, "Coleridge's 'Fears': Problems in Patriotic Poetry" *Clio* 7(1978): 359–73.
31. David Collings sees these tendencies as far more conflictual in "Coleridge Beginning a Career: Desultory Authorship in 'Religious Musings,'" *ELH* 58 (1991): 167–93.
32. Kelvin Everest, *Coleridge's Secret Ministry: The Context of the Conversation Poems, 1795–98* (Sussex: Harvester, 1979); Tim Fulford, *Coleridge's Figurative Language* (New York: St. Martin's Press, 1991), 1–34; Paul Magnuson, *Reading Public Romanticism* (Princeton: Princeton University Press, 1998), 67–94.
33. For contrasting views of the conversation poem's search for an authentic and transcendent poetic voice, see Reeve Parker, *Coleridge's Meditative Art* (Ithaca: Cornell University Press, 1975); Raimonda Modiano, *Coleridge and the Concept of Nature* (Tallahassee: Florida State University Press, 1985), 28–100.
34. On "asking" in a strictly theological context, see Thomas M. Greene, "Coleridge and the Energy of Asking," *ELH* 62 (1995): 907–31.
35. Coleridge to John Thelwall, 21 August 1797, *CL*I:344.
36. Joss Marsh, *Word Crimes: Blasphemy, Culture, and Literature in Nineteenth-Century England* (Chicago: University of Chicago Press, 1998), 7.
37. An idea also pursued in the *Conciones* (*CW* I:65–67)
38. Godwin, *Political Justice*, 761.
39. On the difference between this notion of community and issues of individual moral or religious integrity, see Bernard Williams, "A Critique of Utilitarianism," in *Utilitarianism: For and Against* (Cambridge: Cambridge University Press, 1983), 116–17. On the discussion of "private language" in Wittgenstein, see Saul Kripke, *Wittgenstein on Rules and Private Language* (Cambridge, MA: Harvard University Press, 1982).
40. I take this to be the political extension of Steven Knapp's incisive formulation of the fanatic's epistemology: "an Enlightened fantasy of pre-Enlightened agency." See Knapp, *Personification and the Sublime: Milton to Coleridge* (Cambridge, MA: Harvard University Press, 1985), 81.
41. Thomas Clarkson, *A Portraiture of Quakerism*, 3 vols. (London: Longman, 1806), 1:187.
42. Shelley to Elizabeth Hitchener, 26 January 1812, *Letters* I:238–39.
43. Here I am agreeing with J. Robert Barth's account of the Church's "spirit of tolerance," but I differ from his account of Coleridge's search for a more

"personal, redemptive" religion. See Barth, "Coleridge and the Church of England," in *The Coleridge Connection: Essays for Thomas McFarland* ed. Richard Gravil and Molly Lefebure (New York: St. Martin's Press, 1990), 291, 296.

44. Elie Halévy, *The Growth of Philosophical Radicalism* (Boston: Beacon Press, 1955), 22–23. For a particularly pointed attack on Paley, see *CW* VI: 186–87n.

45. Mill, *Mill on Bentham and Coleridge*; Catherine Gallagher, *The Industrial Reformation of English Fiction: Social Discourse and Narrative Form, 1832–1867* (Chicago: University of Chicago Press, 1985), 187–218.

46. *The Notebooks of Samuel Taylor Coleridge*, ed. Kathleen Coburn, 4 vols. (London: Routledge, 1962): II. entry 2440. A similar argument informs the argument against novels in the third essay of Part I, *CW* IV.1:20–21, and is carried over into the fourth essay's discussion of arrogance.

47. Also relevant here is Coleridge's criticism of "enlightened" readings of the Bible that claim the New Testament to be relevant only for "primitive converts from Judaism" (*CW* VI:37n).

48. On the importance of the Bible as literature in Coleridge's thought see Stephen Prickett, *Romanticism and Religion: The Tradition of Coleridge and Wordsworth in the Victorian Church* Cambridge: Cambridge University Press, 1976), 46–47; Elinor Shaffer, *"Kubla Khan" and The Fall of Jerusalem: The Mythological School in Biblical Criticism and Secular Literature 1770–1880* (Cambridge: Cambridge University Press, 1975). Although Elinor Shaffer is certainly correct to identify Coleridge's affiliation with the German "higher criticism" and its emphasis on the Bible as an individual *interpretation* of God's word rather than a mere recording or reflection of it, we must also see that Coleridge values the imaginative work of the Bible as a textual object: a representation that is neither a transcendent truth nor a psychological evocation of it.

49. Coleridge, in fact, continually understood logic itself in religious terms, just as he considered religion as logic: logic is suspended between "delusions of superstition" and "sophisms of a faithless sensuality" (*CW* XII:197).

50. Coleridge, *Biographia Literaria*, ed. James Engell and W. Jackson Bate, vol. VII of *Collected Works* (1983), VII:2:6.

51. Coleridge, "Apologetic Preface to 'Fire, Famine, and Slaughter,'" *Poetical Works*, 606. A version of this defense of toleration appears in *Biographia Literaria*, 1:198.

52. John Henry, Cardinal Newman, *Apologia Pro Vita Sua: Being a History of His Religious Opinions* (New York: Sheed and Ward, 1946), 64.

53. Mill, *Mill on Bentham and Coleridge*, 145–46.

54. Coleridge, *On the Constitution of the Church and State*, ed. John Colmer, vol. X of *Collected Works* (1976), 24, 46. All further references to this works are noted parenthetically as *CW* X, followed by the page number.

55. Raymond Williams, *Culture and Society 1780–1950* (New York: Columbia University Press, 1958), 49–70.

4 SECT AND SECULAR ECONOMY IN THE IRISH NATIONAL TALE

1. Lady Morgan, *Dramatic Scenes from Real Life*, 3 vols. (1833; New York: Garland Press, 1979) 1:282. All further references to this work are from volume 1 and are noted parenthetically in the text by page number.
2. Morgan, *The Wild Irish Girl*, introduced by Brigid Brophy (London: Pandora Press, 1986), 54.
3. *Ibid.*, 40.
4. Anne Plumpetre, *Narrative of a Residence in Ireland* (London: Henry Coburn, 1817), 347.
5. John Wilson Croker, Review of *Waverly*, *The Quarterly Review* 11 (1814):355.
6. Francis Jeffrey, "Miss Edgeworth's Tales," *The Edinburgh Review* 28 (August 1817): 398; Jeffrey, "Miss Edgeworth's *Tales of Fashionable Life*," *The Edinburgh Review* 20 (July 1812): 119.
7. William Butler Yeats, introduction to *Representative Irish Tales*, vol. VI of *Collected Works*, ed. William H. O'Donnell (New York: Macmillan, 1989), 29, 32.
8. Maria Edgeworth and Richard Lovell Edgeworth, *Essay on Irish Bulls*, in *Tales and Novels by Maria Edgeworth*, 20 vols. in 10 (New York: Harper, 1835), 1:95; Maria and Richard Lovell Edgeworth, *Practical Education*, 2 vols. (1798; New York: Garland Press, 1974), I:VII–VIII.
9. Richard Lovell Edgeworth, preface to *Popular Tales*, in vol. IV of *Tales and Novels*, 3–4.
10. Maria Edgeworth, *Castle Rackrent and Ennui*, 63. All further references to this works are noted parenthetically in the text by page number.
11. Croker, Review of *Tales of Fashionable Life*, *The Quarterly Review* 7 (June 1812): 341.
12. William Stephen, Review of *Tales of Fashionable Life*, *The Quarterly Review* 2 (August 1809): 148.
13. Sir Walter Scott, *Waverly Novels*, vol. I, General Preface. All further references to Scott's novels are from this edition. I follow the convention of quoting by chapter number in parentheses; I also adjust chapter numbers where necessary to conform to modern editions.
14. Terry Eagleton, *Heathcliff and the Great Hunger: Studies in Irish Culture* (London: Verso, 1995), 176.
15. Mary Jean Corbett, "Another Tale to Tell: Postcolonial Theory and the Case of *Castle Rackrent*," *Criticism* 36 (Summer 1994): 383.
16. Suvendrini Perera, *Reaches of Empire: The English Novel from Edgeworth to Dickens* (New York: Columbia University Press, 1991), 31.
17. See Katie Trumpener's account of the national tale as a a record of "the violence done to Ireland" by "the crushing forces of the modern state" in "National Character, Nationalist Plots: National Tale and Historical Novel in the Age of *Waverly*, 1806–1830," *ELH* 60 (1993): 706, 712; for a contrasting view, see Ina Ferris's account of the national tale as a more subversive "rearrangement of relations and positions" in "Narrating Cultural Encounter:

Lady Morgan and the Irish National Tale," *Nineteenth-Century Literature* (1996): 287–303.

18. On "patriotism by assimilation," see C. A. Bayly, *Imperial Meridian: The British Empire and the World, 1780–1830* (London: Longman, 1989), 77–89.

19. Adam Smith, *The Wealth of Nations*, ed. Edwin Cannan, intr. Max Lerner (New York: Modern Library, 1937), 385. Smith credits Hume's *Political Discourses* (1752) as the first investigation of the economy on these terms. For a different reading of Edgeworth's relation to Smith, see Marilyn Butler, introduction to *Castle Rackrent and Ennui*, 28.

20. Karl Marx, *A Contribution to the Critique of Political Economy* (Moscow: Progress Publishers, 1970), 138–40.

21. Smith, *Wealth of Nations*, 745.

22. Marx, *Contribution*, 72, 33.

23. Maria Edgeworth, *Harrington, A Tale*, vol. 1 of *Harrington, A Tale* and *Ormond, A Tale*, 2 vols. (London: R. Hunter, 1817), 6. All further references to this work are noted parenthetically in the text by page number.

24. Michael Ragussis, "Representation, Conversion, and Literary Form: *Harrington* and the Novel of Jewish Identity," *Critical Inquiry* 16 (Autumn 1989), 124.

25. Maria Edgeworth, *Belinda*, vols. XI and XII of *Tales and Novels*, XII: 10.

26. For explorations of this perspective, see Catherine Gallagher, *Nobody's Story: The Vanishing Acts of Women Writers in the Marketplace 1670–1820* (Berkeley: University of California Press, 1994), 204–38; Teresa Michals, "Commerce and Character in Maria Edgeworth," *Nineteenth-Century Literature* 49 (1994): 1–20.

27. *Harrington*'s plot contains so many details that resemble well-known aspects of the young Jeremy Bentham's life – from the fear of ghosts to the nursemaid's theft – that it is tempting to see Bentham as a model for the novel's hero.

28. Etienne Dumont to Richard Lovell Edgeworth, 4 October 1806, Bentham manuscripts, University College London, no. 174.5.

29. Morgan, *The Missionary* (1811; reprint, with an introduction by Dennis R. Dean Delmar, NY: Scholar's Facsimiles and Reprints, 1981).

30. Edgeworth, *The Absentee*, ed. W. J. McCormack and Kim Walker (Oxford: Oxford University Press, 1988), 133–4. All further references to this work are noted parenthetically in the text by page number.

31. For Maria Edgeworth's brief notes for an essay on the "Genius and STYLE of Burke", see Appendix III, *The Absentee*, 282.

32. My term "nation-effect" echoes Roland Barthes's term "reality effect," a "narrative *luxury*," he asserts, that typifies the techniques of realist fiction. See *The Rustle of Language*, trans. Richard Howard (New York: Hill and Wang, 1986), 141.

33. George Wilhelm Friedrich Hegel, *Philosophy of Right*, trans. T. M. Knox (London: Oxford University Press, 1967), 192–93. See also Foucault's account of Frederick the Great, "the meticulous king of small machines, well-trained regiments, and long exercises" in *Discipline and Punish*, 136.

34. Bernard Williams, *Moral Luck: Philosophical Papers 1973–1980* (Cambridge: Cambridge University Press, 1981), 20–39.
35. On the logic of limited liability and its relation to Richardson's *Clarissa*, see Sandra Macpherson, "Lovelace Ltd.," *ELH* 65 (1998): 99–121.
36. Maria and Richard Lovell Edgeworth, Review of John Carr, *The Stranger in Ireland*, *The Edinburgh Review* 10 (April 1807): 47.
37. For a different account – one that views the nurse as a sponsor of national tradition – see Trumpener, *Bardic Nationalism*, 193–241.
38. See Mary Jean Corbett, "Public Affections and Familial Politics: Burke, Edgeworth, and the 'Common Naturalization' of Great Britain," *ELH* 61 (1994): 894; W. J. McCormack, *Ascendancy and Tradition in Anglo-Irish Literary History from 1789 to 1939* (Oxford: Oxford University Press, 1985), 165.
39. Christopher Ricks, *Keats and Embarrassment* (Oxford: Clarendon Press, 1974).
40. For a contrasting account of the blush and its connection to conventional modesty see Ruth Bernard Yeazell, *Fictions of Modesty: Women and Courtship in the English Novel* (Chicago: University of Chicago Press, 1991).
41. *Hansard*, 2d series, vol. xvi (1827), col. 815. For an extensive discussion of the Nugent heritage, see McCormack, *Ascendancy and Tradition*, 141–45.
42. Elizabeth Inchbald, *A Simple Story* (Oxford: Oxford University Press, 1967), 3; J. C. D. Clark, "Religious Affiliation and Dynastic Allegiance in Eighteenth-Century England: Edmund Burke, Thomas Paine, and Samuel Johnson," *ELH* (Winter 1997): 1035.
43. My explanation draws heavily from William McCormack's superbly informative appendix to *The Absentee*. See Appendix ii, *The Absentee*, 276–81.
44. Edgar E. MacDonald, ed., *The Education of the Heart: The Correspondence of Rachel Mordecai Lazarus and Maria Edgeworth* (Chapel Hill: University of North Carolina Press, 1977), 14.
45. *Ibid.*, 22, 26, 35.
46. Brooke's name may also be intended to remind us of Charlotte Brooke, who published her *Reliques of Irish Poetry* in 1789.
47. See John Guillory, *Cultural Capital: The Problem of Literary Canon Formation* (Chicago: University of Chicago Press, 1993), especially 85–133.
48. Georg Lukács, *The Historical Novel*, trans. Hannah and Stanley Mitchell (1962; Lincoln: University of Nebraska Press, 1983), 30, 32.
49. *Ibid.*, 48.
50. In particular, see Welsh's view of Scott's emphasis on "prudence," a combination of individual and collective psychology, realism, and romance, in Alexander Welsh, *The Hero of the Waverly Novels* (1963; Princeton: Princeton University Press, 1992), 1–20. Judith Wilt, in *Secret Leaves: The Novels of Walter Scott* (Chicago: The University of Chicago Press, 1985), 1–17, echoes this account in her views on the value of tradition and moderation in the Waverly novels.
51. Lukács, *The Historical Novel*, 52.
52. *Ibid.*, 60.
53. Ina Ferris, *The Achievement of Literary Authority: Gender, History, and the Waverly Novels* (Ithaca: Cornell University Press, 1991); Fiona Robertson, *Legitimate*

Histories: Scott, Gothic, and the Authorities of Fiction (Oxford: Clarendon Press, 1994).

5 WORDSWORTH AND "THE FRAME OF SOCIAL BEING"

1. William Wordsworth to John Scott, 18 April 1816, *The Letters of William and Dorothy Wordsworth: The Middle Years*, 2 vols., ed. Ernest De Selincourt (Oxford: Oxford University Press, 1937), II:734. Further references to this edition are cited parenthetically in the text by volume and page number, and abbreviated as *MY*.
2. Wordsworth to Thomas Poole, 13 March 1815, *MY* II:646.
3. Wordsworth to Daniel Stuart 7 April 1817, *MY* II:784.
4. Sir J. T. Coleridge, *A Memoir of the Rev. John Keble* (Oxford: James Parker, 1869), 258. See also Christopher Wordsworth, *Memoirs of William Wordsworth, Poet Laureate*, 2 vols. (London: Edward Moxon, 1851), II:355–57.
5. Wordsworth, *The Excursion* (9.784–5), vol. v of *The Poetical Works of William Wordsworth*. All further references to this work are noted parenthetically in the text by book and line number, and abbreviated where necessary as *E*. References to Wordsworth's other poems are from *The Poetical Works*, with the exception of *The Prelude* and *The Pedlar*.
6. Wordsworth, *The Prelude* (3.440). References to *The Prelude* are to the 1805 version, unless otherwise noted. All further references to this work are noted parenthetically in the text by volume and page number.
7. John Keble, *Sermons, Academical and Occasional* (Oxford: John Henry Parker, 1847), 138.
8. Stephen Gill, *William Wordsworth: A Life* (Oxford: Oxford University Press, 1990), 418.
9. Stephen Gill, *Wordsworth and the Victorians* (Oxford: Clarendon Press, 1998), 63.
10. Matthew Arnold, *Essays in Criticism, Second Series* (London: Macmillan, 1888), 136.
11. Harold Bloom, *The Visionary Company* (Ithaca: Cornell University Press, 1961), 195–96.
12. M. H. Abrams, *Natural Supernaturalism*, 65, 91.
13. Kenneth Johnston, *Wordsworth and "The Recluse"* (New Haven: Yale University Press, 1984), 292. Paul Sheats essentially takes this view in *The Making of Wordsworth's Poetry, 1785–1798* (Cambridge, MA: Harvard University Press, 1973).
14. Paul de Man, "Wordsworth and the Victorians," in *The Rhetoric of Romanticism* (New York: Columbia University Press, 1984), 91–92.
15. Marjorie Levinson, *Wordsworth's Great Period Poems: Four Essays* (Cambridge: Cambridge University Press, 1986), 16, 34, 37.
16. Thomas Pfau, *Wordsworth's Profession: Form, Class, and the Logic of Early Romantic Cultural Production* (Stanford: Stanford University Press, 1997). For other accounts of Wordsworth's connections to political and religious

dissent, see Heather Glen, *Vision and Disenchantment* Nicholas Roe, *The Politics of Nature: Wordsworth and Some Contemporaries* (New York: St. Martin's Press, 1992); Anne Janowitz, *Lyric and Labour in the Romantic Tradition* (Cambridge: Cambridge University Press, 1998).

17. James Chandler, *Wordsworth's Second Nature*; Robert Griffin, *Wordsworth's Pope* (Cambridge: Cambridge University Press, 1996); Peter Manning, *Reading Romantics* (Oxford: Oxford University Press, 1990), 273–99; Robert Ryan, *The Romantic Reformation*, 80–118; Richard E. Brantley, *Wordsworth's Natural Methodism* (New Haven: Yale University Press, 1975).

18. Wordsworth to James Losh, 4 December 1821, in *The Letters of William and Dorothy Wordsworth: The Later Years*, 2 vols., ed. Ernest de Selincourt and Helen Darbishire (Oxford: Clarendon Press, 1939), II:58. Further references are cited parenthetically in the text by volume and page number, and abbreviated as *LY*.

19. Chandler, *Wordsworth's Second Nature*; see also David Bromwich, *A Choice of Inheritance* 43–78.

20. For this psychological dimension of Burke's thought, see Chandler, *Wordsworth's Second Nature*, 198, 202. Chandler, I would suggest, is probably right about Burke – but his assessment of Wordsworth is open to doubt.

21. Wordsworth to Sir George Beaumont, 10 November 1806, *MY* 1:77.

22. Wordsworth, *Poetical Works*, III:508–22.

23. Wordsworth, "Speech at the Laying of the Foundation Stone of the New School in the Village of Bowness," in *The Prose Works of William Wordsworth*, 3 vols., ed. W. J. B. Owen (Oxford: Clarendon Press, 1974), III:294. All further references to prose works are noted parenthetically in the text by volume and page number, and abbreviated as *WPr*.

24. In a letter to Francis Wrangham – where he argues against Catholic emancipation – Wordsworth thinks of the church to which he is "tenderly attached . . . not the less on account of the pretty little spire of Brompton Parish Church, under which you and I were made happy men, by the gift from providence of two excellent wives." See Wordsworth to Wrangham, April 1809, *MY*1:291.

25. Kenneth Johnston offers a reading of the Gothic church's significance as a ruin, and poetry as a "substitute cathedral"; see Johnston, *Wordsworth and "The Recluse*," XXIII, 245.

26. The difference between *The Temple* (1633) and *The Recluse* is that Herbert imagines himself building a church out of poems; Wordsworth imagines his poems to be built into a church.

27. Wordsworth, *Poetical Works*, V:1–2.

28. *Oxford English Dictionary*, 2nd edn. (Oxford: Oxford University Press, 1989), s.v. "excursion."

29. Franco Moretti, *Atlas of the European Novel 1800–1900* (London: Verso, 1998). My argument differs substantially from the account of *The Excursion* in Michael Wiley's *Romantic Geography: Wordsworth and Anglo-European*

Spaces (New York: St. Martin's Press, 1998), where he sees Wordsworthian geography as yet another dimension of the opposition between the poet's early radicalism and later conservatism.

30. See Wordsworth to William Pasley, 28 March 1811, *MY* 1:472–3. Pasley argued for perfecting accurate maps of British dominions to aid in military and legislative "prudence" and the prevention of unnecessary "risk" to the national population. See C. W. Pasley, *Essay on the Military Policy and Institutions of the British Empire* (4th edn., 1812; London: John Weale, 1847), 183, 213, 219. In Edgeworth's *The Absentee*, Count O'Halloran has a volume of "Pasley on the Military Policy of Great Britain" in his library, "marked with many notes of admiration" (117).

31. Geoffrey Hartman, *Wordsworth's Poetry, 1787–1814* (Cambridge, MA: Harvard University Press, 1987), 300.

32. John O. Hayden, ed., *Romantic Bards and British Reviewers* (Lincoln: University of Nebraska Press, 1971), 39, 42; Bloom, *The Visionary Company*, 193.

33. Hartman, *Wordsworth's Poetry*, 301.

34. Alan Richardson, *Literature, Education, and Romanticism: Reading as Social Practice, 1780–1832* (Cambridge: Cambridge University Press, 1994), 100–03; Celeste Langan, *Romantic Vagrancy*, 227–28.

35. Samuel Taylor Coleridge to John Thelwall, 13 May 1796, in *Collected Letters*, 1:216; William H. Galperin, *Revision and Authority in Wordsworth: The Interpretation of a Career* (Philadelphia: University of Pennsylvania Press, 1989), 29–30.

36. Hoxie Neale Fairchild, *Religious Trends in English Poetry*, 5 vols. (New York: Columbia University Press, 1949), III:208.

37. John Wilson, *The Recreations of Christopher North* (New York: D. Appleton, 1869), 190.

38. Critics such as E. P. Thompson have astutely claimed that the figure of the Solitary may represent John Thelwall or even the poet's own revolutionary *alter ego* from which he seeks to achieve a principled distance. See E. P. Thompson, "Hunting the Jacobin Fox," *Past and Present* 142 (1994): 132–39. Kenneth Johnston identifies him with Joseph Fawcett, author of *The Art of War* (1795). See Johnston, *The Hidden Wordsworth: Poet, Lover, Rebel, Spy* (New York: W. W. Norton, 1998), 242. Wordsworth discusses Fawcett in the Fenwick notes on the poem. See *The Fenwick Notes of William Wordsworth*, ed. Jared Curtis (London: Bristol Classical Press, 1993), 80.

39. Nicholas Roe, *Wordsworth and Coleridge: The Radical Years* (Oxford: Clarendon Press, 1988), 15–37; Roe, *The Politics of Nature: Wordsworth and Some Contemporaries* (New York: St. Martin's Press, 1992), 101–16. See also Kenneth Johnston's account of Cambridge radicalism in *The Hidden Wordsworth*, 175–87.

40. I take the term "therapy" from Langan's account in *Romantic Vagrancy*, 227ff.

41. Galperin, *Revision and Authority*, 44. See also Alison Hickey, *Impure Conceits: Rhetoric and Ideology in Wordsworth's "Excursion"* (Stanford: Stanford University Press, 1997).

42. Pierre Bourdieu, *Language and Symbolic Power*, ed. and intr. John B. Thompson, trans. Gino Raymond and Matthew Adamson (Cambridge, MA: Harvard University Press, 1990), 115, 121.

43. For a contrasting, more or less deconstructive, account of the Wanderer's "imposition of patterns on individual experiences," see Frances Ferguson, *Wordsworth: Language as Counter-Spirit* (New Haven: Yale University Press, 1977), 227.

44. I am describing a logic that bears some resemblance to the way that François Ewald understands the emergence of "solidarity" in the modern state to involve the idea of society preceding itself. See Ewald, *L'Etat providence* (Paris: Bernard Grasset, 1986), 326–27.

45. Wordsworth to Catherine Clarkson, December 1814, *MY*II:618.

46. Wordsworth, *The Pedlar*, 324–25, in *The Pedlar, Tintern Abbey, The Two-Part Prelude*, ed. Jonathan Wordsworth (Cambridge: Cambridge University Press, 1985). All further references to this work are noted parenthetically in the text by line number, and abbreviated where necessary as *P*.

47. The lines are altered slightly in *The Excursion*: "but wandering thoughts were then / A misery to him; and the Youth resigned / A task he was unable to perform."

48. John Calvin, *On the Christian Faith: Selections from the Institutes, Commentaries, and Tracts*, ed. John T. McNeill (New York: Bobbs-Merrill, 1957), 50, 51.

49. E. P. Thompson, "Disenchantment or Default?," 149–81.

50. John Herman Merivale, "Wordsworth's *Excursion, a Poem*," *The Monthly Review*, 2nd series 74 (February 1815), in *The Romantics Reviewed: Contemporary Reviews of British Romantic Writers*, ed. Donald Reiman, 3 parts in 9 (New York: Garland, 1972), Part A, 732.

51. See Mitchell Dean, *The Constitution of Poverty: Towards a Genealogy of Liberal Governance* (London: Routledge, 1991).

52. David Simpson, *Wordsworth's Historical Imagination: The Poetry of Displacement* (New York: Methuen, 1987), 201.

53. Alan Liu, *Wordsworth: The Sense of History* (Stanford: Stanford University Press, 1989), 322, 325.

54. See Hickey, *Impure Conceits*, 123.

55. Wordsworth, *Poetical Works*, v:473.

56. Andrew Bell, *An Analysis of the Experiment in Education, Made at Egmore, Near Madras*, 3rd edn. (London: T. Bensley, 1807), 2, 5.

57. Thomas Southwood Smith, *The Divine Government*, 5th edn. (Philadelphia: J. B. Lippincott and Company, 1866), 120. Wordsworth speaks of Smith's "valuable Work" in a letter to Thomas Powell, 28 June 1838 *LY*II:948.

58. Richard Yates, *The Basis of National Welfare, Considered in Reference Chiefly to the Prosperity of Britain and the Safety of the Church of England* (London: F. C. and J. Rivington, 1817), 29, 18, 49–66.

59. Thomas Laqueur, *Religion and Respectability: Sunday Schools and Working Class Culture 1750–1850* (New Haven: Yale University Press, 1976). See especially Laqueur's comments (220–22) on the Sunday school's emphasis on a system

of obedience determined by the position of persons within the school's structure rather than *who* a person is in advance of participation.

60. David M. Thompson, "The Religious Census of 1851," in *The Census and Social Structure*, ed. Richard Lawton (London: Frank Cass, 1978); Ian Hacking, *The Taming of Chance* (Cambridge: Cambridge University Press, 1990), 26–27.

61. D. V. Glass, *Numbering the People* (Farnborough: Heath, 1973), 15.

62. Frank D. McConnell, *The Confessional Imagination: A Reading of Wordsworth's Prelude* (Baltimore: Johns Hopkins University Press, 1974), 4.

63. For Kenneth Johnston, this phase of Wordsworth's career repeatedly displays "human mental consciousness" as "radically independent of material limitation." Johnston, *Wordsworth and "The Recluse"*, 15.

64. William Cowper, *The Poems of William Cowper* (London: Joseph Dent, 1931), 361.

65. Jean-Joseph Mounier, *On the Influence Attributed to Philosophers, Free-Masons, and to the Illumination the Revolution of France* (1801; Delmar, NY: Scholars' Facsimiles and Reprints, 1974), 120–21.

66. Robert Lowth, *Lectures on the Sacred Poetry of the Hebrews* (Andover, MA: Codman Press, 1829), 23. For relevant readings of the primitive association between poetry and religion, see Alan Bewell, in *Wordsworth and the Enlightenment: Nature, Man, and Society in the Experimental Poetry* (New Haven: Yale University Press, 1989), and Elinor Shaffer, *"Kubla Khan" and the Fall of Jerusalem*.

67. Joseph Kishel studies the relationship between the Essay and the Chartreuse passage, arguing that Wordsworth's object is to join the earthly with the spiritual. See "Wordsworth and the Grande Chartreuse," *Wordsworth Circle* 12 (Winter 1981): 82–88.

68. Readings of the "Essay" traditionally emphasize its attempts to mold and control its audience. See, for example, Charles Rzepka, *The Self as Mind: Vision and Identity in Wordsworth, Coleridge, and Keats* (Cambridge, MA: Harvard University Press, 1986), 63–64.

69. John Wilson, "Wordsworth's Sonnets and Memorials," *Blackwood's Edinburgh Magazine* 12 (August 1822), in Reiman, *The Romantics Reviewed*, Part A, 118.

70. Nancy Easterlin, *Wordsworth and the Question of "Romantic Religion"* (Lewisburg, PA: Bucknell University Press, 1996), 116–51; Barbara Gates, "Wordsworth's Mirror of Morality: Distortions of Church History," *The Wordsworth Circle* 12 (1981): 129–32.

71. *The Fenwick Notes*, ed. Curtis, 35.

72. Wordsworth, *Poetical Works*, III:557.

73. Review of Christopher Wordsworth, *Memoirs*, *The Gentleman's Magazine* 190 (August 1851): 111.

74. Review of *Ecclesiastical Sketches* and *Memorials of a Tour*, *Literary Chronicle* (14 December 1822), in Reiman, *The Romantics Reviewed* Part A, 588.

75. All references to the *Ecclesiastical Sonnets* are noted parenthetically by book and sonnet number.

76. For Bede's account, see *Ecclesiastical History of the English People*, trans. Leo Shirley-Price, ed. and intr. D. H. Farmer (Harmondsworth: Penguin, 1990), 106–07.

77. Sharon Turner, *The History of the Anglo-Saxons from the Earliest Period to the Norman Conquest*, 3 vols., 5th edn. (London: Longman, 1828), 1:332–333, 333n.

78. See Trumpener, *Bardic Nationalism*, 3–34, 67–127.

79. Wordsworth to Richard Sharp, 16 April 1822, *LY* 1:65–66.

80. Wordsworth, *Poetical Works*, III:557.

81. On the relation between freedom and constraint in Wordsworth's sonnets, see Jonathan Hess, "Wordsworth's Aesthetic State: The Poetics of Liberty," *Studies in Romanticism* 33 (1994): 3–29.

82. My account agrees in some respects with Regina Hewitt's "Church Building as Political Strategy in Wordsworth's Ecclesiastical Sonnets," *Mosaic* 25 (1992): 31–46, but I differ from her explanation of the church as "social control."

83. Wordsworth, *Poetical Works* III:556.

84. Ann L. Rylstone, in *Prophetic Memory in Wordsworth's Ecclesiastical Sonnets* (Carbondale: Southern Illinois University Press, 1991), argues that the sonnets represent an "integration of nature and the church" (3) but I differ from her "general emphasis on common experience" (5) that depends upon synthesizing the "phenomenal and spiritual" (29).

85. For examples of these arguments, see Thomas McFarland, *Romanticism and the Forms of Ruin: Wordsworth, Coleridge, and Modalities of Fragmentation* (Princeton: Princeton University Press, 1981), 182, 186; Liu, *Wordsworth: The Sense of History*, 463.

6 "CONSECRATED FANCY": BYRON AND KEATS

1. See Martin Aske, "Magical Spaces in 'The Eve of St. Agnes,'" *Essays in Criticism* 31 (1981): 196–209; Philip Martin, *Byron: A Poet Before His Public* (Cambridge: Cambridge University Press, 1982).

2. Lord Byron to Robert Charles Dallas, 7 September 1811, *Byron's Letters and Journals*, ed. Leslie Marchand, 12 vols. (Cambridge, MA: Harvard University Press, 1973–83), 2:92. Further references to this work are noted in parentheses by volume and page number and abbreviated as *BLJ*.

3. John Keats, *The Fall of Hyperion: A Dream*, canto 1, lines 1–18. All quotations from the poems are taken from *The Complete Poems of John Keats*, edited by Jack Stillinger (Cambridge, MA: Harvard University Press, 1978), and are cited parenthetically by line number.

4. C. M. Woodhouse, "The Religion of an Agnostic," *The Byron Journal* 6 (1978): 26–33; Byron to Thomas Moore, 4 March 1822, *BLJ* IX:118–19.

5. Robert Ryan, *The Romantic Reformation*, 150.

6. Bernard Beatty, "Fiction's Limit and Eden's Door," in *Byron and the Limits of Fiction*, ed. Bernard Beatty and Vincent Newey (Liverpool: Liverpool University Press, 1988), 33.

7. Byron, *Don Juan* (7:6,8:18) vol. v of *The Complete Poetical Works*. For Byron's frequent condemnation of "cant," see Lady Blessington, in *Conversations of Lord Byron*, ed. Ernest J. Lovell, Jr. (Princeton: Princeton University Press, 1969), 12, 29.

8. Byron to James Wedderburn Webster, 25 September 1813, *BLJ* III:120.

9. Alvin B. Kernan, "*Don Juan*: the Perspective of Satire," in *Romanticism and Consciousness: Essays in Criticism*, ed. Harold Bloom (New York: W. W. Norton, 1970), 345; on Byron's skepticism, see Michael Cooke, *The Blind Man Traces the Circle: On the Patterns and Philosophy of Byron's Poetry* (Princeton: Princeton University Press, 1969), 144.

10. Jerome McGann, *The Romantic Ideology: A Critical Investigation* (Chicago: University of Chicago Press, 1983), 8, 11, 123–30.

11. See, for example, Robert Gleckner's account of the poet's "pessimistic, nihilistic view of the world," in *Byron and the Ruins of Paradise* (Baltimore: Johns Hopkins University Press, 1967), 106.

12. Byron to John Murray, 5 September 1811, *BLJ* II:91n.

13. For a more comprehensive view of Byron's parliamentary career, see Malcolm Kelsall, *Byron's Politics* (Sussex: Harvester, 1987), 34–56. Although I agree with Kelsall in finding Byron's politics to be less radical than those adopted by the corresponding societies, my reading differs from his account of the poet's merely defensive posture on behalf of aristocratic Whigs.

14. Byron, *The Complete Miscellaneous Prose*, ed. Andrew Nicholson (Oxford: Oxford University Press, 1991), 41. Further references to this work are noted in parentheses and abbreviated as *BPr*.

15. Byron, *The Complete Poetical Works*, vol. II. All further references to *Childe Harold* are noted parenthetically in the text by canto and stanza number; other works are noted by canto and line number. References to notes to *Childe Harold* are noted parenthetically in the text and abbreviated as *BP* II.

16. In a note to this stanza, Hobhouse glossed the lines with a quote from Drummond's *Academical Questions* that concludes, "he who will not reason, is a bigot; he who cannot, is a fool; and he who dares not, is a slave." *BP* II:256.

17. Byron to Annabella Milbanke, 15 February 1814, *BLJ* IV:60.

18. Hansard, 2nd series, vol. II (1820), col. 473.

19. Kelsall, *Byron's Politics*, 75.

20. John Cam Hobhouse, *Historical Illustrations to Childe Harold* IV (London, 1818), 321–22.

21. *BP* II:283n. See also Byron's note to stanza 73 of canto 2, where Greeks are analogized to Irish Catholics and Jews "throughout the world" (*BP* II:201n).

22. R. C. Strong and J. A. van Dorsten, *Leicester's Triumph* (Leiden: Leiden University Press, 1964), 3; quoted in Richard Helgerson, *Forms of Nationhood:*

The Elizabethan Writing of England (Chicago: University of Chicago Press, 1992), 53.

23. Nigel Leask, *British Romantic Writers and the East: Anxieties of Empire* (Cambridge: Cambridge University Press, 1992), 13.

24. Robert Southey, *Thalaba the Destroyer* (1801; Oxford: Woodstock, 1991); Thomas Moore, *Lallah Rookh*, in *Thomas Moore's Complete Poetical Works* (New York: Thomas Crowell, 1895), 368–479.

25. Richard C. Sha, *The Visual and Verbal Sketch in British Romanticism* (Philadelphia: University of Pennsylvania Press, 1999), 188; Anne Janowitz, *England's Ruins: Poetic Purpose and the National Landscape* (Cambridge, MA: Basil Blackwell, 1990), 42; Vincent Newey, "Authoring the Self: *Childe Harold* III and IV," in *Byron and the Limits of Fiction*, ed. Beatty and Newey, 178.

26. Jerome Christensen, *Lord Byron's Strength: Romantic Writing and Commercial Society* (Baltimore: Johns Hopkins University Press, 1993), 186–87.

27. In the second edition of the poem, Byron reveals his mistaken naming of the convent as "Our Lady of Punishment" rather than "Our Lady of the Rock." Byron reveals that he mistook *Pena* (rock) for *Pena* (punishment); but insists upon the appropriateness of his mistake: "I may well assume the other sense from the severities practised there" (BP II:187).

28. Peter Manning, *Byron and His Fictions* (Detroit: Wayne State University Press, 1978), 29–30.

29. Madame De Stael, *Corinne, or Italy*, trans. Sylvia Raphael (Oxford: Oxford University Press, 1998), 353–54.

30. I refer to Allen Grossman's suggestion that "the poem is the destiny of the reader." See Grossman, *Summa Lyrica*, in *The Sighted Singer: Two Works on Poetry for Readers and Writers*, with Mark Halliday (Baltimore: Johns Hopkins University Press, 1992), 213. Also see Grossman's other highly relevant comments on how poetry "administers our powers" to act as the mediation of diversity (284–86).

31. Guillory, *Cultural Capital*, 90.

32. John Barnard, *John Keats* (Cambridge: Cambridge University Press, 1987), 39; David Perkins, *The Quest for Permanence: The Symbolism of Wordsworth, Shelley, and Keats* (Cambridge, MA: Harvard University Press, 1959), 226–28; M. H. Abrams, *Natural Supernaturalism*, 124. For related accounts of Keats's humanized religion, see Ronald A. Sharp, *Keats, Skepticism, and the Religion of Beauty* (Athens: University of Georgia Press, 1979), and Helen Vendler's account of the poet's "radical secularization of the Christian myth of the divine," in *The Odes of John Keats* (Cambridge, MA: Harvard University Press, 1983), 265.

33. Jerome McGann, *The Beauty of Inflections* (Oxford: Oxford University Press, 1985), 17–65.

34. Marjorie Levinson, *Keats's Life of Allegory: The Origins of a Style* (London: Basil Blackwell, 1988), 5.

35. See Daniel P. Watkins, *Keats's Poetry and the Politics of the Imagination* (Rutherford; NJ: Fairleagh Dickinson University Press, 1989).

36. Paul Hamilton, "Keats and Critique," in *Rethinking Historicism: Critical Readings in Romantic History* (London: Basil Blackwell, 1989), 128.

37. Jeffrey N. Cox, *Poetry and Politics in the Cockney School: Keats, Shelley, Hunt, and Their Circle* (Cambridge: Cambridge University Press, 1998), 90,117.

38. Nicholas Roe, *Keats and the Culture of Dissent*, 135, 172, 225–26. See Robert Ryan's earlier study, *Keats: The Religious Sense* (Princeton: Princeton University Press, 1976); Ryan's study, giving much less attention to the poems, makes a case for Keats's adoption of a "natural religion" (23).

39. John Milton, *The Reason of Church Government*, in *Complete Poems and Major Prose*, 668. I am grateful to Robin Grey for alerting me to this allusion.

40. On the significance of Milton in Keats's political thinking see Barnard, *John Keats*, 58.

41. Keats to John Hamilton Reynolds, 3 May 1818, *The Letters of John Keats*, 1:281–82. All further references to this work are noted parenthetically by volume and page number and abbreviated as *KL*.

42. Jeffrey N. Cox argues that Keats wrote this poem in a social setting that may have emphasized the importance of establishing a particular set of skeptical beliefs. This was a sonnet, Cox suggests, that Keats wrote in a "competition" with Leigh Hunt, who wrote "To Percy Shelley, on the Degrading Notions of Deity." See Cox, *Poetry and Politics*, 110–11.

43. Keats to George and Georgiana Keats, 19 February 1819, *KL*II:62–63,65. For a brief discussion of this letter – and a relationship drawn between Lewis Way's chapel and *The Eve of St. Agnes* – see Robert Gittings, "Rich Antiquity," in *Twentieth-Century Interpretations of "The Eve of St. Agnes"*, ed. Allan Danzig (Englewood Cliffs, NJ: Prentice Hall, 1971).

44. Keats regards the reviewers as allies even when they are against him, writing to George and Georgiana Keats, "You will be glad to hear that Gifford's [i.e., Croker's] attack upon me has done me service – it has got my Book among several *Sets*." Keats to George and Georgiana Keats, 18 December 1818, *KL*II:9.

45. See Keats to Leigh Hunt, 10 May 1817, *KL*I:137; Keats to George and Thomas Keats 14(?) February 1818, *KL*I:227.

46. Horace Smith, "Nehemiah Muggs," in *Gaieties and Gravities, a Series of Essays, Comic Tales, and Fugitive Vagaries*, 3 vols. (London: Henry Coburn, 1825), II:54.

47. *Hansard*, 2nd series, vol. XIX (1828), col. 129.

48. Jack Stillinger's influential reading of the poem demonstrates Keats's skeptical attitudes about the "false lure" of the "visionary imagination." See Stillinger, *The Hoodwinking of Madeline and Other Essays on Keats's Poems* (Urbana: University of Illinois Press, 1971), VII, 86. Other accounts of Keats's skepticism include Stuart M. Sperry, *Keats the Poet* (Princeton: Princeton University Press, 1973).

49. Michel de Certeau, "What We Do When We Believe," in *On Signs*, ed. Marshall Blonsky (Baltimore: Johns Hopkins University Press, 1985), 192, 94.

50. Review of *Lamia* [etc.], *New Monthly Magazine* 14 (September, 1820): 247. Reiman suggests that this review may have been written by Thomas Noon Talfourd.
51. Levinson, *Keats's Life of Allegory*, 135.
52. *Ibid.*, 143, 151.
53. *Ibid.*, 152.
54. Richard Moran, "Seeing and Believing: Metaphor, Image, and Force," *Critical Inquiry* 16 (Autumn 1989): 100, 110.
55. Peter Manning, "Childe Harold in the Marketplace: From Romaunt to Handbook," *MLQ* 52 (1991): 176.
56. Herbert G. Wright, "Has Keats's 'Eve of St. Agnes' a Tragic Ending?" in *Twentieth-Century Interpretations of "The Eve of St. Agnes"*, ed. Danzig, 12.
57. Georges Bataille, *Theory of Religion*, trans. Robert Hurley (New York: Zone Books, 1992), 24.
58. Leon Waldoff refers, for example, to Keats's "aggressively self-critical attitude" towards the deceptions of the imagination in this poem; see his *Keats and the Silent Work of the Imagination* (Urbana: University of Illinois Press, 1985), 175.
59. Stillinger, *The Hoodwinking of Madeline*, 46–66.
60. Keats, *Lamia*, part 1, line 305. All further references to *Lamia* are noted parenthetically in the text by part and line number.
61. Watkins, *Keats's Poetry*, 142.
62. For a contrasting emphasis on the importance of conformity in *Lamia*, see Paul Endo, "Seeing Romantically in *Lamia*," *ELH* 66 (Spring 1999): 111–28.
63. Keats to George and Georgiana Keats, 17–27 September 1819, *KL*II:194, 186, 189.
64. *Complete Poems*, 359.
65. Some critics, that is, assume that all the objects that Lamia creates disappear with her: see, for example, Bruce Clarke's claim that Apollonius effectively removes Lamia and her "scene," in "Fabulous Monsters of Conscience: Anthropomorphosis in Keats's *Lamia*," *Studies in Romanticism* 24 (Spring 1990): 564.
66. Keats to Benjamin Robert Haydon, 10 January 1818, *KL*I:203.
67. Keats to Benjamin Robert Haydon, 10 May 1817, *KL*I:141–42.
68. Keats to Benjamin Bailey, 8 October 1817, *KL*I:170; Keats to George and Georgiana Keats, 2 February 1819 to 30 April 1819, *KL*II:102–3.
69. "Myth," Allen Grossman writes, "is somebody else's religion." Grossman, *Summa Lyrica*, 322.
70. *The Notebooks of Samuel Taylor Coleridge*, II:2807.
71. See, for example, James Hill, "Experiments in the Narrative of Consciousness: Byron, Wordsworth, and *Childe Harold*, Cantos 3 and 4," *ELH* 53 (Spring 1986): 122–23. For Byron's comments on the *Lyrical Ballads* and the "dose" of "Wordsworth physic" administered by Shelley, see Thomas Medwin, *Conversations of Lord Byron*, ed. Ernest Lovell (Princeton: Princeton University Press, 1966), 194.

7 CONCLUSION: THE INQUISITORIAL STAGE

1. Tilottama Rajan writes convincingly of drama's traditional status as a "communal mode" that "assumes a shared ideology and an affective link between words and the world outside them." See Rajan, *The Supplement of Reading: Figures of Understanding in Romantic Theory and Practice* (Ithaca: Cornell University Press, 1990), 304.
2. Carlson, *In the Theater of Romanticism*; Jewett, *Fatal Autonomy*.
3. Lord John Russell, *Don Carlos*. All references to this work are noted parenthetically in the text by page number.
4. Edward Peters, *Inquisition* (New York: The Free Press, 1988), 212.
5. Russell, however, admits no familiarity with Schiller's dramas.
6. *Hansard*, 1st series, vol. XXXIV (1816), cols. 747–48.
7. Thomas Clarke, *History of Intolerance; With Observations on the Unreasonableness and Injustice of Persecution, and on the Equity and Wisdom of Unrestricted Religious Liberty*, 2 vols. (London: B. J. Holdsworth, 1820–23), II:456, 488.
8. *The Monthly Review* 91 (1820): 396.
9. Review of *Don Carlos; or, Persecution*, in *The Monthly Review* 100 (1823): 75.
10. Russell, *An Essay on the History of the English Constitution From the Reign of Henry VII to the Present Time* (London: Longman, 1865), 77.
11. See Steven Mullaney, "Lying Like Truth: Riddle, Representation, and Treason in Renaissance England," *ELH* 47 (1980): 32–47.
12. Preface to *The Cenci*, in *Shelley's Poetry and Prose* 238. All further references to the introductory material are noted parenthetically in the text by page number; references to the verse text are noted parenthetically by act, scene, and line number.
13. Scrivener, 187; Stuart Sperry, "The Ethical Politics of Shelley's *The Cenci*," *Studies in Romanticism* 25 (1986): 411–27.
14. Shelley to Robert Southey, 17 August 1820, *Letters* II:230–31.
15. Byron to Douglas Kinnaird, 22 November 1820, *Letters and Journals*, VII:236. Further references to this work are abbreviated as *BLJ*.
16. Byron to Augusta Leigh, 5 October 1821, *BLJ* VIII:233.
17. Shelley to Thomas Medwin, 20 July 1820, *Letters* II:219.
18. Jerrold E. Hogle, *Shelley's Process*, 154.
19. Michael Kohler, "Shelley in Chancery: The Reimagination of the Paternalist State in *The Cenci*," *Studies in Romanticism* 27 (1998):545–89.
20. Shelley to Thomas Medwin, 1 May 1820, *Letters*, II:189.
21. Shelley to Horace Smith, quoted in Donald Reiman, "Wordsworth, Shelley, and the Romantic Inheritance," 13.
22. *The Fall of Jerusalem* won Byron's praise as "the best" of the books he was reading in Italy in the Summer of 1820; see Byron to John Murray, 22 July 1820, *BLJ* VII:138.
23. See *Letters*, II:102n. Although he took an interest in Milman's work, Shelley suspected Milman of authoring an attack on *Laon and Cythna* in *The Quarterly Review*. See *Shelley's Poetry and Prose*, 391n.

24. See, for example, Ginger Strand and Sarah Zimmerman, "Finding an Audience: Beatrice Cenci, Percy Shelley, and the Stage," *European Romantic Review* 6 (Winter 1996): 262.
25. Henry Hart Milman, *Fazio: A Tragedy in Five Acts* (New York: David Longworth, 1818), 38. All further references to this work are noted parenthetically in the text by page number.
26. Roger Blood, "Allegory and Dramatic Representation in *The Cenci*," *Studies in Romanticism* 33 (1994): 355–89.
27. Byron to Thomas Moore, 19 September 1821, *BLJ* VIII:216.
28. Leslie Marchand, *Byron: A Biography* (New York: Knopf, 1957), 933.
29. "Licentious Productions in High Life," *The Investigator* 5 (October 1822), in Reiman, *The Romantics Reviewed*, part B, 1182–84.
30. According to Harold Bloom, for example, Cain is a figure for the poet, a "deliberate criminal seeking the conditions for his art by violating the moral sanctions of his society." See Bloom, *The Visionary Company*, 253.
31. Roger D. Lund, "Irony as Subversion: Thomas Woolston and the Crime of Wit," in *The Margins of Orthodoxy: Heterodox Writing and Cultural Response, 1660–1750*, ed. Roger D. Lund (Cambridge: Cambridge University Press, 1995), 170–94.
32. John Matthews, "Lord Byron," *Blackwood's Edinburgh Magazine*, (February, 1822) in Reiman, *The Romantics Reviewed*, part B, 181.
33. The relationship between *Cain* and the issue of blasphemous libel has been explored in Peter A. Schock, "The 'Satanism' of *Cain* in Context: Byron's Lucifer and the War Against Blasphemy," *Keats–Shelley Journal* 44 (1995): 182–215. This account differs from mine primarily in that it concentrates on Byron's conscious manipulation of his text in order to avoid the legal charge of blasphemy.
34. "Lord Byron's Sardanapalus, &c.," *The British Critic*, 2nd series 17 (May 1822), in Reiman, *The Romantics Reviewed*, part B, 315.
35. "Licentious Productions," in Reiman, *The Romantics Reviewed*, part B, 1177, 1181, 1184.
36. Byron, *Lord Byron's Cain*, ed. T. G. Steffan (Austin: University of Texas Press, 1968), 385. References to verse text are cited parenthetically by act, scene, and line number.
37. "Cases of Wolcot v. Walker; Southey v. Sherwood; Murray v. Benbow; and Lawrence v. Smith," *The Quarterly Review* 27 (April 1822): 123–38.
38. Byron to Douglas Kinnaird, 15 November 1821, *BLJ* IX: 60.
39. Byron to Thomas Moore, 19 September 1821, *BLJ* VIII: 216.
40. I quote in these examples from the King James version.
41. Francis Jeffrey, "Lord Byron's Tragedies," *The Edinburgh Review* 35 (February, 1822) in Reiman, *The Romantics Reviewed*, part B, 932.
42. Byron, *The Complete Poetical Works*, VI:310. All references to the verse text are from this edition and are noted parenthetically in the text by stanza number.
43. Although Stuart Peterfreund has written on the legalistic aspects of the poem, he emphasizes primarily the correspondence between the poem's

characters and actual historical figures. See Peterfreund, "The Politics of Neutral Space in Byron's Vision of Judgment,'" *MLQ* 40 (1979): 275–91.

44. Robert Southey, *A Vision of Judgment* and Byron, *The Vision of Judgment* (London: William Dugdale, 1824), 11, 12, 15, 17.
45. Indeed, it could be said that *The Vision of Judgment* accords with the work of Southwood Smith (discussed above in chapter 5), and John Austin's *The Province of Jurisprudence Determined* (1832).
46. Byron, *The Complete Poetical Works*, vol. v.
47. See Jeffrey Cox, *Poetry and Politics in the Cockney School*, 82–122.

Selected bibliography

Abrams, M. H. *Natural Supernaturalism: Tradition and Revolution in Romantic Literature.* New York: W. W. Norton, 1971.

Arnold, Matthew. *Essays in Criticism, Second Series.* London: Macmillan, 1888.

Austen, Jane. *Mansfield Park.* Edited by Kathryn Sutherland. Harmondsworth: Penguin, 1996.

Barbauld, Anna Laetitia. *An Address to the Opposers of the Repeal of the Corporation and Test Acts.* London: J. Johnson, 1790.

Barlow, Joel. *The Political Writings of Joel Barlow.* 1796; reprint, New York: Burt Franklin, 1971.

Barnard, John. *John Keats.* Cambridge: Cambridge University Press, 1987.

Barth, J. Robert. "Coleridge and the Church of England." In *The Coleridge Connection: Essays for Thomas McFarland.* Edited by Richard Gravil and Molly Lefebure. New York: St. Martin's Press, 1990.

Bataille, Georges. *Theory of Religion.* Translated by Robert Hurley. New York: Zone Books, 1992.

Batho, Edith. *The Later Wordsworth.* Oxford: Oxford University Press, 1933.

Beatty, Bernard, and Vincent Newey, eds. *Byron and the Limits of Fiction.* Liverpool: Liverpool University Press, 1988.

Bell, Andrew. *An Analysis of the Experiment in Education, Made at Egmore, Near Madras.* 3rd edn. London: T. Bensley, 1807.

Bentham, Jeremy. *Church of Englandism and its Catechism Examined.* London: Effingham Wilson, 1818.

    The Works of Jeremy Bentham. 11 vols. Edited by John Bowring. Edinburgh: William Tate, 1843.

    Chrestomathia. Edited by M. J. Smith and W. H. Burston. Oxford: Clarendon Press, 1983.

Bewell, Alan. *Wordsworth and the Enlightenment: Nature, Man, and Society in the Experimental Poetry.* New Haven: Yale University Press, 1989.

Blackstone, William. *Commentaries on the Laws of England.* 4 vols. 1765–1769; reprint, Chicago: University of Chicago Press, 1979.

Bloom, Harold. *The Visionary Company: A Reading of English Romantic Poetry.* Ithaca: Cornell University Press, 1961.

    Shelley's Mythmaking. Ithaca: Cornell University Press, 1969.

Boulger, James D. *Coleridge as Religious Thinker*. New Haven: Yale University Press, 1961.

Bourdieu, Pierre. *Language and Symbolic Power*. Edited and introduced by John B. Thompson. Translated by Gino Raymond and Matthew Adamson. Cambridge, MA: Harvard University Press, 1990.

Brantley, Richard E. *Wordsworth's Natural Methodism*. New Haven: Yale University Press, 1975.

Bromwich, David. *A Choice of Inheritance: Self and Community from Edmund Burke to Robert Frost*. Cambridge, MA: Harvard University Press, 1989.

Burchell, Graham, Colin Gordon, and Peter Miller, eds. *The Foucault Effect: Studies in Governmentality*. Chicago: University of Chicago Press, 1991.

Burke, Edmund. *Reflections on the Revolution in France*. Edited by J. G. A. Pocock. Indianapolis: Hackett, 1987.

    Works of the Right Honourable Edmund Burke. 16 vols. London: C. and J. Rivington, 1826.

Butler, Marilyn. *Romantics, Rebels, and Reactionaries: English Literature and its Background, 1760–1830*. Oxford: Oxford University Press, 1981.

    Jane Austen and the War of Ideas. Oxford: Clarendon Press, 1987.

Byron, George Gordon, Lord. *Lord Byron's Cain*. Edited by T. G. Steffan. Austin: University of Texas Press, 1968.

    Byron's Letters and Journals. Edited by Leslie Marchand. 12 vols. Cambridge, MA: Harvard University Press, 197–83.

    The Complete Poetical Works. Edited by Jerome McGann. 7 vols. Oxford: Clarendon Press, 1980–93.

    The Complete Miscellaneous Prose. Edited by Andrew Nicholson. Oxford: Clarendon Press, 1991.

Carlson, Julie. *In the Theater of Romanticism: Coleridge, Nationalism, Women*. Cambridge: Cambridge University Press, 1994.

"Cases of Wolcot v. Walker; Southey v. Sherwood; Murray v. Benbow; and Lawrence v. Smith." *The Quarterly Review* 27 (April 1822): 123–38.

Chandler, James. *Wordsworth's Second Nature: A Study of Poetry and Politics*. Chicago: University of Chicago Press, 1984.

    England in 1819: The Politics of Literary Culture and the Case of Romantic Historicism. Chicago: University of Chicago Press, 1998.

Christensen, Jerome. *Coleridge's Blessed Machine of Language*. Ithaca: Cornell University Press, 1981.

    Lord Byron's Strength: Romantic Writing and Commercial Society. Baltimore: Johns Hopkins University Press, 1993.

Clark, J. C. D. *English Society, 1688–1832: Ideology, Social Structure, and Political Practice During the Ancien Régime*. Cambridge: Cambridge University Press, 1985.

Clark, Timothy. *Embodying Revolution: The Figure of the Poet in Shelley*. Oxford: Clarendon Press, 1989.

Clarke, Thomas. *History of Intolerance; with Observations on the Unreasonableness and Injustice of Persecution, and on the Equity and Wisdom of Unrestricted Religious Liberty*. 2 vols. London: B. J. Holdsworth, 1820–23.

Clarkson, Thomas. *A Portraiture of Quakerism*. 3 vols. London: Longman, 1806.

Coleridge, Samuel Taylor. *Poetical Works*. Edited by Ernest Hartley Coleridge. Oxford: Oxford University Press, 1912.

　The Collected Letters of Samuel Taylor Coleridge. Edited by Earl Leslie Griggs. 6 vols. Oxford: Oxford University Press, 1956–71.

　The Notebooks of Samuel Taylor Coleridge. 4 vols. Edited by Kathleen Coburn. London: Routledge, 1962.

　The Collected Works of Samuel Taylor Coleridge. 16 vols. General editor Kathleen Coburn. Princeton: Princeton University Press and London: Routledge and Kegan Paul, 1969–2001.

Colley, Linda. *Britons: Forging the Nation 1707–1837*. New Haven: Yale University Press, 1992.

Colmer, John. *Coleridge: Critic of Society*. Oxford: Clarendon Press, 1959.

Cottom, Daniel. *The Civilized Imagination: A Study of Ann Radcliffe, Jane Austen, and Sir Walter Scott*. Cambridge: Cambridge University Press, 1985.

Cowper, William. *The Poems of William Cowper*. London: Joseph Dent, 1931.

Cox, Jeffrey N. *Poetry and Politics in the Cockney School: Keats, Shelley, Hunt, and Their Circle*. Cambridge: Cambridge University Press, 1998.

Croker, John Wilson. "Miss Edgeworth's *Tales of Fashionable Life*." *The Quarterly Review* 7 (June 1812): 329–42.

　Review of *Waverly*. *The Quarterly Review* 11 (1814): 355.

Dawson, Paul M. S. *The Unacknowledged Legislator: Shelley and Politics*. Oxford: Clarendon Press, 1980.

Dean, Mitchell. *The Constitution of Poverty: Towards a Genealogy of Liberal Governance*. London: Routledge, 1991.

De Man, Paul. *The Rhetoric of Romanticism*. New York: Columbia University Press, 1984.

Donzelot, Jacques. *The Policing of Families*. Translated by Robert Hurley. New York: Random House, 1979.

Duncan, Ian. *Modern Romance and Transformations of the Novel: The Gothic, Scott, Dickens*. Cambridge: Cambridge University Press, 1992.

Dyer, George. *The Complaints of the Poor People of England*. 1793; Oxford: Woodstock Books, 1990.

Edgeworth, Maria. *Harrington, A Tale* and *Ormond, A Tale*. 2 vols. London: R. Hunter, 1817.

　Tales and Novels by Maria Edgeworth. 20 vols. in 10. New York: Harper, 1835.

　The Absentee. Edited by W. J. McCormack and Kim Walker. Oxford: Oxford University Press, 1988.

　Castle Rackrent and Ennui. Edited by Marilyn Butler. Harmondsworth: Penguin, 1992.

Edgeworth, Maria, and Richard Lovell Edgeworth. "Carr's *Stranger in Ireland*." *The Edinburgh Review* 10 (April 1807): 41–60.

　Practical Education. 2 vols. 1798; reprint, New York: Garland Press, 1974.

Ellison, Julie. *Delicate Subjects: Romanticism, Gender, and the Ethics of Understanding*. Ithaca: Cornell University Press, 1990.

Empson, William. "The Last of the Catholic Question – Its Principle, History, and Effects." *Edinburgh Review* 49 (March 1829): 218–72.

Ewald, François. *L'Etat providence*. Paris: Bernard Grasset, 1986.

Ferguson, Frances. *Wordsworth: Language as Counter-Spirit*. New Haven: Yale University Press, 1977.

    Solitude and the Sublime: Romanticism and the Aesthetics of Individuation. New York: Routledge, 1992.

Ferris, Ina. *The Achievement of Literary Authority: Gender, History, and the Waverly Novels*. Ithaca: Cornell University Press, 1991.

Fish, Stanley. *The Trouble With Principle*. Cambridge, MA: Harvard University Press, 1999.

Foucault, Michel. *Discipline and Punish: The Birth of the Prison*. Translated by Alan Sheridan. New York: Vintage, 1979.

Frend, William. *Considerations on the Oaths Required by the University of Cambridge*. London: J. Deighton, 1787.

Furneaux, Philip. *An Essay on Toleration*. London: T. Cadell, 1773.

Furniss, Tom. *Edmund Burke's Aesthetic Ideology*. Cambridge: Cambridge University Press, 1993.

Galperin, William H. *Revision and Authority in Wordsworth: The Interpretation of a Career*. Philadelphia: University of Pennsylvania Press, 1989.

Glen, Heather. *Vision and Disenchantment: Blake's "Songs" and Wordsworth's "Lyrical Ballads"*. Cambridge: Cambridge University Press, 1983.

Godwin, William. *Enquiry Concerning Political Justice*. Harmondsworth: Penguin, 1985.

    Mandeville. Edited by Pamela Clemit. Vol. VI of *The Collected Novels and Memoirs of William Godwin*. London: William Pickering, 1992.

    St. Leon: A Tale of the Sixteenth Century. Edited by Pamela Clemit. Oxford: Oxford University Press, 1994.

Grossman, Allen, with Mark Halliday. *The Sighted Singer: Two Works on Poetry for Readers and Writers*. Baltimore: Johns Hopkins University Press, 1992.

Guillory, John. *Cultural Capital: The Problem of Literary Canon Formation*. Chicago: University of Chicago Press, 1993.

Hansard Parliamentary Debates, 1st series, vol. XXXV (1800); vol. XXXIV (1816).

Hansard Parliamentary Debates, 2nd series, vols. II–XX (1820–29).

Hartman, Geoffrey. *Wordsworth's Poetry, 1787–1814*. New Haven: Yale University Press, 1964; reprint, Cambridge, MA: Harvard University Press, 1987.

Haydon, Colin. *Anti-Catholicism in Eighteenth-Century England, c. 1714–80*. Manchester: Manchester University Press, 1993.

Hazlitt, William. *The Complete Works of William Hazlitt*. 21 vols. Edited by P. P. Howe. New York: A. M. S. Press, 1967.

    The Spirit of the Age, or, Contemporary Portraits. New York: Chelsea House, 1983.

Hegel, George Wilhelm Friedrich. *Philosophy of Right*. Translated by T. M. Knox. London: Oxford University Press, 1967.

Hempton, David. "Religion in British Society 1740–1790." In *British Politics and Society from Walpole to Pitt 1742–1789*. Edited by Jeremy Black. London: Macmillan, 1990.

Henriques, Ursula R. Q. *Religious Toleration in England 1787–1833*. Toronto: University of Toronto Press, 1961.

Hewitt, Regina. "Church Building as Political Strategy in Wordsworth's Ecclesiastical Sonnets." *Mosaic* 25 (1992): 31–46.

Hickey, Alison. *Impure Conceits: Rhetoric and Ideology in Wordsworth's "Excursion"*. Stanford: Stanford University Press, 1997.

Hobbes, Thomas. *Leviathan*. Edited by C. B. Macpherson. Harmondsworth: Penguin, 1968.

Hobhouse, John Cam. *Historical Illustrations to Childe Harold* IV. London, 1818.

Hobsbaum, Eric. *Nations and Nationalism*. Cambridge: Cambridge University Press, 1990.

Hogle, Jerrold E. *Shelley's Process: Radical Transference and the Development of His Major Works*. New York: Oxford University Press, 1988.

Hume, David. *Political Essays*. Edited by Knud Haakonssen. Cambridge: Cambridge University Press, 1994.

Hurd, Richard. *Letters on Chivalry and Romance*. In *Augustan Reprint Series*. Vols. CI–CII. 1762; reprint, Los Angeles: Augustan Reprint Society, 1963.

Ignatieff, Michael. *A Just Measure of Pain: The Penitentiary in the Industrial Revolution*. New York: Columbia University Press, 1978.

Janowitz, Anne. *England's Ruins: Poetic Purpose and the National Landscape*. Cambridge, MA.: Basil Blackwell, 1990.

Jeffrey, Francis. "Pamphlets on the Catholic Question." *Edinburgh Review* 11 (October 1807): 116–44.

"Miss Edgeworth's *Tales of Fashionable Life*." *The Edinburgh Review* 20 (July 1812): 109–26.

"Miss Edgeworth's Tales." *The Edinburgh Review* 28 (August 1817): 390–418.

"O'Driscol's *History of Ireland*." *Edinburgh Review* 46 (October 1827): 433–70.

Jewett, William. *Fatal Autonomy: Romantic Drama and the Rhetoric of Agency*. Ithaca: Cornell University Press, 1997.

Johnson, Claudia. *Jane Austen: Women, Politics, and the Novel*. Chicago: University of Chicago Press, 1988.

Equivocal Beings: Politics, Gender, and Sentimentality in the 1790s: Wollstonecraft, Radcliffe, Burney, Austen. Chicago: University of Chicago Press, 1995.

Johnston, Kenneth. *Wordsworth and "The Recluse"*. New Haven: Yale University Press, 1984.

Keats, John. *The Letters of John Keats*. Edited by Hyder Edward Rollins. 2 vols. Cambridge, MA.: Harvard University Press, 1958.

The Complete Poems of John Keats. Edited by Jack Stillinger. Cambridge, MA: Harvard University Press, 1978.

Keble, John. *Sermons, Academical and Occasional*. Oxford: John Henry Parker, 1847.

Kelsall, Malcolm. *Byron's Politics*. Sussex: Harvester, 1987.

Kennedy, James. *Conversations on Religion with Lord Byron and Others*. London: John Murray, 1830.

Knapp, Steven. *Personification and the Sublime: Milton to Coleridge*. Cambridge, MA: Harvard University Press, 1985.

Literary Interest: The Limits of Anti-Formalism. Cambridge, MA: Harvard University Press, 1993.

Kramnick, Isaac. *Republicanism and Bourgeois Radicalism*. Ithaca: Cornell University Press, 1990.

Langan, Celeste. *Romantic Vagrancy: Wordsworth and the Simulation of Freedom*. Cambridge: Cambridge University Press, 1995.

Laqueur, Thomas. *Religion and Respectability: Sunday Schools and Working Class Culture 1750–1850*. New Haven: Yale University Press, 1976.

Leask, Nigel. *The Politics of the Imagination in Coleridge's Critical Thought*. London: Macmillan, 1988.

Levinson, Marjorie. *Wordsworth's Great Period Poems: Four Essays*. Cambridge: Cambridge University Press, 1986.

Keats's Life of Allegory: The Origins of a Style. London: Basil Blackwell, 1988.

Levy, Leonard. *Blasphemy: Verbal Offense Against the Sacred, from Moses to Salman Rushdie*. New York: Knopf, 1993.

Liu, Alan. *Wordsworth: The Sense of History*. Stanford: Stanford University Press, 1989.

Locke, John. *Two Treatises of Government*. Edited by Peter Laslett. Cambridge: Cambridge University Press, 1960.

A Letter Concerning Toleration. Buffalo: Prometheus Books, 1990.

Lukács, Georg. *The Historical Novel*. Translated by Hannah and Stanley Mitchell. Boston: Beacon Press, 1962; reprint, with a preface by Fredric Jameson, Lincoln: University of Nebraska Press, 1983.

Macpherson, C. B. *The Political Theory of Possessive Individualism: Hobbes to Locke*. Oxford: Oxford University Press, 1962.

Magnuson, Paul. *Reading Public Romanticism*. Princeton: Princeton University Press, 1998.

Makdisi, Saree. *Romantic Imperialism: Universal Empire and the Culture of Modernity*. Cambridge: Cambridge University Press, 1998.

Mallock, W. H. "The Logic of Toleration," *The Nineteenth Century* 5 (January 1879): 64–88.

Manning, Peter. *Byron and His Fictions*. Detroit: Wayne State University Press, 1978.

"Childe Harold in the Marketplace: From Romaunt to Handbook." *MLQ* 52 (1991): 170–190.

Marchand, Leslie. *Byron: A Biography*. New York: Knopf, 1957.

Marsh, Joss. *Word Crimes: Blasphemy, Culture, and Literature in Nineteenth-Century England*. Chicago: University of Chicago Press, 1998.

Martin, Philip. *Byron: A Poet Before His Public*. Cambridge: Cambridge University Press, 1982.

Marx, Karl. *A Contribution to the Critique of Political Economy*. Moscow: Progress Publishers, 1970.

McCalman, Ian. *Radical Underworld: Prophets, Revolutionaries, and Pornographers in London, 1795–1840*. Cambridge: Cambridge University Press, 1988.

McClure, Kirstie M. "Difference, Diversity, and the Limits of Toleration." *Political Theory* 18 (August 1990): 361–91.

McConnell, Frank D. *The Confessional Imagination: A Reading of Wordsworth's Prelude.* Baltimore: Johns Hopkins University Press, 1974.

McCormack, W. J. *Ascendancy and Tradition in Anglo-Irish Literary History From 1789 to 1939.* Oxford: Oxford University Press, 1985.

McFarland, Thomas. *Coleridge and the Pantheist Tradition.* Oxford: Oxford University Press, 1969.

McGann, Jerome. *The Romantic Ideology: A Critical Investigation.* Chicago: University of Chicago Press, 1983.

The Beauty of Inflections. Oxford: Oxford University Press, 1985.

Mill, John Stuart. *Mill on Bentham and Coleridge.* Edited by F. R. Leavis. 1950; reprint, Westport, CT: Greenwood Press, 1983.

On Liberty and Other Essays. Edited by John Gray. Oxford: Oxford University Press, 1991.

Milman, Henry Hart. *Fazio: A Tragedy in Five Acts.* New York: David Longworth, 1818.

"Pulpit Eloquence," *The Quarterly Review* 29 (April 1823): 301–21.

Milton, John. *Complete Poems and Major Prose.* Edited by Merritt Y. Hughes. New York: Macmillan, 1985.

Moore, Thomas. *Thomas Moore's Complete Poetical Works.* New York: Thomas Crowell, 1895.

Moran, Richard. "Seeing and Believing: Metaphor, Image, and Force." *Critical Inquiry* 16 (Autumn 1989): 87–112.

Moretti, Franco. *Atlas of the European Novel 1800–1900.* London: Verso, 1998.

Morgan, Lady. *The Missionary.* 1811; reprint, with an introduction by Dennis R. Dean, Delmar, NY: Scholar's Facsimiles and Reprints, 1981.

Dramatic Scenes from Real Life. 3 vols. 1833; reprint, New York: Garland Press, 1979.

The Wild Irish Girl. Introduced by Brigid Brophy. London: Pandora Press, 1986.

Morrow, John. *Coleridge's Political Thought: Property, Morality, and the Limits of Traditional Discourse.* London: Macmillan, 1990.

Mounier, Jean-Joseph. *On the Influence Attributed to Philosophers, Free-Masons, and to the Illuminati on the Revolution of France.* 1801; reprint, Delmar, NY: Scholars' Facsimiles and Reprints, 1974.

Newman, Gerald. *The Rise of English Nationalism: A Cultural History, 1720–1830.* New York: St. Martin's Press, 1987.

Newman, John Henry. *Apologia Pro Vita Sua: Being a History of His Religious Opinions.* New York: Sheed and Ward, 1946.

Paine, Thomas. *Rights of Man.* In *The Thomas Paine Reader.* Ed. Michael Foot and Isaac Kramnick. Harmondsworth: Penguin, 1987.

Parker, Reeve. *Coleridge's Meditative Art.* Ithaca: Cornell University Press, 1975.

Parliamentary History of England, vol. xv (1753); vol. xxii (1790); vol. xxviii (1798).

Parnell, Henry. "Divided Allegiance of the Catholics." *Edinburgh Review* 43 (November 1825): 125–63.

Pasley, C. W. *Essay on the Military Policy and Institutions of the British Empire*. 4th edn., 1812; reprint, London: John Weale, 1847.

Perera, Suvendrini. *Reaches of Empire: The English Novel from Edgeworth to Dickens*. New York: Columbia University Press, 1991.

Pfau, Thomas. *Wordsworth's Profession: Form, Class, and the Logic of Early Romantic Cultural Production*. Stanford: Stanford University Press, 1997.

Plumpetre, Anne. *Narrative of a Residence in Ireland During the Summer of 1814, and that of 1815*. London: Henry Coburn, 1817.

Pocock, J. G. A. *Virtue, Commerce, and History*. Cambridge: Cambridge University Press, 1985.

Poovey, Mary. *Making a Social Body: British Cultural Formation 1830–64*. Chicago: University of Chicago Press, 1995.

A History of the Modern Fact: Problems of Knowledge in the Science of Wealth and Society. Chicago: University of Chicago Press, 1998.

Price, Richard. *Political Writings*. Edited by D. O. Thomas. Cambridge: Cambridge University Press, 1991.

Prickett, Stephen. *Romanticism and Religion: The Tradition of Coleridge and Wordsworth in the Victorian Church*. Cambridge: Cambridge University Press, 1976.

Words and the Word: Language, Politics, and Biblical Interpretation. Cambridge: Cambridge University Press, 1986.

Priestley, Joseph. *An Address to Protestant Dissenters of All Denominations, On the Approaching Election of Members of Parliament*. London, 1774; reprint, Boston: Thomas and John Fleet, 1774.

Letters to the Right Honourable Edmund Burke, Occasioned by his Reflections on the Revolution in France. Birmingham: Thomas Pearson, 1791.

Political Writings. Edited by Peter Miller. Cambridge: Cambridge University Press, 1993.

Priestman, Martin. *Romantic Atheism: Poetry and Freethought, 1780–1830*. Cambridge: Cambridge University Press, 1999.

Pyle, Forest. *The Ideology of Imagination: Subject and Society in the Discourse of Romanticism*. Stanford: Stanford University Press, 1995.

Radcliffe, Ann. *A Journey Made in the Summer of 1791 through Holland and the Northern Frontier of Germany*. London: G. G. and J. Robinson, 1795.

The Italian. Edited by Frank Garber. Oxford: Oxford University Press, 1968.

The Romance of the Forest. Edited by Chloe Chard. Oxford: Oxford University Press, 1986.

A Sicilian Romance. Edited by Alison Milbank. Oxford: Oxford University Press, 1993.

The Castles of Athlin and Dunbayne: A Highland Story. Edited by Alison Milbank. Oxford: Oxford University Press, 1995.

Ragussis, Michael. "Representation, Conversion, and Literary Form: *Harrington* and the Novel of Jewish Identity." *Critical Inquiry* 16 (Autumn 1989): 113–43.

Figures of Conversion: "The Jewish Question" & English National Identity. Durham, NC: Duke University Press, 1995.

Rawls, John. "Justice as Fairness: Political not Metaphysical." *Philosophy and Public Affairs* 14 (Summer 1985): 223–51.
Political Liberalism. New York: Columbia University Press, 1993.
Reeve, Clara. *The Old English Baron.* Edited by James Trainer. Oxford: Oxford University Press, 1967.
Reiman, Donald. *The Romantics Reviewed.* 3 parts in 9. New York: Garland Publishing, 1972.
"Wordsworth, Shelley, and the Romantic Inheritance." *Romanticism Past and Present* 5 (1981): 6.
Richardson, Alan. *Literature, Education, and Romanticism: Reading as Social Practice, 1780–1832.* Cambridge: Cambridge University Press, 1994.
Ricks, Christopher. *Keats and Embarrassment.* Oxford: Clarendon Press, 1974.
Robertson, Fiona. *Legitimate Histories: Scott, Gothic, and the Authorities of Fiction.* Oxford: Clarendon Press, 1994.
Robinson, David. "The Catholic Question." *Blackwood's Edinburgh Magazine* 18 (July 1825): 6–20.
Robinson, Robert. *Ecclesiastical Researches.* Cambridge: Francis Hodson, 1792.
Roe, Nicholas. *Keats and the Culture of Dissent.* Oxford: Clarendon Press, 1997.
Rousseau, Jean Jacques. *Political Writings.* Edited by Alan Ritter. New York: Norton, 1988.
Russell, Lord John. *Don Carlos; or, Persecution. A Tragedy, in Five Acts.* 2nd edn. London: Longman, 1822.
An Essay on the History of the English Constitution From the Reign of Henry VII to the Present Time. London: Longman, 1865.
Ryan, Robert. *Keats: The Religious Sense.* Princeton: Princeton University Press, 1976.
"Byron's *Cain*: The Ironies of Belief." *The Wordsworth Circle* 21 (1990): 41–45.
The Romantic Reformation: Religious Politics in English Literature, 1789–1824. Cambridge: Cambridge University Press, 1997.
Rzepka, Charles. *The Self as Mind: Vision and Identity in Wordsworth, Coleridge, and Keats.* Cambridge, MA: Harvard University Press, 1986.
Said, Edward. *The World, The Text, and the Critic.* Cambridge, MA: Harvard University Press, 1983.
Sandel, Michael. "Judgemental Toleration." In *Natural Law, Liberalism, and Morality.* Edited by Robert P. George. Oxford: Clarendon Press, 1996.
Schama, Simon. *Citizens: A Chronicle of the French Revolution.* New York: Alfred A. Knopf, 1989.
Schmitt, Cannon. *Alien Nation: Nineteenth-Century Gothic Fictions and English Nationality* Philadelphia: University of Pennsylvania Press, 1997.
Schneewind, Jerome. "Bayle, Locke, and the Concept of Toleration." In *Philosophy, Religion, and the Question of Intolerance.* Edited by Mehdi Aminazavi and David Ambuel. Albany: State University of New York Press, 1997.
Scott, Sir Walter. *The Waverly Novels Centenary Edition.* 25 vols. Edinburgh: Adam and Charles Black, 1877.
Sha, Richard C. *The Visual and Verbal Sketch in British Romanticism.* Philadelphia: University of Pennsylvania Press, 1999.

Shaffer, Elinor. *"Kubla Khan" and The Fall of Jerusalem: The Mythological School in Biblical Criticism and Secular Literature 1770–1880*. Cambridge: Cambridge University Press, 1975.

Sharp, Ronald A. *Keats, Skepticism, and the Religion of Beauty*. Athens: University of Georgia Press, 1979.

Shelley, Percy Bysshe. *The Letters of Percy Bysshe Shelley*. Edited by Frederick L. Jones. 2 vols. Oxford: Clarendon Press, 1964.

Shelley's Poetry and Prose. Edited by Donald J. Reiman and Sharon B. Powers. New York: W. W. Norton, 1977.

Simpson, David. *Wordsworth's Historical Imagination: The Poetry of Displacement*. New York: Methuen, 1987.

Romanticism, Nationalism, and the Revolt Against Theory. Chicago: University of Chicago Press, 1993.

Singer, Brian C. J. *Society, Theory, and the French Revolution: Studies in the Revolutionary Imaginary*. New York: St. Martin's Press, 1986.

Siskin, Clifford. *The Work of Writing: Literature and Social Change in Britain, 1700–1830*. Baltimore: Johns Hopkins University Press, 1998.

Smith, Adam. *The Wealth of Nations*. Edited by Edwin Cannan. Introduction by Max Levner. New York: Modern Library, 1937.

The Theory of Moral Sentiments. Edited by D. D. Raphael and A. L. Macfie. Indianapolis: Liberty Classics, 1982.

Smith, Sydney. "Ingram on Methodism," *Edinburgh Review* 11 (January 1808): 341–62.

Smith, Thomas Southwood. *The Divine Government*. 5th edn. Philadelphia: J. B. Lippincott and Company, 1866.

Southey, Robert. *Joan of Arc, an Epic Poem*. Bristol: Joseph Cottle, and London: J. Robinson, 1796.

"The Progress of Infidelity." *The Quarterly Review* 28 (January 1823): 493–536.

The Book of the Church. 2 vols. London: John Murray, 1824.

"The Roman Catholic Question – Ireland." *The Quarterly Review* 38 (January 1828): 535–98.

The Life of Wesley and the Rise and Progress of Methodism. 2 vols. London: Oxford University Press, 1925.

Thalaba the Destroyer. 1801; reprint, Oxford: Woodstock, 1991.

Southey, Robert. *A Vision of Judgment* and Lord Byron, *The Vision of Judgment*. London: William Dugdale, 1824.

Stephen, William. Review of *Tales of Fashionable Life*. *The Quarterly Review* 2 (August 1809): 146–54.

Stillinger, Jack. *The Hoodwinking of Madeline and Other Essays on Keats's Poems*. Urbana: University of Illinois Press, 1971.

"Superstition and Knowledge." *The Quarterly Review* 29 (1823): 440–75.

Taylor, Charles. "Atomism." In *Philosophy and the Human Sciences: Philosophical Papers*. Cambridge: Cambridge University Press, 1985.

Taylor, Isaac. *Fanaticism*. London: Holdsworth and Ball, 1833.

Thomas, Keith Vivian. *Religion and the Decline of Magic*. New York: Scribner, 1971.

Thompson, E. P. "Disenchantment or Default? A Lay Sermon." In *Power and Consciousness*, edited by Conor Cruise O'Brien and William Dean Vanech. London: University of London Press, 1969.

Trilling, Lionel. *The Opposing Self: Nine Essays in Criticism*. New York: Viking Press, 1950.

Trumpener, Katie. "National Character, Nationalist Plots: National Tale and Historical Novel in the Age of *Waverly*, 1806–1830." *English Literary History* 60 (1993): 685–731.

    Bardic Nationalism: The Romantic Novel and the British Empire. Princeton: Princeton University Press, 1997.

Tully, James. "Governing Conduct." In *Conscience and Casuistry in Early Modern Europe*. Edited by Edmund Leites. Cambridge: Cambridge University Press, 1988.

Turner, Sharon. *The History of the Anglo-Saxons from the Earliest Period to the Norman Conquest*. 3 vols. 5th edn. London: Longman, 1828.

Viswanathan, Gauri. *Outside the Fold: Conversion, Modernity, and Belief*. Princeton: Princeton University Press, 1998.

Walpole, Horace. *The Castle of Otranto*. In *Three Gothic Novels*. Edited by Peter Fairclough. Harmondsworth: Penguin, 1968.

Walzer, Michael. *On Toleration*. New Haven: Yale University Press, 1997.

Warburton, William. *The Alliance Between Church and State, or, the Necessity and Equity of an Established Religion and a Test-Law Demonstrated*. London: Fletcher and Gyles, 1736.

    The Divine Legation of Moses. 4 vols. 1738–65; reprint, New York: Garland Press, 1978.

Watkins, Daniel P. *Keats's Poetry and the Politics of the Imagination*. Rutherford, NJ: Fairleagh Dickinson University Press, 1989.

Welsh, Alexander. *The Hero of the Waverly Novels*. 1963; reprint, Princeton: Princeton University Press, 1992.

Williams, Anne. *Art of Darkness*. Chicago: University of Chicago Press, 1995.

Williams, Bernard. "A Critique of Utilitarianism." In *Utilitarianism: For and Against*. Cambridge: Cambridge University Press, 1983.

Williams, Raymond. *Culture and Society 1780–1950*. New York: Columbia University Press, 1958.

Wilson, A. N. *God's Funeral*. New York: Norton, 1999.

Wilson, John. "Dr. Phillpotts and Mr. Lane on the Coronation Oath.," *Blackwood's Edinburgh Magazine* 24 (July 1828): 1–28.

    The Recreations of Christopher North. New York: D. Appleton, 1869.

Wilt, Judith. *Secret Leaves: The Novels of Walter Scott*. Chicago: University of Chicago Press, 1985.

Wordsworth, Christopher. *Letters to M. Gondon on the Destructive Character of the Church of Rome*. London: Francis and John Rivington, 1847.

    Memoirs of William Wordsworth, Poet Laureate. 2 vols. London: Edward Moxon, 1851.

Wordsworth, William. *The Letters of William and Dorothy Wordsworth: The Middle Years.* 2 vols. Edited by Ernest De Selincourt. Oxford: Oxford University Press, 1937.

The Letters of William and Dorothy Wordsworth: The Later Years, 2 vols. Edited by Ernest De Selincourt and Helen Darbishire. Oxford: Clarendon Press, 1939.

The Poetical Works of William Wordsworth. 5 vols. Edited by Ernest de Selincourt and Helen Darbishire. Oxford: Clarendon Press, 1952.

The Prose Works of William Wordsworth. 3 vols. Edited by W. J. B. Owen. Oxford: Clarendon Press, 1974.

The Prelude: 1799, 1805, 1850. New York: W. W. Norton, 1979.

The Pedlar, Tintern Abbey, The Two-Part Prelude. Edited by Jonathan Wordsworth. Cambridge: Cambridge University Press, 1985.

The Fenwick Notes of William Wordsworth. Edited by Jared Curtis. London: Bristol Classical Press, 1993.

Yates, Richard. *The Basis of National Welfare, Considered in Reference Chiefly to the Prosperity of Britain and the Safety of the Church of England.* London: F. C. and J. Rivington, 1817.

Index

314

CAMBRIDGE STUDIES IN ROMANTICISM

GENERAL EDITORS
MARILYN BUTLER, *University of Oxford*
JAMES CHANDLER, *University of Chicago*